ZM6

Oxford Bibliographical Society
Publications

THIRD SERIES VOLUME VIII

Printing Historical Society

PUBLICATION No. 18

THE FIFTEENTH-CENTURY PRINTING PRACTICES OF JOHANN ZAINER, ULM, 1473–1478

CLAIRE M. BOLTON

THE OXFORD BIBLIOGRAPHICAL SOCIETY
OXFORD

PRINTING HISTORICAL SOCIETY
LONDON

2016

Published by the Oxford Bibliographical Society *care of* the
Bodleian Library, Oxford OX1 3BG
in association with the the Printing Historical Society *care of*
St Bride Library, Bride Lane, London EC4Y 8EE

© 2016 Oxford Bibliographical Society

ISBN 978-0-901420-59-6

Inquiries about the Oxford Bibliographical Society
and its publications should be addressed to
the Honorary Secretary at the
Bodleian Library

British Library Cataloguing in Publication Data
A catalogue record for this book is available
from the British Library

Typeset by Anne Joshua, Oxford
Printed in Great Britain by
Henry Ling Limited, The Dorset Press,
Dorchester DT1 1HD

CONTENTS

LIST OF ILLUSTRATIONS

LIST OF TABLES

ABBREVIATIONS

This listing includes all the Catalogues and Bibliographies consulted as Primary Sources for this research.

ADB Steiff, K., 'Günther und Johannes Zainer', *Allgemeine Deutsche Biographie*, Bd. 44 (Leipzig, 1898) (repr. Berlin, 1967–1971), pp. 672–674

AGB *Archiv für Geschichte des Buchwesens*, vol. 1– , ed. Historische Kommission des Börsenvereins des Deutschen Buchhandels (Frankfurt, 1956)

AUG Hubay, Ilona, *Incunabula der Staats- und Stadtbibliothek Augsburg* (Wiesbaden: Inkunabelkataloge Bayerische Bibliotheken, 1974)

BL The British Library, London

BMC *Catalogue of books printed in the XVth century now in the British Museum*, vols. 1–4, ed. A. W. Pollard; vols. 5–8, ed. Victor Scholderer; vol. 9–10, ed. G. D. Painter (London: Trustees of the British Museum, 1908–2005) (vols. 1–10 lithographic reprint 1963), vol. 11, ed. Lotte Hellinga ('t Goy-Houten: Hes & de Graaf, 2007)

Bod-inc. Coates, Alan . . . [et al] with the assistance of Carolinne White and Elizabeth Mathew; blockbooks, woodcut and metalcut single sheets by Nigel F. Palmer; an inventory of Hebrew incunabula by Silke Schaeper. *Catalogue of books printed in the XVth century now in the Bodleian Library*, 6 vols. (Oxford: Oxford University Press, 2005)

BSB Bayerische Staatsbibliothek, Munich

BSB-Ink Hertrich, Elmar, ed., *Bayerische Staatsbibliothek Inkunabelkatalog*, vols. 1–5 (Wiesbaden: Reichert, 1988), vol. 6, ed. Bettina Wagner (Wiesbaden: Reichert, 2005), vol. 7, ed. Bettina Wagner, in Zusammenarbeit mit Claudia Bubenik . . . [et al.] (Wiesbaden: Reichert, 2009)

C Copinger, W. A., Supplement to Hain's *Repertorium bibliographum*, 2 vols. (London, 1895–1902)

CUL Cambridge University Library

GOFF Goff, Frederick, R., *Incunabula in American libraries. A third census of fifteenth-century books recorded in North American collections* (repr. New York: Bibliographical Society of America, 1964)

GW *Gesamtkatalog der Wiegendrucke*, Kommission für den Gesamtkatalog der Wiegendrucke; vols. 1–8 (Leipzig, 1925–40); second revised impression, vols. 1–7 (Stuttgart: Hiersemann, 1968), vol. 8 (Stuttgart: Hiersemann, 1978, vol. 9, 1991; vol. 10, 2000; vol. 11, pts. 1 and 2, 2003)

H Hain, Ludwig, *Repertorium bibliographicum in quo libri omnes ab arte typographica inventa usque ad annum MD typis expressi . . . recensentur* (Stuttgart and Paris, 1826–38, repr. Milan: Görlich, 1966)

ISTC *Incunabula Short Title catalogue.* All the entries in this thesis are identified by their ISTC number. The number comprises two letters and eight figures, with the second letter indicating the initial of the author. Titles and authors' names follow format used by ISTC. Although recent, and therefore not used by earlier scholars, this is the only database/inventory that is comprehensive in that every edition printed in the fifteenth century is included. To help to identify a particular edition, e.g. one cited in an earlier article with perhaps only a Hain number (H), a *Gesamtkatalog* number (*GW*) or a Goff number, a concordance is supplied to these three catalogues as an Appendix. The ISTC is also accessible online through the British Library's website at http:/blpc.bl.uk/catalogues/istc/index.html and the *Illustrated Incunable Short Title Catalogue* is available as a CD-Rom, 2nd edition (London: Primary Source Media in association with The British Library, 1998)

MMW *Catalogus van de incunabeln,* Museum Meermano-Westreenianum (The Hague, 1920)

na not after

OATES Oates, J. C. T., *A catalogue of the XVth century books in the University Library, Cambridge* (Cambridge: Cambridge University Press, 1954)

OTTO Hubay, Ilona, *Incunabula in der Benediktinerabtei Ottobeuren* (Wiesbaden: Anton Konrad, 1987)

R Reichling, Dietrich, *Appendix ad Hainii-Copingeri Repertorium bibliographicum,* 6 parts (Munich: I. Rosenthal, 1905–1911)

SBU Breitenbruch, Bernd, *Die Inkunabeln der Stadtbibliothek Ulm* (Weissenhorn: Anton Konrad, 1987)

SHEP Sheppard, L. A., *Catalogue of XVth century books in the Bodleian Library* (unpublished card catalogue and only available in the library)

UBW Hubay, Ilona, *Incunabula der Universitätsbibliothek Würzburg* (Wiesbaden: Harrassowitz, 1966)

VD *Verzeichnis der im deutschen Sprachbereich erschienenen Drucke des XVI. Jahrhunderts,* 25 vols. (Stuttgart: Hiersemann, 1983–2000)

VGT *Veröffentlichungen der Gesellschaft für Typenkunde des XV. Jahrhunderts,* new edn (Osnabrück: Otto Zeller, 1966)

W Walsh, James, E., *A catalogue of the fifteenth-century books in the Harvard University Library,* 5 vols. (New York: Center for Medieval and Early Renaissance Studies, State University of New York at Binghampton, 1991–1997)

ACKNOWLEDGEMENTS

Many people have given support and encouragement throughout the research and writing of this book.

My thanks are due to Dr Alan Coates and the staff at the Bodleian Library who were endlessly patient in answering my requests for books, to Dr Bettina Wagner who always eased my visits to the BSB in Munich, to Herr Appenzeller in Ulm who allowed me to photograph Zainer's editions in great detail and to other librarians and archivists in Augsburg, The Hague, London, Manchester, Mainz, Memmingen, Reading, Windsor, and Würzburg.

To Guy Hutsebaut, at the Plantin-Moretus Museum who memorably lent us a screwdriver, gave us the freedom of the Museum, and then left for the day. To Nicholas Smith at Cambridge University Library who let me use Philip Gaskell's wooden press. To St Bride Library who supplied the image of a printing press from Fertel's 1723 manual.

To those who kindly took the time to answer my various queries along the way, including Mike Anderson, Lotte Hellinga, Hans-Jörg Künast, Alan May, Peggy Smith, Andrew Honey, James Mosley and Stan Nelson.

To Ursula Hinske-Gengnagel for good food and help with German translations; to Ruth Barnes for her input about fifteenth-century fabrics; to Jo De Baerdemaeker for a fine drawing (Figure 4.13) and to David for putting up with me throughout. Nigel Palmer and Scott Mandelbrote read the text for the Oxford Bibliographical Society and corrected a number of errors.

My apologies to those I have not listed specifically.

1 INTRODUCTION

This research starts from the basic hypothesis that the end products of printing, in this case the copies of the editions printed, show evidence in their page layout and retain clues on their leaves that can give information about the printing methods used and the operation of the press. By interpreting these clues much can be revealed about fifteenth-century printing practices and the presses used, and sometimes more than has hitherto been discussed by scholars. The term 'printing practices' is used here to cover both the pre-planning, design aspects as well as the technical book-production aspects of fifteenth-century printing.[1] It comprises the design of the page; the length of the line, the number of lines and the width of the margins, as well as the mechanics of how the type was set, how the formes were imposed, how the type was inked, how the paper was prepared, how the sheets of paper were printed – whether one leaf or two at a time and how register was achieved.

Unfortunately there is a dearth of evidence about the technical aspects of fifteenth-century printing. It is not known how the first printers printed. There are no descriptions of method, no contemporary accounts of printing and no illustrations of the press, which might show its mechanics, for the first fifty years. The earliest illustration of a printshop and press does not occur until the end of the century in an edition of *Danse macabre* printed by Mathias Huss in Lyon in 1499 and it is lacking in detail, particularly of critical parts of the press (see Figure 1.1).[2]

The earliest printing manual was written by Joseph Moxon in 1683, over two hundred years after the first printed book was completed in the 1450s.[3] Moxon is an invaluable source for printing methods, and will be drawn on frequently in this study, but the time lapse has to be kept in

---

[1] Lotte Hellinga, 'Analytical bibliography and the study of early printed books with a case study of the Mainz Catholicon', *Gutenberg-Jahrbuch*, 64, 1989, pp. 47–96 (p. 52) applies the term 'practice' to relate to what happened regularly in a particular printing house.

[2] *Danse macabre*, 1499 (id00020500).

[3] Joseph Moxon, *Mechanick exercises on the whole art of printing*, ed. Herbert Davis and Harry Carter, 2nd edn, repr. (New York: Dover, 1978). A comprehensive list of printing manuals is supplied in P. Gaskell, G. Barber, and G. Warrilow, 'An annotated list of printers' manuals to 1850', *Journal of the Printing Historical Society*, 4 (1968), pp. 11–31. None of the manuals give any more help with understanding the fifteenth century than Moxon. The earlier German manuals, by Hornschuch, *Orthotypographia*, eds. M. Boghardt, Frans A. Jannsen, W. Wilkes (Leipzig, 1608, German translation 1634, repr. Darmstadt: Renate Raeke, 1984), J. L. Vietor, *Formatbüchlein*, eds. M. Boghardt, Frans A. Janssen, W. Wilkes (n.pl: 1653, repr. Darmstadt: Renate Raeke, 1983), and Georg Wolffger, *Neu-aufgesetztes Format-Büchlein*, eds. M. Boghardt, Frans A. Janssen, W. Wilkes (Graz: 1673, repr. Darmstadt: Renate Raeke, 1987) concentrate more on correcting signs, symbols, case-lays, imposition schemes, histories of famous printers, etc. but make no mention of the workings of the press, how to cast type, etc., as detailed by Moxon.

Figure 1.1. The first illustration of a printshop, showing press and compositor, from *Danse macabre*, printed by Mathias Huss in Lyon in 1499. (Reproduced from James Moran, *Printing presses*, Faber & Faber, 1973.)

mind. Although there are no contemporary descriptions of printing practice for the incunable period, snippets of information can be gleaned from other sources such as contemporary correspondence that in passing mentions a visit to a printshop or, as with the Amerbach correspondence, where Johann Amerbach writes on all subjects including occasionally aspects of running his printshop in Basel.[4]

There are many different aspects to the history of printing in the incunable period. Some scholars discuss incunables in general as Konrad Haebler does with his important contribution to the understanding of early printed books and how they were produced.[5] Others focus on a

---

[4] Barbara C. Halporn, *The correspondence of Johann Amerbach. Early printing in its social context* (Ann Arbor: University of Michigan, 2000) is perhaps the most easily accessible version of Amerbach's letters. However the letters refer to activity from the 1480s, a decade after that being discussed here with Zainer. The full correspondence can be found in Alfred and Jenny Beat R. Hartman, eds., *Die Amerbachkorrespondenz,* vol. 1 (Basel: Universitätsbibliothek, 1942). This latter publication has (in 2002) completed its twelfth volume, under Hartman's editorship, with letters into the late sixteenth century. The first two volumes, covering the period 1481–1524, are the most relevant for incunabulists.

[5] Konrad Haebler, *Handbuch der Inkunabelkunde* (Leipzig: Hiersemann, 1925) and in English translation, *The study of incunabula,* trans. L. Osborne (New York: Grolier Club, 1933).

particular aspect. Many scholars have concentrated on Johann Gutenberg. There are a large number of articles and books, sometimes contradictory, as the authors have stated their various theories about Gutenberg,
his life, his invention, his lawsuits, what he might and might not have
printed, and some on how he might have done it.[6] Some scholars have
researched the texts of the earliest printed editions and their transmission,
or made an analysis of the language as printed in the texts. Although such
textual considerations have not been the focus of this present study, the
results can sometimes help throw light on technical points.[7] Other work
has concentrated on the type and typefaces being used by the first
printers. The pioneering work of Henry Bradshaw, Robert Proctor,
Alfred Pollard and Konrad Haebler helped to differentiate the early
typefaces, by which some of the first printers and their presses were able to
be identified.[8]

However it still remains that there is little factual information about
fifteenth-century printing practices. This means that making a study, as
hypothesised above, of copies of the editions to look for clues and evidence
for printing practice, could prove valuable. Lotte Hellinga states that a
'relatively small number of studies have been undertaken of printing
house practice relating to selected items and printers'.[9] The aim of this
study is to provide some sound evidence for fifteenth-century printing
practice, and begin to fill a gap in our knowledge.

It was decided to concentrate on the editions of one printer in particular, Johann Zainer, and to make a detailed study of his work by noting
and recording aspects of his printing practice though his first years, from
1473–1478.[10] Zainer was chosen for this study because he was a clumsy
printer, leaving many marks on his printed pages.[11] Because his printing
showed less technical expertise than many of his contemporaries, his
editions could provide more clues about his printing practice than might
be found in the editions of other printers. It was essential to examine

[6] Janet Ing, *Johann Gutenberg and his Bible* (New York: Typophiles, 1988) gives a succinct summary
of the most influential works about Gutenberg. Guy Bechtel, *Gutenberg et l'invention de l'imprimerie*
([Paris]: Fayard, 1992) writing some four years after Ing, provides a very throrough account of
Gutenberg and his invention.

[7] For example Christa Bertelsmeier-Kierst, *'Griseldis' in Deutschland. Studien zu Steinhöwel und Arigo*
(Heidelberg: C. Winter, 1988). Some implications of the findings in this study for printing practice are
discussed in Chapters 2 and 4.

[8] Paul Needham, *The Bradshaw method. Henry Bradshaw's contribution to bibliography.* The seventh
Hanes Foundation Lecture (Chapel Hill: University of North Carolina, 1988).

[9] Lotte Hellinga, *BMC*, vol. 11, p. 2.

[10] 1478 was the year of the death of Heinrich Steinhöwel, Zainer's financial and editorial backer –
see next section 'Johann Zainer'.

[11] Wytze Hellinga, *Copy and print in the Netherlands* (Amsterdam: Federatie der Werkgeversorgisa-
tiën in het Boekdrukkersbedrijf, 1962), p. 154, describes a number of examples of bad practice found
in the works of early printers, such as bad register, slurred impression, offset, etc. Zainer showed all of
these and more.

actual copies of the editions, and to look at as many copies as possible of each edition within the time frame. Looking at multiple copies helped ensure that one could get the best picture possible of how Zainer printed; for example a mark or blind impression or spelling error found in one copy, could be checked to see if it occurred in other copies, and all the various pieces of information built into the aggregate picture.

The primary aim was to understand how Zainer worked at his press; to get alongside him and follow his thought processes as he approached the planning, typesetting and printing of his editions. As a practising letterpress printer, I am bringing my 35 years experience of designing and printing books, and working on hand presses, to aid my understanding of Zainer and his practices. Another aim has been to put Zainer into context with his contemporaries and, having established some of Zainer's printing practices, to see if some other fifteenth-century printers were working in a similar manner. This is not a history of Zainer's press, or a history of printing in Ulm, Augsburg or southern Germany. This chapter gives an overview of Zainer and sets him in the context of printing in the fifteenth century. It also looks at the methodology of the study in recording the information from the editions, and the other Primary Sources, the incunable catalogues and bibliographies. Chapter 2 gives a broad overview of what was discovered by using this inductive approach, and the next four chapters explore in more detail four different aspects of Zainer's printing practices.

JOHANN ZAINER

Johann Zainer was the first printer in Ulm, in southern Germany, his first dated edition being issued from there in January 1473.[12] In the first six years of his press in Ulm Johann printed around 50 different editions, including both books and broadsides.[13] It is not known exactly how long before 1473 he had been printing in Ulm. Johann, along with his brother Günther Zainer, had started printing with Johann Mentelin in Strassburg

---

[12] Peter Amelung's important exhibition catalogue *Der Frühdruck im deutschen Südwesten, 1473–1500* (Stuttgart: Würtembergische Landesbibliothek, 1979) or in English translation by Ruth Schwab-Rosenthal, *Peter Amelung's Johann Zainer, the elder and younger* (Los Angeles: K. Karmiole, 1985) contains much biographical detail about Johann Zainer, the history of his press, the typefaces that he used and background information about some of the editions that he printed. Amelung brings together the early history of printing in Ulm, with a quick overview of other towns of south-west Germany, drawing on material from Ulm Stadtarchiv, histories of Ulm in the Middle Ages, and art history, as well as from earlier histories of Ulm printing such as G. W. Zapf, *Älteste Buchdruckergeschichte Schwabens* (Ulm, 1791) on the history of printing in Swabia, and K. D. Hassler, *Die Buchdrucker-Geschichte Ulm's* (Ulm, 1840, new edn, Nieuwkoop, 1965) on the history of book printing in Ulm. Amelung's *Der Frühdruck* has been the principal source for biographical detail about Johann Zainer.

[13] It is difficult to give an exact number because many of these editions have only attributed dates. A list of Zainer's editions is given under *Bibliography – Primary Sources, section 1*.

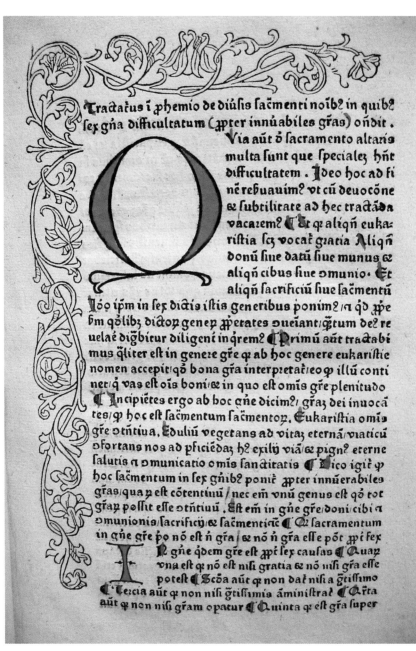

Figure 1.2. A typical incipit page printed by Zainer. Page [b4r] from Albertus Magnus, *Summa de eucharistiae sacramento*, 1474, with woodcut border and initials. (Ulm Stadtbibliothek.)

and the brothers both married Strassburg wives.[14] Probably in late 1467 the brothers moved to Augsburg and Günther became the first printer there with the printing of his first book in March 1468, *Meditationes vitae Christi*.[15]

Johann worked in Augsburg with his brother until sometime in 1472 when he moved to Ulm and set up a press there, the first in that city.[16] His move to Ulm was probably due to the influence of Dr Heinrich Steinhöwel, described as one of the most important humanist writers in Swabia at that time. Steinhöwel had lived and worked in Ulm since 1450, where he was the city doctor.[17] However he was also interested in the new humanist thinking to the extent that he translated and edited humanist texts.[18] One was Petrarch's *Historia Griseldis* which he had translated into German in 1461. Steinhöwel saw the advantages of the new printing technology and used Günther Zainer to print some of his books for him in Augsburg; *Apollonius* and *Historia Griseldis*, the first of these, were both printed by Günther in 1471.[19]

By the end of 1472 Steinhöwel had been instrumental in setting up Johann Zainer as his *Hausdrucker* in Ulm.[20] It seems that right from the beginning Steinhöwel was responsible for much of the editorial selection of Zainer's texts, for writing and translating, as well as financing the operation. Although there is no documentary proof of this, Amelung suggests that Steinhöwel's close involvement can be clearly seen. Zainer's first dated edition was a text written by Steinhöwel, as were six of the twelve editions he printed in his first year.[21] The woodcut borders on the first pages of three of these editions include Steinhöwel's coat-of-arms.[22]

---

[14] Amelung, *Der Frühdruck*, p. 15.

[15] Bonaventura, *Meditationes vitae Christi*, 1468 (ib00893000).

[16] Amelung, *Der Frühdruck*, p. 15.

[17] F. J. Worstbrock, 'Frühhumanismus in Deutschland' in Helmut Gier and Johannes Janota, eds., *Von der Augsburger Bibelhandschrift zu Bertolt Brecht* (Weissenhorn: Anton H. Konrad, 1991), pp. 168–174 (p. 172). More information about Steinhöwel can be found in Gerd Dicke's entry in *Die deutsche Literatur des Mittelalters: Verfasserlexikon*, vol. 9 (Berlin: de Gruyter, 1995), pp. 258–278, and H. O. Burger, *Renaissance–Humanismus–Reformation. Deutsche Literatur im europäischen Kontext* (Bad Homburg: Berlin-Zurich, 1969).

[18] Bertelsmeier-Kierst, p. 150.

[19] Apollonius de Tyro, *Historia Apolloni regis Tyri* [German] 1471 (ia00925000) and Francesco Petrarca, *Historia Griseldis* [German], 1471 (ip00402850).

[20] Worstbrock, p. 173.

[21] *Büchlein der Ordnung* (is00762800) was written by Steinhöwel and was the first German book to be printed about the plague. See Karl Sudhoff, 'Der Ulmer Stadtarzt und Schriftsteller Heinrich Steinhöwel' in Arnold C. Klebs and Karl Sudhoff, eds., *Die ersten gedruckten Pestschriften* (Munich: Münchner Drucke, 1926). The other editions with texts written, edited or translated by Steinhöwel are *Deutsche Chronik*, 1473 (is00765000); *Historia Griseldis* (Latin) 1473 (ip00402000), *Historia Griseldis* (Swabian) [1473] (ip00403000); *Von den erlauchten Frauen*, 1473 (i00720000); *Historia Griseldis* (German), [c.1473] (ip00404000).

[22] Amelung, p. 15, and also P. Amelung, 'Humanisten als Mitarbeiter der Drucker am Beispiel des Ulmer Frühdrucks', in Fritz Kraft and Dieter Wuttke, eds., *Das Verhältnis der Humanisten zum Buch* (Boppard: Bolt, 1977), pp. 129–144.

His financial underwriting of the press may have helped Johann start on a fairly large scale and also perhaps encouraged Johann's rate of production.[23] Steinhöwel's financial commitment must have involved large sums of money. Wolfgang Reuter compares the sums of seven hundred guilders paid for the purchase of equipment for a printing shop in Augsburg around 1473 as the equivalent to seven years' salary for Heinrich Steinhöwel. Many of Zainer's editions were richly illustrated. In the first year alone he used two separate alphabets of woodcut initials, six individually cut, large initials, six woodcut borders that ran on two sides of a page, and commissioned over 80 woodcut illustrations for one edition and 10 for another; all indications of a large financial commitment. This was only the first year. From 1473 until 1478 the press continued the rapid rate of production with an editorial policy heavily influenced by Steinhöwel.[24]

The other strong influence on Zainer's printing came from the Dominican order in Ulm. One of the brothers, Felix Fabri, produced indexes for at least two of Zainer's books, both written by the Dominican Leonardus de Utino, his *Sermones de sanctis* in 1475 and *Sermones quadragesimale* in 1478.[25] Zainer continued to be the sole printer for the Dominicans in Ulm until the decline of his press in the early 1480s.[26] It is not known who financed the printing of these religious books.

When Steinhöwel died in 1478 Johann lost both his main editor and his main financial backer. His brother Günther died in the same year, removing any support he might have had from him and his press. Johann's press began to decline from that period, both financially and editorially. He continued printing until 1482 – then there are no imprints of his between 1483 and 1486.[27] He seems to have sold some of his type and woodcut initials to Heinrich Knoblochtzer, perhaps to pay off his debts.[28] In 1486 he started printing again, with new type faces, and ran the press until 1493, when he left Ulm for Augsburg. No known printed editions were printed by Zainer after that date. In 1496 his son, also named Johann Zainer, printed his first edition in Ulm. Zainer the younger continued to print for some years, and was still listed as a printer

---

[23] Wolfgang Reuter, 'Zur Wirtschafts- und Sozialgeschichte des Buchdruckgewerbes im Rheinland bis 1800', *Archiv für Geschichte des Buchwesens*, 1 (1958), pp. 642–736 (p. 665).

[24] Amelung, *Der Frühdruck*, p. 18.

[25] Amelung, *Der Frühdruck*, pp. 19–20. *Sermones de sanctis*, 1475 (il00158000) and *Sermones quadragesimales,* 1478 (il00146000). As an interesting side comment that gives an indication of the link between the two men, a copy of Zainer's edition of Pelagius' *De planctu ecclesiae*, 1474 (ip00249000) in Ulm Stadtbibliothek, shelfmark 14975, has marginal notes in Brother Felix Fabri's handwriting.

[26] Amelung, *Der Frühdruck*, p. 19.

[27] Amelung, *Der Frühdruck*, p. 22.

[28] Amelung, *Der Frühdruck*, p. 23.

in Ulm archives in 1518; his last edition was printed in 1522.[29] He died in early 1541.

When the Zainer brothers had begun learning to print in Strassburg in the 1460s it was very early in the days of the new technology – less than ten years after the printing of the 42-line Bible in Mainz. Strassburg had strong early printing connections. Gutenberg had lived there between 1434 and 1444 while he was experimenting with his 'work of the books'.[30] Mentelin had his printshop there, and may have started printing as early as 1458.[31] Heinrich Eggestein and Mentelin's son-in-law Adolf Rusch began printing in the 1460s. Other printers, who later set up in other cities, had connections with the city. It is not known exactly when the brothers began to work with Mentelin, but they were well enough established in Strassburg to marry daughters of Strassburg citizens and become citizens themselves; Günther in 1463 and Johann in 1465.[32]

This early period must have been one of flux in printing technique. The neophyte printers would have had to adapt and innovate to establish for themselves a practical method of working. The knowledge they acquired had only just begun to spread from Mainz, accelerated by the sack of that city in 1462, when those with printing knowledge moved from town to town, taking what they had learnt with them. By the end of the 1460s printing had been established in seven German and three Italian towns or cities – a small body of specialist workers in the new technology.[33] With so few proponents it is not surprising that there is little knowledge of how these early printers worked – how they made their type letters, how they set their type, how they made their impressions of type onto paper with their presses, and how they accurately registered their pages.

THE AUGSBURG CONNECTION

Augsburg, the Zainer brothers' destination around 1467, had long been an established literary centre, important for its manuscript production.[34] It quickly embraced the new printing technology and, by the time Johann left the city to move to Ulm in 1472, printing in Augsburg had expanded

---

[29] VD. Index, vol. 3, p. 320 lists 13 editions attributed to Zainer printed after 1500, with *Revocation* (BSB 4° Polem. 3341(14)) being printed in 1522.

[30] Bechtel, pp. 317 and 577.

[31] Ferdinand Geldner, *Die deutschen Inkunabeldrucker. Ein Handbuch der deutschen Buchdrucker des XV. Jahrhunderts nach Druckorten.* 2 vols. (Stuttgart: Hiersemann, 1968–1970), p. 56.

[32] Amelung, *Der Frühdruck*, p. 15.

[33] Margaret B. Stillwell, *The beginning of the world of books 1450–1470* (New York: The Bibiliographical Society of America, 1972), pp. 66–67.

[34] Johannes Janota, 'Von der Handschrift zum Druck', in Helmut Gier and Johannes Janota, eds., *Augsburger Buchdruck und Verlagswesen von den Anfängen bis zur Gegenwart* (Wiesbaden: Harrassowitz, 1997), pp. 125–139 (p. 125). Janota's article is one of over 42 essays included in this comprehensive study of the history of Augsburg printing.

and his brother Günther was no longer the only printer there. Johann Schüssler set up his press in 1470 and Johann Bämler shortly after. A press in the monastery of St Ulrich and St Afra had been established in 1472, perhaps with Anton Sorg running it.[35] Other printers including Johannes Wiener and Jodocus Pflanzmann followed later and by 1478 there were nine presses working in the city and 278 different editions had been printed there.[36] Printing in both German language and local Swabian dialect was an important part of Augsburg work; it has been estimated that over 27 per cent of German-language incunables were printed in the city.[37]

Another characteristic of the Augsburg printers was the use of woodcut initials and woodcut illustrations, printed along with the text. Günther Zainer was the first person after the printing of Fust and Schoeffer's *Psalter* of 1457 (ip01036000) to use ornamental printed initials.[38] He printed his first woodcut-illustrated edition, Jacobus de Voragine's *Legenda aurea* (ij00156000), in 1471 with 131 woodcuts.[39] Falk Eisermann states that 'The first to experiment with a combination of words and images on a single leaf was Günther Zainer, the first Augsburg printer and creator of an influential style of book illustration'.[40]

Johann Zainer, only 60 kilometres away in Ulm, kept in touch with this fast growing network of printers in Augsburg, and Ulm too became an important book printing city in the south-west Swabia region of Germany. Amelung describes Ulm as a city predestined to be a book production centre.[41] It was a successful trading centre and, according to Arthur Hind, was famous in the late fourteenth and early fifteenth centuries as the chief centre for the printing and distribution of playing cards.[42] With the building of new Ulm Minster in the fifteenth century the city had also become a centre for craftsmen, artists and woodcarvers.

Johann's editions include many of the characteristics of Augsburg printing such as his combination of type and illustrations, his use of printed woodcut initials and the design of his type faces. But although

---

[35] Geldner, pp. 132–139.

[36] Hans-Jörg Künast, 'Entwicklungslinien des Augsburger Buchdrucks von den Anfängen bis zum Ende des Dreissigjährigen Krieges', in Helmut Gier & Johannes Janota, eds., *Augsburger Buchdruck und Verlagswesen von den Anfängen bis zur Gegenwart* (Wiesbaden: Harrassowitz, 1997), pp. 3–21 (p. 11).

[37] Künast, p. 5, footnote 18.

[38] S. H. Steinberg, *Five hundred years of printing*, new edn, rev. John Trevitt (London: British Library and New Castle: Oak Knoll, 1996), p. 24.

[39] Sheila Edmunds, 'New light on Johannes Bämler', *Journal of the Printing Historical Society*, 22 (1993), pp. 29–53 (p. 33).

[40] Falk Eisermann, 'Mixing pop and politics', in Kristian Jensen, ed., *Incunabula and their readers* (London: British Library, 2003), pp. 159–177 (p. 164).

[41] Amelung, *Der Frühdruck*, p. 2.

[42] Arthur Hind, *An introduction to a history of the woodcut* (London: Constable, 1935), p. 304.

being influenced by Augsburg it is quite likely that Zainer worked with
Ulm woodcut artists for his editions. The style of Zainer's woodcuts for
his Aesop's *Vita et fabulae* is so close to that of the carvings of Ulm
Minster's choir stalls, completed in 1474 that they may have been cut by
the same carver or at least by someone who was strongly influenced by the
carvings.[43] Hind adds that for two decades between 1470 and 1490 'Ulm
possessed illustrators more gifted than any in the same period in
Augsburg'.[44]

Steinhöwel continued regular contact with Augsburg and some of his
editions were still printed there. Günther Zainer printed an edition of
Steinhöwel's translation of *Historia Griseldis* in 1471 and another edition in
1473.[45] In 1472 Johannes Bämler printed another edition in Augsburg.[46]
Then Johann Zainer printed three editions, one in Latin, one in the local
Swabian dialect, and one in a more modern German, in Ulm in 1473.[47]
Later in 1478 Bämler printed another edition.[48] There were other over-
lapping editions being printed in both cities by the brothers. Günther
printed *Rationale divinorum officiorum* in 1470 and Johann printed it in 1473
and again in 1475.[49] The design and the layout of these last three editions
are remarkably similar and the typefaces are almost identical. These are
not printers working in isolation but practitioners in regular contact with
each other.

ZAINER'S TYPEFACES

Thirteen different typefaces have been ascribed to Johann Zainer's press
through its entire period of production.[50] From 1473 until 1478, the period
of this study, Zainer used five different typefaces. Classifying and identifying incunable typefaces with no standard body size or given name is
confusing, and a number of systems have been used to help clarify the
matter. The *BMC* gives descriptions of Zainer's typefaces and names the
first five as Types 116, 110, 117, 96 and 136.[51] Today these faces have the

---

[43] Amelung, *Der Frühdruck*, p. 3. Aesop, *Vita et fabulae* [*c.*1476–77] (ia00116000).

[44] Hind, p. 304.

[45] Francesco Petrarca, *Historia Griseldis*, 1471 (ip00402850) and 1473 (ip00492900).

[46] This edition is part of a compilation printed by Bämler in April 1472 and listed as part of
(il00126000) – it is not known if Bämler had any financial support from Steinhöwel or perhaps from
Hector or Georg Mülich, or Jacob Hämerlin as conjectured by Edmunds, p. 34. See also Curt Bühler,
'The fifteenth-century editions of Petrarch's *Historia Griseldis* in Steinhöwel's German translation', *The
Library Quarterly*, 15 (1945), pp. 231–236.

[47] Francesco Petrarca, *Historia Griseldis*, 1473 (Latin edn) (ip00402000); (Swabian dialect edn)
(ip00403000) and (German edn) (ip00404000).

[48] Francesco Petrarca, *Historia Griseldis*, 1478 (ip00404600).

[49] Guillelmus Duranti, *Rationale divinorum officiorum*, 1470 (id00404000); 1473 (id00407000); 1475
(id00408000).

[50] Amelung, *Der Frühdruck*, p. 42.

[51] *BMC*, vol. 2, p. 518.

initals G or R added to designate a gothic or roman type face. The figures refer to the standard incunabulists' measure in millimetres over 20 lines of text. The *GW* used another system and from the beginning in 1925, for the first two volumes, the typefaces used by each printer were given a chronological number, starting with 1 for their earliest used face. From volume three onwards the *GW* uses the 20-line measurement system. Another system was introduced by Konrad Haebler, based on the upper case 'M' (or 'Qu' for roman founts) intended for classifying larger typefaces, ones usually used for headlines which could not be measured over 20 lines of text.[52] The VGT illustrates and enumerates all the typefaces found in fifteenth-century editions.[53] Both Haebler's 'M' list and the VGT list are design based. Amelung refers in his text to Zainer's typefaces by number, following the early *GW* system, the first five being numbered Type 1, 2, 3, 4 and 5. (To cover all bases he also uses all the other systems when first introducing Zainer's types). Although a chronological number might be simpler it is not helpful in keeping the size of a particular face in mind when reading or writing. It was decided to use just one system when referring to Zainer's faces for the purposes of this study, the incunabulists' method of measurement over 20 lines of text for naming the types, as this is the system most commonly used by scholars. A table of Zainer's typefaces is also included here for reference.

Table 1.1. Showing Zainer's first five typefaces as classified by different systems

20 lines	Amelung/*GW*	M	VGT (page ref.)
116 mm	1	15 & 56	475, 479, 530
110 mm	2	(Qu) 109	476, 479
117 mm	3	15	477, 479
96 mm	4	25	478, 479
136 mm	5	27	478, 480, 482

The body size of Type 116G is 5.8mm and that of Type 110R is 5.5mm. In today's terms of describing type sizes by their standardised points, i.e. *c.*72 points to the inch for the English and American point sizes, Type 116G and Type 117G are about 17 points and Type 110R equates to about 16 points. Type 96G, with a body size of 4.8mm is about 14 points and Type 136G, with a body size of 6.8mm is just over 19 points.

---

[52] Konrad Haebler, *Typenrepertorium der Wiegendrucke*, repr. (Nendeln/Liechtenstein and Wiesbaden: Kraus, 1968).
[53] VGT.

Typeface designs

The designs of Johann's first three typefaces, used between 1473 and 1477, are very close to those of his brother Günther, another factor indicating the continuing relationship between the brothers through this period. The type designs are so close that it is most likely that Johann borrowed the matrices, or the punches and made his own matrices, with a few variations, and then, with his own slightly smaller mould cast his own founts of type letters.[54]

Type 116G is a gotico-antiqua (= fere-humanistica) face and is basically the same design, although on a slightly smaller body, as Günther's Type 117G (Figure 1.3).[55] Interestingly the brothers' gotico-antiqua typeface designs are very close to those used by Mentelin in Strassburg, with whom they had learnt to print.

The gotico-antiqua face is, as its name suggests, a face with elements of both the more upright Germanic gothic or textura face and the more rounded roman or antiqua face. Type 116G started with pointed ascenders and descenders to the f, h and s (termed 116* in *BMC*) but after being used for Zainer's first three editions these were replaced with letterforms with shorter ascenders and descenders.[56] An h with a short right leg (termed Type 116a in *BMC*) was used for a time later in 1473 but was then replaced by an h with a tailed leg (termed Type 116b in *BMC*).[57] Type 116G was used from 1473 to 1476.

Type 110R is a roman (antiqua) face (Figure 1.4). It was only used as a text face twice in 1473, and afterwards occasionally for headlines until 1476. Again it is very close in design to a typeface of Günther's, his Type 107R that he only used for one edition, *Etymologiae*.[58]

Johann first used his Type 117G in 1476. It is again similar in style to a typeface of Günther's, his Type 118G (Figure 1.5).[59] Writing about the transition from manuscript to print in Augsburg, Johannes Janota shows the close relationship between the scribes and the printers.[60]

---

[54] Amelung, *Der Frühdruck*, p. 32. Amelung states that in 1493, when he had stopped printing, Johann moved back to Augsburg and earned a living casting and manufacturing type, so this may well have been a skill he had from the beginning of his printing life.

[55] Amelung, *Der Frühdruck*, p. 43. See also A. F. Johnson, *Type designs*, new rev. edn (n.p: Deutsche, 1966), pp. 6–24, who gives clear descriptions of the differences between these early gothic typeface designs.

[56] *BMC*, vol. 2, p. 518. *BMC* is the only source of the variations of Type 116G and bases its attribution of dates to some undated edition of the use of the variants.

[57] Giovanni Boccaccio, *De claris mulieribus*, 1473 (ib00720000).

[58] Isidorus, *Etymologiae*, 1472 (ii00181000).

[59] *BMC*, vol. 2, pp. ix and 518. Notes in *BMC* show that Günther's Type 118G was also used by other Augsburg printers after his death. It appears in an edition by Ambrose Keller in 1479 (p. 361) in the headlines of an edition by Bämler in 1479 (p. 330), by Kästlin in one edition in 1481 (p. 362), and by Blaubirer in 3 editions from 1480–81 (p. 360). However these are not all the same body size so perhaps they borrowed the punches to make their own matrices, and then cast their own founts.

[60] Janota, 'Von der Handschrift', p. 138.

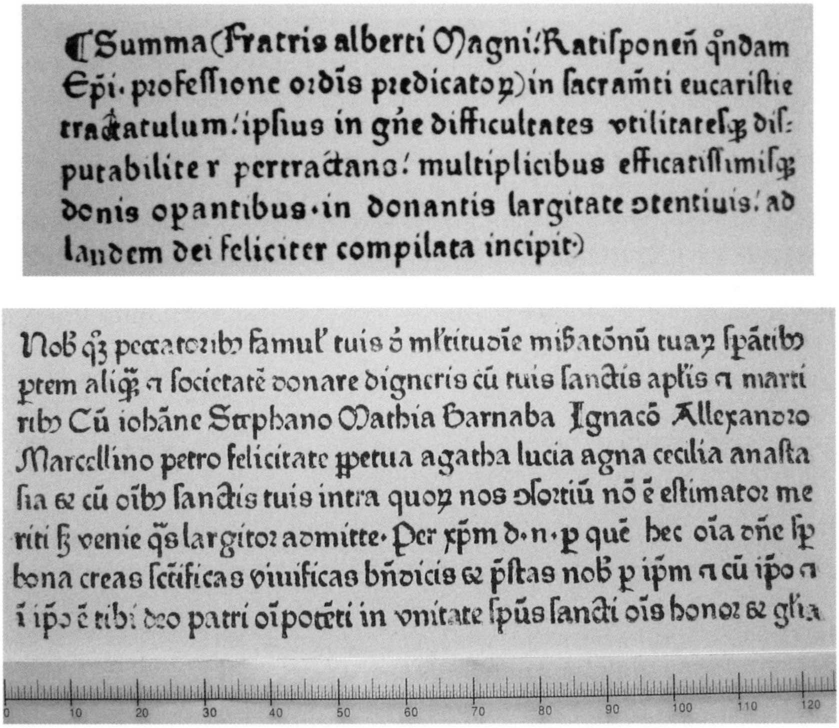

¶Summa Fratris alberti Magni. Ratisponen qndam
Epi. profeſſione ordis predicatox in ſacramti eucariſtie
tractatulum ipſius in gñe difficultates vtilitateſx diſ:
putabiliter pertractans multiplicibus efficatiſſimiſx
donis opantibus in donantis largitate otentiuis ad
laudem dei feliciter compilata incipit)

Nob qz peccatoribz famul tuis o mltituoie miſatonu tuax ſpatibz
prem aliqz a ſocietate donare digneris cu tuis ſanctis aplis a marti
ribz Cu iohane Stephano Mathia Barnaba Ignaco Allexancro
Marcellino petro felicitate ppetua agatha lucia agna cecilia anaſta
ſia ez cu oibz ſanctis tuis intra quox nos oſortiu no e eſtimator me
riti ſz venie qs largitor admitte. Per xpm d. n. p que bec oia one ſp
bona creas ſctificas viuificas bñoicis ez pſtas nob p ipm a cu ipo a
i ipo e tibi deo patri oipoteti in vnitate ſpus ſancti ois honor ez glia

Figure 1.3. Johann Zainer's Type 116G (above) and Günther Zainer's Type 117G (below). Both examples taken from *BMC*.

He suggests, quoting Carl Wehmer, that Günther was working closely with scribe Heinrich Molitor and that the design of Type 118G was based on Molitor's hand.[61] It has a much larger looking face on the body than the old Type 116G, but, being of almost the same body size it could be, and was, used alongside Type 116G.[62] Type 117G was used as a text type set in the same line together with Type 116G (with Type 110R used separately for the headlines) in an undated edition *Documenta moralia*.[63] It was only in use for a short time and only to print five editions, one of which is dated, *Die vierundzwanzig goldenen Harfen,* which carries the year [14]76 in the colophon.[64] The other editions using Type 117G carry no date but, because Type 117G was never used again by

[61] Carl Wehmer, 'Augsburger Schreiber aus der Frühzeit des Buchdrucks', *Beiträge zur Inkunabelkunde*, N.F.2 (1938), pp. 108–127 (p. 121).

[62] The difference in body size between 116G and 117G is only 1mm over 20 lines. Therefore the difference in body size between pieces of type from each of the two faces is only 0.05mm, barely discernable, and a difference which would not have caused any problems, if the faces were being set together in the same line, when locking up the forme.

[63] Cato, *Documenta moralia* [*c*.1476] (ic00320000).

[64] Johannes Nider, *Die vierundzwanzig goldenen Harfen* [14]76 (in00224000).

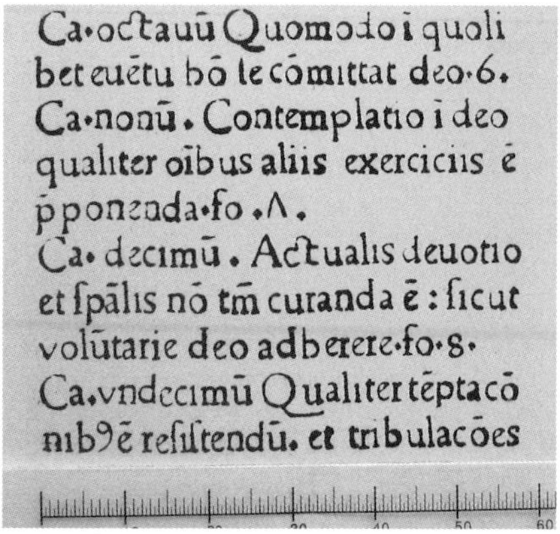

Ca·octauũ Quomodoi quoli
bet euẽtu bõ le comittat deo·6·
Ca·nonũ· Contemplatio i deo
qualiter oĩbus aliis exerciciis ẽ
pponẽdada·fo ·Λ·
Ca· decimũ · Actualis deuotio
et fpãlis nõ tm curanda ẽ : ficut
volũtarie deo adberere·fo·8·
Ca·vndecimũ Qualiter teptacõ
nib9ẽ refiftendũ· et tribulacões

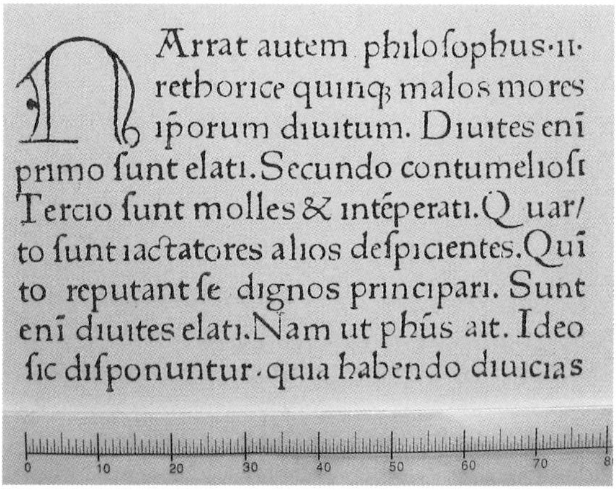

Arrat autem philofophus·11·
rethorice quinq̃; malos mores
iporum diuitum. Diuites eni
primo funt elati. Secundo contumeliofi
Tercio funt molles & inteperati. Q uar/
to funt iactatores alios defpicientes. Qui
to reputant fe dignos principari. Sunt
eni diuites elati. Nam ut phũs ait. Ideo
fic difponuntur · quia habendo diuicias

Figure 1.4. Johann Zainer's Type 110R (above) and Günther Zainer's Type 107R
(below). Both examples from *BMC*.

Zainer in any other editions, they were presumably printed around the
same time as *Die goldenen Harfen*. The size of the face may have proved a
problem because it was wide and would have taken up more space on
the page than Type 116G, therefore requiring much more paper for
printing a book.[65] Because it was in use for such a short time and was
replaced by Type 96G, a significantly smaller face, its uneconomic use
of space may have been a factor in its demise.[66]

---

[65] Paper costs were a major part of the total cost of book production. L. Febvre and H.-J. Martin,
The coming of the book (London: New Left Books, 1976), p. 114, suggest that about half the overall cost
of producing an edition in the fifteenth century was paper.

[66] A rough count made of the number of characters over three lines of text of both Type 116G and
117G showed that Type 117G took up approximately 20 per cent more space on the line than Type
116G.

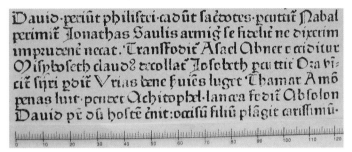

Figure 1.5. Johann Zainer's Type 117G (above) and Günther Zainer's Type 118G (below). Both examples from *BMC*.

Type 96G was introduced sometime during 1477. It is a less rounded face and more compact than Types 116G and 117G, and has some unusual letterforms in the uppercase such as the A and M. It is used on its own for the undated *Legenda aurea* [not after 1477] and in *Sermones quadragesimales* dated March 1478, and with Type 136G, Zainer's first type designed specifically for headlines, in *Calendarium* for 1477–1552 with a printed date 1478 (Figure 1.6).[67] Type 136G is a standard rotunda in style.

With the introduction of Type 96G and Type 136G the earlier typefaces (116G, 110R and 117G) are never seen again. Typefaces wear and need replacing. In the *BMC* Introduction Pollard states that the 'type-metal used in the fifteenth century appears to have been very soft, and the printer who desired to go on using the same fount was obliged to provide

---

[67] Jacobus de Voragine, *Legenda aurea* (ij00088400); Leonardus de Utino, *Sermones quadragesimales*, 9 Mar 1478 (il00158000) and Jacob Pflaum, *Calendarium 1477–1552*, 1478 (ip00542000). A copy of *Legenda aurea* in the BSB has a manuscript purchase note of 1477.

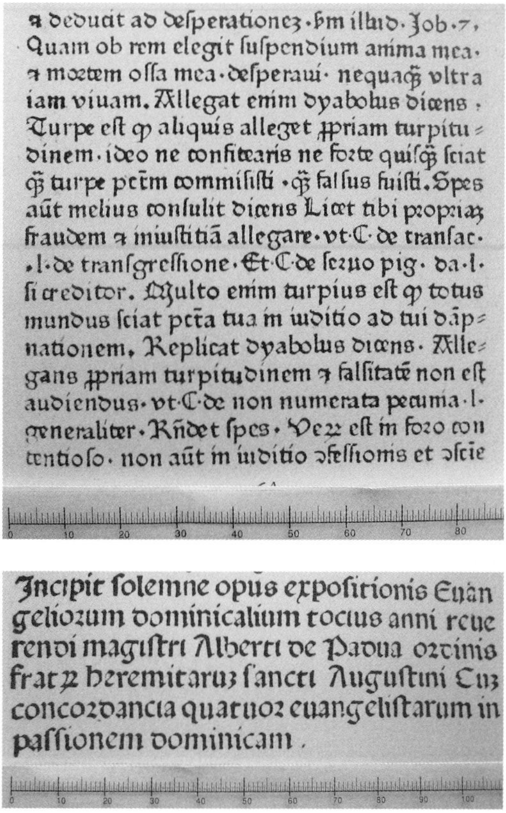

a deducit ad desperatione3 · sm illud · Job · 7 ·
Quam ob rem elegit suspendium anima mea ·
7 moetem ossa mea · desperaui · nequacq vltra
iam viuam. Allegat enim dyabolus dicens ·
Turpe est cp aliquis alleget ppriam turpitu =
dinem · ideo ne confitearis ne forte quisqg sciat
cp turpe petm commisisti · cp falsus fuisti. Spes
aut melius consulit dicens Licet tibi proprias
fraudem 7 iniustitia allegare · vt·C·de transac ·
· l · de transgressione · Et·C·de seruo pig · da · l ·
si creditor. Multo enim turpius est cp totus
mundus sciat peta tua in iuditio ad tui daps
nationem. Replicat dyabolus dicens · Alle=
gans ppriam turpitudinem 7 falsitate non est
audiendus · vt·C·de non numerata pecunia · l ·
generaliter · Rndet spes · Ve22 est in foro con
tentioso · non aut in iuditio confessionis et oscie

Incipit solemne opus expositionis Euan
geliozum dominicalium tocius anni reue
rendi magistri Alberti de Padua ordinis
fratz heremitaru3 sancti Augustini Cu3
concozdancia quatuoz euangelistarum in
passionem dominicam ·

Figure 1.6. Johann Zainer's Type 96G (above) and Type 136G, designed specifically for headlines (below). Both examples from *BMC*.

for its renewal. This could be effected either by periodical recasting of the type in bulk, or by frequent additions to the fount supplementing a diminishing stock of any particular sort'.[68] He cites two printers, Grüninger in Strassburg and De Gregoriis in Venice, who melted down their old type to make new founts in their place. Evidence from the San Ripoli press in the late 1470s, on the purchase of metal, shows that they did not buy huge quantities of lead, which would suggest that they may have been melting down their old type for re-use.[69] Because Zainer's

[68] *BMC*, vol. 1, p. xv.

[69] Melissa Conway, *The 'Diario' of the printing press of San Ripoli 1476–1484* (Florence: Leo S. Olschki, 1999) includes many of the purchases made by the press. This is not a comprehensive account book but from the entries it can be seen that a total of 109lbs of tin were purchased but only 20lbs of lead. The proportions of these metals are not correct for use as type metal because lead is the main component with only a little tin added to help the flow of the molten metal. When re-melting old type metal some of the tin is lost, so extra is needed to top up.

earlier types are never found in use again after the new ones had been introduced he too may have melted down his old worn type to recast as the new faces.

Zainer was a prolific printer, producing around thirteen editions in his first year. This research concentrates on 244 copies, represented in 38 editions which Zainer printed between the years 1473 and 1478. These are listed in *Bibliography – Primary Sources, section 1*. It was decided to put a limit on the number of editions being studied to keep this research within manageable proportions. Also, the first years of his printing, when Zainer established himself in his own workshop, were thought most likely to have been the period when he might have been more experimental in his approach. Limiting the number of editions enabled more copies of each edition to be looked at, giving a greater chance for comparison. Single sheet broadsides and almanacs printed in the first five years have been omitted from the core of this study because it was felt they did not bring enough evidence of printing practice. The dated *Papal Bull* of 1478 was omitted because there is only one copy in the Mazarine Library in Paris and also it was a small edition of six leaves.[70] However some copies of other editions, printed by Zainer after 1478, were also examined to see if he was still practising the same methods in later years, and whether some of the measurements and data noted in his early books remained the same.

The problem of Zainer's undated editions

Many of Zainer's editions are undated. From 1473 until 1478 (or an assigned date that includes 1478) there are a total of 51 editions attributed to Zainer of which only 18 have a date printed within the book. This made it difficult to decide which editions to include for this study.[71] The undated editions do have dates assigned to them in catalogues, based on various sources of information. The dates used in this study are all taken from ISTC. Variations in typeface can help date undated editions and is one method used by bibliographers when approaching dating problems. Other information may come from external factors, such as a list of books for sale, or a note made by the purchaser or rubricator.

For Zainer's first two years chronological variations in some of the letterforms in his Type 116G and his ornamental initials have been used

[70] Sixtus IV, Pont. Max., *Bulla 21 Mar.1478* (is00542500).

[71] 1478 was chosen as this was the year when both Zainer's brother and Heinrich Steinhöwel died, both people who had given much support to the early years of his press as mentioned above.

[72] *BMC*, vol. 2, p. 518. Also Amelung, *Der Frühdruck*, p. 88, states that the undated, Thomas Aquinas, *De periculis contingentibus* (it00316000) was printed in the second form of Type 116G.

by bibliographers to attribute dates to some of the editions.[72] In early 1474, he printed a list of editions that he was offering for sale, and this has been used, along with the typographical evidence to firm up some of the attributed dates.[73] In 1476 he introduced Type 117G, used only for a short period, which helps attribute dates to four more undated editions, by linking them with the one dated edition printed in Type 117G. Up to *c*.1477, and the printing of the *Decameron,* there are 30 editions, some dated and some with attributed dates, whose inclusion in this study was certain. Also certain for inclusion was the dated edition of *Sermones,* printed in 1478.

The main problem came with the editions Zainer printed from 1477 onwards using his new Type 96G, firstly on its own and then with Type 136G for headlines. There are no dated editions for 1477 and only two for 1478. There are 17 editions with assigned dates of *c*.1477, *c*.1478, 1478–80, and not after 1478. As four of these editions had a purchase note from the first buyer giving a good indication of year, they were added to the list.

This still left thirteen editions, all with a possible 1478 date and all using the same typefaces. It was decided to see if any other chronological indicators could be found. It had been noted that Zainer changed his pattern of quiring through the years. This will be explored more fully in Chapter 2, *Initial Observations and Basic Findings*, but at this stage it was decided to include all editions quired in either 10s, or alternate 8s and 10s, as well as one edition quired in 8s for comparison. This gave rise to the consequence that one edition, Johannes Nider, *Praeceptorium divinae legis* (in00205000) with a date of [not after 1479] in ISTC was included because it was quired in alternate 8s and 10s.

Having selected 38 from the possible 51, and not using all the 51 editions could mean that any statistical information could be affected. When comparing statistics with those found by other scholars the figures were always compiled with both 38 editions and 51 editions to see if the results were seriously affected.

The format of the 38 selected editions

Almost all Zainer's editions were printed in folio format, i.e. one sheet of paper folded in half after printing to give two leaves/four pages. For the editions selected for this research Zainer printed one quarto edition, 28 chancery-folio editions, one median-folio edition, seven royal-folio editions and one imperial-folio edition.[74] Haebler states that the two main

---

[73] *Advertisement for 15 books printed in 1473* [before 9 April 1474] (iz00016500).

[74] Philip Gaskell, *A new introduction to bibliography* (Oxford: Oxford University Press, 1972), p. 67, lists the common four main paper sizes used in the fifteenth century: imperial (500 × 740mm), royal (445 × 615mm), median (345 × 515mm) and the smallest (the one used by Zainer for his small folios) chancery (315 × 450mm).

Table 1.2. The percentage of Zainer's editions in different formats, printed between 1473 and 1478, compared with the percentages found by Smith in the periods 1470–74 and 1475–79 from her survey of printers generally.

	Period	Folios		Quartos		Octavos		Total editions
Zainer	1473–78	37	97.30%	1	2.70%		2.38%	38
Smith	1470–74	180	55.70%	123	38.10%	13	4%	316
	1475–79	303	61.30%	174	35.20%	14	2.80%	491

paper sizes in the incunable period were royal and median sizes.[75] This does not seem to be correct as Paul Needham states that both median and imperial sizes of paper were uncommonly used in incunables and suggests that Haebler's information was 'quite unreliable'.[76] Needham also adds for interest that a median sheet of paper is almost exactly half the size of an imperial sheet and that chancery is half that of royal.[77] From measuring the dimensions of the leaves of Zainer's smallest folios, some of which have untrimmed deckle edges, and some that have a turned-in corner that had escaped the binder's trim, it was clear that they all could have come from chancery-size paper.[78]

Margaret Smith looked at formats of 4,194 different editions printed during the incunable period.[79] Zainer printed over 97 per cent of his editions in folio format, a much higher percentage than was found in the work of other printers, as shown by Smith for the 1470s, where almost 60 per cent of editions were in folio format (Table 1.2). All the 28 chancery-size folios are printed with one column of text on each page. His other editions are all on larger paper: his median-, royal- and imperial-folio editions are all printed with two columns of text to a page. He printed no editions with marginal notes and none with more than two columns. Smith comments that single-column editions were in the majority across all incunables, whatever format.[80] However for folio format she shows an occurrence rate for single columns of 59.3 per cent

---

[75] Haebler, p. 49.

[76] Paul Needham, 'Res papirea: sizes and formats of the late medieval book', in Peter Rück, ed., *Die Rationalisierung der Buchherstellung in Mittelalter und in der frühen Neuzeit* (Marburg an der Lahn: Institut für historische Hilfswissenschaften, 1994), pp. 123–145 (p. 125, footnote 10).

[77] Needham, 'Res papirea', p. 126.

[78] Zainer also printed two quarto editions, possibly one octavo, and five broadsheets, none of which are being included in this research.

[79] Margaret M. Smith, *Form and its relationship to content in the design of incunables* (Cambridge: unpublished thesis, 1983), p. 70.

[80] Smith, Figure 5.2, p. 177.

[81] Smith, Figure 5.3, p. 179.

and 45.7 per cent for the periods 1470–74 and 1475–79 respectively.[81] This compares with 78 per cent for Zainer, between 1473 and 1478 and shows that his use of single columns was much higher than that of his contemporaries.

This may have a purely practical explanation; setting two columns of text on as small a leaf as a chancery-folio edition would make for a very narrow measure, and difficulties for the compositor, with a big increase in word breaks and/or hyphenation to fit the text to the line.[82] Smith also comments on line length and its relation to type size for both single- and double-column editions. Her figures show that Zainer was working with a slightly larger type size than the mean and to a slightly shorter line length for the period.[83] The mean text-type size found by Smith was 111mm over 20 lines and the line length was 121mm, whereas Zainer's type size was 116/117mm and his line length 110mm. His later Type 96G, used from 1477, was smaller than the mean, although he still kept the same line length. As with Zainer, Smith also found that the relationship between type size and line length was flexible.[84]

The subject matter of Zainer's editions

This research is not primarily about the texts that Zainer printed, it is much more about his printing practices. However Smith established that there was a strong link between some subject matter and the layout on the page, such as whether in single or double columns. Some writers have made some general comments about the layout of the first printed books in their following of the manuscript tradition. Curt Bühler described the practice of printers in Bologna, particularly of legal books, working to the double-column practice used by the calligraphers.[85] Haebler stated that, although the design of the type page was at the printer's discretion to begin with, the manuscript tradition would have had an influence.[86] He added that almost all Bibles and liturgical books were printed in double columns, apart from Psalters where the text was set in long lines right across the page. More recently Paul

---

[82] A rule of thumb used by printers is that the type will fit comfortably into a line that is twice the length in pica ems as the body size of type in pica points, i.e. 12 point type will fit comfortably into a 24 pica line. Zainer's Type 116G is *c*.17 point and the 110mm line of his chancery folios is almost 26 picas long. He was already quite tight in setting one column of that size type to that measure, even tighter in his two columns which measure only 83mm/16 pica ems wide. For the median-folio column width of 66mm/16 pica ems the measure is extremely tight.

[83] Smith, Figure 4.9, p. 161.

[84] Smith, p. 154.

[85] Curt Bühler, *The fifteenth-century book* (Philadelphia: University of Pennsylvania Press, 1960), p. 46 and Curt Bühler, *The university and the press in fifteenth-century Bologna* (Notre Dame, Indiana: Mediaeval Institute, University of Notre Dame, 1958), pp. 17–18.

[86] Haebler, *Incunabula*, p. 84.

Needham discusses how different the same text would look, in typeface design and size and in page size, if printed in the 1460s and then later in the 1480s and 1490s.[87]

Smith's figures supply some statistical evidence. They show that double columns were in the minority across all subjects taken as a whole. However, where the subject matter was medicine, law, Bibles or encyclopaedias, over 50 per cent of the editions (and for Bibles and encyclopaedias over 95 per cent) were printed in double columns.[88] She also found that the majority of royal folios had double columns, although the majority (61.3 per cent) of all double columns were printed on median size paper.[89] Smith does not give a separate breakdown of figures for chancery-folio editions.

Zainer printed 76 per cent of the editions being studied here as chancery folios, the smallest size in this format. They were all printed as single columns and covered a range of subjects; theology, humanist literature, history, and philosophy. The one median folio he printed is set in double columns, and is humanist literature. 100 per cent of his larger editions, the seven royal, and one imperial folio, are religious texts set in double columns. These figures for Zainer sit quite comfortably alongside Smith's findings.

Of these 38 editions Zainer printed seven in German (18 per cent) including one in Swabian dialect, 30 (79 per cent) in Latin and one, Aesop's *Vita et fabulae*, in both German and Latin (2.6 per cent).[90] These figures are close to that found by Smith with Latin 72.3 per cent, vernacular 25.4 per cent and other, including two languages in one edition (2.2 per cent).[91] One of the editions in German is a religious text, Nider's *Die vierundzwanzig goldenen Harfen,* but the other editions in German are historical, medical and literary (Table 1.3).

Zainer used his gotico-antiqua faces, Types 116G, 117G, and 96G for texts in both his Latin and German editions. He used his roman face Type 110R only for printing in Latin; in two Latin editions, *De adhaerendo Deo* and *Historia Griseldis.*[92] It was also used for text in the Latin broadsheet *Vitae huius compendiosa descriptio* (ip00419700) and for headlines in four other editions, the quarto *Büchlein der Ordnung (Pest Regiment)* (is00763000) *De planctu ecclesiae* (ip00249000) *Sermones de sanctis* (il00158000) and

---

[87] Paul Needham, 'The changing shape of the Vulgate Bile in fifteenth-century printing shops', Paul Saenger and Kimberley van Kampen, eds., *The Bible as book; the first printed editions* (London and New Castle: British Library and Oak Knoll, 1999), p. 54.

[88] Smith, p. 193.

[89] Smith, p. 198.

[90] Curt Bühler, '*Griseldis',* pp. 231–236, for an account of Zainer's Swabian edition of *Griseldis* (ip00403000).

[91] Smith, p. 144.

[92] Albertus Magnus, *De adhaerendo Deo* [*c*.1473] (ia00218000).

Table 1.3. The languages of Zainer's editions.

Language	Chancery	Median	Royal	Imperial	Quarto	Total
Latin	22		7	1		30
German	4	1			1	6
Swabian	1					1
Lat & Ger	1					1
Total	28	1	7	1	2	38

Table 1.4. The percentage use of different typefaces for different languages by Zainer for printing his editions compared with the percentage use found by Smith for other printers.

	Typeface used	Latin	Vernacular
Zainer	roman	100%	0%
	gotico-antiqua	82.90%	17.10%
Smith – Germany	roman	100%	0%
	gotico-antiqua	95.10%	4.90%

Documenta moralia. Zainer's use of his roman face only for Latin texts is, at 100 per cent, exactly the same as found by Smith for use of roman founts in Germany. However he had a lower use of his gotico-antiqua faces for Latin texts, at 82.9 per cent, than found by Smith at 95.1 per cent, and consequently a higher use of them for German texts at 17.1 per cent compared with Smith's 4.9 per cent (Table 1.4).[93]

The number of copies in an edition

It is not easy to find much information about the size of edition for incunable editions. Occasionally some detail was supplied in the colophon of the edition. Pollard noted information from colophons that showed, for example, that printer Johannes de Spira printed 300 copies in Venice of Cicero's *Epistolae ad familiares* in 1469 (ic00504000) and 300 copies of a second edition (ic00505000) later in the same year.[94] Phillipo de Lavangia stated in his colophon that he had printed an edition 300 copies of the same text in 1472 in Milan (ic00511500).[95] Other information about possible size of an edition can sometimes be found in other documents such as account books or correspondence. The San Ripoli

---

[93] Smith, p. 145.

[94] Alfred W. Pollard, *An essay on colophons with specimens and translations* (Chicago: Caxton Club, 1905), pp. 33 and 36.

[95] Pollard, *Colophons*, p. 150.

Press *Diario* states that 400 copies of their *Donatus* were taken to Domenico the paper merchant for him to sell on 14 November 1476.[96] There are numerous further entries in the *Diario* about sales and the printing of books in both small and large quantities. 100 copies of Antoninus Florentinus *Confessionale* (ia00847000) were taken to Mariano in Florence for sale on 24 October 1477 and 400 copies of *Ars morendi* (ia01102000) were supplied on 3 July 1979.[97]

Much of the information is about Italian editions and it is more difficult to find details about German printers and those that were near to Zainer in time. In 1473 Peter Schoeffer in Mainz is thought to have printed 360 copies on paper and 40 copies on vellum of Pope Gregorius IX, *Decretales* (ig00447000).[98] The introductory notes in the British Library catalogue state that an especially commissioned Breviary, printed by Georgius de Spira in 1480, was in an edition of 400 copies.[99]

Uwe Neddermeyer has collated information about editions for which there are some known figures, and includes details about one edition by Zainer.[100] This has come from a document held in Augsburg Stadtarchiv. In the document Günther is standing surety for Johann, to his godparents, the family Rottengater of Ulm, for the supply of enough paper for Johann to print 525 copies of de Utino's *Sermones de tempore*.[101] In fact there is no evidence, in the form of a printed edition, or even a fragment from the edition, that Johann ever printed *Sermones de tempore*. Johann printed the companion volume, de Utino's *Sermones de sanctis* (il00158000) in 1475.[102] This is the only clue to the size of Zainer's editions, but it does indicate that he was working on quite a large scale. Neddermeyer offers figures from other printers but there are few that are close to Zainer in either time or place.

The size of Zainer's printing workshop

There is no information about Zainer's printing workshop, either its location or how many presses he had. Unfortunately the Tax books and Register of citizens for Ulm between 1474 and 1499, which might have

---

[96] Conway, *Diario*, p. 92 [f. 1r].

[97] Conway, *Diario*, p. 134 [f. 26r] and p. 176 [f. 60r].

[98] Gottfried Zedler, 'Über der Preise und Auflagenhöhe unser älteste Druck', *Beiträge zum Bibliotheks- und Buchwesen* (1913), pp. 267–288 (p. 281).

[99] BMC, vol. 2, p. xi. *Breviarium ratisbonense*, 1480 (ib01176000), *BMC*, vol. 2, p. 485.

[100] Uwe Neddermeyer, *Von der Handschrift zum gedruckten Buch: Schriftlichkeit und Leseinteresse im Mittelalter und in der frühen Neuzeit: Quantitative und qualitative Aspekte* (Wiesbaden: Harrassowitz, 1998), vol. 2, p. 755.

[101] Neddermeyer, p. 755, footnote 23, with reference to the information being supplied by Hans-Jörg Künast, sourced from Augsburg SB, 2° Cod. Aug. 390, ff. 265v–266r. With thanks to Hans-Jörg Künast for sending me a copy of the text of the original document and helping with further information.

[102] If this document did relate to the 1475 *Sermones de sanctis*, an edition of 243 leaves, then the paper order, for which Günther was standing surety, would have been at least 65,000 sheets.

given some information about Zainer's relative wealth and standing, are missing.[103] The first evidence that Zainer lived in Ulm is found in a document when he was admitted, along with his brother, to the Roman Brotherhood of the Holy Ghost on 15 June 1478.[104] Zainer described himself in the colophons of his editions as being from Reutlingen until he was established as an Ulm citizen in 1481; the first colophon where he makes his status clear as an Ulm citizen is in the colophon of Bonaventura's *Sermones* (ib00949000).[105] Zainer is listed as a debtor in a debtors' book of 1481 and 1488, but again there is nothing from the earlier period.[106] However the large number of copies, 525, being contemplated for an edition of *Sermones* suggests that he had a largish establishment.

There is some information about the number of presses installed at the monastery of SS Ulrich and Afra in Augsburg in 1472. Two presses were made, then five more were purchased from Schüssler, and there was also mention of a further six royal-size presses, along with all the necessary type, paper, punches and typecasting instruments.[107] This would seem like a large amount of equipment and in his article about Augsburg printing Scholderer suggests that the three volume edition of Vincentius Bellovacencis, *Speculum historiale,* 1474 (iv00284000), was printed on the six royal presses, working with two presses for each volume.[108] There is nothing to tell whether either Zainer brother had an establishment of this size, but the figures are worth bearing in mind; Schüssler had five presses to dispose of, and the monastery was acquiring up to twelve different presses, all close by, in Augsburg at the same time, the early 1470s. This suggests that half-a-dozen or more presses could have been the norm, but this remains speculation.

PRIMARY SOURCES

Bibliographies and Catalogues

This study is based on a combination of different approaches as it attempts to come to a closer understanding of the printing practices in the fifteenth-century. It brings together the recorded results from direct observation, and the noted and recorded empirical measurements of

---

[103] Peter Amelung, 'Der Ulmer Buchdruck im 15. Jahrhundert. Quellenlage und Forschungs-stand', *Villes d'imprimeries et moulins à papier du XIVe au XVIe siècle* (Bruxelles: Crédit Communal de Belgique: 1976), pp. 25–38 (p. 26).

[104] Amelung, *Der Frühdruck*, p. 21.

[105] Amelung, 'Der Ulmer Buchdruck', p. 31, footnote 18.

[106] Amelung, 'Der Ulmer Buchdruck', p. 28.

[107] Victor Scholderer, 'Notes on early Augsburg printing', *The Library*, 5th series, 6 (1951), 1–6 (p. 5).

[108] Scholderer, p. 6. This was a particularly large edition and not typical of SS Ulrich and Afra undertakings.

Zainer's editions, together with the bibliographical information already available from catalogues. Further light on interpreting the data comes from practical experiments and the findings of other scholars.

Before any observations could be made copies of the editions had to be located, as well as the relevant information that was available about the editions in the incunable catalogues and bibliographies. Both the editions and their relevant catalogues serve as Primary Sources for this study. Bibliographies and catalogues of incunables are essential tools for any student of early printing. The bibliographies aim to list all existing incunables, usually either by country or throughout the world. The information they list is not usually copy-specific but will list the edition by title, author, place and date of printing, printer, and if appropriate, translator. The catalogues are library specific and vary in the quality of information they provide.

When beginning this study the first source for discovering which editions had been printed by, or attributed to, Zainer, and for locating where copies of his editions were held was the ISTC.[109] The ISTC lists all known incunable editions by author with a unique 'i' number, and includes all other bibliography and major incunable catalogue numbers for each edition. It also provides lists of locations of copies of each edition, although not completely comprehensive as it is still under construction. This database will be the one universal bibliography for all known incunable editions. It is searchable online under author, title, printer, place of printing, year, etc., British Library shelfmark, ISTC number and other bibliographical references, such as Hain or *GW* and Goff.[110] Links from ISTC to the Bayerische Staatsbibliothek's website are in the process of being added.[111]

With this core information, the catalogues of incunable collections in various libraries were consulted to discover more details about individual copies. The British Library catalogue [*BMC*], gives the most detailed bibliographic information of any of the catalogues, and has provided essential information for this study. It gives text of incipit and colophon, format, quiring details, number of leaves, whether leaves are numbered, leaf dimensions, number of columns, number of lines (including headline or not), text-area dimensions, pin holes, blind impressions (some) type face(s), use of printed initials or spaces left, use of printed borders, printed woodcuts as well as extra notes about other features in the edition, and

---

[109] The *Illustrated incunabula short title catalogue on CD-Rom,* 2nd edn (London: Primary Source Media in association with The British Library, 1998). The ISTC is also accessible online at http://blpc.bl.uk/catalogues/istc/index.html

[110] H; *GW*; GOFF.

[111] *BSB-Ink* is accessible online at www.bsb-muenchen.de in a wide number of fields including date, printer, place, author, title, collational formula, provenance, and binding details.

biographical notes about the printer. Also, and of particular interest to the printing historian, it is arranged in 'Proctor order', after Robert Proctor who was responsible for its arrangement, largely chronologically; by printing countries, then by printing places, by printer and by edition.

One or two other catalogues from all those consulted are mentioned here as they provided extra information beyond the basics. The Bodleian Library incunable catalogue gives the size of the bound book and leaf size, and information about provenance and binding.[112] The incunable catalogue of the Bayerische Staatsbibliothek in Munich provides a very useful concordance which lists printing places with the printers working there and their editions in chronological order as well as providing links between BSB and Hain, *GW*, Goff and Copinger bibliographies, with *BMC* and an internal *BSB-Ink* shelfmark.[113]

Bernd Breitenbruch's catalogue of incunabula in the city library in Ulm, where Zainer started printing, includes fifty copies of editions printed by Zainer.[114] It gives details about provenance and binding, with over one-third of the collection coming from the libraries of the Dominican and Franciscan orders in Ulm, and many of these copies also being bound in Ulm.

The editions; measuring and recording the data

Having located the editions and the relevant information available from catalogues the next step was to make observations and record the data. The observations fall into two categories; basic empirical data and other details concerning printing quality and techniques.

Basic empirical data

When printing a book, basic design decisions have to be made such as format, the width of the text area, typeface, the number of lines to a page, the positioning of the text and the size of the margins, and leaf size.[115] Every edition studied for this research, printed both by Zainer and by other printers, had these basic features measured and recorded. 313 copies of 71 different editions printed by Zainer, and 246 copies of 213 editions by 46 other printers, have been recorded. A full list of these editions, with their catalogue reference numbers and shelfmark is given in *Bibliography – Primary Sources*. For some of the Zainer editions it has been possible to record only one copy, because only one exists, but for others up to thirteen copies have been recorded. Being able to look at more than one copy makes it possible to check if there is any variation between the

[112] *Bod-inc.*
[113] *BSB-Ink.*
[114] Bernd Breitenbruch, *Die Inkunabeln der Stadtbibliothek Ulm* (Weissenhorn: Anton Konrad, 1987) [SBU].
[115] See *Glossary*.

copies, for instance in the text-width measurement or in the position of point holes or other marks on a certain leaf.

Other data and relevant details

Apart from recording the basic layout data, other details were also noted when, and if, they occurred – things that probably occurred during the printing process. Some of these details were meant to be there and come under the area of 'quality control', such as quality of inking, imposition and registration, and depth of impression of the type.[116] Others were caused by some part of the printing process, such as point holes that only occurred on some of his large folios.

There were other details that were not meant to be there, and could be counted as printers' errors. This latter category includes inked spacing material, blind impressions of type, cloth impression marks, inking problems such as set-off and off-set, frisket bite where the edge of the paper mask covered an edge of the text, finger prints, smudged printing, and inked string marks.[117] The presence of a deckle edge on the fore edge or foot of any leaves was also noted because this could give a clue as to the original size of the sheet on which the book was printed.

Measuring

The basic data described above, i.e. width and depth of text area, margins, leaf size, was all measured and recorded in millimetres. When measuring the margins, the central gutter (the margin between the text areas on a sheet) is the most important one because it is the only margin of which the final size was decided by the printer – a clue to his thinking at this design decision stage. It is also the most difficult to measure accurately because often the pages are not folded exactly, or the binding is too tight to get right into the centre of the fold for measuring. It was found that the most accurate figure could be obtained, where binding allowed, by measuring the width of the margin either side of the fold line in the central gutter on a conjugate pair of leaves in the centre of a quire, to get the total measurement between the two blocks of text. It has to be remembered, when measuring text areas, that one can only measure what can be seen on the page; there may be type metal set in the forme, beyond the visible length of the line of printed type letters on the page. Some letters are cast on quite wide bodies, perhaps a half millimetre wider than the actual letter shape seen on the page, or the set line of type may have spacing added at either end beyond the visible printed type. None of these can be measured, unless they have been inked and printed in error and therefore do appear on the leaf.

[116] See *Glossary*.
[117] See *Glossary*.

The number of lines was noted and, because the number of lines on a page often varied through an edition, a note was made of the page that had had its lines counted. The type face was identified following *BMC*. Where there were evident point holes they were measured in millimetres with their distance from the text and their distance from each other. Occasionally a corner or edge of paper was found turned in where it had escaped trimming during the binding process. Careful unfolding and measurement of these often showed the original size of the sheet, and gave an indication of how much had been trimmed off.

The accuracy of the measurements

There can be differences in these 'empirical' measurements. The dimensions of the text area printed on the same leaf in different copies of the same edition can vary. This can be due to a number of different factors. The cause most usually discussed by bibliographers for different dimensions of text area is paper stretch; the movement in the paper when or since the book was printed. Paper was damped before printing, to soften the fibres and make them more receptive to the printing ink. When paper is damped it expands, and then contracts when it dries, not always to the original size. Later storing in more or less damp conditions can affect the dimensions, and drying out the sheet when under pressure will keep it at the expanded size.

Fredson Bowers states that difference in paper shrinkage is one of the factors that can affect measurements of type areas.[118] Gaskell also discusses paper shrinkage and his implication is that it does not make a vital difference, more that it is something about which the bibliographer must be aware. He states that shrinkage was generally more pronounced across the chain lines than along them and gives figures of about 1 per cent and occasionally as high as 2.5 per cent.[119] Alfred Pollard writing in *BMC* also discusses variations in type size depending on the paper. He states that if paper is damped vigorously and then dried quickly it will shrink more than if it is handled gently. He adds that there can be differences with various thicknesses of paper and he cites an extreme example of a type measure in an edition printed by C.W. which differed between 110 and 104.5mm, because various thicknesses of paper were used in the same copy.[120] Pollard makes a useful point that the differences in measurements are not really a problem once one recognises the different factors that can affect them.

---

[118] Fredson Bowers, 'Bibliographical evidence from the printer's measure', *Studies in Bibliography*, 2 (1949–50), pp. 154–169 (pp. 163–4).

[119] Gaskell, p. 13.

[120] *BMC*, vol. 1, pp. xx–xxi, with reference to C.W.'s printing of Alanus de Insulis, *Distinctiones dictionum theologicum* [not after 1473] (ia00169000).

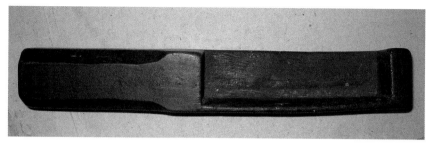

Figure 1.7. Wooden composing stick made to a fixed measure, date unknown. (Plantin-Moretus Museum, Antwerp.)

Apart from the stretching/contracting of paper there are other factors that might have caused differences in measurements of text areas. It is not known how Zainer was setting his type, if he was using a composing stick or setting directly into a galley or tray. If he had been using a stick it would most likely have been one cut from wood to a fixed measure (Figure 1.7). Bowers suggests that when composing sticks were being used, being handmade articles, they might easily have varied in width by a millimetre or two, although nominally being of the same size.[121] His study was based on his measurements taken from 'some hundreds of books', almost exclusively confined to the printing of Restoration play quartos. However his observations of fixed measures from setting type with fixed setting sticks show the tolerances to which the printer was working in the sixteenth and early seventeenth century.

Whether fixed or adjustable, sticks were likely to vary by as much as two millimetres even when intended to be used in setting the same width of text-areas. This is understandable when the difficulties are taken into account either of two compositors adjusting their sticks identically or of the artisan carving two wooden fixed sticks to give an absolutely precise opening for each.[122] Bowers suggests that up to two millimetres can be taken as normal. He also describes the difficulties of establishing whether two different sticks have been used, where the difference might be as little as one millimetre, and the importance of measuring across lines with similar letters at the end and the beginning to achieve an accurate a measurement as possible.[123] Bowers also suggests a further reason that might cause differences in text width; that of differences in tightness of lock up.[124] When all the lines that comprise the text block for a page of an edition are set, everything is 'locked-up' by some method so they will not

[121] Bowers, p. 154.
[122] Bowers, p. 155.
[123] Bowers, p. 155.
[124] Bowers, pp. 163–4.

move or fall over when being printed. It is not known what method of
lock-up was used in the fifteenth century but this is also a factor that
should be borne in mind.

The quality of the data

The other things noted were more subjective, such as quality of inking —
whether a page was over inked, under inked, unevenly inked, showed ink
bleed, had set-off or off-set in varying degrees, and they are more difficult
to record. Because it is difficult to quantify such things as unevenness of
inking, only the most obvious examples were noted.

There also might be a danger of seeing what one wants to see to help
build up a case for a particular pattern of work. To avoid this, only things
that were very obvious have been recorded. The doubtful, nebulous, or
perhaps-might-be-there, have not been recorded. This can be a difficult
rule to adhere to if, for example, a certain mark has been found in one
edition, and perhaps might be visible in a second. One wants it to be
there, to begin to establish a pattern, but if it was not clearly visible then it
was not included.

The importance of viewing more than one copy of an edition is also vital
to try to ensure as accurate a record of the data as possible. Also, when
looking for the kind of clues being studied here, it is useful to discover
whether they occur in more than one copy. Many of these clues are
technical errors and part of discovering Zainer's working practice, apart
from noting the errors, is to see if there is any consistency to them.
Examples might be whether an inked rising space showed in more than
one copy, or whether a point hole was in the same position in relation to
the text in more than one copy. Where it has only been possible to see one
copy of an edition the information has not been used for later interpretation.

One is dealing with artefacts that have been around for over 500 years
and much may have happened to them in the time. Some copies have
never left home, and there is great satisfaction, for example, in looking at a
book in Ulm library that had been printed in Ulm and then bound there
almost immediately after printing, and had then spent most of its life in a
monastery there before moving to the city library. This kind of book, in a
contemporary binding and kept in good condition, should give the best
and most accurate data.

Other books have had a more adventurous time, and often to their
detriment. One copy of an edition in the BSB had been so trimmed that it
had no margins left at all. Other copies of editions sometimes have leaves
or quires missing. There are very few surviving broadsheets. These single
sheets such as almanacs, only of relevance for a year, were regularly used
to line the bindings of other books, when their original use was past, and

from where many have been rescued during conservation work in the last century. The Zainer editions in John Rylands Library had all, bar one, been rebound in 1894 in tight navy morocco, gold tooled for the Library and with the edges of their leaves neatly trimmed and gilded. Many of them had been washed, sometimes to the extent of making the hand colouring bleed. Needless to say there was little evidence left for the researcher. The transient nature of some of this evidence, even after it has been recorded, is remarked on by David Paisey in his article on blind impressions.[125] Where known, the state and age of the binding was noted to give background information for later interpretation of the data.

One might wonder, given some of the circumstances described above, whether it is possible to base serious research on such apparently haphazard data. If enough copies of the editions are looked at and due care is taken about the quality of what is recorded then yes, these splendid artefacts can give up their secrets and reveal something about the process of their creation. This shows the importance of looking at as many copies as possible to build up a solid and representative database. Within the limits of finance and time frame this has been done for this present study.

Photography is not allowed in many libraries. However the libraries in Ulm, Augsburg, Mainz and Meermano-Westreenianum in The Hague all allowed photographs to be taken. This visual record is important as an *aide memoire* for the researcher as well as to illustrate this text. Where possible a photographic record of a sample page, the incipit or any other factors was made.

Interpreting the data

From studying the various data it was hoped that patterns would emerge, giving evidence of working practice. Sometimes a clear pattern emerged immediately but usually the bare figures needed collating and interpreting to see if there was a pattern; it was not until the various factors were brought together that a pattern could be seen. The results are given in later chapters. Sometimes, even after the information was tabulated, the results could be confusing. For this kind of data extra information was needed, and practical experiments were conducted to help provide this.

PRACTICAL EXPERIMENTS

This study is primarily about practice – how Zainer printed – so some practical experiments were undertaken. Practical experience of over 35

---

[125] In his article 'Blind printing in early continental books', in A. L. Lepschy, J. Took and D. Rhodes, eds., *Book production and letters in the western European Renaissance* (London: Modern Humanities Research Association, 1986), pp. 220–233 (pp. 221–222), David Paisey cites examples of marks in some editions described in *BMC* as originally standing out clearly. These were subsequently found to have vanished due to rebinding or environmental changes.

years working as a printer can only go so far and did not cover some of the points that arose about fifteenth-century practice. For example working an iron handpress has a very different feel from working a wooden press. Further, in trying to interpret some of the more confusing data collected, it was thought that only a practical experiment could show whether a hypothesis could have credence or not.

Practical experiments, and their results, have to be considered carefully. They can have strengths and weaknesses. One of the strengths of experiments is that they can help throw new light on aspects of practice. However this has to be balanced with their weakness. One has to recognise the impossibility of trying to recreate fifteenth-century printing conditions in the twenty-first century. When considering the costs of fifteenth-century printing, Michael Pollak had the differences in press, type, paper and working conditions of the incunable period, compared to those of the twentieth century, very much in mind as he explored the possible man hours involved in printing an incunable.[126] He suggests that working on a wooden hand-press with pressure being applied through a wooden screw, with hand-cast type, hand-made linen-rag paper, damp, soft packing, hand-mixed ink, in a workshop with little light and probably no heat during the winter is going to be very different from printing today on an iron hand press with machine-cast type, perhaps hand-made linen-rag paper but more probably cotton-rag paper, and probably a firm packing and machine-mixed ink.

Frans Janssen also discusses the pros and cons of trying to recreate the fifteenth century, in particular as pertaining to an early printing press.[127] He states that, through the process of both building and operating a wooden press, new insights can be brought to understand the early printing process. However he also discusses the problems of accuracy, and how difficult it is to find a proper representation of an early press on which to base the reconstruction. The most accurate, he suggests, is a drawing by Pieter Jansz Saenredam dated 1628, 150 years later than the period of this study.[128]

For the experiment on testing the balance of the platen on a wooden press (see Chapter 4, *Blind Impressions from (bearer) Type*) a major hurdle was that there are no surviving fifteenth-century wooden presses to use.[129]

---

[126] Michael Pollak,'Production costs in fifteenth-century printing', *The Library Quarterly*, 39 (1969), pp. 318–330.
[127] Frans Janssen, 'Reconstructions of the common press', *Technique and design in the history of printing* ('t Goy-Houten: Hes & de Graaf, 2004), pp. 273–285.
[128] Janssen, 'Reconstructions', p. 278, illustration 8.
[129] Philip Gaskell, 'A census of wooden presses', *Journal of the Printing Historical Society*, 6 (1970), pp. 1–31 and Frans Janssen, 'Inventaire des presses typographiques en bois conservées aux Pays-Bas et en Belgique', in A. R. A. Croiset van Uchelen, ed., *Hellinga Festschrift: Forty-three studies in bibliography presented to Dr Wytze Hellinga* (Amsterdam: Israel, 1980), pp. 302–316, both provide lists of

There are two seventeenth-century wooden presses in the Plantin Museum in Antwerp but they are not in working order. However it was possible to use the wooden press in Cambridge University Library constructed in 1969 under Philip Gaskell's direction, following the model described in Stower's manual of 1808 with an old fashioned box hose.[130] Although acknowledging that this press may not have been anything like Zainer's it did provide an opportunity to work with a wooden press, with a screw for lowering the platen and delivering impression – a totally different mechanism for printing than with a nineteenth-century Albion iron hand-press with springs and levers.

Similar problems arise with paper (see Chapter 5, *Cloth Impressions*). Fifteenth-century paper, made from linen rag, is not freely available for experimental purposes (although one original Zainer leaf in the author's possession was subjected to a cautious damping experiment to measure paper stretch, it was not thought necessary to print on that paper or try anything more invasive). Other papers used were those available to hand in the print shop – some heavily sized, eighteenth-century, account-book paper made from linen rag, and a variety of papers, hand made and mould made, from both cotton rag and flax fibres (these are specified later). It was felt that, although the lack of fifteenth-century paper might give slightly different results, it would not invalidate the experiment and, with these limitations in mind, that the experiments could help under-stand some of the fifteenth-century practices.

This combination of information from primary sources together with that from the practical experiments form the basis of this study, along with the background information from the secondary sources, which is discussed in the relevant chapters.

surviving wooden presses at their time of writing – not all the presses listed have survived to today as described by Janssen and Gaskell.

[130] Janssen, 'Reconstructions', p. 281, reference to Caleb Stower, *The printer's grammar* (London: 1808, repr. London: Gregg, 1965), pp. 302–345.

2 INITIAL OBSERVATIONS AND BASIC FINDINGS

This chapter concentrates on basic findings that come firstly from initial observation of Zainer's editions and secondly from recorded measurements made from his editions. Some points raised in this chapter are dealt with in more detail in Chapter 3, *Type and Ems*, Chapter 4, *Blind impressions from (bearer) Type*, Chapter 5, *Cloth Impressions* and Chapter 6, *Points and Point Holes*, and some other points need further research and are beyond the scope of this study. The following will be discussed in this chapter: inking, impression quality, printing the reiteration, the use of woodcut elements, the number of lines per page, the size of the centre margins, the use of skeletons and quiring patterns. The first three items give evidence of Zainer's skill as a printer because they involve how successfully he managed to ink his type when printing his pages. The other factors are all items about which Zainer would have had to make a design decision during the planning stage at the beginning of every project. Discovering how he approached his editions can help understand how he operated as a printer and throw light on his printing practices.

From direct observation

Before taking any measurements, some information about Zainer's printing practices can be gained solely from looking at the pages of his editions. Evidence from the pages can tell us about the quality of his inking, the evenness of impression and the accuracy of his register. The quality of production of many of Zainer's editions is not good. Admittedly the quality of production of many editions printed in the fifteenth century is poor, but Zainer's work seems to stand out as being consistently poorer than many, perhaps most. Individually each small example of poor presswork may not seem too bad, and not every fault is found in every edition, but when taken together they add up to a printer whose work was, at best, uneven in quality. A comparison of Johann's presswork to that of his brother Günther, especially when comparing copies by each brother of the same text such as Duranti's *Rationale divinorum officiorum*, shows that Günther was by far the more skilled pressman. Günther's press work is generally cleaner, crisper, straighter, and seems to show more overall control by the printer than that of Johann – it is interesting to think that they both learnt to print at the same printshop.

Inking

Ink needs to be distributed evenly over the type; too much ink and the letter shapes will be distorted by surplus ink filling in the counters or bulking up the strokes, and too little makes the text less legible. Ink needs to be of the correct consistency for the job, the paper and the weather. C. H. Bloy suggests that most of the fifteenth-century printers would have made their own ink and gives evidence from The San Ripoli press and their purchases of linseed oil and turpentine and pigments to support this statement.[1] The first mention found of a specialist ink maker was in Paris in 1522, and many printers were their own ink makers until the mid nineteenth century.[2]

Moxon describes the problems that could be found with poor quality ink.[3] He states that the provision of good ink is the responsibility of the master printer, in charge of the printing house. If other oil is added to eke out the pure linseed oil, not only will the ink have a tendency to yellow but it will also take longer to dry, causing set-off.[4] The ink will also dry slowly if the oil has not been boiled long enough. Not enough blacking will result in a pale brown, rather than a true black ink. Zainer's editions show many of the inking problems described by Moxon. Although there is no documentary evidence for Zainer it seems that he could have made his own ink and so any problems due to ink quality would have been his responsibility.

Zainer would have been using ink balls to distribute ink over the forme of type. Evidence of his use of ink balls has been found once or twice in his editions, where the ink ball has missed inking a part of the forme, leaving an under-inked area. The printed page reveals the curve of the ink ball between the inked and un-inked area. The clearest example found is on leaf [c7v] in the Bodleian copy of *De adhaerendo Deo* (Figure 4.1).

There is some variation in the inking coverage of the printed text through the pages of all the copies. Some text areas are inked more blackly than others and sometimes there is an un-evenness of ink application over the text. Ideally the ink coverage should be the same throughout every copy of the edition. This entails a careful eye and quality control from one print run of one sheet to the next and also through every print run. This is not easy to achieve and Zainer did not achieve it. Variation in inking coverage can be found, from one page to the next within a copy and from one page in a copy of an edition to the same

---

[1] C. H. Bloy, *A history of printing ink, balls and rollers, 1440–1850* (London: Wynkyn de Worde Society, 1967), p. 5. Conway, *Diario*, p. 321, lists the purchases of linseed oil and on p. 322 the purchase of *pecie grecha* and *pecie nera*, all necessary ingredients for ink making.

[2] Bloy, p. 66.

[3] Moxon, pp. 82–86.

[4] Moxon, p. 83.

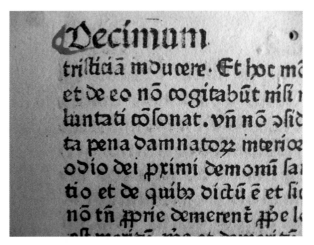

Figure 2.1. Ink bleed showing as brown/yellow staining through the paper behind the text in a page from *Praeceptorium* [not after 1479], not easy to capture in a photograph. (Ulm Stadtbibliothek.)

page in another copy of that edition. For most of his printing the differences in ink coverage are not huge but they are noticeably present and suggest that even inking was not his top priority.

One of the results of over inking can be ink bleed, especially if the ink quality is not all it should be. As Moxon stated, poor quality oil takes longer to dry and causes yellow stains in the paper. An example of yellow staining can be seen at Figure 2.1. The same happens if the type has been over inked; the ink will take longer to dry on the page, allowing more time for it to soak into the paper, and it will stain through to the other side. Ink bleed occurs in a number of Zainer's editions, often caused by over-inking, and was noted particularly in copies of the Latin edition of *De claris mulieribus*.

There is considerable extraneous distribution of ink throughout Zainer's editions. Examples have been found of marks from inky fingerprints, inked spacing, inked furniture, inked string, smudged letters, slurred letters, inked shoulders of letters at the head and foot of the text block, and inked hairs caught up with the type. One or two of these anomalies suggest a failure in his printing method, and the others carelessness of the workman and lack of quality control.

One failure of printing technique is suggested in the high number of printed marks from inked, raised, spaces found (see examples at Figure 3.6). Spacing should not rise to a height where it both receives ink and then prints. That this happens in Zainer's printing suggests that the lock-up of his forme was not tight enough. Loose lock-up suggests some

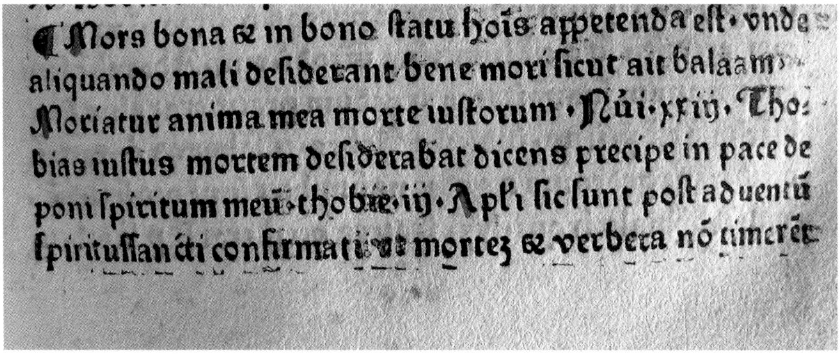

Figure 2.2. Inked shoulders at foot of leaf [i1r] of *Aurea Biblia*, 1476. (Ulm Stadtbibliothek.)

unevenness in the type setting and irregular line lengths; if lines of type are not set consistently to the same degree of tightness in the composing stick some lines will be slightly longer than others, making it impossible to lock the forme up securely. It also suggests that his quality control through a print run was not all it might be. If he had checked each page as it came off the press, and noted the inky mark from raised spacing, he could have corrected it. However, even where there is obvious inked spacing as in a headline of an edition, the same mark has often been found in all copies of that edition looked at, indicating that Zainer had not noticed the mark, or that, if he had noticed the mark, he did not think it of any import.

Another failure of technique is the high incidence of printed shoulders at the head and foot of the text block (Figure 2.2). Either the packing should have been slightly harder or there should have been slightly less pressure when printing, or all the shoulders of the type should have been filed down. Moxon suggests that inking the 'beards' of the type (as he terms the lower portion of the shoulder) is a fault, caused perhaps by running the bed of the press in too far or not far enough, and so causing the platen to tilt, and exerting unequal pressure on the head or foot of the type area.[5] He also states that when the matrices are struck they should have a deep enough drive to avoid the type letters 'bearding' later.[6] He discusses the possibility of the beards being scraped off as part of dressing the letters before sending them to the printer (Figure 2.3).[7] Zainer's matrices (and consequently his type) may have had a shallow depth of

[5] Moxon, p. 271.

[6] Moxon, p. 24. Monotype casters work to a depth of drive of 1.27mm (*Monotype super caster manual* (London: [The National Committee of the Monotype Users' Associations], 1972, p. 18.2)). Inked shoulders can be caused by poor press work, too soft a packing or shallow depth of drive.

[7] Moxon, p. 188. The footnote states that chamfering the beards with a plane was done in later centuries.

Figure 2.3. A row of the letter m cast at different times from Granjon's Large Ascendonica matrices. Note the different angles on the shoulders from having been filed down at different times. When similar type letters were observed being planed at Stephenson & Blake typefoundry, the letters of one sort were all placed in a long stick, and were all filed at the same time. (Plantin-Moretus Museum.)

drive. The examples of so-called 'fallen type' found in two Zainer editions both show the impressions of letters with square, not sloping shoulders, and a depth of drive of 1mm (further discussion about this fallen type and the shape of fifteenth-century type is given in Chapter 3). The high occurrence of printed shoulders (or Moxon's 'bearding') in Zainer's editions may have had a number of different causes, but all of them can be described as failure of technique.

There are a number of instances of smudged type on Zainer's printed pages. This suggests that he was not managing to lay the paper on, or lift it off, the type cleanly, and that there had been some movement during this operation; the paper should not make any contact with the inked type until the precise moment of printing. Smudged type does not happen all the time, which suggests it was not as a result of a poor usual method of positioning the paper, but is more likely due to occasional carelessness of the pressman. As well as the slightly smudged type there are some occasions of smearing that look as though they have been caused when the paper had dragged across the inked letters as it was being removed. One example was noted on leaf [B3v] in the Ottobeuren copy of the 1475 edition of *Sermones de sanctis* where the direction of the drag lines suggest that when the sheet was being lifted up and away from the platen the head of the forme would have been nearest to the

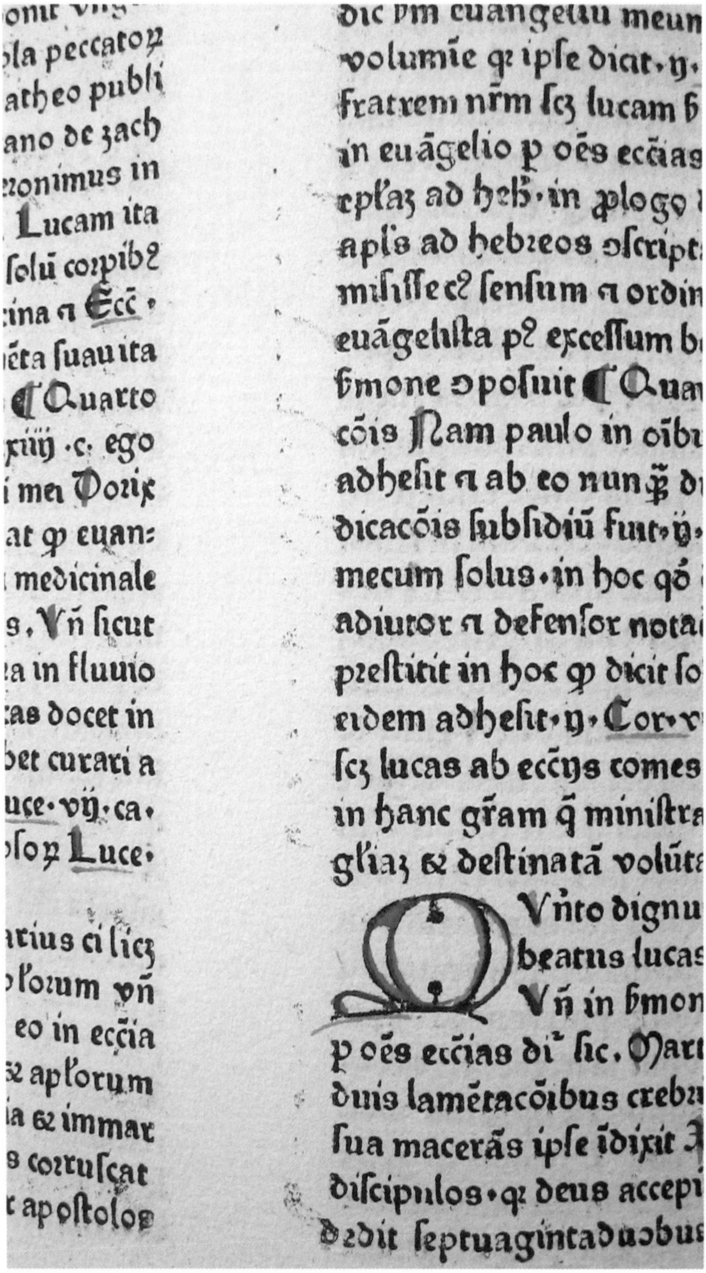

Figure 2.4. Ink marks in inter-columnar margin of leaf [B3v] *Sermones,* 1475, from where the paper was slightly dragged across the inked letters instead of being lifted off cleanly after printing. (Ottobeuren Abbey.)

hoc non habent
nde dicit mgr fen
gando fcim aug.
·credere deum·ez
dere deo·eft crede
1 fcripturis·vel
Credere deo ez re:
um·eft crede ipm
ozem omniu crea:
m effentia Vn ad
credere qz eft·Sed
ι in eum tende cu
tis in deum a in,
dunt deu·fcz effe
ιoc eft verbis ti?
deu·l·omnia que
humanitate·Lo
eum pzemiffioe
mones ez danati
з in deu qz fic ten
n amas·bm aug·
fi pzter credulita
aatb·vlt·Signa
ec feqnter in noie
ιeo fides di*ppale
ιce poffum? epb.
utu fidei·in quo
znea extinguere
poficoe fup iuue

rndit alexander· qz artius illos includent·
Cum igitur angufta viaz incipet obdurare
mollibus bituminibus·quod tam humano
laboze fieri non potuit·rogauit deum ifrľ.
vt illud opus compleret·Et ecce nutu diui:
no ppter credulitate eius·pzerupta montiu
ad leinuicem accefferunt· ez factus eft locus
immeabilis·Vt ait iofeph?·Deus quid fa:
cturus eft pzo fidelibus fuis ondit·cum tm
pzo infidelibus fecit·Exemplum etiam ha :
bemus in centurione· cui pzo falute fui dep
canti finaliter vnfum fuit·Vade ez ficut cre
didifti fiat nbi·

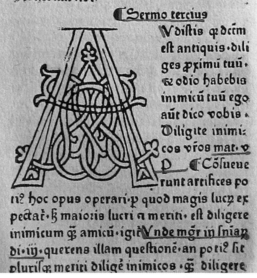

¶Sermo tercius
Vdiftis qz dicm
eft antiquis·dili
ges pzimu tuu·
ez odio habebis
inimicu tuu ego
aut dico vobis·
Diligite inimi:
cos vros mat·v
D ¶Cofueue
runt artifices po
ni? hoc opus operari·p quod magis lucz ex
pectat·§ maiozis lucri a meriti· eft diligere
inimicum qz amicu·igit Vnde mgr in fniaz
di·iij·querens illam queftione·an potiz fit
plurifqz meriti diliqe inimicos ·qz diligere

Figure 2.5. Marks from inky string in the inter-columnar margin of page [a6v] in *Quadragesimale*, 1476. There is no sign of any impressions from the string here, but the mark looks exactly the same as one I made when using string to support a sheet of paper. (Ulm Stadtbibliothek.)

'puller'[8] (Figure 2.4). Some further examples, with drag lines in the same direction were found through quires [n] and [o] in the Bodleian copy of *Liber Bibliae*.[9] These could suggest the action of the puller when

[8] Leonardus de Utino, *Sermones de sanctis*, 1475 (il00158000) OTTO 269, shelfmark Inc. 130. Moxon (p. 292) describes the press being operated by two men, the beater on the far side of the press inking the type and the puller, on the near side, laying on and removing the paper and winding in the press and pulling the bar.

[9] Berchorius, *Liber Bibliae*, 1474 (ib00336000) *Bod-inc.* B-155, shelfmark Auct. 6 Q 1.22.

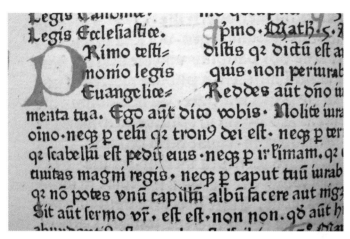

Figure 2.6. A hair, caught up in the type, inked and printed on page [x4v] of copy of *Sermones quadragesimales*, 1478. (Meermano-Westreenianum/Museum van het Boek.)

lifting the printed sheet off the forme. It is not known what method Zainer was using to lay his paper on and lifting it off the forme – this will be discussed later in Chapter 6, *Points and Point Holes*.

Other inky marks, appearing to have been made by a piece of string, have been found in all of Zainer's royal folios, except the 1473 edition of *Rationale divinorum officiorum*. It could be that the string was part of a paper holding apparatus intended to support the damp sheet of paper, which because of its size would have had a tendency to sag in the middle, when being laid on the press.[10] These marks do not occur in the chancery folios. They look very like those made personally when the string picked up ink by mistake and printed on the paper. The marks vary in length, are sometimes inked and sometimes just impressed, and run down the inter-columnar margins. One example can be seen on leaf [a6v] in the Ulm copy of *Quadragesimale*, 1476 (Figure 2.5).[11] Zainer is not the only printer in whose editions possible string marks have been found and similar marks, both in the inter-columnar and outer margins, have been found in two editions printed by Adolf Rusch, his *Catholicon* and *Speculum naturale*, although with these editions the marks are heavily impressed rather than inked.[12] Another mark noted was from an inked hair, which was either lying on the type or was locked up in the type forme and printed on the sheet (Figure 2.6).

[10] It is not known how the early printers manipulated their sheet of paper on and off the press. This will be discussed more fully in Chapter 6, *Points & Point Holes*.

[11] Johannes Gritsch, *Quadragesimale*, 1476 (ig00491000) SBU 246, shelfmark 14984.

[12] Johannes Balbus, *Catholicon* [*c*.1470] (ib00022000) and Vincent of Beauvais, *Speculum naturale* [*c*.1476] (iv00492000).

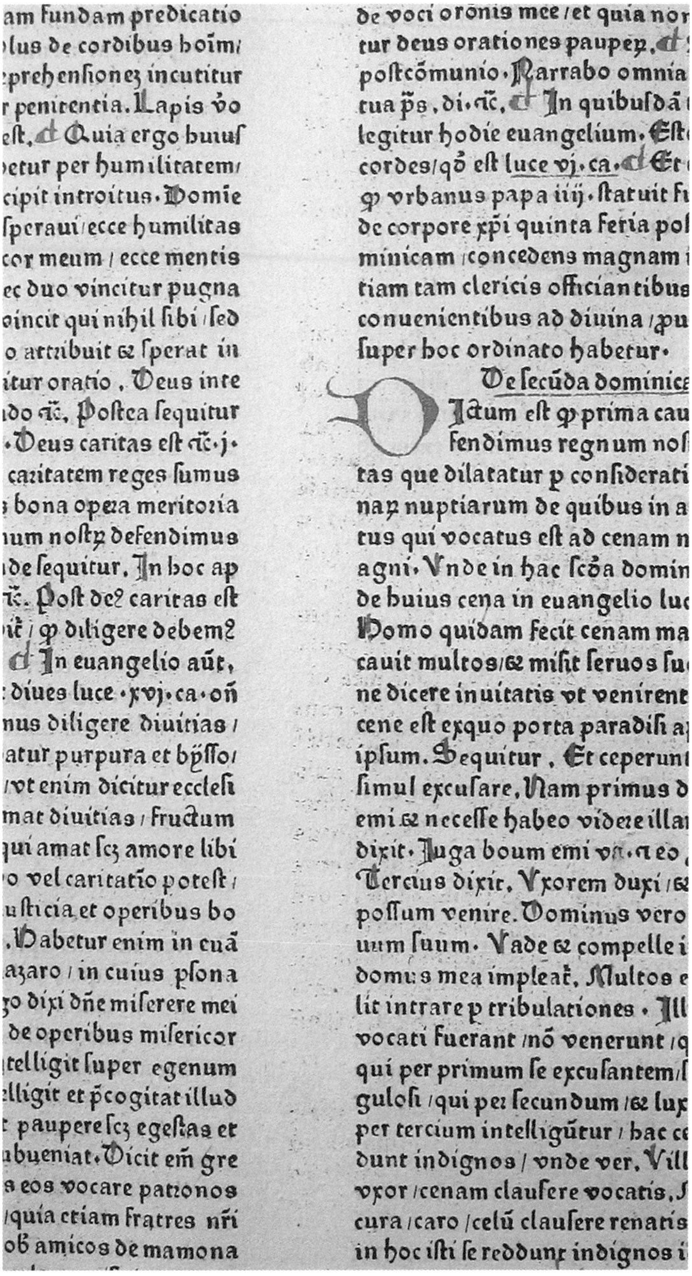

Figure 2.7. *Rationale divinorum officiorum*, 1473. Page [z6r] showing set-off from [z6v] in the inter-columnar margin. (Ottobeuren Abbey.)

Apart from all these, smaller inking anomalies which have been noted occasionally in some editions, there are also the more regular examples that occur in every edition examined. Almost all Zainer's pages show set-off; spots and flecks of ink marks across the paper. From practical experience this would have been caused by stacking the freshly printed sheets on top of each other while the ink is still wet. As the pile increases, so does the weight of the paper pressing down, and ink from the newly printed sheets transfers onto the sheet above it in the stack. Interleaving with waste sheets can prevent this, as can piling the paper in small heaps that do not get too heavy. Examples of set-off have been found in every copy of every edition printed by Zainer that have been examined.[13] Occasionally the set-off marks are so clear that all the lines of text can be seen, although not always clearly enough to read.[14] A very clear example was found in the Bodleian copy of chancery folio *De mysterio missae,* where on leaf [f4v/7r] can be seen the crooked set-off imprint of [f7v/4r].[15] This example gives evidence that Zainer was printing both conjugate leaves at the same time for his chancery folios. Another example where the set-off was clear enough to be able to identify the origin of the text can be seen in the Ottobeuren copy of royal folio *Rationale divinorum officiorum* (Figure 2.7).[16] Moxon describes the method of stacking newly printed sheets in a 'Heap' and then also (alarmingly) suggests how a Heap that was slipping sideways could be righted by driving it into an upright position.[17] This latter remedy must have caused considerable smudging of the inked sheets.

Along with set-off, almost all the copies looked at also have at least one example of off-set. Off-set occurs when ink from a freshly printed leaf is set off onto the tympan or backing sheet during the printing of the reiteration. If the sheet is always placed exactly in the same position the ink building up on the tympan does not mark (off set) on to the first printed side. However if the register is inaccurate and the sheet varies in its position, the ink build up on the tympan will mark the first printed side of the leaf as it off sets from the tympan (Figure 2.8 and 2.8a). To avoid this, the printer either has to renew the top packing sheet frequently, or regularly wipe it clean, or print the reiteration when the first side's ink has dried. Off-set will always be found on the side of the sheet that has been printed first,

---

[13] Interestingly the press work of his brother Günther is much cleaner with little of the set-off, smudging and slurring that is found in Johann's editions.

[14] Unfortunately none of Zainer's set-off marks are as clear as some of those made by Caxton (or his binder?) which show noticeable clarity. They are described by Sanae Ikeda in 'Caxton's Printing of Christine de Pisan's Fayttes of armes and of chyualrye', *Journal of the Early Book Society,* 10 (2007), pp. 186–200.

[15] Albertus Magnus, *De mysterio missae,* 1473 (ia00287000); *Bod-inc.* A-124, shelfmark Auct. 6 Q 4.3(1).

[16] Guillelmus Duranti, *Rationale divinorum officiorum,* 1473 (id00407000); OTTO 149, shelfmark Inc. 200.

[17] Moxon, p. 297 and p. 306.

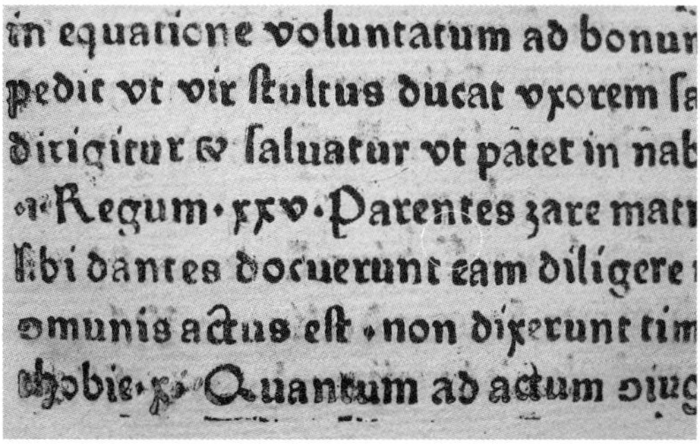

> in equaticne voluntatum ad bonur
> pedit vt vir ſtultus ducat vxorem ſa
> diriqitur & ſaluatur vt patet in nat
> ⁊ᵗRegum·xxv·parentes zare matı
> ſibi dantes docuerunt eam diligere ⁊
> omunis actus eſt ·non dixerunt tim
> thobie·p·Quantum ad actum oiu͡g

Figure 2.8. Typical evidence of off-set on page [i4r] of *Aurea Biblia*, 1476, seen as smudged areas in the background. Page [i4r] was printed first, and the verso [i4v] second, while ink from [i4r] was still wet. Some ink from [i4r], caused by pressure from some letters in [i4v], was set-off on to the packing sheet and then off-set back onto [i4r]. (University of Reading Library.)

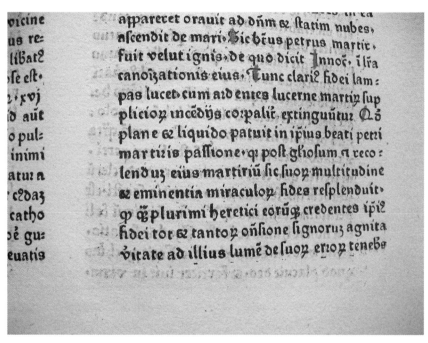

Figure 2.8a. Off-set on page [o3r] of *Sermones*, 1475, seen clearest as smudged greyer, reversed, letter shapes to left and foot of column caused by wet ink and poor register when printing page [o3v]. There are also a few blacker speckles and spots of ink, scattered across the page, caused by set-off. (Ulm Stadtbibliothek.)

and where there has been poor register. Some examples of off-set are clearer than others, depending how wet the ink was from the first printing, and how good the register has been.[18]

Some of these marks from inking errors can be confusing and difficult to distinguish, especially as some of them can occur at the same time. Ink bleed will usually always show a yellow 'halo' round the letter shapes. Set-off can show on either side of the leaf and can vary from a few specks of ink on the page to a full imprint in reverse, of the other side of the leaf to the one where the set-off occurs. Off-set only occurs on the first side printed. It is most usually noted as partial letter forms from the second side, appearing behind the printing of the first side. The letter shapes have slightly fuzzy edges and if they could be read, would be in reverse (set-off would be right-reading if it could be read). If the ink coverage has been uneven these marks will only show on part of the page where there has been too much ink – they are most unlikely to occur if the ink coverage is correct and even.

Impression and impressed marks

The forme is placed on the press, the type inked, paper laid on top with some packing material and the whole positioned under the platen, and then the bar pulled to bring the platen down and make an impression of type onto the paper. If the forme is not positioned centrally on the bed of the press the platen will tilt and give an uneven impression. The depth of the impression will vary with the kind of material used for packing, the quality of the paper, and the dampness of both paper and packing, as well as how hard the bar is pulled. Zainer used a fairly deep impression, suggesting that he was working with soft packing. Nothing out of the ordinary has been noted – his impression is generally even across the leaves and with no noticeable lightness to any one corner.

Despite the suggestion above that the regular occurrence of inked shoulders might have been caused by a tilted platen there is no strong evidence of this. If his impression had been particularly heavy or the packing very soft the result would have shown by all the shoulders of his type letters inking and marking the sheet in every line. This has not been found. There is some variation in depth of impressions from one copy of an edition to another but much of this could be caused by later pressing and binding.

As well as the impression of the type block on the leaf other impressed marks have also been noticed. Impressed string marks were noted above.

---

[18] Richard-Gabriel Rummonds shows some helpful photographs of inking defects in *Printing on the iron handpress* (New Castle and London: Oak Knoll and the British Library, 1998), pp. 281–285. (Confusingly he uses the term 'offset' for 'set-off', and 'second impression set-off' for 'off-set' as defined in *Glossary* below). Most of these defects can be found in Zainer editions.

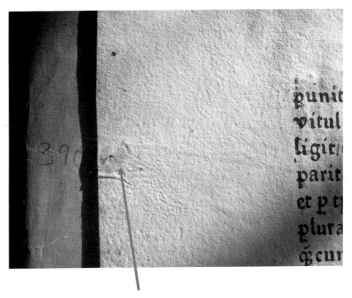

Figure 2.9. Mark of impressed circle round a point hole on leaf [o8v] from *Liber Bibliae*. (Claire Bolton.)

There are also marks from impressed type and impressed fabric marks which will be discussed in Chapter 4, *Blind Impressions from (bearer) Type* and Chapter 5, *Cloth Impressions*. In addition there are marks of which the cause is not known. These are listed here for the record:

(i) at the foot and occasionally at the edge of the page, but never all the way round the text area, there is often a blind impressed line marking the paper. The line can be between *c.*20mm to *c.*80mm long. These impressed lines have been noted, often quite a number of times, in almost every edition. They are usually located within 10–15 mm of the text. Sometimes they are found in a similar position in many copies of an edition. It could be part of the paper holding apparatus – perhaps a frisket or the edge of a frame. These marks look very similar to those discussed by Walter Partridge in his comments about the *Catholicon*.[19] Partridge suggests the marks may have been made by bearer strips or footsticks. It is difficult to comment on this as there is no evidence of how the type was locked up in the forme in the 1460s or if footsticks were being used at that time.

(ii) another mark is an impressed circle around a point hole (see Figure 2.9). This example is in a leaf [o8] (property of the author) from *Liber*

---

[19] Walter Partridge, 'The type-setting and printing of the Mainz Catholicon', *The Book Collector*, 35 (1986), pp. 21–52 (pp. 30–32) and illustrated at Figures 13 and 15.

Bibliae but two other similar examples were found in the BSB copy of Mentelin's *Summa theologiae*.[20] On leaf [e1r] the pinhole is located 68mm below the foot of the text and 2mm in from the right-hand edge of the text. It is at the centre of a circle measuring 5.5mm across, and this time the circle is inked. A similar inked circle with a pinhole in the centre was found on [f6v] of the same copy. Another example was found in the Bodleian Library's copy on leaf [I10] of Caxton's *Receuil des histoires de Troyes*.[21] The circle always surrounds a pinhole suggesting that it results from the paper holding apparatus, but so far there is not enough evidence to say what the cause might be.

(iii) a knobbly mark, measuring *c*.7mm across, as though made by the head of a rose-head nail, found on leaves in quire [g] in the British Library copy of the *Decameron*.[22]

Register

To achieve accurate register when printing, three positions have to be fixed; the position of the forme on the bed of the press, the position of the type in the forme and the position of the paper as it meets the forme. The first two will be considered in more detail below in the section 'Skeletons' and the last will be considered in Chapter 6, *Points and Point Holes*. The present section will consider Zainer's record in achieving accurate register and what it can tell about his method of working.

Zainer was not very good at achieving accurate register (Figure 2.10). There are many examples of poor register throughout the copies of his editions, where the text printed on the reiteration has not lined up accurately with the text printed on the first side of the sheet. Sometimes, and most commonly, there is movement sideways, usually by only one or two millimetres but occasionally by as much as 20 or 30mm. Sometimes there is movement vertically and sometimes the page is crooked. Some editions seem to have more instances of poor register than others; the two editions of *De claris mulieribus*, *De mysterio missae* and the 1475 edition of *Sermones* have noticeably more occurrences of poor register, whereas the 1473 edition of *Rationale divinorum officiorum* has hardly any.[23]

The examples of poor register give clues to one aspect of his printing methods – how many pages he printed at one time, and support the evidence found from ink set-off marks above. They show that he usually printed two conjugate chancery-folio, and median-folio, pages at the same time. However, this is not always the case and there are a few examples

[20] Thomas Aquinas, *Summa theologiae* [not after 1463] (it00208000); *BSB-Ink* T-286, shelfmark 2° Inc.s.a.1146a.

[21] Le Fevre, *Le receuil des histoires de Troyes*, 1473 (il00117000) *Bod-Inc.* L-060, shelfmark Arch. D.1.

[22] Giovanni Boccaccio, *Decameron* [*c*.1476] (ib0073000); *BMC*, vol. 2, p. 520, shelfmark IB.9108A.

[23] Latin edition of Boccaccio, *De claris mulieribus*, 1473 (ib00716000).

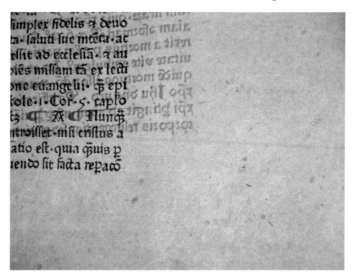

Figure 2.10. Evidence of poor register on leaf [Q8] of *Sermones quadragesimales*, 1478, clearly visible with show through from verso. (Ulm Stadtbibliothek.)

where he only printed one page at a time in his chancery folios. For example in the preliminary table of the Bodleian Library's copy of *Summa de eucharistiae sacramento* the text printed on page [b1r] is crooked but the text is printed straight on its conjugate page [b10v].[24] Similar examples occur through this quire and also quire [a] with pages [b2r/b9v] and [a2v/a3r] that show the contents table of this edition was printed one page at a time. Another example was found in the CUL copy of the Latin edition of *Historia Griseldis* where on page [a1r] the text is straight and, on the same side of the sheet, its conjugate page [a10v], the text is crooked, proving they were not printed at the same time.

Similar evidence of poor register shows that Zainer printed a single page at a time for his imperial and royal folios. In the Bodleian Library's copy of his first royal folio, *Rationale divinorum officiorum,* the text printed on conjugate pages [l5v] and [l6r] is straight, but on their verso the text on [l6v] is crooked and on [l5r] is straight.[25] Another example, which also shows four pages of text were printed separately, is found in the John Ryland's Library copy of *Liber Bibliae.* Here the text on page [h8r] is very crooked, but is backed up perfectly by [h8v] which is also crooked and both are neatly lined up on the same point holes. Neither of the sides of

[24] Albertus Magnus, *Summa de eucharistiae sacramento*, 1474 (ia00335000); *Bod-inc.* A-149, shelfmark Auct. Q sup.2.25.

[25] *Bod-inc.* D-183, shelfmark Auct. 5 Q 2.21. Generally the register is very good through this copy, with small neat point holes. Only occasionally it can be seen that points are used twice which could imply more than one positioning of paper onto press.

the [h8]'s conjugate page, [h4r] and [h4v], are aligned with each other nor with [h8r/h8v]. One of the copies of *Liber Bibliae* in the BSB in Munich also has pages that are backed up crookedly, for example [n1v] and [n10r], which shows that the pages can only have been printed one side of a leaf at a time.[26]

Although the accuracy of his register varies between editions there does not seem to be a chronological basis for the variation. Poor register was particularly noted the German edition of *De claris mulieribus*, 1473, and in the royal folio *Sermones*, 1478, which does not suggest that he improved with experience. The methods Zainer might have used to achieve accurate register will be discussed later.

Printed initials, illustrations and borders

Another aspect of Zainer's printing that is noticeable when looking at his editions, is his use of printed decorative initials and borders, and illustrations. As stated in Chapter 1, Johann, like his brother Günther and other printers in Augsburg, produced many richly illustrated editions. He had woodcut initials in various sizes, both as sets of initials and as one-off initials, woodcut borders, and woodcut illustrations. The *BMC* lists these and Amelung also gives details.[27] All of these would have added to the costs of producing his editions and to the time involved in the printing. All the above elements were generally printed at the same time as the text; the evidence being that everything, text and initial etc. lines up. They would have had to be fitted into the forme, integrated with the lines of set type, which had to have their lengths adjusted to fit, and inked and printed at the same time. The technical restrictions this involved will be discussed more fully in Chapter 3, *Type and Ems*. Apart from the costs of having the woodcuts made there was also the cost of extra paper when using woodcut illustrations. For editions such as *De claris mulieribus* with *c.*180 woodcuts, or Aesop's *Vita et fabulae* with *c.*200 woodcuts, the space taken by the woodcuts involved the use of more paper by 11 per cent and 15 per cent, respectively, than if the editions had not been illustrated.

The editions have a varied combination of these decorative elements, although seven of them (18 per cent of total 38) have no printed decoration of any kind (Table 2.1). Eleven editions (29 per cent) only have printed initials, fourteen (37 per cent) have a border on the first page with an initial, and of these, twelve have initials through the edition. Four editions (10 per cent) have border, initials and woodblock illustrations. Printed initials were the most common printed decoration and appear in 82 per

---

[26] *BSB-Ink* B-29, shelfmark Clm. 28359.

[27] *BMC*, vol. 2, p. 519, and Amelung, *Der Frühdruck*, pp. 61 and 65. *BMC* confusingly classes four different sets of initials under one heading and gives another set two different reference numbers. This is unravelled in the *Appendix*.

Table 2.1. Zainer's use of wood cut initials, borders and illustrations. (Because there is some overlap across the categories the totals come to more than 100 per cent.)

Decorative element	No. of editions	%		No. of editions	%
Only spaces for initials	7	18	spaces total	11	26
Initials and spaces	5	11	initials total	31	82
Initials only	11	29	woodblock total	5	8
Initials and illustrations	1	2	borders total	14	37
Initials and borders	14	37			
initials, illustrations and borders	4	10	some decoration	31	82

cent of the editions. Zainer used eight different sets of initials through this period; all, except the set used for Aesop's *Vita et fabulae*, were used for more than one edition.

Zainer's use of printed initials in 82 per cent of his editions is very high when compared with their overall use as given by Smith. Smith's figures show a 31.5 per cent use of printed initials for the whole incunable period and a usage of 5.9 per cent for the 1470s.[28]

The editions with no printed decoration are the two earliest editions of *De periculis*, the *Decameron* and four editions at the end of the period of this study, *Postilla*, *Praeceptorium*, *Vitae sanctorum* and Magnus' *Sermones*.[29] Although having no printed initials, in each of these editions Zainer has left space for an initial to be inserted by hand. As a printer it would have been as just easy for him to have set the initial along with the text as to have set the space in the forme. It is not known why he did not use initials when he still had them and evidence from some later editions after 1478, such as Nider's *Sermones* and the *Biblia Latina*, shows that he still used printed initials later on.[30]

The initials all had quite a short existence. The first set, *BMC*'s [1a], was only used in four editions in 1473, and was then replaced with a wider version, *BMC*'s [1b], that was only used in six editions in 1474 and part of 1475, before being replaced with a third variant, *BMC*'s [1c], that was used for ten editions in 1475 and 76.[31] There may be some overlap in their use as initials of both [1b] and [1c] are found in one or two later editions. Notes in *BMC* take this chronology to help assign a date to [c.1475] edition

---

[28] Smith, *Form*, pp. 221 and 223.

[29] Thomas Aquinas, *De periculis contingentibus* (it00316000) and (it00317000); Albertus Magnus, *Sermones* (ia00331000); Johannes Herolt, *Postilla* (ig00650000); Hieronymous, *Vitae sanctorum* (ih002000).

[30] Johannes Nider, *Sermones* [1478–80] (in00216000) and *Biblia Latina*, 1480 (ib00567000). Amelung, p. 66, states that the two large sets of initials were sold in 1483.

[31] *BMC*, vol. 2, p. 519.

of *De periculis* (it00318000) as it contains initials from [1b] and had to be printed before *Aurea Biblia* (ir00012000) which uses initials [1c] and has a printed date of 17 June 1475, and I have found no evidence that goes against these suggestions.[32]

Of the smaller, and less ornate, initials Zainer had at least two if not three of some letters. The same initial often occurs twice on a page, and two slightly different versions of the same will be used. Sometimes this second initial is a very close copy of the first, with barely discernable differences, but he also has alternate initials with quite different designs. In *Vocabularius Bibliae,* for instance, there are five different designs of initial E and four of initial S.[33] The lines are quite fine in these initials and, being most probably cut from wood, were vulnerable and could damage easily, as can be seen by the broken lines that occur in some printings.

Five of the editions are illustrated with woodblocks; the two German editions of *Historia Griseldis*, the German and Latin editions of *De claris mulieribus* and *Vita et fabulae*. The woodblocks are cut to fit within the text area; they measure the same width as the text and are 14 lines of text deep, so that they can be printed at the same time as the text. However on two occasions this did not happen; once in the 12-leaf, Swabian dialect edition of *Historia Griseldis* and once in the German edition of *De claris mulieribus*. In *Historia Griseldis* unfortunate planning had resulted in his using the same block twice, on the same side of the same sheet [a6r/7v]. To get round the problem he made up the forme with text and the block in place on [a6r] and a block-size space on [a7v] for his first print run. He then reprinted the sheet with just the block, now in position on leaf [a7v]. His problems with register on this second print run can be seen in Figure 2.11 from the two Ulm Stadtbibliothek copies; in one case he printed the block over the text and in the other it is too far away from it, and in both examples the block is crooked.[34] When he printed the German edition the block, still being used twice, was positioned on opposite sides of the leaf [a6/7]; on [a6r] and then on [a7r], perhaps planned deliberately so that the problem was avoided.

In *De claris mulieribus* the block on page [o8r] is missing. Zainer has inserted a bearer line along the top of the space where the block should have been, but the block is not there. I have not yet come across a copy with the block in position, although the remaining 79 other woodcuts are all printed. The German edition of *De claris mulieribus* has two of the blocks printed on the wrong leaves; blocks on [k2v] and [k7v] have been interchanged by mistake. The Ulm copy has manuscript notes to explain this, and the British Library and Würzburg copies have printed paper

---

[32] *BMC*, vol. 2, p. 523.

[33] Henricus de Hassia, *Vocabularius Bibliae* [*c.*1476] (ih00037000).

[34] SBU 414 and 415; shelfmarks 14993 and 14993,1.

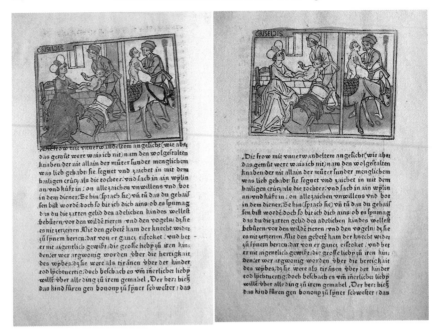

Figure 2.11. Page [a7v] from two copies of *Historia Griseldis*, showing variation in register when the block was printed in a second print run. The printing of the woodblock over the text in the left hand example is proof of a second printing for the block. (Ulm Stadtbibliothek.)

correction labels pasted under the woodblocks – presumably this was an error not discovered until after the printing of the whole edition had been completed.[35] Having a large number of woodblocks to organise, and get in the correct position, as well as the text is another factor for the printer to have to manage. *De claris mulieribus* only had 79 blocks but Aesop's *Vita et fabulae* has over 200 woodcuts which could have brought logistical problems.

Decorative borders (including two initials that are part of a border) feature on the first page of text in 17 of the 38 editions, an occurrence rate of almost 45 per cent. This again seems a high incidence of use of borders. Smith does not comment on the use of woodcuts on the incipit but gives a rate of 9.3 per cent for the use of woodcuts on a title page.[36] Some of Zainer's were especially cut for just one use in one edition, and others were used at the most in three separate editions. Zainer does not use any borders after 1476.

---

[35] Breitenbruch, p. 105 gives the folio references as Bl. 90b and 95b.
[36] Smith, *Form*, p. 258.

It is not known who the artist was for the initials, borders or illustrations but there is a strong probability that they were cut in Ulm. At the time Zainer began printing in the city, Ulm was coming to the end of the construction of its Minster. John Syrlin was the woodcarver responsible for the carving of Ulm Minster's magnificent choir stalls, which were completed at the end of 1474, and his workshop also supplied paintings and joinery.[37] Ursula Koch stated that the style of the carvings of the choir stalls is so close to the woodcuts in *Vita et fabulae* that they were either a product of Syrlin's workshop or produced by someone who was strongly influenced by them.[38] Koch also points out that to manage such a large undertaking as the 200 Aesop woodcuts would have needed a specialist workshop with enough woodcutters to do the work within the short time frame.[39]

Foliation

Foliation, the numbering of the leaves, was fairly rare in early printed books. Smith gives an occurrence rate for the entire incunable period of 23 per cent for headlines, which might include a folio or chapter number, and 10.3 per cent for foliation, with an occurrence rate of 6.6 per cent for headlines and 2.1 per cent for foliation for the period 1470–79.[40] Zainer had a much higher use of both headlines and folio numbers than this. Of his 38 editions 34 per cent have headlines giving either Chapter, Sermon or Book numbers to aid the reader navigate through the edition. 21 per cent of the 38 editions were foliated; seven editions with folios printed in Roman numerals and one with folios printed in Arabic numerals. The folio number was printed on the recto page and the word 'folio' on the verso.

> *Editions with leaves numbered with Roman numerals on recto*
> *De claris mulieribus* (German: *Von den erlauchten Frauen*)
> *De claris mulieribus* (German), [*c.*1473]
> *De claris mulieribus* (Latin), 1473
> *Summa de eucharistiae sacramento*, 1474
> *Rationale divinorum officiorum*, 1473
> *Documenta moralia*, [not after 1476]
> *Decameron*, [*c.*1476]
> *Vitae sanctorum*, [*c.*1478–80]
>
> *Edition with leaves numbered with Arabic numerals on the recto*
> *Legenda aurea*, [not after 1477]

---

[37] Franz Härle, *Das Chorgestühl im Ulmer Münster* (Ulm: Armin Vaas, 2000), p. 10.

[38] Koch, Ursula, *Holzschnitte der Ulmer Äsop-Ausgabe des Johann Zainer* (Dresden: Verlag der Kunst, 1961), p. 42.

[39] Koch, p. 41.

[40] Smith, *Form*, p. 223. See also Margaret M. Smith, 'Printed foliation: forerunner to printed page-numbers?', *Gutenberg-Jahrbuch*, 63 (1988), pp. 54–70.

Accurate numbering of the folios requires care and attention – the printer has to remember to change the numbers with every forme, and also ensure that the new number is inserted correctly and the right way up. Zainer did seem to manage this for the most part when he was working with Roman numerals: there are only a couple of slight errors in *Summa de eucharistiae sacramento* and *Documenta moralia*. However he seems to have had severe problems with his one excursion into Arabic numerals. From personal experience of handling page numbers it is probable that his problems are more due to carelessness when making up a new forme and forgetting to check the new folio numbers, rather than his inability to comprehend Arabic numerals. In *Legenda aurea* (ij00884000) in quire [i] he has number 27 instead of 72 and 37 instead of 73. In quire [l] he prints 89 instead of 98. The leaves in quire [m] are numbered successively 99, 100, 200, 200, 103, 105, 105, 310 instead of what one might expect, 99, 100, 101, 102, 103, 104, 105, 106. In quire [r] he omits number 147 and 148, uses 149 twice and then is a page out for the remainder of the edition. In quire [R] leaf 356 is numbered 635. In quire [V] the word 'folio' is set at the head of the recto leaf [V4r] instead of on the verso [V7v] and the number 379 set at the head of the verso leaf [V7v] instead of on the recto [V4r]. Zainer did not number the pages of his later reprints of this edition.

FROM RECORDED MEASUREMENTS

Tolerances in measurements that might be expected

Measuring is a large part of this study but before basing anything on the recorded figures it is important to know if there might be differences in dimensions from one copy to another of the same edition, and if so how large the differences were, and if they might affect the result of any findings or conclusions.

One line from two different Zainer editions was measured through a number of copies to see what difference in line length might be encountered. Five copies of *De adhaerendo Deo*, line 10 on leaf [a1r] were measured and the line varied in length between 110mm and 111.25mm. Five copies of *Vitae sanctorum* had line 3 of leaf [a1v] measured, and a difference in line length between 111 and 112mm was found. The maximum difference found in these two editions was 1.25mm, which is less than 1 per cent over the whole line length of *c*.110mm, and also much less than the extreme example of 4.5mm cited by Pollard in *BMC*.[41]

---

[41] *BMC*, vol. 2, pp. xx–xxi.

Practical experiments

Experiment 2.1

To discover to what extent the paper damping and drying process might have affected the dimensions of Zainer's printing, two practical experiments were undertaken.[42]

The first experiment was to see by how much paper expands when dampened and contracts when dried. A modern hand-made paper from flax fibres, Barcham Green Chatham was used as flax (linen) would have been the most likely fibre source for Zainer's printing papers in the fifteenth century.

The paper was damped by being placed between other damp sheets of paper, being placed in a plastic bag to retain the moisture and left under a light weight for 24 hours. The aim was to give enough time for the fibres to absorb the moisture evenly. The following day the sheets were printed with a text block. Two measurements of the printed text area were taken and marked on the sheet; 216.5mm across the width of the text and 121mm down 21 lines of text.

The paper was then left to dry on a flat surface with no restraint. When the paper was dry the marked measurements were re-measured giving 215mm by 120mm. This showed that in this instance the damped flax-fibre paper shrunk by 1mm over a measure of 120mm – approximately one per cent.

Experiment 2.2

This second experiment was made to see if fifteenth-century paper will expand and shrink to a similar amount as a modern paper. A leaf of fifteenth-century flax-fibre paper from Zainer's 1474 edition Petrus Berchorius, *Liber Bibliae* was used.

As this sheet already had text printed on it the text area was measured before the paper was damped. The width across the two columns of text measured 83mm / 22.5mm gutter / 84mm, and the depth of the left hand column was 286mm.

The sheet was damped by being placed between other damp sheets of paper, being placed in a plastic bag and left under a light weight for 24 hours, after which time the leaf was re-measured. The width of the text area on the damp paper was 83.5mm / 23mm gutter / 84.5mm across the columns and the depth was 287.5mm. The leaf was then allowed to dry on a flat surface and the measurements taken again, when they were found to have returned to the original dimensions. This showed that the amount of expansion in the fifteenth-century paper that Zainer had used was very close to that of the modern paper, about 1mm over 120mm. However this

---

[42] Date of experiments 14 August 2006 and 5 September 2006.

does not take into account the different methods of drying at the time or since, variations in binding, re-binding, handling and storage since, which can all affect the size of a sheet of paper. What it does show is that there will be some variation of a millimetre or two and that as long as one is aware that paper stretch might be a factor one can be fairly relaxed about minor differences in measurements.

Having taken and recorded the measurements from several copies of the 38 editions, certain points emerged and began to make a pattern. As the recorded measurements accumulated, it was obvious that patterns were there, giving evidence of how Zainer approached his work. The points discussed in this section are all basic points about which Zainer would have had to make a decision before he started printing.

One of the most noticeable factors was the consistency of Zainer's line length which measured *c.*110mm for almost all his single-column chancery folios and *c.*83mm across each column in his double-column royal folios. Table 2.2 lists the dimensions of text areas in Zainer's folios on chancery-size and royal-size paper and it can be seen that there was very little difference in the length of his lines of type within each size category. Given the differences that might be caused by paper stretch or shrink, as discussed above in Experiments 2.1 and 2.2, or in setting method, the figures seem to suggest that Zainer was working to a fixed measure for almost all his chancery-folio editions.[43] The same situation arises with the royal folios where the width of the columns is fixed at 83mm in all of them, and the total width of two columns plus their inter-columnar margin is very close to 190mm.

As mentioned earlier, it is not known how the early printers were supporting their type during the process of composition. Type letters are very unstable and when being assembled into lines, and the lines into pages of text, some kind of support is needed. Apart from the need for support during the composition of the text, there also needs to be some method of accurately producing lines that are all exactly the same length. As mentioned under 'Inking' if lines vary in length from one to the next, even by a millimetre, it will be impossible for the printer to lock up the forme tightly, because the furniture will bind on the longer line and the shorter lines will not get any pressure. During the printing process individual letters can work loose and move, either sideways or upwards as 'work-ups'.

We do not know what Zainer used as a typesetting tool. The San Ripoli press was using some kind of wooden holder for composing type in 1483,

[43] The line length changes to *c.*116mm for the two editions with his larger Type 117 (Aesop's *Vita et fabulae* and Nider's *Vierundzwanzig goldene Harfen*) and there is one anomaly, Nider's *Praeceptorium divinae legis* that has a line length of *c.*127mm.

Table 2.2. Dimensions of text areas in Zainer's chancery and royal folios, showing how generally consistent they were. The figures in brackets are the text height including headline. Figures for the text width of the royal folios are given as: text width of first column/width of inter-columnar margin/text width of second column = total width of text area.

Date	Author	Title	Text area (in mm)	
			Height	Width
Chancery folios				
1473	Heinrich Steinhöwel	*Deutsche Chronik*	180	111
[1473]	Thomas Aquinas	*De periculis contingentibus*	186	110
1473	Albertus Magnus	*De mysterio missae*	197	110
[c.1473]	Johannes de Castello	*De adhaerendo Deo*	186	110
1473	Francesco Petrarca	*Historia Griseldis* [Latin]	164	110
[c.1473]	Francesco Petrarca	*Historia Griseldis* [Swabian]	196	110
[c.1473-74]	Francesco Petrarca	*Historia Griseldis* [German]	196	110
1473	Giovanni Boccaccio	*De claris mulieribus* [Latin]	196	110
[1473]	Giovanni Boccaccio	*De claris mulieribus* [German]	191(196)	110
[1474]	Thomas Aquinas	*De periculis contingentibus*	186	110
1474	Albertus Magnus	*Summa*	193(205)	111
[1475]	Thomas Aquinas	*De periculis contingentibus*	190	111
1475	Antonius Rampigollis	*Aurea Biblia*	197(203)	109
1475	Thomas Aquinas	*Quaestiones*	199(204)	111
[c.1476]	Albertus de Ferraris	*De horis canonics*	198	112
[c.1476]	Thomas Aquinas	*De periculis contingentibus*	190	110
[c.1476]	Albertus de Ferrariis	*Vocabularis Bibliae*	197	110
1476	Antonius Rampigollis	*Aurea Biblia*	196(202)	110
[not after 1476]	Dionysius Cato	*Documenta moralia*	198(204)	111
[14]76	Johannes Nider	*Die 24 goldenen Harfen*	195(200)	117
[c.1476]	Aesop	*Vita et fabulae*	196(200)	116
[not after 1477]	Jacobus de Voragine	*Legenda aurea* [ij00088400]	185(191)	110
[not after 1478]	Jacobus de Voragine	*Legenda aurea* [ij00091000]	191(196)	112
[not after1478]	Albertus Magnus	*Sermones* [ij00331000]	191(198)	112
[c.1478]	Johannes Herolt	*Postilla*	188	111
[c.1478-80]	Hieronymous	*Vitae sanctorum*	198(205)	112
[c.1476]	Jacobus de Voragine	*Legenda aurea* [ij00087000]	195	111
[not after1479]	Johannes Nider	*Praeceptorium*	198(204)	127
Royal folios				
1473	Guillelmus Duranti	*Rationale*	288(305)	83/23/83=189
1474	Petrus Berchorius	*Liber Biblae moralis*	290(299)	84/23/83=190
1475	Guillelmus Duranti	*Rationale*	289	84/25/84=193
[14]75	Johannes Gritsch	*Quadragesimale*	290(300)	84/23/84=191
1475	Leonardus de Utino	*Sermones de sanctis*	290(297)	190
[14]76	Johannes Gritsch	*Quadragesimale*	287(297)	190
1478	Leonardus de Utino	*Sermones de sanctis*	287(291)	188

but the word used in the *Diario, 'uno compositoio'*, could mean anything used for composing type.[44] In the illustration of the printshop in *Danse macabre* (see Figure 1.1) it looks as though the compositor is holding a stick in his hand, and is also filling a tray, complete with centre division and handle, with type letters. A composing stick, made to a fixed measure would help ensure the setting of lines of equal length. Zainer may have used a composing stick, made from wood and to a fixed measure, similar to those found in the Plantin-Moretus Museum, (see Figure 1.7).[45] Alternatively Zainer may have set the type directly into a tray, similar to the galley and slice as described by Moxon.[46] He could have achieved lines of type set to the same length if the tray was filled out with pieces of furniture, leaving a central space with the correct text area for the lines of type to be inserted.

Evidence of loose locking up of the forme can regularly be seen in Zainer's printing with raised, inked spaces (as discussed earlier), as wavy lines of text, or slipped letters. This suggests that it would have been impossible for Zainer to have lifted such a loosely-locked forme off the press or the stone because the loose letters would have fallen out and the whole forme would have collapsed. This evidence of loose lock-up suggests that Zainer might have been making up his formes on a tray or galley, so he could have moved them around the printshop easily. A further thought is that he might not have locked up his type in a chase, as was used later on and until the present day, but have left the type locked up as a forme on the tray for printing and perhaps printed from this tray. This is speculation – it is not known how Zainer set his type, but the evidence on his printed pages often shows very loose lock-up; so loose that any a printer would have been wary of moving such formes around without some firm support underneath.

Zainer's length of line changed slightly to *c.*116mm when he started to use a new typeface, Type 117G, as a text face at sometime in 1476, but he then returned to *c.*110mm when the smaller Type 96G was introduced in *c.*1477–78.[47] Whatever equipment Zainer was using to fill with type while he was setting his pages, it seems to have been consistently producing page after page of text, through many editions, year after year, to almost the same measure.

[44] Conway, p. 263, f. [118r] of the original has an entry for 22 October 1483 of 3s 4d paid to Jacopo [the joiner] for *uno compositoio*.

[45] Examination of the wooden composing sticks in the Plantin-Moretus Museum, all of fixed measures, showed that they had a fairly rough finish. One gets the impression that if two sticks had been made to the same measure there could easily be a millimetre or two of difference in their 'fixed' widths – the difference that Bowers in 'Bibliographical evidence', p. 155 stated could be counted as normal between two sticks of the same width.

[46] Moxon, p. 34, with illustrations on pp. [36], 222 and 401.

[47] Earlier discussion of text-size and line-length relationship can be found in Chapter 1, under section 'the format of Zainer's editions' and Smith, *Form*, p. 154.

Number of lines

Ideally the number of lines on each page should be decided at the planning stage of an edition. The printer, if printing a new edition, has to work out how many lines of text, set to his chosen width, he can fit on a page, and then calculate the number of pages he will need for the edition. This is basic copyfitting or casting-off copy. At the crudest level it is quite possible to set a few lines of text to get the feel of how the type face 'fits' to the line, and do a quick word count. From there it is possible to make a very passable estimate of how much text will fit on a page, and how many pages would be needed for the entire text. The calculations may be out by a word or two but rarely much more than that. When using a typeface that has been used before and is familiar, this feel for the fit of the face is much easier. Copyfitting is even easier with lines of tabular work, as one only has to count lines, not estimate words in a line.

However it seems that the first printers did not find copyfitting easy. Pollard makes this clear in the notes to *BMC*, vol. 1 where he states 'Comparatively few early books keep rigorously to the same number of lines . . . all the way through, . . .'.[48]

Lotte Hellinga has contributed to our knowledge about methods of copyfitting employed in the fifteenth century in a number of articles discussing the use of 'printer's copies', both printed and manuscript, that have survived showing the compositors' marking up on the copy.[49] In particular her article on preparing texts for printing gives a clear step-by-step description of the procedures necessary.[50] Having a copy of the text prepared for the printer, marked up and divided into pages and quires, would make the whole procedure of printing the book a much safer venture. Evidence from Amerbach's correspondence shows that he was having printer's copies especially written out for him to use.[51] There is no evidence of any printer's copies relating to editions by Johann Zainer although there is a manuscript in the BSB (Cgm 1137) in Steinhöwel's handwriting that was used as the basis of Günther's edition of Rodericus' *Der Spiegel des menschlichen Lebens* (ir00231000).[52]

It is easier for the printer always to have the same number of lines of

---

[48] *BMC*, vol. 1, p. xix.

[49] Lotte Hellinga, 'Notes'; 'Manuscripts in the hands of printers', in Joseph B. Trapp, ed., *Manuscripts in the fifty years after the invention of printing: some papers read at a colloquium at the Warburg Institute on 12–15 March 1982* (London: Warburg Institute, 1983), pp. 3–11; and 'Compositors and editors: preparing texts for printing in the fifteenth century', *Gutenberg-Jahrbuch*, 75 (2000), pp. 152–159.

[50] Hellinga, 'Compositors', p. 154.

[51] Halporn, p. 24. A letter from Adolf Rusch to Amerbach in September 1485 discusses having 'the Augustine copied out'.

[52] Janota, 'Von der Handschrift', p. 134. My observations when comparing Steinhöwel's manuscript with the printed edition showed that the text of the manuscript was followed for the printed edition but that there were no marks giving evidence of it having been used as a printer's copy.

type in the forme – it saves time when making up the forme if the text blocks are always the same size, without having to fill out with lines of spacing material, and it helps to keep the press balanced. One tries to copyfit so that every page has the same number of lines. Zainer did aim at a standard number of lines to a page, but did not always achieve it. His royal folios are the most consistent with two columns each of 50 lines, occasionally rising to 51 or 52 where there is a headline included. This suggests that if he was only setting and printing the text on one side of one leaf at a time, he could have worked progressively through the text, setting the quires page by page from the beginning to the end, i.e. in seriatim, and not have had any copyfitting problems at all. However the chancery folios are not so consistent. Although Zainer seems to have aimed at a standard 34 lines to a page, or 35 with the headline, the line count varies throughout every edition.

The most obvious variation in number of lines can be found on the leaves in the centre of the quire. These centre leaves often have a fewer number of lines than the rest of the quire, although occasionally the number of these might be more. For example in the 1476 edition of *Aurea Biblia* quire [k] has leaves with 33 or 34 lines but the centre inner pages [k5v/6r] have 32 lines.[53] However in the same edition in quire [n] where again all the leaves have 33 or 34 lines, the centre inner pages [n5v/6r] have 36 lines each.

A more extreme example of reduced number of lines in the centre of the quire can be seen in another edition. Quire [a] of *Vocabularius Bibliae* has the following number of lines on the outermost leaves of the quire:

Outer side of sheet		Inner side of sheet	
[2r/9v]	34/33 lines	[9r/2v]	32/33 lines
[3r/8v]	33/32 lines	[8r/3v]	32/33 lines
[4r/7v]	32/31 lines	[7r/4v]	31/32 lines

but the innermost pages have fewer lines:

[5r/6v]	28/29 lines	[6r/5v]	23/24 lines.

These adjustments from the standard number of lines in his chancery folios suggest a link with his copyfitting. Evidence discussed has shown that Zainer was printing his chancery folios two conjugate pages at a time. As many of his quires comprise 20 pages this would have entailed his setting the text for page [1r] and [10v] together and estimating what text was printed on the intervening pages. The evidence from the different number of lines on various pages in his quires suggests that he might have printed the outermost leaves of the quire first and then worked towards the centre, and when finally arriving at the centre leaves, have had to do

[53] Antonius Rampigollis, *Aurea Biblia*, 1476 (ir00014000).

some rapid re-calculation of the number of lines on a page.[54] This evidence corroborates that of Lotte Hellinga who found that work almost always began with the first outer forme and progressed from the outside inwards and stated that these findings agreed with what Haebler had inferred for early Italian editions.[55]

As stated above there are no known examples of printers' copy for Zainer so we have no evidence of how he planned his copyfitting. However there are two books where he reprinted the text; occasions where he would have had the chance to use the first edition as a printer's copy when setting the reprint. The first of these is with the four different editions he printed of Thomas Aquinas *De periculis contingentibus*.[56] None of the four editions has a printed date but all have an assigned date, one each year from 1473 to 1476. The text runs to approximately 420 lines and is printed on 13 pages of an 8-leaf pamphlet. In all the editions both sides of the first leaf and the last side of the last leaf are blank. The text is almost exactly the same for all four editions but the type was reset for each. The beginning and ending words on each pair of conjugate pages are the same for the [1473] and [1474] editions, although the spellings and use of contractions varies considerably between them. It is possible that his compositors might have been working by the sheet and the [1473] edition could have been used as a model for [1474]. The [1475] edition differs in the beginning and ending words and the [1476] edition differs again from all the previous editions. The first two editions have spaces left for initials to be added by hand later, and the last two editions have printed initials. In all the editions there are a different number of lines on the pages, throughout each edition and also when comparing one edition to another (Table 2.3).

One would think with around 420 lines of text and only 13 pages to print them on Zainer might have been able to do the mathematics, and work with his standard 34 lines to a page, for 12 pages, giving 408 lines, with the extra 11, 13, 15 or 18 lines on the last short page. This last page, [8v], would have had to have been printed on its own because its conjugate page, [1r], was blank. 34 lines of text on each conjugate page would have provided equally balanced formes of type, with just the single page to be printed separately. Instead Zainer varies the number of lines

---

[54] Other information discussed in Chapter 4, *Blind Impressions from (bearer) Type*, adds to this suggestion that Zainer started setting from the outer leaves of his quires and worked towards the centre.

[55] Lotte Hellinga, 'Notes', p. 69, found that in Italian books the type-page in the centre leaves of a gathering was noticeably adjusted to fit the copy, inferring that this meant they were printing by formes from the outer to the inner of the quire. Haebler also stated that with German books the copy adjustment was done by use of abbreviations and that this only happened at the end of a gathering – therefore German printers were working sequentially through their quires.

[56] Thomas Aquinas, *De periculis contingentibus* [*c.*1473] (it00316000); [*c.*1474] (it00317000); [*c.*1475] (it00318000); [*c.*1476] (it00319000).

Table 2.3. The number of lines on conjugate leaves in four different editions of *De periculis contingentibus.*

Conjugate leaf	Date	[1473]	[1474]	[1475]	[1476]
	Forme	Number of lines			
8v / 1r	inner	0 / 0	0 / 0	0 / 0	0 / 0
1v / 8r	outer	0 / 34	0 / 34	0 / 32	0 / 34
7v / 2r	inner	32 / 33	32 / 33	34 / 34	34 / 34
2v / 7r	outer	32 / 32	32 / 32	33 / 32	33 / 32
6v / 3r	inner	32 / 33	32 / 33	32 / 34	33 / 32
3v / 6r	outer	32 / 33	32 / 32	33 / 33	34 / 33
5v / 4r	inner	31 / 32	31 / 31	31 / 31	32 / 32
4v / 5r	outer	32 / 33	32 / 33	32 / 32	31 / 32
Total lines		**421**	**419**	**423**	**426**

right through all the editions. In the [1473] edition only one forme has conjugate pages of type set with the same number of lines; the [1474] edition has three, the [1475] edition has four and the [1476] edition has two. The remainder all have uneven numbers of lines of type and for all of them he would have had to add lines of spacing material at the foot to fill out the space in the forme. One might think that he could have used the first edition as an exemplar and then adjusted the number of lines on each leaf of the later editions to give a more balanced printing experience, but the evidence here suggests that he did not.

A similar situation can be found with Zainer's two editions of Rampigollis' *Aurea Biblia,* printed in 1475 and 1476. The type was reset for the 1476 edition, as shown by the numerous alterations of spellings and contractions. The quiring of the two editions is exactly the same, with the 1476 edition following the pattern of the 1475 edition. The text only agrees roughly at the beginning and end words on the pages. The number of lines on each leaf varies considerably between editions, and only in two quires do both editions have the same number of lines on the same leaves. Zainer could have achieved more balanced formes with 34 lines per page by removing a line where he had 35 and adding to where he only had 33 lines on a page. It remains a puzzle as to why Zainer did not work in a more balanced and logical printer's manner, especially for the 1476 edition where he was likely to have had the 1475 edition to use as a printer's copy. The situation suggests anarchy in the print room, a completely free hand given to the compositors, and little attention to detail by proof reader or overseer. Hellinga states that despite the casting-off done by the master printer 'a compositor had the final hand in making the text.'[57] Perhaps this is an example of compositors let loose.

A variation in the standard number of lines was also found by David Rogers in editions from Günther Zainer's workshop.[58] It seems that he also had problems with copyfitting and Rogers found examples of extra lines being added on a second print run, extra single leaves being added to accommodate missing text, and evidence of proof corrections forcing words onto another leaf, and so causing changes in the line count. Rogers counted 56 occasions in more than 100 books [?editions] printed by Günther where he had had to add or remove an extra leaf to accommodate mis-fitted text. In the 38 editions in this present study only 10 examples of extra leaves in editions printed by Johann have been noted, eight in his royal folios and two in his chancery folios.

One explanation may be that he only had a small fount of type, perhaps only enough for four or eight pages of text. If Zainer had had enough type to set the type for the whole 20 pages of text in the quire at one time he could have avoided irregular pages, but this does not really explain why he did not even out the number of lines in these reprint editions.[59]

CENTRAL GUTTER

A further measurement taken was that of the central gutter, the total margin(s) between the two text blocks, on either side of the centre fold line of the sheet, in Zainer's chancery folios. This full measurement can only be seen, and measured, across the centre pages of a quire. Unlike the outer margins, which can vary depending on later trimming and binding over the years, this central gutter was a dimension fixed by the printer. It is a difficult measurement to take accurately, being in the centre of the sheet within a bound book. If the binding is tight and with its back heavily rounded then it is almost impossible to get an accurate measure. For best accuracy the margins on both sides of a centre fold of the sheet in the middle of a quire have to be measured to establish the total distance between the two text blocks on each leaf. This is especially important if, as sometimes, the leaf has not been folded accurately in half by the binder. The central gutter of the royal folios is not being considered here. Evidence suggests that Zainer was printing these

---

[57] Lotte Hellinga, 'Manuscripts', p. 5.

[58] David Rogers, 'A glimpse into Günther Zainer's workshop, c.1476', *Buch und Text im 15. Jahrhundert. Arbeitsgespräch in der Herzog August Bibliothek vom 1. bis 3. März 1978* (Hamburg: Hauswedell, 1981), pp. 145–163 (pp. 147–150).

[59] It is sometimes possible to estimate the size of a fount if a recognisable damaged letter can be noted, being used more of less often, in successive pages of text. If this letter is used in every leaf there is some evidence for it coming from a small fount, with the printer having to distribute his type from one forme before setting the type for the next. It has not been possible to find such evidence for Zainer.

editions one leaf at a time and therefore the centre margin could vary depending on the accuracy of the positioning of paper on the type for printing.

Table 2.4 lists Zainer's chancery folios and one median folio, the *Decameron*, with the widths of the central gutter. The figures shown vary because they come from measuring different copies with different ease of access in to the spine. However, even with varying figures, the changes in the size of this central gutter can clearly be seen and this could indicate a change in working practice at a particular point in time. Some of the early editions have printed dates in their colophons which help to place them chronologically. The typefaces used for these editions as discussed in Chapter 1 under 'Zainer's typefaces' have also been added as they can also help indicate a chronology for some of the undated editions.

Three editions dated 1473, including his earliest, firmly dated, chancery-folio *Deutsche Chronik*, all have a narrow central gutter of approximately 66–70 millimetres.[60] Two other editions, *De periculis contingentibus* and *De adhaerendo Deo*, which are both undated, also have this same gutter measurement. It is therefore possible that these two might have been printed at the same time as the other three.

However there are also two further dated editions from 1473 with a wider central gutter measurement of approximately 86–90 millimetres. This wide gutter then continues to be used for 16 chancery folios, of which six have printed dates, over the next three years, so it seems possible that the editions with the wider gutter and dated 1473 were printed after those with the narrow gutter, which belong to his first period of printing.

Zainer reverts to the narrow gutter probably in 1477 when printing his last edition using Type 117G, the *Decameron*.[61] From this edition onwards he continues to set his formes with the narrow gutter for all the remaining, undated, editions studied for this book. It is not known what was in the space of the central gutter in the type forme – it might have been wooden furniture or metal spacing, or he might have been setting his type directly into a tray or galley with a fixed centre. What is noticeable is that Zainer, although changing his central gutter dimension once, and then a few years later changing it back, was working to the same basic measurements for all his chancery-folio editions. It would seem that he decided on the basic dimensions for printing his text on chancery-size paper; the text

---

[60] Heinrich Steinhöwel, *Deutsche Chronik*, 1473 (is00765000).

[61] There has been some discussion about the dating of the *Decameron*. *BMC* (vol. 2, p. 520) originally suggested that it was printed earlier, *c.*1473, because of its lack of initials and uneven line endings. Amelung's work on Zainer's typefaces places the *Decameron* later, *c.*1477 (*Der Frühdruck*, p. 44). In Table 2.4 it seems to be the odd one out. It has been positioned here so it links with the other uses of Type 117G and the other uses of a narrow margin. It is most unlikely that Johann was using Type 117G in 1473, which could have enabled the *Decameron* to be part of the earlier group of Zainer's editions with narrow margins.

Table 2.4. Measurement across the central gutter, between the two text areas on a sheet in Zainer's chancery- and median-folio editions. The table gives a suggested chronology for the editions, based on printed dates in colophons, use of text typeface and changes in width of central gutter.

Date	Title	Text type	Approximate centre margin measurement in mm
1473	*Deutsche Chronik*	116*	65–67
[1473]	*De periculis contingentibus*	116a	66–70
1473	*De mysterio missae*	116*a	66–69
[c.1473]	*De adhaerendo Deo*	110	66–70
1473	*Historia Griseldis* [Latin]	110	64–70
[not before 15 Aug 1473]	*De claris mulieribus* [German]	116*ab	87–88
[c.1473]	*Historia Griseldis* [Swabian]	116ab	86–87
1473	*De claris mulieribus* [Latin]	116ab	87–88
[c.1473–74]	*Historia Griseldis* [German]	116ab	88
[1474]	*De periculis contingentibus*	116ab	86
1474	*Summa*	116ab	87
[1475]	*De periculis contingentibus*	116b	87–89
17jun1475	*Aurea Biblia*	116b	87
1475	*Quaestiones*	116b	86–88
[c.1476]	*De horis canonics*	116b	87–89
[c.1476]	*De periculis contingentibus*	116b	88–90
[c.1476]	*Vocabularius Bibliae*	116b	87–90
1476	*Aurea Biblia*	116b	87
[not after 1476]	*Documenta moralia*	116b/117	88–90
[14]76	*Die 24 goldenen Harfen*	117	88–90
[c.1476–77]	*Vita et fabulae*	117	87
[c.1476]	*Decameron*	117	67–70
[not after 1477]	*Legenda aurea* [ij00088400]	96	67–70
[not after 1478]	*Legenda aurea* [ij00091000]	96	68–70
[not after 1478]	*Sermones* [ia00331000]	96	67–70
[1478]	*Postilla*	96	68–70
[c.1478–80]	*Vitae sanctorum*	96	68–70
[c.1476]	*Legenda aurea* [ij00087000]	96	67–70
[not after 1479]	*Praeceptorium*	96	67

width, the number of lines and the gutter, and then he stayed with that decision apart from a slight alteration to the gutter. Similarly with his royal folios where, although the central gutter alters, the width of columns, number of lines and inter-columnar margin remain the same.

There seems to be no obvious reason as to why Zainer changed from a narrow central gutter to a wider one. His original narrower margin allows good access to enable the reading of the text in the inner area of the pages, even in a thick edition. He might have changed to a wider margin for aesthetic reasons but to my eye the wider margin tends to give his pages a clumsy look with so much space on the inner margin. The extra *c.*20mm added to the width of the whole text area, but this extra text area should not have caused him technical printing problems; he could have printed both layouts, the bifolia with both the narrow and the wide central gutters, with the same size press and platen without noticing much difference.

SKELETONS

The measurements discussed above also show that the printing area on one leaf of Zainer's royal folios is almost exactly the same as that on his chancery bifolium (see Figure 2.12). This suggests that if the press had a large enough platen to print the full area of text on a royal-folio leaf, it could manage to print the full area of text of two conjugate chancery-folio leaves at one time.

The existence of so many almost identical measurements points to Zainer working with a fixed skeleton; a fixed forme of furniture in a supporting frame or chase, with the same space allowed for the type block, and the whole then located in the same position on the bed of the press time for every print run.[62] Other evidence from bearer type, discussed in Chapter 4, also points to Zainer working with a fixed skeleton. Lotte Hellinga suggested that 1473 was not too early for skeleton formes and that the use of fixed dimensions may have helped Zainer handle all his woodcut elements.[63] Rogers also commented on Günther working to a standard page size for more than 30 editions, whatever length of text he was printing.[64] Günther's central gutter measurements in 10 of his chancery folios were all between 66mm and 70mm, so perhaps he was also working with a fixed skeleton.

We do not know how many presses Johann Zainer had. If he had had more than one press, and if, as seems likely, he was working with fixed skeletons, it would have been easy to have used any press to print any page from any edition without needing to adjust anything. We do not know if he printed more than one edition at a time. However there is also

---

[62] It is all too easy to make mistakes when printing a complicated item such as a multi-section book. It is important to fix as many of the variables as possible. One method of reducing the chances of making a mistake in imposition is to work with a fixed skeleton (or two skeletons, one for the outer forme and one for the inner forme). Gaskell, *Bibliography*, pp. 109–110, states that it was possible to print an entire edition using one skeleton, only imposing the new forme when the old one came off the press, and suggests that it may indicate a shortage of type, or other constituent part of the skeleton.

[63] Personal communication 23 February 2007.

[64] Rogers, p. 150.

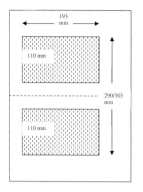
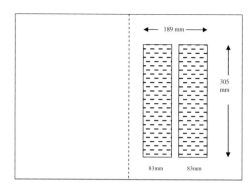

text area

Figure 2.12. Diagram showing (left) dimensions of text area in a conjugate pair of leaves from a chancery folio and (right) the similar text area on one leaf from a royal folio.

a suggestion from the unusual combination of 'ff' and 'C' used as a bearer line in *Aurea Biblia*, 1476, *Documenta moralia*, [c.1476] and *Quadragesimale*, 1476, that all three editions might have been in print at the same time.[65] Also he was a prolific printer and would have needed enough press capacity to cope with his output. These factors, plus the note of his projected print run of 525 copies of *Sermones de sanctis* in 1475 in the letter between Johann and Günther mentioned in the *Introduction*, all suggest that it is very likely that he had more than one press.[66]

Johann would also most likely have worked to some kind of fail-safe system of orientation where he always placed the forme on the bed of the press, facing in the same direction, i.e. with the head of the forme always in the same position on the bed.[67] He would then have always placed the paper for printing with the head of the sheet in the same place. There is no proof that Zainer always fed to the head, but the evidence of large variation in the foot margins of his editions suggests that his most consistent feed-edge of the paper was the head. When working with his chancery folios he could have fed both sides of the bifolium to the same head position by simply turning the sheet over.

With the royal and imperial folios Zainer would have had to reverse the position of the forme and the feed-edge when printing the reiteration of a single leaf. This, also, would have been simpler to do with a second press, and would have helped to avoid imposition problems. He could have

---

[65] See Chapter 4, *Blind Impressions from (bearer) Type*.
[66] More information is given in Chapter 4, *Blind Impressions from (bearer) Type*.
[67] Gaskell, *Bibliography*, p. 127, states that it was necessary to have rules for the orientation of the formes so as to avoid mistakes in imposition. This has also been found from my personal experience.

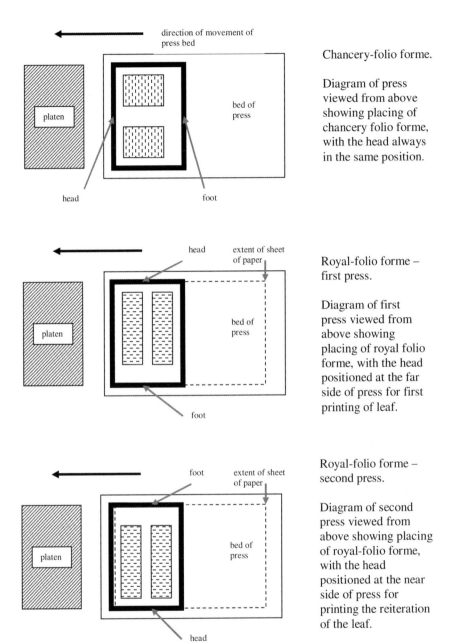

direction of movement of
press bed

platen

bed of
press

head   foot

Chancery-folio forme.

Diagram of press
viewed from above
showing placing of
chancery folio forme,
with the head always
in the same position.

head   extent of sheet
of paper

platen

bed of
press

foot

**Royal-folio forme –
first press.**

Diagram of first
press viewed from
above showing
placing of royal folio
forme, with the head
positioned at the far
side of press for first
printing of leaf.

foot   extent of sheet
of paper

platen

bed of
press

head

**Royal-folio forme –
second press.**

Diagram of second
press viewed from
above showing placing
of royal-folio forme,
with the head
positioned at the near
side of press for
printing the reiteration
of the leaf.

Figure 2.13. Diagrams showing various orientations of the forme on the press bed.

printed the first side of the page on a first press, with its fixed positions and feeding to the head on the far side of the press, and then printed the reiteration on a second press, with its fixed positions reversed so the head was on the near side of the press. Once the method of working was established it need never have changed, and was one element of book printing that he could fix firmly. Diagrams showing this are given in Figure 2.13.

Scholderer suggests that the six presses, purchased especially to print royal-size paper at SS Ulrich and Afra in Augsburg meant that two presses could be used for printing each of the three large volumes of their *Speculum* – perhaps one was set up for the outer formes and the other for the inner.[68] This would have been the safest way to proceed, especially when dealing with such a large edition as the *Speculum*.

QUIRING

To convert the separate printed sheets of paper into a book they have to be folded, and gathered together into quires. The number of sheets being gathered into each quire is another basic decision that has to be made by the printer before any printing starts. A number of factors can affect the decision on how many leaves will be in a quire. Firstly, as discussed above under 'Number of Lines' and taking into consideration the printing capacity of his press, the printer has to estimate how much space the lines of type will take and then calculate how many leaves will be needed for the whole edition. He then has to try to divide the number of sheets, folded into leaves, evenly into quires through the book. The binding has a better chance of survival if the quires are of similar thickness. There is also the thickness of the paper to be taken into consideration. If the paper is too thick then it is difficult to fold more than three or four sheets comfortably together.

Gaskell states that most fifteenth-century quires consisted of up to five sheets (10 leaves).[69] Haebler states that 'gatherings in 8s gradually became the norm through the incunable period'.[70] These slightly contradictory statements leave open the question of when the change from quiring in 10s to quiring in 8s might have occurred. Smith recorded the number of leaves in the quire as part of her 1983 research, but the data was not included in her final thesis and she did not correlate the figures to any dates.[71] Using her basic data the figures were extracted based on five-year blocks. The data is illustrated in the graphs at Figure 2.14 and 2.15.

[68] Scholderer, 'Notes', p. 6.
[69] Gaskell, *Bibliography*, p. 82.
[70] Haebler, *Incunabula*, p. 53.
[71] My grateful thanks to Margaret Smith for access to her unpublished data.

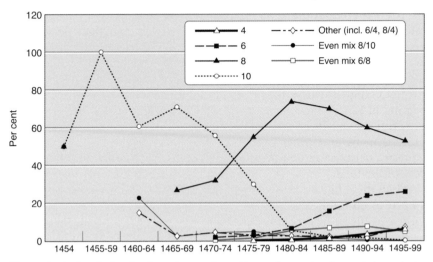

Figure 2.14. Graph showing how the number of leaves in a quire changed through the incunable period.

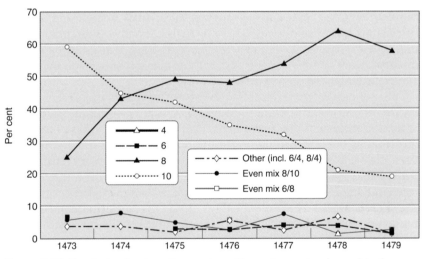

Figure 2.15. Graph showing how the number of leaves in a quire changed in the years from 1473 to 1479.

Figure 2.14 shows the number of editions in each category, as a percentage of those editions which had enough quires to show a pattern, for each period. Over 22 per cent of the total editions did not have enough quires, or no information was listed in the *GW* so these editions have not been included in these calculations. The information from the remaining

78 per cent of editions (in total 3,258 editions) shows, as Haebler intimated, that there was a gradual rise in editions printed in 8s to their becoming the majority at some time between 1474 and 1479. But this does not tell the whole story and it is interesting to see when the change from quiring in 10s to quiring in 8s came about.

Smith's figures show that over the entire period, from 1454 to 1499, quiring in 8s was the most popular, being represented by 53 per cent of the editions counted. After that there is a big drop to 16 per cent for quiring in 6s and then to 11 per cent for quiring in 10s. The other patterns, of quiring in 4s, 12s, or mixed 6/8s or 8/10s, are all under 5 per cent of the total.

When these figures are broken down to blocks of five-year periods and looked at chronologically it can be seen that the earliest editions were quired in 10s with some others, such as 12s and 14s, and some 8/10s mix being introduced in the early 1460s. By the late 1460s quiring in 8s increased and continued to increase to over 50 per cent of the editions through the 1470s, and peaked at 74 per cent in the early 1480s. At the same time the number of editions quired in 10s had a rapid decline from 56 per cent in the early 1470s to only 5.5 per cent by the early 1480s, and to less than 1 per cent by the end of the century. The change from predominantly quiring in 10s to predominantly quiring in 8s happened through the 1470s and by the early 1480s that change was complete. Some other quirings emerged; quiring in 6s became popular, rising to 26 per cent by the end of the century and there was a slight increase in all the other combinations.

To try to establish at what point in the 1470s this change occurred, the figures were also extracted to single years from 1473 to 1479 (Figure 2.15). From this graph it can be seen that in 1473 quiring in 10s was still the most used but by 1474 quiring in 8s and 10s were almost equal. For the next three years, from 1475 to 1477, quiring in 8s rose and quiring in 10s diminished, gradually. For the last two years, 1478 and 1479, this process accelerated to 58 per cent being in 8s and only 19 per cent being quired in 10s. These figures suggest that the change from quiring in 10s to 8s happened from 1475 onwards.

Zainer's changeover period, from quiring in 8s to quiring in 10s, seems to occur a little later than the average shown in Figure 2.15. In his first three years, from 1473 to 1476, his editions are still printed predominantly in quires of 10 leaves. Mixed in with the 10s are some 8s with an occasional 6 or 12. The 12-leaf quires only occur in his royal or imperial folios. There are also some odd single sheets let into some of the 10-leaf quires; perhaps caused by poor copyfitting or an error in composition.[72]

---

[72] *Rationale divinorum officiorum*, 1473, has an extra leaf (half sheet) added in quire [d] and *De mysterio missae* has a half leaf, with only 17 lines of text on each side, added in quire [k]. *Liber Bibliae* had an extra leaf added in both quires [h] and [i].

Where there is a table of contents it is often found in a quire of a smaller or larger number of leaves than the rest of the edition. This material was usually printed in a separate quire(s) from the body of the text, and then could be bound either at the beginning or the end of the copy, at the whim of the binder or eventual owner. Occasionally there is a particularly small quire within the edition because the text has come to the end of a section. *De planctu ecclesiae*, has quire [n] of only four leaves with the short remaining length of text from that section of the book.[73] In the two copies of this edition in the Bodleian one has the 8-leaf table bound at the end and the other has it at the beginning.[74] Despite some occasional variation in quire sizes, the editions to 1476, especially the chancery folios, are substantially quired in 10s.

A first change seems to come at some time during *c*.1477 with the printing of the *Decameron* where there is a very definite change in the pattern of the quires from 10s to alternating 10s and 8s. In all there are eight different editions that have this pattern of alternating 10s and 8s. The royal folio *Sermones quadragesimales*, 1478, has also been included here as it does alternate, but in blocks of five or six quires of 8 leaves and then of 10 leaves. This alternating 8 and 10 quiring is unusual and only occurs in 4.7 per cent of the editions as recorded by Smith.

After what might be considered a transitional period of printing in quires of alternating 8s and 10s, there is a second change as Zainer starts to print his editions almost solely in quires of 8 leaves. There are 21 editions quired almost totally in 8s.[75] Some of these changes are illustrated in Table 2.5 which shows the pattern of quiring in Zainer's editions. Only four of the 21 editions that are quired in 8s are given in this table.

Zainer is slightly late in his change over to quiring in 8s at sometime after 9 March 1478 when the dated edition *Sermones quadragesimales* (quired still in 8s and 10s) was completed. Zainer's next firmly dated edition is *Biblia Latina* (ib00567000) of 29 January 1480, quired in 8s – as are two other dated editions for that same year, *Scala coeli* (ig00311000) and *Vocabularius ex quo* (iv00363350).

We do not know the dates of printing for any of the other editions printed either in 8s and 10s, or solely in 8s, between March 1478 and January 1480. However the change in quiring patterns is so marked that it raises the question as to whether it could be used, along with other aspects such as changes in type face and in centre margin dimensions, to suggest a firmer date for some editions that previously had only an approximate

---

[73] Alvarus Pelagius, *De planctu ecclesiae*, 1474 (ip00249000).

[74] Shelfmarks Auct. 5 Q 1.11 and Auct. Q sub.fen. 1.8.

[75] Only seven of these editions include a quire of 10 leaves, and then there is only one 10-leaf quire in each edition. There are also very occasional 6-leaf and 12-leaf quires but by far the majority of the quires in these editions are 8s.

Table 2.5. The chronological changes in the number of leaves in quires in Zainer's multi-quired folio editions in this study, plus two further editions quired in 8s. Key to symbols: § = 2; ○ = 4; ◇ = 6; × = 8; ● = 10; ▲ = 12 leaves per quire

Title	Date
Quired in 10s	
Deutsche Chronik	1473
De mysterio missae	1473
De adhaerendo Deo	[c.1473]
Claris (latin)	1473
Claris (german)	[1473]
Rationale	1473
Summa	1474
Liber Bibliae	1474
De planctu ecclesiae	1474
Rationale	1475
Quadragesimale	1475
Aurea Biblia	1475
Sermones	1475
Quaestiones	1475
Quadragesimale	1476
Aurea Biblia	1476
Vocabularius Bibliae	[c.1476]
Documenta moralis	[na1476]
Goldene Harfen	[1476]
Vita et fabulae	[c.1476-77]
Quired in 8s and 10s	
Decameron	[c.1476]
Legenda aurea [jj00088400]	[na1477]
Legenda aurea [jj00091000]	[na1478]
Sermones [ia00331000]	[na1478]
Vitae sanctorum	[c.1478-80]
Sermones quadragesimales	1478
Postilla	[1478]
Praeceptorum	[na1479]
Quired in 8s	
Legenda aurea [jj00087000]	[c.1476]
Sermones [ia00332000]	[c.1478-80]
Sermones – Nider	[c.1478-80]
Sermones [ia00333000]	[c.1478-80]

date assigned to them.[76] The question about the date of printing of the *Decameron* was mentioned earlier as part of the discussion about Zainer's change in width of his central gutter. The information about quiring can also be added to the previous data, and because it is quired in alternating 8s and 10s it is somewhat more likely that it was printed after his *Vita et fabulae,* dated *c.*1476–77, which is quired almost exclusively in 10s. Also both editions are printed in the new Type 117.

Nider's *Praeceptorium* has assigned dates of 'not after 1479' and 'not after 1480'; a period when Zainer was only printing editions in 8s. *Praeceptorium* is quired in alternate 8s and 10s and therefore might have an earlier date of '*c.*1478'. Two of Zainer's editions of Voragine's *Legenda aurea* are quired in alternating 8s and 10s, 'not after 1477' and '*c.*1478', and the third, '*c.*1476', only in 8s. Again it could be that this latter edition was printed '*c.*1478', and after the other two editions and not '*c.*1476' as suggested by ISTC and Goff. Zainer printed three editions of Albertus Magnus *Sermones* (ia00331000), (ia00332000) and (ia00333000), all with assigned dates of [1478–80]. The first of these is quired in 8s and 10s and the other two in 8s, which suggests that (ia00331000) could have been printed before the other two. The last two editions have exactly the same quiring pattern.[77]

If one assumes that the changes in pattern of quiring do have a chronological basis then it could be also worthwhile considering whether these changes could indicate an alteration in some other practice: the method of working at the press, the purchase of a bigger two-pull press, that would have enabled the printing of two royal-folio leaves at a time rather than one, or more staff to do the typesetting.

There is little other corroborative evidence but data about typesetters exists for the *Decameron* where Bertelsmeier-Kierst shows from textual analysis that at least two different typesetters were working on the edition.[78] However they were working in blocks of three or four quires at a time, and one large block of sixteen quires, and not on alternating quires (Table 4.8).[79] There is no obvious link with the pattern of quiring and the work of the compositors for this edition.

In the royal folio, *Sermones quadragesimales,* 1478, there is evidence from the patterns of point holes that indicates that four different tympans, and perhaps presses, were being used.[80] However the pattern of using different

[76] Zainer changed his skeleton to working with a narrower centre margin at some time in 1476–77, between printing Aesop's *Vita et fabulae* and the *Decameron,* when he changed his quiring pattern from 10s to alternating 8s and 10s.

[77] It would be interesting to make a detailed study of these three editions of Albertus Magnus' *Sermones* to see if the differences in quiring are linked to any other technical or textual variations.

[78] Bertelsmeier-Kierst, pp. 249–253. More about the significance of this is given in Chapter 4, *Blind Impressions from (bearer) Type.*

[79] Bertelsmeier-Kierst, p. 250.

[80] A full discussion of Zainer's use of point holes and through this edition in particular will be given in Chapter 6, *Points & Point Holes.*

tympans in no way tallies with the quiring pattern of 8s and 10s in this edition and therefore it seems unlikely that Zainer was quiring this way because of a different way of working at the press.

Zainer was not alone in changing his quiring pattern from 8s to 10s in the 1470s, although his quiring in alternate 8s and 10s was very unusual and is represented by less than 5 per cent of all the editions surveyed by Smith. Some quiring patterns by other printers were examined to see if they were quiring in alternate 8s and 10s. These were not easy to find and would require a complete survey of every printer's quiring pattern which is beyond the scope of this research. However one or two examples were found. His brother Günther printed two editions in quires of alternate 8s and 10s; *Legenda aurea* in 1472 and *Rationale divinorum officiorum* in 1475. Anton Sorg printed *Expositio* in 1476 in 8s and 10s and Anton Koberger printed volume 3 of the *Summa theologica* in 1478 in alternate 8s and 10s, but the other volumes had a different pattern, and after 1481 he quired almost exclusively in 6s. It would be interesting to see if the gradual change over to 8s as the norm occurred along with the spread of a two-pull press, but again this is a question that can only be raised and not answered in this book.

OUTER MARGINS AND LEAF DIMENSIONS

Having considered the dimensions of Zainer's type areas in his different size editions, and the width of his central gutters, there remains a further point for discussion – the large amount of white paper left in the outer margins of his editions. Unlike the width of the central gutter, the final dimensions of the copies are not determined by the printer. When deciding on the type block area, the printer has to allow enough paper for the outer margins as well as for some trim. If one takes the standard paper sizes and compares their area with the area of type being printed on them in Zainer's editions, only approximately one third of the original sheet area is taken up by printed text (Table 2.6). Some of the surplus paper is later trimmed by the binder to give the dimensions seen in the finished copies. Zainer was not alone in having wide margins and the margins of incunables, especially the outer margins, were generous, perhaps unnecessarily so considering the costs of paper. The lavish size of margins in incunables was remarked on by Pollard in his notes to *BMC*, vol.1.[81]

Some of the copies of Zainer's editions examined for this study were still in their original bindings, and from measuring these and comparing with the approximate dimensions of the original sheet some idea of how much

---

[81] *BMC*, vol. 1, p. xix.

Table 2.6. The percentage of the sheet area used for printed text in various sizes of Zainer's editions.

	Chancery	Median	Royal	Imperial
Dimensions	315 × 450mm	345 × 515mm	445 × 615mm	500 × 740mm
Sheet area	1420 sq. cm	1800 sq. cm	2700 sq. cm	3700 sq. cm
Text area	440 sq. cm	600 sq. cm	960 sq. cm	1200 sq. cm
Text area as % of sheet area	30%	33%	35%	32.40%

the binder trimmed off can be estimated. Copies in later second or third bindings are not being considered here, but it was thought useful to bring together the information from original bindings.

The BSB has two copies of the 1475 *Rationale divinorum officiorum*, both in original bindings bound by Konrad Dinckmut in Ulm.[82] As a royal folio its original sheet size would have been *c.*445 × 615mm. Although both copies were bound by Dinckmut, there are slight differences in the finished dimensions; one has a finished sheet size of 405 × 568mm and the other 400 × 558mm, a difference in trim of 40 × 45mm on the first and 45 × 50mm on the second copies. This shows that Dinckmut had trimmed approximately 20–25mm off all sides; the head, foot and fore-edge of the books when he was binding them. Other Dinckmut bindings of Zainer royal folios show very similar amounts of trim although none are exactly the same (Table 2.7). The amount trimmed off is approximately 15 per cent of the original sheet. Without knowing exactly the original paper size it is difficult to be accurate in describing how much has been trimmed. In his article about some proof leaves that had come from Günther Zainer's workshop, and later used as pastedowns, David Rogers gives the dimensions of a proof bifolium, with deckle edges on all sides, as 310 × 445mm – a slightly smaller sheet, by 5mm each way, than the commonly accepted 315 × 450mm for chancery-size paper.[83]

The chancery folios show a similar amount of trim with about 18 per cent of the original sheet being removed. There are two copies of *Vierundzwanzig goldene Harfen* in the BSB, both in Dinckmut bindings.[84] These two show similar trim from head and foot of *c.*15mm but one copy has *c.*30mm removed from the fore-edge, which seems an unusually large amount, whereas the other has a more average *c.*20mm.

---

[82] *BSB-Ink* D-328; shelfmarks 2° Inc.c.a.368 and 2° Inc.c.a.368a. Breitenbruch, pp. 31–35, discusses some of the Dinckmut bindings in the Ulm Stadtbibliothek and illustrates some of the tools used in his workshop.

[83] Rogers, p. 160 in caption.

[84] *BSB-Ink* N-179, shelfmarks 2° Inc.c.a.509 and 2° Inc.c.a.509a.

Table 2.7. Bindings by Konrad Dinckmut of Zainer editions showing the amount of paper trimmed from original sheet size. Other contemporary bindings of Zainer's editions, not listed here, show trimming between 5% and 27% for chancery folios and 15% and 20% for a royal folio. (All measurements are approximate and in millimetres.) This is probably too small a sample from which to make any definitive conclusions, but the average of c.18% of the sheet being trimmed off seems quite wasteful.

Title	Library	Trimmed dimensions of full sheet	Amount trimmed	Head	Foot	Fore-edge	% of sheet trimmed
Royal folios – 445 × 615mm							
Rationale divinorum officiorum, 1475	BSB	405 × 568	40 × 45	20	20	22.5	15%
	BSB	400 × 558	45 × 50	22.5	22.5	25	17%
Quadragesimale, 1475	SBU	405 × 562	40 × 53	20	20	26.5	16%
Sermones, 1475	BSB	410 × 552	35 × 63	17.5	17.5	31.5	16%
	SBU	407 × 560	38 × 55	19	19	27.5	16%
Quadragesimale, 1476	BSB	405 × 560	40 × 55	20	20	27.5	16%
	SBU	392 × 564	53 × 51	26.5	26.5	25.5	18%
Sermones, 1478	SBU	406 × 560	39 × 55	19.5	19.5	27.5	16%
Median folio – 345 × 515mm							
*Decameron, [c.1476]	BL	327 × 462	18 × 43	9	9	21.5	16%
Chancery folios – 315 × 450mm							
De claris mulieribus, [Latin] 1473	UBW	304 × 424	11 × 26	5.5	5.5	13	9%
Quaestiones, 1475	BSB	286 × 410	29 × 40	14.5	14.5	20	17%
Goldene Harfen, [14]76	BSB	285 × 410	30 × 40	15	15	20	18%
Goldene Harfen, [14]76	BSB	285 × 390	30 × 60	15	15	30	22%
Vocabularius Bibliae [c.1476]	BSB	290 × 400	25 × 50	12.5	12.5	25	19%
Aurea Biblia, 1476	BSB	285 × 390	30 × 60	15	15	30	22%
Vitae sanctorum, [c.1478]	BSB	299 × 420	16 × 30	8	8	15	11%
Postilla super epistolas, [1478]	BSB	281 × 410	17 × 40	8.5	8.5	20	19%
Postilla super epistolas, [1478]	BSB	275 × 400	40 × 50	20	20	25	22%
Praeceptorium [na1479]	BSB	301 × 432	14 × 28	7	7	14	9%
Imperial folio – 500 × 740mm							
*De planctu ecclesiae, 1474	SBU	478 × 642	22 × 98	11	11	49	17%

* These volumes not bound by Dinckmut but are contemporary Ulm bindings from a different binder

Another clue to original sheet size can sometimes be gleaned from folded-in edges of paper that have escaped the binder.[85] These can be carefully folded out and measured to reveal how much has been removed. One example in the John Rylands library copy of *Documenta moralia*, with a sheet measuring *c.*300 × 442mm, had a fold-in of 7mm on the foot and fore-edges, which would have brought the sheet up to an original dimension of a chancery-folio sheet, *c.*315 × 450mm. Another fold-in was found on a leaf in a BSB copy of *Legenda aurea* [not after 1477] showed 12mm on the fore edge and 16mm at the foot.[86] This was on a second binding as the sheet size for this copy was a neat *c.*252 × 374mm. A 3mm fold-in was found in a copy of 1475 *Aurea Biblia*, bound in the nineteenth century for the Bodleian Library. These fold-ins, are fairly rare but help add to the picture of how much a binder might remove, and how much margin the printer might need to allow.[87]

It seems that the size of the sheets of paper supplied to, or used by, Zainer were not uniform. Although Zainer may have been using chancery-size paper for his small folios, variation in size within an edition has been found. Presumably the binders' trimming is intended to remove the uneven deckle edges from the book.[88] However in almost every copy of Zainer's editions examined there remains a leaf or two showing a deckle edge. More deckle edges occur in those copies that are still in their original bindings than those that have been rebound later, which might entail a second or third trim. Even in the Dinckmut bindings, where a good 20mm was removed from all sides of the books, a number of leaves with deckle edges have survived. Occasionally there are sheets, only one or two in a quire, which are significantly smaller than the rest. In *Vitae sanctorum*, the sheet [h2/7] is much smaller. It measures 285 × 388mm compared with a full chancery-size sheet of 315

---

[85] W. M. Gnirrep, J. P. Gumbert and J. A. Szirmai, eds., *Kneep en binding: en terminologie voor de beschrijving van de constructies van oude boekbanden* (The Hague: Koninklijke Bibliotheek, 1992) use the word *snijoor*, meaning 'cut ear' for these.

[86] *BSB-Ink* I-68, shelfmark 2° Inc.s.a.1247.

[87] Interestingly three of the above Dinckmut bindings in the BSB have pastedown leaves from other Zainer editions. One copy of *Vierundzwanzig goldene Harfen* (2° Inc.c.a.509d) has a leaf from *De horis canonicis*, and one copy of *Vitae sanctorum* (2° Inc.s.a.650) and one copy of *Praeceptorium* (2° Inc.s.a.917) both have leaves from Zainer's *Decameron* as pastedowns. This gives evidence of a link between the two Ulm workshops of Zainer and Dinckmut from 1476 to 1479. John Flood, 'Early editions of Arigo's translations of Boccaccio's *Decameron*', in Anna L. Lepschy, John Took, Dennis E. Rhodes, eds., *Book production and letters in the western European renaissance. Essays in honour of Conor Fahy* (London: Modern Humanities Research Association, 1986), p. 81, adds to this link with information about a pastedown leaf found in the British Library's copy of Zainer's *Decameron* (in most probably an Ulm binding) from Zainer's [not after 1477] edition of *Legenda aurea*. Amelung, *Der Frühdruck*, p. 191, also comments on waste from Zainer's editions being used in Dinckmut bindings.

[88] Personal correspondence 15 June 2007. Nicholas Pickwood suggests that the binders would trim down to the smallest size of paper being used but took care to leave some deckles on the shortest leaves – 'cutting to show proof'.

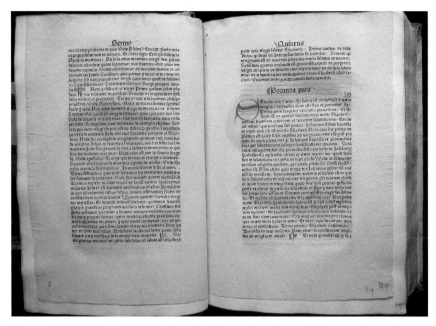

Figure 2.16. Bifolium [d4v/5r] printed on the smaller size and different colour of paper, indicating different paper stock, in the centre of quire [d] in *Expositio evangeliorum* [1480]. (Ulm Stadtbibliothek.)

× 450mm and shows deckle on all edges, having escaped any trimming by the binder in seven out of the eight copies looked at.[89] Other examples can be found with four out of five sheets in quires [c] and [d] of *De mysterio missae* which show foot and fore-edge deckle where they have escaped the binder's trim. A further example of small leaves in the centre of the quire was also found in a later edition, *Expositio evangeliorum,* and is illustrated in Figure 2.16.[90] This copy had been trimmed to give a sheet size of 298 × 432mm (removing *c.*17mm from the height and *c.*18mm from the width) but not enough had been trimmed from the foot or fore edges to disguise the fact that some sheets were smaller. The smaller sheets are also a different quality of paper although it was not possible to identify the watermark.

From brief notes made of watermarks and quality of paper it is clear that Zainer used different papers, and often mixed paper sources through

[89] The eighth copy (SBU 277, shelfmark 52722) had been trimmed to an extremely small size giving a sheet dimension of 243 × 348mm which had removed any sign of any deckles.

[90] Albertus de Padua, *Expositio evangeliorum* [*c.*15 June 1480] (ia00340000). SBU 26, shelfmark 15083.

an edition.[91] This could be an explanation of the existence of the much smaller sheets in some of his editions. Perhaps he hoped or assumed that after the binder had trimmed the book the differences would all be cut away and so would not show. This is only a small look at the amount of paper trimmed by the binder. It is another factor that had to be addressed by the printer; he had to allow for trim when deciding on the layout of the text on the page. This is an area that could fruitfully be taken further with a comprehensive survey of contemporary bindings, from different binders.

These basic observations suggest a printer working in a hurry, so much so that his press work was smudged, his register erratic and his inking uneven. Some of these factors may not have much significance on their own, but when added to the whole may help build up a picture of Zainer's printing practices. Some of the factors noted; his working to fixed measures, his sometimes irregular number of lines to a page, whether he was working seriatim or by formes, and the variety of point-hole patterns will be explored in greater depth in the next chapters.

---

[91] Lotte Hellinga in her study of the printing house of Nicolaus Ketelaer and Gherardus in Utrecht, 1473–75, in 'Problems about technique and methods in a fifteenth-century printing house', *Villes d'imprimerie et moulins à papier du XIVe siècle. Colloque International*, Collection Pro Civitate series no. 43 (Brussels: Crédit Communal de Belgique, 1976), pp. 301–313 (p. 312–313), noted a mix of papers being used through editions. She also found links between the different paper stocks used and the individual presses working in the printshop.

3 TYPE AND EMS – WORKING TO FIXED MEASURES

TYPE – A THREE-DIMENSIONAL THING

Zainer was printing with metal type, individual letters cast at the head of a piece of metal – a technology that was under 20 years old when he set up his press in Ulm, and a technology that was to last for the next 500 years. The face of the letter is inked and is printed on the page; it is the print from the face of the type which is seen on the page. This face is cast from a matrix, usually made of copper, which has had the letter shape struck into it from a steel punch. The face of the type is what can be seen and is usually the first thing to be considered when trying to identify an unknown piece of printing. But type is more than this. It is also a physical thing that can be picked up and held in the hand – it is a three-dimensional object with height, depth and width (see Figure 3.1).

Harry Carter makes this point in his account of early typefounding when he discusses the problem that most bibliographers have in thinking of type as being more than the face of the type.[1] He stresses the importance of understanding that the face is supported by a '3-dimensional thing', the type body. The body size (in depth and height) of a piece of type is dictated by the mould, in which the type is cast, which is fixed in these dimensions, and in width by the matrix, to which the mould is adjusted for each letter being cast. A mould was usually kept for one particular typeface. Later the different founts of type began to be known by their mould size, such as 'Paragon' or 'Cicero' or 'Pica', but these terms varied from founder to founder and a fount of type from one founder cast for instance with a Pica size mould could vary from a fount cast with nominally the same mould from a different founder. Carter describes the efforts of Christopher Plantin in 1563 to relate his various typefaces to their appropriate moulds as evidenced in the inventories of the Plantin-Moretus Museum.[2]

Through the centuries printers tried to resolve the problems of chaotic type sizes. Fournier and Didot in France introduced different point systems in the eighteenth century, based on point sizes measuring 0.349 and 0.376, but these systems were not adopted in the UK or the

---

[1] Carter, p. 5.
[2] Carter, p. 8, footnote 3. The detailed story and interpolation of the Plantin-Moretus Museum's archive of documents and artefacts is given in Leon Voet, *The Golden Compasses*, 2 vols. (Amsterdam: Van Gendt, 1969) which was not published at the time Carter was writing.

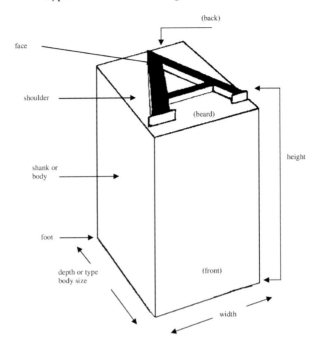

Figure 3.1. Diagram showing the different parts of a piece of fifteenth-century type.

USA. At the end of the nineteenth century the Anglo-American point system was adopted as standard in these countries. The type bodies were measured in points of *c*.72 points/6 picas to one inch.[3] This system remains in use to the present day, although when used to describe today's computer founts the points now relate to the typeface as seen on the page and not the body of the letter.

As discussed in the *Introduction*, there were no standard type sizes in the fifteenth century, but that is not to say that the printers were not working to a standard. As will be explored in this chapter, evidence has been found that shows that fifteenth-century printers were working to a basic measure when setting their type and imposing their formes. Unfortunately there is only a little surviving evidence from the fifteenth century as to what type physically looked like or how it was made.

Perhaps some of the earliest type survivals are 222 pieces of type, dating to late fifteenth or early sixteenth century, that were found in the river Saône in France in the mid-nineteenth century. They lay largely ignored

---

[3] Andrew Boag, 'Typographic measurement: a chronology', *Typography papers*, 1 (1996), pp. 105–121, provides a neat chronology of systems of typographic measurement. A further account of the history of standardisation of type sizes can be found in G. Willem Ovink, 'From Fournier to metric, and from lead to film' (parts 1 and 2) *Quaerendo*, 9 (1979), no. 2, pp. 95–127 and no. 4, pp. 283–327.

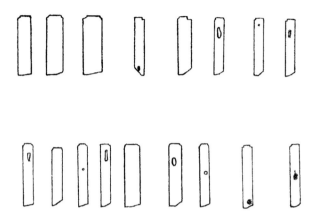

Figure 3.2. Outline of shapes of some of the type, dating from the fifteenth or sixteenth century, found in the river Saône. Redrawn from Maurice Audin, *Les types Lyonnais primitives*. None of the type pieces illustrated by Audin show a groove in the foot although most have a curiously angled foot.

until Maurice Audin made a detailed study of them in the 1950s.[4] The letters showed a variety of different faces, so had come from different founts. They also ranged in height from over 27 mm to just under 22 mm. Their body sizes ranged from 6.5 mm to 3.1 mm. Apart from variation in size they also varied in body shape. Some had sloping shoulders at the top, many had a sloping foot, one or two had a nick in the side and some had a hole pierced through (Figure 3.2). None had a groove in the foot as was usual in later centuries. The collection seems to raise more questions than it answers and Audin concluded that the first fifty years of type-founding and printing were experimental, no one method worked for every printer, and that the many different printers came up with different solutions of how to make type that would print onto paper.[5]

Other information about the shape and size of pieces of fifteenth-century type can also be gleaned in the very rare examples where a loose letter has fallen on top of the type set in the forme and has been printed along with it, making an impression into the paper. These pieces of 'fallen type', as they are called, show pieces of type of various heights and shapes. Perhaps the earliest example is one found in the Pelplin copy of the 42-line *Bible* and described by Paul Schwenke.[6] Here the piece of type lies at

[4] Maurice Audin, *Les types Lyonnais primitifs* (Paris: Bibliothèque Nationale, 1955).
[5] Audin, 'Types', p. 22.
[6] Paul Schwenke, *Untersuchungen zur Geschichte des ersten Buchdrucks* (Berlin, 1900), p. 25.

the foot of the left-hand column of page [e6r]. Adolf Schmidt was a
librarian in Darmstadt and wrote a series of three, wide-ranging, articles
in 1897, based on the observations he had made of the copies in the
Darmstadt library. He covered many aspects of printing practice, and
mentions some examples of fallen type.[7] Helmut Presser showed an
illustration of another example and Talbot Reed listed some further
examples discovered by other scholars.[8] Reed described and gave an
illustration of a piece of fallen type discovered in 1875 by Jean Madden;
this example also being later cited by Updike and Audin.[9] Reed also
mentioned another example of fallen type found by Henry Bradshaw in
CUL.[10] Scholderer brought in another example in 1927.[11] The height of
all these letters varies and again some of the letters have evidence of a hole
through the shank; the pieces of type found by Madden, Schmidt and
Scholderer all show a circular indentation in the shank and it is these
indentations that have been interpreted as evidence of holes.

These examples of fallen type are few and during this research others
have come to light. The first was found by on leaf [q4v] in a copy in the
BSB of Zainer's *Summa de eucharistiae sacramento,* 1474 (Figure 3.3).[12] The
mark lies across the centre of the page, three lines up from the foot of the
text. It has a heavy coat of ink at one end where the face of letter was,
indicating that it had been part of the forme of type, and having been
inked, had been pulled out by the action of the ink on the ink balls during
the inking process, and lay unnoticed on the type matter when the paper
was lowered for printing. The fallen type has left a beautiful crisp
impression of a piece of type lying on its side, and offers detail for the
printing historian. The total height of the piece of type was 21mm, with
the letter projecting only 1mm above the shoulder of the type body −
quite a shallow depth of drive. The foot of the letter is flat and there is no
evidence of a groove in the foot. There are no visible shoulders to the
letter, and no nicks in the side of the body. The depth of the impression
was slight, perhaps only a millimetre or less, implying a thin letter such as
'l' or 't' or 'i'. The ink on the letter only covers the top two-thirds of the
face, implying a letter with some ascender but no descender. Another

---

[7] Adolf Schmidt, 'Untersuchungen über die Buchdruckertechnik des 15. Jahrhunderts', *Central-blatt für Bibliothekswesen,* 14 (1897), pp. 14−27; 57−65; 153−175 (pp. 63−64).

[8] Helmut Presser, 'Abdruck einer Type von 1482', *Gutenberg-Jahrbuch,* 35 (1960), pp. 118−121 (p. 118) and Talbot Baines Reed, *A history of the old English letter foundries* (Oxford: Oxford University Press, 1887), p. 9.

[9] Reed, p. 24, Fig. 5. This illustration is repeated by Daniel Updike, *Printing Types,* 2nd edn (London: Oxford University Press, 1937) and also by Maurice Audin, 'Types du XVe siècle', *Gutenberg-Jahrbuch,* 29 (1954), pp. 84−100 (p. 87).

[10] Reed, p. 21.

[11] Victor Scholderer, 'Early Bolognese type-faces in Germany', *Gutenberg-Jahrbuch,* 2 (1927), pp. 127−133 (p. 130).

[12] *BSB-Ink* A-156, shelfmark 2° Inc.c.a.206a.

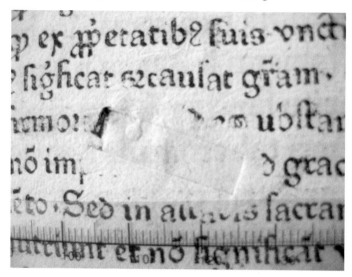

Figure 3.3. Imprint of a piece of 'fallen type', measuring 21mm high and 5.8mm wide. It shows a 2.5mm diameter raised round dome formed by an indentation or perforation through the shank, on leaf [q2v] of Zainer's edition of *Summa de eucharistiae*, 1474, shelfmark *BSB-Ink 2° Inc.c.a.260a*. (Bayerische Staatsbibliothek, Munich.)

aspect in this piece of fallen type is that on the shank of the letter there is a raised domed circle on the sheet, formed by an indentation or a perforation in the shank of the type when it was onto the paper. The circle measures 2.5mm diameter and is about 0.5mm from the edge of the type and 4mm from the top.

The second recently discovered also comes from another edition printed by Zainer. There are two pieces of fallen type on a single leaf [T7v] from his *Biblia Latina* printed in 1480.[13] The *Biblia Latina* was printed with Zainer's Type 96G for the text and Type 136G for the headings. Both pieces of fallen type on this leaf are of Type 96G (Figure 3.4). The first, in the foot of the left-hand column, shows a crisp impression of a piece of type, inked at the head, with no ascender or descender, with square shoulders, 21mm high and a hole through the shank. The second example, lying towards the top of the right-hand column, is not so clear, but still shows a hole in the shank. It is interesting to see that six years after printing *Summa* using Type 116G in 1474, Zainer was still working with a typeface (this time his Type 96G) that stands to the same height as his earlier type, and that his type still had holes in the

---

[13] The leaf is in ownership of Lenore Rouse, and currently on loan to the Rare Books and Manuscripts Department, The Catholic University of America, Washington D.C. I am very grateful to Mike Anderson for drawing my attention to this recent discovery.

Figure 3.4. Leaf [T7v] from Zainer's *Biblia Latina*, 1480 (ib00567000) with impressions from two pieces of fallen type, one in each column. The piece in the foot of left-hand column has square shoulders and shows a circle formed by an indentation or perforation. It has seriously interrupted the printing of the text around it. There may have been another letter lying partially beneath this one. The piece in the right-hand column is also perforated and seems to show some kind of twisting or damage, or marks caused by creases in the paper. (The Catholic University of America, Rare Books and Manuscripts Department, Washington D.C.)

shanks – this suggests that Zainer was perhaps working to his own standard type height through this period. It is also interesting to note that all three indentations are located to one side of the shank rather than centrally. The other examples of fallen type which have similar circular indentations are listed in Table 3.1.

Table 3.1. List of different pieces of 'fallen type', with perforations found in different editions.

Date	Title	ISTC	Shelfmark	Printer	Place	Library	Leaf	Height	Source
[before 1471]	*Sententiarum, vol.4*	il00479000	[not known]	Heinrich Eggestein	Strassburg	Darmstadt	[171v]	[not known]	Schmidt
1474	*Summa eucharistiae*	ia00335000	2° Inc.c.a.260a	Johann Zainer	Ulm	BSB	[q2v]	21mm	Bolton
[c.1475]	*Liber in laudem Mariae*	ip00468000	Inc. 3 A.4.9	Nicholas Goetz	Cologne	CUL	[b4v]	24mm	Bradshaw
[1478–79]	*Digestum novum*	ij00567000	[not known]	Berthold Ruppel	Basel	Darmstadt	[46r]	21mm	Schmidt
1479	*De morali lepra*	in00191000	[not known]	Konrad Winters	Cologne	BN Paris	[not known]	24mm	Madden
1480	[single leaf] *Biblia Latina*	ib00567000	[not known]	Johann Zainer	Ulm	Catholic University of America	[T7v]	21mm	
1481	*Rudimenta grammatices*	ip00318730	IA.1265	Johannes de Nördlingen	Strassburg	BL	[not known]	23mm	Scholderer
1482	*Reise in das gelobte Land*	it00491000	Ink. 230	Johann Schoensperger	Augsburg	Mainz StB	[not known]	22mm	Presser

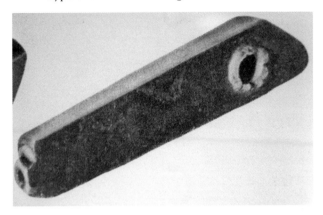

Figure 3.5. Illustration from Audin's article in *Gutenberg-Jahrbuch*, 1954, showing the rough metal edges around a hole bored through a piece of type (with an angled foot) found in the River Saône. (*Gutenberg-Jahrbuch*)

There has been discussion amongst scholars as to whether the type really was perforated. Scholderer suggested that the indented marks seen in the fallen type are not from holes and that they were similar to pin marks found in later machine-cast type.[14] However he also puts forward the argument that if the indentations were holes, and had been used for threading the type letters on to wires, why were there unthreaded letters, fallen on the type forme, causing the impressed marks. Despite this argument, and the daunting thought of drilling or piercing a hole accurately in the thousands of pieces of type in a fount, there also exists other evidence that suggests that some type, for at least a decade between 1471 and 1482, was produced with holes.

Firstly, some of the letters from the river Saône had round holes through them – type with holes does exist as a historic reality. In a separate article about the Lyon types Audin includes photographs of four of the pieces, one of which shows a letter with a round hole through it.[15] His 'Type 11' on this page clearly shows the metal fragments, protruding around the edge of the hole, left from where a drill or punch had exited the shank of the letter.[16] This surely is evidence of type having a hole

---

[14] Victor Scholderer, 'The shape of early type', *Gutenberg-Jahrbuch*, 2 (1927), pp. 24–25 (p. 25).

[15] Audin, 'Types' (p. 90).

[16] James Mosley 'The enigma of the early Lyonnaise printing types', *La Lumitype-Photon: René Higgonet, Louis Moyroud et l'invention de la composition moderne* (Lyon: Musée de l'imprimerie et de la Banque, 1995), pp. 13–28 (p. 23) states that these are the 'best illustrations of these types'. Mosley's article provides a useful recount of what we know today about historical typefounding. (This illustrated piece of type also has an angled foot, as do many of the Lyon type letters and some of the examples of fallen type. It is not proposed to address this question of type with angled feet here as the examples of Zainer's type have flat feet).

bored through (Figure 3.5). The rough edges of metal projecting around the hole would have had to been removed before the letter could have been set in a line of type.

Secondly, there are three pieces of documentary evidence, all coming from the same decade as the examples of fallen type with holes, that support the theory that type, did have holes drilled through the shanks. In the San Jacopo di Ripoli records in Italy the purchase of 'a drill to pierce the letters' in May 1477 is listed at a cost of 2s 4d.[17] We do not know if they did drill holes in their type letters but this is an indication that they might have done so. Another document, this time from Germany, from Augsburg in 1472, gives evidence of a little more than intention. Amongst the list of presses and equipment that Abbot Melchior von Stammheim purchased for the press he was setting up, at his Monastery of SS Ulrich and Afra, was one item for the preparation of 40,000 letters to be used with a Royal-size press, and to be cast, bored and planed, for the price of 60 guilders. He also paid 50 guilders for the casting, boring and planing of some other type letters (perhaps the 'German type for two presses' mentioned in the previous sentence).[18] This document has been drawn on before by scholars including Scholderer in 1951 and more recently by Rolf Schmidt in 1997 when they discussed the history of the SS Ulrich and Afra press in Augsburg.[19] However no one seems to have commented on this very definite statement that the type was being bored as part of its casting and preparation for use. Neil Harris cites another mention of perforated type in a document that also raised little comment when it first surfaced.[20] Harris draws attention to a document from Ferrara dated 12 April 1477 that includes information about printer Enrico selling some pierced letters (*littere bucade*) to printer Frederico who lived in Padua.[21]

Thirdly these indentations are not pin marks, as found in later machine-cast type. Type cast in a hand mould, as were all type letters until the early nineteenth century, would not have had a pin mark, as became common with machine-cast type. The circular indentation in the shank of machine-cast type was caused by a small pin that mechanically

[17] Conway, '*Diario*', p. 108. The entry states '*uno trapano per forar lettere*'.

[18] A facsimile of a 1557 copy of the original document can be seen in Georg W. Zapf, *Augsburg Buchdruckergeschichte*, vol. 1, table 4.

[19] Scholderer, 'Notes', pp. 5–6. Rolf Schmidt gives a full transcription of the text in 'Die Klosterdruckerei von St. Ulrich und Afra in Augsburg (1472 bis 1474)' in *Augsburger Buchdruck*, pp. 141–153 (p. 150). My thanks to Hans-Jörg Künast for confirming that the term '*borcznig und hobel*' in the old German of this document does mean 'boring and planing'.

[20] Neil Harris, 'A mysterious UFO in the Venetian "*Dama Rovenza*" [c.1482]', *Gutenberg-Jahrbuch*, 78 (2003), pp. 22–30 (p.27).

[21] Harris, 'UFO', p. 27, footnote 12, quotes from Angela Nuovo, 'Il commercio librario a Ferrara tra XV e XVI secolo. La bottega di Domenico Sivieri', *Storia della tipografia e del commercio librario*, 3 (1998), p. 27.

helped eject the type from the mould.[22] It could have the type size marked on its end and sometimes a founders' mark for identification. Scholderer was misleading to suggest that the marks found on these fifteenth-century fallen type letters might have been pin marks; perhaps he was confusing the technologies of hand- and machine-cast type.[23]

The existence of a piece of perforated fallen type in Zainer's *Summa* (and pieces in his *Bible* of 1480) indicates that he was using perforated type from at least 1474 until 1480. Unfortunately there is no evidence suggesting why the type was perforated. Holes are usually supplied in items so they can be threaded in some way, but what that way may have been for type letters can only be speculation. Mosley states 'Many early types irrefutably have holes in them, and we must presume that if these were deliberately made, they had a purpose'.[24] This purpose may have been to add stability by threading the letters onto 2.5mm diameter wires, for each line of text, but it seems a complicated procedure. Unless further evidence turns up there will probably be no answer to why type had holes.[25]

Apart from the marks made by pieces of type lying on the forme by mistake there are other marks that give evidence of the type body. The shoulders of the type letters, especially those on the foot of the bottom line were sometimes inked and pressed into the paper, leaving a printed line on the page. Sometimes this line is the full width of the body and sometimes only a partial imprint is made. An example of inked shoulders is shown in Figure 2.2.

---

[22] Updike (p. 13) states 'Nowadays all type is cast by machine'. He later adds (p. 16) 'The *pin-mark* is an indentation on the upper part of the body, made by the pin in casting.' Updike is clearly referring to the pin mark of machine-cast type. John Southward, in *Modern printing*, 2nd edn (London: Raithby Lawrence, 1904), p. 101 states that the pin-mark is only found in machine-made types.

[23] Technically it might be possible to insert something into a hand mould to make a pin mark indentation, but it is highly unlikely that this happened in the fifteenth century. The perfect round domed shape of the impressed mark that was found in the piece of fallen type in Zainer's *Summa* was not formed by anything like a flat pin-mark.

[24] Mosley, p. 28.

[25] There are one or two small pieces of evidence that suggest that something, wire or twine, might have been used to thread the letters together. A blind impressed mark is noted by Walter Partridge (p. 31, Figure 14) in the Gallizia paper copy of the *Catholicon* in the British Library. Partridge suggests the mark was made by twine. In 'Analytical bibliography' (p. 75) Lotte Hellinga recounts James Mosley's thoughts on this mark in the *Catholicon* and other similar marks found in both copies of the British Library' s 34-line Aquinas, *Summa de articulis* (it00273000). Mosley suggests that wire might have been used to bind two lines of type together (in Hellinga 'Analytical bibliography', p. 76). This impressed mark was also noted on page [b6r] in the Bodleian Library's copy of the *Summa de articulis* (shelfmark Auct. 1 Q 5.40) which looked to me as if it had been made by wire rather than twine. However I have not noted any impressed wire marks in any of Zainer's editions, merely marks from perforated 'fallen' type, and, although the evidence is accumulating, I do not feel there is enough to go beyond speculation at the present time.

And spacing

There is also evidence of Zainer's spacing making marks. As with the type letters, in letterpress technology, spacing material is also three-dimensional and has a physical entity; the compositor has to pick up and place pieces of spacing of various widths, between words or to fill out the end of a line. Pieces of spacing are cast in the same mould as the type face, therefore having the same body as the type. They are shorter in height than the type letters so they do not make contact either with the ink or the paper. They are usually cast in a variety of widths and are used to separate the words, or at the end of the line or paragraph to fill out the line, or to fill out a space being left for a later initial to be added by hand. For a printer the spacing material is almost as important as the type; space is essential to support the type letters and to separate the words. It is the careful adjustment of the spacing between words that makes the text more legible, and the lines of even tightness. Sometimes, owing to loose lock up, these spaces rise up during the print run, receive ink and print onto the paper. Their imprints, something that was never meant to be seen on the page, brings further clues about the dimensions of the spacing being cast and used.

Zainer seems to have locked his type up into the forme fairly loosely as many examples of inked spacing, spaces that have worked up during the print run, have been found in the pages of his editions.[26] Examples of em quads, one-eighth em, one-sixth em, and one-quarter em have been found.[27] There is also a curious not quite 2-em space, lying on its side with a v-shaped nick in its side. As it measures 10mm long it is too short to be a full 2-em of Type 116G, which would measure 11.6mm. Examples of some of Zainer's inked spacing material are shown in Figure 3.6. From measuring the spaces found in Aldus' editions Peter Burnhill found evidence of his spacing in varying widths of a half, third, quarter, fifth, sixth, eighth and twelfth of an em.[28] Zainer may have had spacing thinner than the eighth of an em noted but I have not found evidence from inked marks to substantiate this.

---

[26] The examples of Zainer's fallen type also point to loose lock up. The forme must have been locked up loosely enough for the letters to have been pulled from the forme.

[27] Since the standardisation of the point system at the end of the nineteenth century, printers worked and measured in the pica em – equivalent to a 12 point quad, a square of metal with a 12 point body. There was no standard type measure in Zainer's time but he had his typefaces with its associated spacing material and he had quads of the same body sizes as his type. Moxon (p. 170) describes the quadrat as being cast to thicknesses of an n, m, and other larger pieces. On p. 171 he adds that quadrats were cast 'exactly to the Thickness of a set Number of m's or *Body, viz.* two m's thick, three m's thick four m's thick, *&c.*'.

[28] Peter Burnhill, *Type spaces* (London: Hyphen Press, 2003), p. 35.

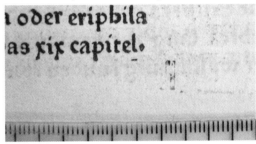

(a) A thin space in the final line, about the one eighth of an em wide.

(b) Two thin spaces, each slightly under 1mm − probably one sixth of an em − wide.

(c) The bottom right hand corners of two ems.

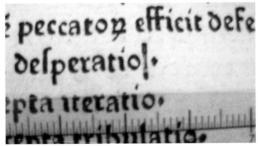

(d) Another thin space, about one eighth of an em.

Figure 3.6. Some examples of inked raised spaces found in Zainer's editions.

WORKING TO FIXED MEASURES – ZAINER

As discussed in Chapter 2 it seems certain that Zainer was working to fixed measurements for setting his type. However, although Zainer had fixed measurements for his text areas, it was not originally clear on what standard unit, if any, these measurements were based. He may have been working to some unit of linear measurement in use in Germany at the time, but he would not have been using millimetres when he decided on his text widths.[29] As a printer it seems likely that he might have been working in the standard measure he had to hand – the square of the body size of his typeface, his printers' em. This might seem obvious to a letterpress printer today, who has been brought up working to measurements based on the pica em, but this has not previously been considered for early fifteenth-century printers.

Zainer definitely had em quads; partially inked and impressed traces of them are visible in a number of his books, as are double-em quads, one-and-a-half em quads and other smaller spacing. As discussed in Chapter 2 it is not known what he was using to set his lines of type. Whatever he used, my measurements of his text areas show clearly that it was of a fixed measure. Later composing sticks, by at least Moxon's time, were adjustable and had to be set to the correct measure for each job. From at least as early as the eighteenth century the method of setting the composing stick to a measure was based on filling it with pica em quads or 'm's lying on their sides.[30] This method of setting the stick, for any job and in whatever size of type, to a measure based on pica ems was continued well into the twentieth century – *Practical printing and binding*, published in conjunction with the London College of Printing in 1965, states:

In normal composition the measure is a specific number of ems of 12 point (or pica).[31]

The measurements of Zainer's text widths were looked at again, and this time measured in ems of his typefaces. To do this em rules were made for each of his typefaces, rulers marked up in ems of each type size.[32] In every

---

[29] Norman Feather, *Mass, length and time* (London: Penguin, 1959), p. 18 states that the metric standard of length was introduced in 1801 by the French National Assembly.

[30] John Smith, *The printer's grammar* (London, 1755, repr. Thoemmes Press: Bristol, 1998), pp. 196–197. Moxon, pp. 40–42, gives a rather vague description of the use of a composing stick that could be adjusted to different measures for whatever width of text matter desired. He also describes (p. 203) how the seventeenth-century compositor sets the stick to the measure given, either by measuring against the copy, or by setting the first line to agree with the copy and tightening the stick to that measure. Unlike Smith in 1755, he does not mention ems.

[31] *Practical printing and binding*, 3rd edn (Watford: Odhams, 1965), pp. 21–22.

[32] The em rule is a standard printer's tool. It is a ruler, which (together with inches and millimetres) can have 8-point, 9-point, 10-point, 11-point and 12-point ems marked up on it. This splendid tool makes counting the number of lines of type in any size a simple job. It can also be used to measure width of type area, spaces for images, etc.

Table 3.2. Zainer's different type sizes and the number of ems in each size of type for the text widths he used.

Type size	Dimension of em	Number of ems in 110mm line	Number of ems in 117mm line	Number of ems in 82mm line	Number of ems in 87mm line	Number of ems in 128mm line
116	5.8mm	19		14	15	
110	5.5mm	20				
117	5.85mm		20			
96	4.8mm	23				27
136	6.8mm					19

edition examined the text width to which Zainer was working was in a full number of ems of the typeface being used. It seems that Zainer was using multiples of the em of his typefaces as the basis for all his text widths. His text width of 110mm equated to 20 ems of Type 110R but also equals 19 ems of Type 116G. The widths of his columns in his royal and imperial folios, c.83mm and 87mm equate to 14 and 15 ems of Type 116G. 23 ems of his later text face, Type 96G, also fit into a 110mm line. All his typefaces fitted to the same fixed measures, each in a multiple of the em quad of its type body, without a problem. These figures are summarised in Table 3.2.

To check the theory further other aspects of Zainer's pages were measured to see if they also were in whole ems. His wood cut initials that were 3-lines of text deep also measured 3 or 4-ems wide; they had been deliberately cut on a 3 × 3- or 3 × 4-em block to use with Type 116G. Similarly with his 4-line, 5-line and 10-line initials; they were all based on multiples of the body of Type 116G. His woodcut illustrations are on blocks that measure 14 lines deep and 19 ems wide, having been made to fit across the 110mm wide text area. Zainer's borders are also cut to a measurement based on the em of Type 116G. The smaller borders in the chancery folios are 4 ems of Type 116G wide, with the section running along the top measuring 27 ems and the section running down the left-hand side measuring 36 ems (Figure 3.7). The larger borders used in the royal folios are 6 ems of Type 116G wide, with 37 ems along the top and 54 ems down the side.

Zainer uses his Type 116G em even further. In two editions he has hanging indents at the start of his paragraphs which project by one em. Margaret Smith states that 'Hanging indents are rarely encountered in incunables, possibly because they required considerable labour to achieve in type.'[33] However Zainer did use them, and it was made

---

[33] Margaret M. Smith, 'The typography of complex texts', *Typography papers*, 1 (1996), pp. 75–92 (p. 84).

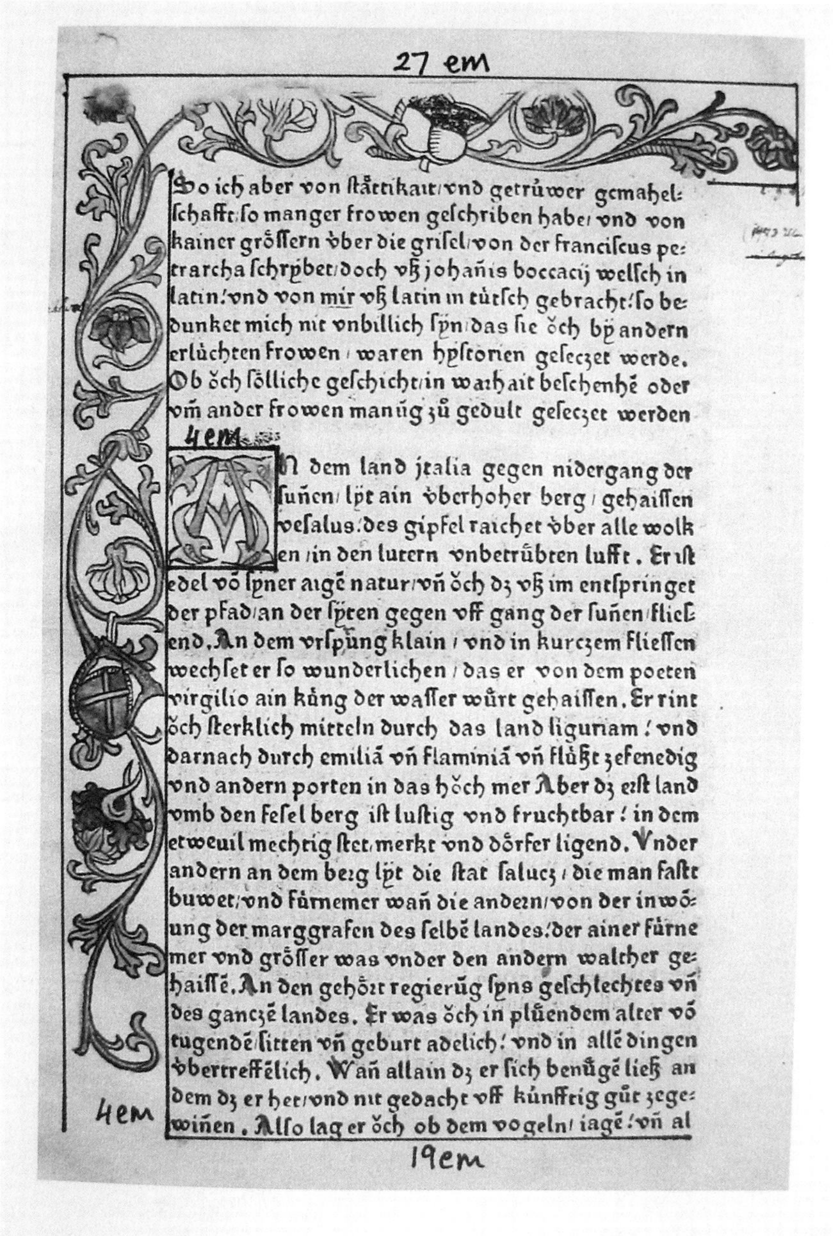

Ðo ich aber von ſtättikait/vnd getrůwer gemahel:
ſchafft.ſo manger frowen geſchriben habe/vnd von
kainer gröſſern vber die griſel/von der franciſcus pe:
trarcha ſchrÿbet/doch vß johañis boccacÿ welſch in
latin.vnd von mir vß latin in tütſch gebracht.ſo be:
dunket mich nit vnbillich ſÿn/das ſie öch bÿ andern
erlüchten frowen / waren hÿſtorien geſeczet werde.
Ob öch ſölliche geſchicht/in warhait beſchenhé oder
vm̃ ander frowen manũg zů gedult geſeczet werden

Iñ dem land italia gegen nidergang der
ſuñen/lÿt ain vberhoher berg / gehaiſſen
veſalus.des gipfel raichet vber alle wolk
en /in den lutern vnbetrübten lufft . Er iſt
edel vö ſpner aigē natur/vñ öch dz vß im entſpringet
der pfad/an der ſpten gegen vff gang der ſuñen/flieſ
end.An dem vrſpũng klain / vnd in kurczem flieſſen
wechſet er ſo wunderlichen / das er von dem poeten
virgilio ain kũng der waſſer wůrt gehaiſſen.Er rint
öch ſterklich mitteln durch das land liguriam / vnd
darnach durch emiliã vñ flaminiã vñ flũßt zefenedig
vnd andern porten in das höch mer Aber dz erſt land
omb den feſel berg iſt luſtig vnd fruchtbar / in dem
etweuil mechtrig ſtet.merkt vnd dörfer ligend. Vnder
andern an dem berg lÿt die ſtat ſaluc; / die man faſt
buwet/vnd fürnemer wañ die andern/von der inwö:
ung der marggrafen des ſelbē landes.der ainer fürne
mer vnd gröſſer was vnder den andern walther ge:
haiſſé.An den gehört regierũg ſpns geſchlechtes vñ
des ganczē landes. Er was öch in plũendem alter vö
tugendē/ſitten vñ geburt adelich/ vnd in allē dingen
vbertreffélich. Wañ allain dz er ſich benůgē ließ an
dem dz er het/vnd nit gedacht vff kũnffig gůt zege:
wiñen . Alſo lag er öch ob dem vogeln/ iagé/vñ al

Figure 3.7. First page from German edition of *Historia Griseldis* showing text, initial and border measured in ems of Type 116G. (Ulm Stadtbibliothek.)

easier because he was working with em quads, and he only had to insert an em quad at the beginning of each line when setting his text. Smith may be wrong in suggesting that hanging indents were difficult – they are slightly tedious to achieve as the compositor has to insert an em at the beginning of every line, they use extra spacing material, and also take up space on the page that might otherwise have held text, but they do not really involve extra labour to achieve.[34] Later on Zainer indents, rather than having hanging indents, and these are by one em quad. An em quad is often inserted as a paragraph break in the text. The central gutters discussed in Chapter 2 of c.70mm and c.90mm work out as 12 ems and 16 ems of Type 116G – it seems likely that Zainer had furniture cut to standard lengths and widths for his skeleton forme, and all based on the em of Type 116G. The inter-columnar margin of the royal folios measures 23mm, 4 ems. His entire method of working, and the design and layout of his page, is in units based on the em of his Type 116G as can be seen in Figure 3.7.

This is a sound logical way of printing, working with every element being based on the same standard unit of measurement, in Zainer's case the em of his Type 116G. Without working in this manner he would not have been able to lock up the various elements, the type, initials and woodblocks, together to print them all at the same time. In an article describing how many of the early woodcut illustrations were square shaped with four square corners, while commenting on the artistic merit of the designs, and that woodcut initial 'I' was the same width as an initial 'M', Helmut Presser did not seem to realise the technical advantage, indeed the necessity, for their being so.[35] The letters and blocks had to be square, or at least be cut to fit to the same measure as the text face so they could be locked up in the forme.

Although writing primarily about Aldus Manutius' Greek types, Nicolas Barker commented on the method of work of early printers and stressed that they had to adopt some standard of measurement, even if it were just within one printing house, so that the forme could be locked up accurately.[36] He had noticed that many of the fifteenth-century printers worked with type sizes that were very similar to each other and lists the most popular sizes in his Table 1.[37] He discusses what the basis for measurement, used by the first printers might have been, and suggests that it could have been the *picco*, a standard measure, and the metal

[34] Another example of hanging indents of one em were noted in Günther Zainer's printing of the *Catholicon* in 1469 (ib00021000).

[35] Helmut Presser, 'Formgesetze im illustrierten Buch des 15. Jahrhunderts', *Gutenberg-Jahrbuch*, 26 (1951), pp. 75–80.

[36] Nicolas Barker, *Aldus Manutius and the development of Greek script and type in the fifteenth century* (Sandy Hook: Chiswick Book Shop, 1985), p. 78.

[37] Barker, p. 80.

Table 3.3. Figures taken from p. 80 of Nicolas Barker's *Aldus Manutius and the development of Greek type*, showing the dimensions of some fifteenth-century type bodies.

Common Fifteenth-Century Type Bodies as fractions of the 6.3mm scale

Fractions	Body	20-line measurement
$1\frac{1}{3}$	8.4mm	168mm
$1\frac{1}{4}$	7.785	157.5
$1\frac{1}{6}$	7.35	147
$1\frac{1}{12}$	6.825	136.5
1	6.3	126
$\frac{11}{12}$	5.775	115.5
$\frac{7}{8}$	5.5125	110
$\frac{5}{6}$	5.25	105
$\frac{3}{4}$	4.725	94.5
$\frac{2}{3}$	4.2	84
$\frac{5}{8}$	3.9375	79
$\frac{7}{12}$	3.675	73.5
$\frac{1}{2}$	3.15	63
$\frac{5}{12}$	2.625	52
$\frac{3}{8}$	2.3625	47

workers' cubit, of Venice and the Levant in the fifteenth and sixteenth century.[38] The *picco* measured 60.3 or 60.4 centimetres, which Barker divides on the basis of the old Roman (duodecimal) scale of 24 to give a digit of 25.2mm. This digit he again divides, this time by 4, to give a basic unit, measuring 6.3mm. When this 6.3mm is split down into fractions of 12 the figures agree remarkably with the various type sizes. Barker's table of common fifteenth-century type bodies is reproduced at Table 3.3. Whether one agrees with Barker's mathematics or not, what is of interest is the suggestion that the early printers were working within some standard. Interestingly Zainer's Type 110R, 116G, 96G, and 136G are all on, or very close to, the figures given in Barker's table, with a proportional link to each other on his scale, which might explain why Zainer was able to interchange his various typefaces to his fixed text widths.

Burnhill also considered how Aldus Manutius was working when he examined four Aldine editions printed between 1495 and 1522. He

[38] Barker, p. 79.

suggests that 'in-house typographic norms had been around since Gutenberg'.[39] As a typographer Burnhill was chiefly examining how Aldus's letters fitted together along with the spacing, but he showed that Aldus was working in ems of his typefaces with the pieces of spacing being proportional parts of the em.[40]

OTHER PRINTERS WORKING IN EMS OF THEIR TYPEFACES

Justified setting

Burnhill shows very clearly that by the end of the fifteenth century Aldus was working in ems of his type for printing his editions but it was not known if other early printers were also working to a standard based on their own em measure. Along with the measuring and recording of editions by printed by Zainer, editions by other printers were also looked at. 246 copies of 213 editions by 46 other printers, dating from 1454 to 1490, have been examined for this research.[41] As can be seen from these totals only a very few of the editions were looked at in more than one copy – none were examined in the same depth as with Zainer's editions, but the aim was to try to establish an overall view of the printing practices of Zainer's contemporaries. Although this is only a small selection from the work of other printers working in the fifteenth century, it is useful for comparison with Zainer.

Amongst the measurements taken were the text widths of all editions looked at, and this was measured in both millimetres and ems. Measuring in ems is not as precise as measuring in millimetres but due care still has to be taken. One can only measure the visible text and often has no idea how much type metal (unseen and unprinted) there might be beyond the printed letter shapes. Zainer, and other printers in the 1470s, were setting justified lines, and therefore only a very slight allowance needs to be made for the type body at either end of a line. It is still safer to measure a line with the letter l, or an ascender or descender at the ends of the lines, to obtain the most accurate reading. With earlier printers, in the 1450s and early 1460s, who were not setting to a justified right hand margin, it is more difficult to know where the end of the line might be. Sometimes the line might be set to the full length of the measure but, more likely than not, spacing is added at the end of the line beyond the visible text. An indication of how much spacing has been added, and what the full line length could be, might be found if there are any inked rising spaces at the end of the line to give a clue.

---

[39] Burnhill, p. 10.

[40] Burnhill, p. 70, gives a table showing the different thicknesses of spacing found in the four different type sizes used to print the four editions.

[41] See *Bibliography – Primary Sources, section 3* for full details.

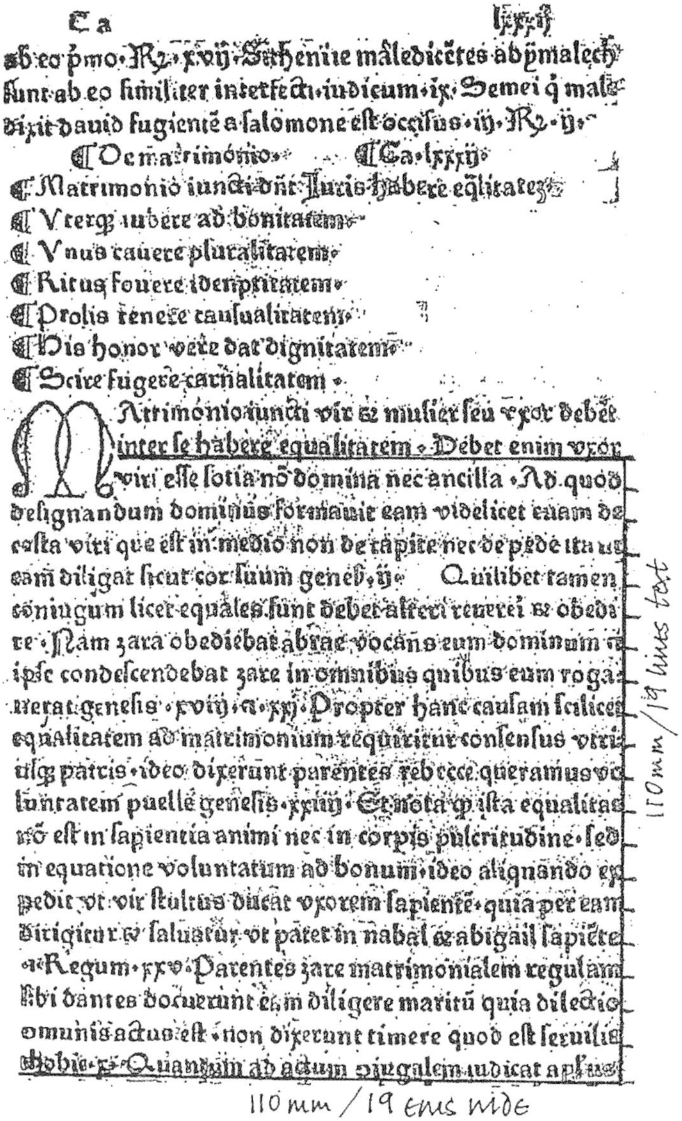

ab eo p̃mo· Rz· xvij·Sicheñie mãledicẽtes ab p̃malech
ſunt ab eo ſimiliter interfecti·iudicum·ix· Semei q̃ male
dixit dauid fugientẽ a ſalomone eſt occiſus·iij· Rz· ij·
    ⁊ De matrimonio·   ⁊ Ca· lxxxij·
⁊ Matrimonio iuncti dñt Iuris habere eq̃litatez·
⁊ Vterg̃ iubere ad bonitatem·
⁊ Vnus cauere pluralitatem·
⁊ Ritus fouere idenptitatem·
⁊ Prolis tenere cauſualitatem·
⁊ Dis honor vere dat dignitatem·
⁊ Scire fugere carñalitatem ·

Matrimonio iuncti vir ⁊ mulier ſeu vxor debẽt
inter ſe habere equalitatem · Debet enim vxor
viri eſſe ſocia nõ domina nec ancilla · Ad quod
deſignandum dominus formauit eam videlicet euam de
coſta viri que eſt in medio non de capite nec de pede ita ut
eam diligat ſicut cor ſuum geñ·ij· Quilibet tamen
coniugum licet equales ſunt debet alteri reuerei ⁊ obedi
re · Nam zara obediebat abrae vocans eum dominum ⁊
ipſe condeſcendebat zare in omnibus quibus eum roga
uerat geneſis · xviij·⁊ xxj· Propter hanc cauſam ſcilice
equalitatem ad matrimonium requiritur conſenſus viri
uſq̃ patris · ideo dixerunt parentes rebecce queramus vo
luntatem puelle geneſis· xxiiij· Et nota q̃ iſta equalitas
nõ eſt in ſapientia animi nec in corpis pulcritudine· ſed
in equatione voluntatum ad bonum· ideo aliquando ex
pedit vt vir ſtultus ducat vxorem ſapientẽ· quia per eam
dirigitur ⁊ ſaluatur vt patet in nabal ⁊ abigail ſapiẽte
·⁊ Regum· xxv·Parentes zare matrimonialem regulam
ſibi dantes docuerunt eã in diligere maritũ quia dilectio
omnis actus eſt ·non dixerunt timere quod eſt ſeruilis
Dobie· z· Quanquam ad actum ciugalem iudicat apl̃us

110 mm / 19 lines text

110 mm / 19 ems wide

Figure 3.8. Page of text from *Aurea Biblia*, 1476, marked up to make an em rule for Type 116G. (University of Reading Library.)

When working with Zainer's editions his type sizes were known and an em rule had been prepared for each of them. With care this can also be done for other printers, and having an em rule for each edition being studied, or each typeface being used, makes the measuring process of various aspects, such as spacing for initials or as paragraph breaks, much easier. If one knows the type size being used it is possible to mark up a strip of paper with a 20-line measure in steps of one-twentieths. A slight allowance might have to be made for paper stretch when comparing an empirically based em rule against the original edition, but the differences will be slight. Another method was also developed to enable the making of a quick check to see if a printer was setting his text to a measure based on his ems. This is also useful but will only work if the printer is doing justified setting with a straight right-hand margin, and is not leading his lines of type. As the em is a proportional measure one can also measure in ems from a photograph of a printed page, if the original is not to hand.

(1) Measure width of text, ideally from a line with an upright stroke at either end, and note the measurement in millimetres.
(2) Run this measurement from the baseline of the bottom line of text up the text – the measured distance should coincide with the baseline of another line of text. Usually this is exact, but occasionally may be 0.5mm out (see Figure 3.8).
(3) Count the number of lines – this is the number of ems to which the printer was working.

Figure 3.8 shows a page of text from Zainer's *Aurea Biblia*, 1476. The length of the baseline of the line at the foot has been measured (1). This measurement is run up the side of the text and comes to the baseline of line 20 when counted from the foot of the text (2). This is 19 lines of type, which means that Zainer's text width measures 19 ems.

For all the printers whose editions were examined, from the *c.*1463 onwards, and who were working with justified setting, the measurements showed clearly that they were working to a measure that was based on the em of their typeface being used. Some of the findings of some of the printers are listed in Table 3.4. This is only a selection but includes printers in various countries, and editions printed in 1460s and 1470s. As well as each having text widths set to multiples of their ems, other factors, as noted with Zainer, were also in ems. All the spaces for decorative initials noted were in ems, from 2×2-em to 13×13-em. If there was a space at the beginning of a new paragraph it would be a 1-em or a 2-em space. I have not included in this list editions printed before 1463, or those with unjustified text, as they need to be considered separately.

Table 3.4. A selection of editions from different printers, from 1463 onwards, in different countries, all working, with justified setting, to a text width based on the em quad of their particular typeface.

Printer	Date	Title	ISTC number	Type size	Text width in mm	Text width in ems
Mentelin	[not after 1463]	*Summa theologica*	it00182000	92	84	18
(Strassburg)	[before Jun 1466]	*Biblia Germanica*	ib00624000	92	88	19
	[not after 1466]	*De arte praedicandi*	ia01226000	92	112	24
	[not after 1466]	*Homiliae super Matt..*	ij00288000	92	112	24
Eggestein	[before May 1466]	*Biblia Latina*	ib00530000	126	89	14
(Strassburg)	[not after 1468]	*Biblia Latina*	ib00531000	126	89	14
		Petrus Lombardus	il00479000	129	77	12
Sweyn. & Pann.	29 Oct 1465	*Opera* [Lactantius]	il00001000	120	133	22
(Subiaco)	12 Jun 1467	*De civitate Dei*	ia01230000	120	71	12
Adolf Rusch	[before Jun 1467]	*De sermonum proprietate*	ir00001000	103	88	17
(Strassburg)	[not after 1473]	*Secretum de contemptu mundi*	ip00412000	103	100	19
Ulrich Han	1468	*De Oratore*	ic00655000	86	105	24
(Rome)	1 Apr 1469	*Tusculanae disputat.*	ic00630000	86	108	25
Gunther Zainer	12 Mar [14]68	*Meditationes vitae*	ib00893000	117	123	21
(Augsburg)	30 Apr 1469	*Catholicon*	ib00021000	117	86	15
	1472	*Etymologiae*	ii00181000	107	123	23
Vindelinus de Spira (Venice)	1469	*Historia naturalis*	ip00786000	110	165	30
Lauer (Rome)	1470	*Quaestiones*	it00182000	128	128	20
Georg Reyser	[c.1470]	*Manuale*	ia01282250	120	126	21
(Würzburg)	[not after 1474]	*Quadragesimale*	ig00493000	93	82	17
Sensenschmidt	[not after 1470]	*Flores*	ib00388000	114	68	12
(Nürnberg)	[c.1470]	*De regulis mandatorum*	ig00204000	114	131	23
	[not after 1474]	*De examinatione doctrinarum*	ig00229000	110	123	22
Sorg	[not after 1473]	*De oculo morali*	ij00390000	103	122	24
(Augsburg)	1475–78	*De consideratione*	ib00368000	103	123	24
Wenssler	[not after 1472]	*Epistolare ad exercitationem*	ib00261000	121	115	19
(Basel)	[not after 1473]	*De consolatione philosophiae*	ib00221800	121	115	19
	[not after 1474]	*Expositio super orationem*	ih00029000	122	115	19
Caxton (Bruges)	1473	*Le receuil*	il00117000	120	126	21
Fyner (Esslingen)	1474	*Expositio in Job*	it00236000	96	130	27
Mansion (Bruges)	1477	*Dits Moraux*	id00274500	162	130	16
Fratrae (Brussels)	1478	*Casus breves*	it00505800	100	110	18

Unjustified setting

It is fairly simple to establish whether editions with justified setting were printed to a fixed em measure. However for the earlier editions, with unjustified setting and where it is impossible to tell how far beyond the visible text the line extends, things are not so simple. Having established fairly certainly that printers by the mid-1460s were working in ems it was decided to discover from how early this method might have been used.

When doing unjustified setting, the printer needs to allow enough space at the end of the line to avoid ending the line with thin spaces, which are liable to slip into the next line. Ideally he will allow at least one em beyond the end of the longest line of text so he can work with thicker pieces of spacing. It is these pieces of spacing at the end of the line that, if they work up during the print run and print, can be clues that give an indication as to what might be in the forme beyond the extent of the text. Some findings about some of these very early editions with unjustified line lengths are brought together here, although more work needs to be done to come to more definite conclusions.

Some editions with unjustified setting did have marks from raised inked spacing at the ends of some of the text lines. The Bodleian copy of Fust and Schöffer's 1459 *Psalterium Benedictinum* has some marks from inked spacing at the ends of lines 1–7 on folio [154v].[42] The lengths of the lines of visible text are between 206 and 211mm, with the inked marks on the printed page extending the line length to *c.*230mm. This line measurement of *c.*230mm equates to 16 ems of Type 286G, the measure it seems to which the printers were working (Figure 3.9) . This 16 em measure is kept to throughout the edition, both on the leaves with the ornamental initials and without. The initials themselves can also be measured in ems of Type 286G; the large 6-line initials indent 6-ems into the body of the text and extend 1 em into the margin, although this 'margin' on the left-hand side is included in the total 16-em measure of the text area. On folio [135r] there is an impressed mark of the left-hand edge of the ornamental initial O. The distance from this mark to the right-hand end of the line is again the measure of 16ems.

Similar evidence of the end of the line was also found in the Windsor copy of the 1457 *Psalter*.[43] The visible text measures about 1 em narrower than the 1459 *Psalter* and a number of possible end-of-line, inked marks were found at *c.*215mm on folios [32v], [33r], [38r], [38v] and [41r] which would suggest a 15-em of Type 286G measure.

The copy of Fust and Schöffer's *Canon Missae*, 1458, using the same type and same initials as the two *Psalters,* has a visible text width of

[42] *Psalterium Benedictinum*, 1459 (ip00106200) *Bod-inc.* P-519, shelfmark Arch. B.a.1.
[43] *Psalterium Romanum*, 1457 (ip00103600), Royal Library Windsor.

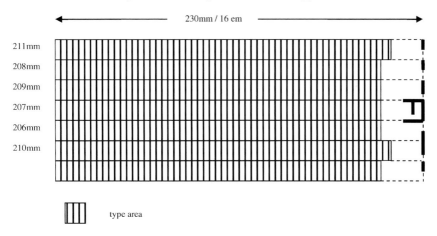

| type area

Figure 3.9. Diagram showing the top 7 lines of text in Bodleian Library copy of *Psalterium Benedictinum*, 1459, leaf [154v]. Line lengths of text vary but evidence from inked rising spaces at the ends of lines show that full line measure was from 19mm to 24mm longer than visible text, giving a set width of 230mm, or 16 ems of Type 286G.

*c.*189–94mm, which is similar to the 1457 *Psalter.*[44] There is no evidence in the Bodleian copy of spacing beyond the end of the text lines but Irvine Masson states that the Vienna copy has raised spacing on some leaves. His description sounds very similar to the marks from the spacing found in the two *Psalters*.

. . . right hand marginal furniture, about a centimetre or more away from the line-ends, there were packed rows of ordinary space-pieces which are occasionally seen printed in the text. They show as narrow rectangles, of type-body height and about as thick as a minim of a letter. As furniture these are tightly stacked end-to-end up the margin, in several courses in contact, whose joints alternate like brickwork. . . .[45]

This evidence in these editions, of spacing material being added to the end of the text line, helps to provide a measurable line length. The line length often extended beyond the visible text by more than one em (14.3mm) and on one occasion spacing of 23mm had been added at the end of the visible text line. With the full line lengths established, it can be seen that Fust and Schöffer were working to a measure based on the em of their Type 286G, from as early as 1457.

Another edition examined showed evidence from the inked spacing in the margin that it was printed to a measure based on its em quad. It is the

[44] *Canon Missae* [*c.*1458] (im00736000) *Bod-inc.* M-284, shelfmark Arch. G.b.4.
[45] Irvine Masson, *The Mainz Psalters and the Canon Missae 1457–1459* (London: Bibliographical Society, 1954), p. 7.

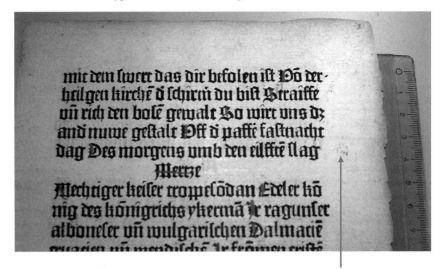

Figure 3.10. Photograph of leaf [2v] of *Türkenkalender* (*BSB-Ink* M-149, shelfmark Rar.1) showing inked mark from raised space in right-hand margin. (Bayerische Staatsbibliothek, Munich.

earliest dated edition printed in German in December 1454, the *Türkenkalender* (it00503500) set in Type 164G, the same as the 36-line Bible type. It comprises six leaves of unjustified setting, with visible lines of text of varying lengths, which makes it difficult to establish if the printer was working to a measure based on an em of Type 164G. On leaf [2v] the lines vary between 109 and 117mm in length. However also on this leaf is a printed mark from a raised em quad, beyond the right hand end of line 5 (Figure 3.10). Measuring the length of this line on the original to include this mark gives a line length of 123mm, the same as 15ems of Type 164G. If this inked piece of spacing is exactly at the right-hand end of the line then this is a very early example of the printer working to a measure based on his em, from at least December 1454.

Figure 3.11 shows the same leaf, photocopied from a facsimile published in 1975 to which its em scale has been added.[46] Although not the exact size of the original, as ems are a proportional measurement, it is still make an em rule from the printed lines of text, and then use it as a measure. Other evidence that the printer was working in ems can be seen on leaf [1r] where there is a 2-line space for an initial that is also 2 ems wide.

Fust & Schöffer's *Constitutiones* of 1460 also shows clear command of the

---

[46] Ferdinand Geldner, *Der Türkenkalender 1454: Faksimile mit Kommentar* (Wiesbaden: Reichert, 1975).

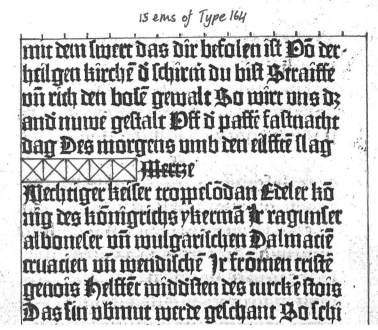

Figure 3.11. Photocopy of leaf [2v] from a facsimile of the *Türkenkalender* with lines added to show how the text might have been set to a 15 em measure of Type 164G, the 36-line *Bible* type. Note 5-em indent for *Mertze* on line 6. (Ferdinand Geldner, *Der Türkenkalender 1454: Faksimile mit Kommentar*, Wiesbaden: Reichert Verlag, 1975.)

use of ems as the basis of their typesetting.[47] Two different typefaces used are Type 91G and Type 118G, the larger for the text and the smaller for the commentary. The basic column width measures *c*.123mm, 27ems of Type 91G. There is a space of 4 lines of Type 91G inserted before the smaller area of text set in Type 118G to a width of *c*.62/3mm, 11 ems of Type 118G. Because of some inked spacing in the middle margins at the head, side and foot of the blocks of Type 118G it was possible to determine that the top margin comprised 4 lines of spacing from Type 91G and the side and foot margins were based on ems of Type 118G. Setting two different sizes of type at the same time and arranging them, as text and commentary, so the correct section of text is beside the correct section of commentary requires considerable control of printing technology. This is sophisticated typesetting, and would not have been possible without the printers having established a sound mathematical foundation to which they could work, and one based on their ems. This is

---

[47] Clement V, *Constitutiones*, 25 June 1460 (ic00710000) *Bod-inc.* C-359, shelfmark Auct. 4 Q 1.4.

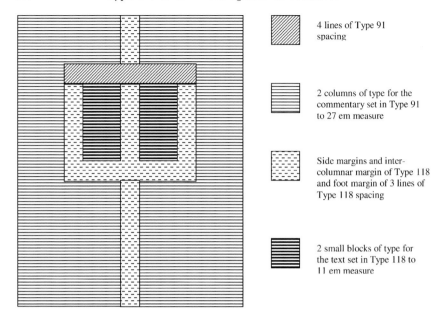

4 lines of Type 91 spacing

2 columns of type for the commentary set in Type 91 to 27 em measure

Side margins and inter-columnar margin of Type 118 and foot margin of 3 lines of Type 118 spacing

2 small blocks of type for the text set in Type 118 to 11 em measure

Figure 3.12. Diagram showing how two different sizes of type and spacing are used to set the pages of text and commentary in Fust and Schöffer's *Constitutiones*, 1460.

illustrated in a diagram at Figure 3.12. With this edition the two typefaces used, Type 91G and Type 118G, have body sizes that are proportional – three lines of Type 118G are almost exactly four lines of Type 91G, so they can be used alongside each other. Smith also found a mathematical link between the typefaces found in Vindelinus de Spira's 1471 edition of *Decretalium* where Type 200G is used for the lead-ins and Type 99G for the text.[48]

Fust and Schöffer's *De vita christiana* also seem to be set to a measure based in ems of Type 91G.[49] Slight marks from inked spaces were noted beyond the end of the line of visible text, at 87mm, giving a text width of 19 ems. However other editions printed by them do not seem to be in ems.

[48] Margaret M. Smith, 'Space-saving practices in early printed books', *Journal of the Printing Historical Society*, 6 (2003), pp. 19–39 (p. 35). Nicolas Panormitanus, *Secunda pars, pars secunda libri Decretalium* (ip00058000).

[49] Augustinus, *De vita christiana* [*c*.1461] (ia01354000). *Bod-inc.* A-606, shelfmark Douce 122(1).

OTHER PRINTERS PERHAPS NOT WORKING IN EMS OF
THEIR TYPEFACES

The Bodleian copy of Fust and Schöffer's *Rationale divinorum officiorum* of 1459 shows no evidence of rising spacing to help determine to which measure they were working.[50] The longest visible line of text measures 91mm, 20 ems but the initial spaces are not all in ems. Some 2-line and 3-line spaces measure 2 and 3 ems wide but others are slightly wider. Evidence might be found in other copies that could give a definite measure for the text width. Their 48-line *Bible* of 1462 is also unjustified setting, with a visible line length of *c*.89–90mm. However a few inked rising spaces suggest a full line length of *c*.94mm, 16 ems of Type 118G.[51] As with their *Rationale,* this edition also has initial spaces of different widths, and not all in ems of Type 118G. Again evidence from a different copy might help clarify line lengths.

The small group of editions printed in the *Catholicon* type, Type 82G, also bring questions. These three editions have been subject to lengthy discussion over many decades. Lotte Hellinga's account of 1989 admirably brings all the arguments together.[52] However this can be looked at again to add what has been discovered, in terms of ems, and whether the printer was working with them, for these editions. In the *Catholicon* and in the Bodleian copy of the 34-line edition of *Summa de articulis* blind impression marks were noted beyond the end of the lines of visible text.[53] The whole line length, including the blind-impressed spacing, measures 87 mm in both editions, 21 ems of Type 82G. However some of the spaces for initials in the *Catholicon* measure in ems and some do not. The 36-line edition of *Summa de articulis* showed no sign of any blind impressed spaces, but did show a couple of inked spaces at the end of a couple of lines, at a line length of *c*.83mm – 20 ems.[54] The *Dialogus rationis* brings its own problem. It is set in the same typeface as the other two editions but the lines are either leaded, or cast on a larger body making it Type 95G. The line length, indicated by raised inked spacing, is *c*.83mm – 20 ems of Type 82G or 18 of Type 95G.[55] However the last word in the edition, 'AMEN', on [b12r] has each letter spaced and the spacing between each letter is exactly 3 ems of Type 95G, which suggests that the type is not leaded but is more likely cast on the larger body, and that ems of Type 95G were being used.

[50] Guillelmus Duranti, *Rationale divinorum officiorum*, 6 Oct. 1459 (id00403000) *Bod-inc.* D-178, shelfmark Auct. 4 Q 1.3.

[51] *Biblia latina*, 14 August 1462 (ib00529000).

[52] Lotte Hellinga, 'Analytical bibliography', pp. 47–96.

[53] Balbus, *Catholicon* [*c*.1460–69] (ib00020000) *Bod-inc.* B-010, shelfmark Auct. 2 Q inf.1.31(a) and Aquinas, *Summa de articulis* [*c*.1460–69] (it00273000) *Bod-inc.* T-117, shelfmark Auct. 1 Q 5.40.

[54] Aquinas, *Summa de articulis* [*c*.1460–69] (it00272950) SBU 538, shelfmark 15296.

[55] Matthaeus de Cracovia, *Dialogus rationis* [*c*.1460–69] (im00367000) SBU 357, shelfmark 15297.

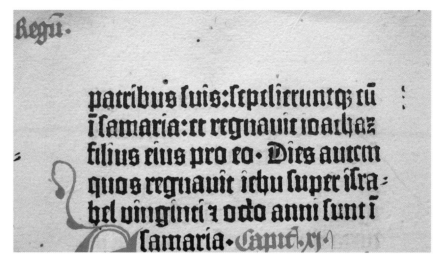

Figure 3.13. Raised and inked space, 96mm from LH of text, on line 1 of page [C5r] of the 36-line *Bible*. (Plantin-Moretus Museum.)

Another printer working at the same time was Johann Mentelin in Strassburg. The earliest edition ascribed to him is his 49-line *Bible*, dated '*c*.1461'.[56] It is not set in ems of his typeface, the text is unjustified and neither the line length nor the initial spaces measure in ems. However by 1463 his *Summa theologica* has justified setting and the line length of 83mm equals 18 ems of his text type, Type 92G.[57] This implies a change in practice during these three years, and his later editions are all set in ems.

Examples of clear marks of inked spacing at the end of lines have also been found in the 36-line *Bible* but here the evidence they give is more confusing. The lines of visible text vary in length between 86 and 89mm and all three copies examined, in the Plantin-Moretus Museum, Würzburg University Library and the BSB in Munich, show inked marks from raised spacing beyond the visible text in the right-hand margin (Figure 3.13).[58] The marks indicate a line length of 96mm but this does not equate to a round number of ems of Type 164G. Further ink marks from raised spacing were found in the BSB copy at the foot of the right-hand column of page [T4v]. This column has only 34 lines of printed text with a rubric having been added in red ink later for the last three lines. The printer had filled out the foot of the column with two lines of spacing, some of which has raised and made ink marks on the page, now slightly obscured by the

---

[56] *Biblia latina*, [*c*.1461] (ib00528000).
[57] Aquinas, *Summa theologica* [not after 1463] (it00208000).
[58] *Biblia latina* [*c*.1459–60] (ib00527000); *BSB-Ink.* B-409, shelfmark 2° Inc. s a.197m; UBW Hubay 983, shelfmark I.t.f.1; ANT O.B.6.11.

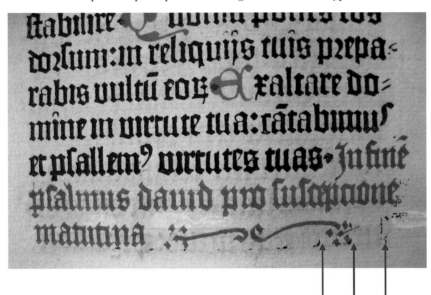

Figure 3.14. Foot of page [T4v] of the 36-line *Bible* (*BSB-Ink* B-409, shelfmark Rar.111a) with inserted spacing in last two lines at foot of right-hand column. Marks show rising spaces 8mm wide and a full line length of 96mm. The red has been added by hand. (Bayerische Staatsbibliothek, Munich.)

red (Figure 3.14). The bottom right-hand corners two of the pieces of spacing have made clear marks, and there are other vertical marks from large pieces of spacing, that when measured were established to be 8mm apart. The furthest out right-hand mark again gives a line length of 96mm, which gives an uncomfortable measure of 11½ ems of Type 164G. However if the spaces were 8mm wide, as suggested by the marks on [T4v] (rather than 8.2mm wide if they were a Type 164G em) then 12 of them would have provided a neat 96mm measure.

Further confusion can be found when measuring the spaces for initials; the spaces for 2-line initials are different widths, some are 17mm wide and some are 15mm wide, suggesting that the printer was not using standard spacing for his initial spaces, and was inconsistent in what he did use. Perhaps the printer of the 36-line *Bible* was working to a set width of 96mm, as suggested by all the inked spacing marks in right-hand margin, and this measure might have been based on pieces of spacing 8mm wide, slightly under the full width of a Type 164G em quad, as seen at the foot of leaf [T4v].

Other editions printed with Type 164G were examined to see if evidence for the full length of the line could be found, and to what

Table 3.5. List of different editions of Donatus' *Ars minor* that seem to have spaces left for initials measured in ems.

Library	Date	ISTC	Edition	Personal examination
Paris BN		(id00314800)	27-line	
Munich		(id00314900)	27-line	yes
London		(id00315000)	27-line	
Munich	[*c.*1454–56]	(id00315100)	27-line	yes
Munich		(id00315600)	28-line	yes
Oxford	[*c.*1455]	(id00316000)	30-line	yes
London		(id00316100)	30-line	
Washington DC		(id00316200)	30-line	

measure they were set. Without some evidence from raised spacing in the margin it is difficult to be certain to what measure texts might have been set. Some fragments of early editions of Donatus's *Ars minor* were looked at, both in the original and as photographs. This was frustrating as the survivals are fragmentary, with often only a portion of the text page remaining, or the ends of the lines missing. It was not possible to establish an accurate line length for any of them. Where there were spaces for initials it was possible to check if these were in based on the em. The following all seem to have clear 2×2-em spaces for initials. Beyond this it is impossible to say with any certainty whether the printer was using his em as a basis for these editions or not

The 42-line *Bible* also brings questions with it. A few possible marks from raised spacing have been noted in the right-hand margin of the Bodleian and BSB copies, but not in any way the same number as noted in the 36-line *Bible*. None of the marks occurred in the same position in relation to the text. This means that it is impossible to establish a line length. The length of the visible lines of text vary from between 86 and 91mm – 91mm seems to be the longest printed line. Of course the printer may not have had as much spacing beyond the visible text as was seen in the 36-line *Bible* or the *Psalters*, or *Canon Missae*. One or two inked marks were noted at the end of the lines that looked as though they had been made from a thin piece of card. Slipping a piece of card in at the end of a slightly loose line is a well established printers' 'bodge' to tighten the line and these marks could perhaps suggest that the full line length was 91mm.

Although trying to establish that the line length was based on an em quad is doubtful for this edition it is still possible to measure the ems, using the lines of type as a guide. Measuring ems also brings a small problem as the first nine pages of the *Bible* were printed with Type 147G, the tenth page with Type 141G and from the eleventh page onwards Type 140G was used – three different type bodies entails three different em rules. Once equipped with the em measurement it is possible to measure the spaces that had been left for initials. If the printer was using the square of his typeface as a basis for working the initial spaces should be square. The spaces for initials for the first eleven pages are not square. Six lines of Type 147G measure 44.1mm, but the width of the space only measured 42mm. Similarly four lines of Type 147G measure 29.5mm, but the space for the initial was 28mm. However when printing the pages with Type 140G all the spaces for initials were square. This suggests that the printer might have been using the square of Type 140G as his basis for working from page eleven onwards in the *Bible* but not in the previous pages.

Although there is no certain established line length the longest measured line of 91mm does equal 13 ems of Type 140G, but only *c.*12½ ems of Type 147G; another indicator that the printer might have been using Type 140G as his standard for the latter part of the *Bible*.

EVIDENCE FROM SPACING IN EARLY PROOF SHEETS

Apart from the raised inked spacing found in some of the editions discussed above there are also other examples of inked and printed raised spacing in some early proof sheets, from an *Ars minor* edition and the 36-line *Bible*, that have been found by other scholars.[59] The proofs were discovered, amongst other fragments, being used to reinforce the binding of a book in the Jagiellonian Library in Cracow.[60] They are all printed in Type 164G and have been the subject of much research, especially by Carl Wehmer, who analysed the various states of the type face and papers used.[61] Despite Wehmer's meticulous scrutiny, and his mention of technical aspects as regard to the column setting, he does not seem to comment on the significance of the other marks on the leaves – the inked spacing material. As these proof sheets all show rare evidence of spacing material being used in the 1450s they were thought relevant to this discussion.

Leaf [2] is a sheet with two columns of 40 lines of text, thought to be a proof for the 36-line *Bible*, and has pieces of spacing, both in the right-hand margin and in the inter-columnar margin. At first glance the

[59] Donatus, *Ars minor* (id00314650).

[60] Jan Pirożyńsky, 'Early imprints from the Gutenberg press in the Jagiellonian Library', *Polish libraries today*, vol. 6 (2005), pp. 30–34. The leaves are located under Jagiellonian Library shelfmark Inc.2267, and are leaves 2, 3 and 4.

[61] Carl Wehmer, *Mainzer Probedruck in der Type des sogenannten astronomischen Kalenders für 1448* (Munich: Leibniz, 1948).

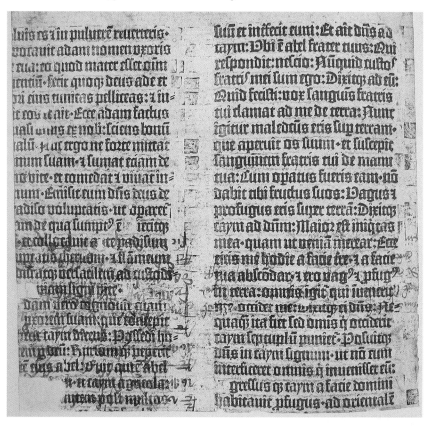

Figure 3.15. Housed in the Jagiellonian Library, Cracow, shelfmark Inc.2267. Leaf [2] is a proof sheet for the 36-line *Bible*, [*c*.1458] and shows raised and inked spaces in the margins. (Reproduced from Carl Wehmer, *Mainzer Probedruck in der Type des sogenannten astronomischen Kalenders für 1448* (Munich: Leibniz, 1948).)

spacing is a complete jumble and of different sizes (see Figure 3.15). The spaces on the outer edge of the right-hand margin are mostly of Type 164G but are not square; they seem to be 7mm wide, the same width as Type 140G used in the 42-line *Bible*. There are quite a few other pieces of spacing 7mm deep, and in various widths in the inter-columnar margin and a few that seem to be 6mm high. One wonders, in these early days, where spacing from a different type body had come – perhaps the printer had Type 140G and 120G in the print shop as well as Type 164G or perhaps this is evidence that all the type came from one printer. There only seems to be one em, the Type 140G em, and there seems to be no other square spacing and no evidence of an em quadrat of Type 164G.

At a second glance a straight line 'divide' in the spacing can be seen in both margins, perhaps between spacing filling out a line length and then spacing inserted as the margin. The pieces may not be spaces at all. As they have printed, with no great evidence of very heavy impression they are probably full type height and could perhaps be upside-down type letters. Whether this evidence, of how the printer assembled his spacing in the forme for a proof sheet, bears any relation to how he might have assembled his spacing for printing the real page is impossible to tell. The final *Bible* had 36 lines set to a narrower measure so there was obviously some adjustment between proof stage and actual printing. He would have needed a better fitting basis for lock-up to print multiple copies than is shown in this proof. This proof is printed on paper from about the same period as the *Astronomical Calendar* [*c.*1458], so was printed at least three years after the *Türkenkalender*.[62]

The other proof sheets, with printed spacing are equally perplexing. There are three proof sheets from a 27-line edition of Donatus's *Ars minor,* also dating to *c.*1458 of which two, leaves [3] and [4] show raised spaces. They are both illustrated, in their actual size, in Wehmer's *Mainzer Probedruck*.[63] Page [3a] shows a printed space at the end of almost every line in the right-hand margin. None of the pieces of spacing are square. Again they are Type 164G high but Type 140G wide (Figure 3.16). Page [4a] has at least two pieces of spacing at the end of every line (Figure 3.17). Again not a single piece is square. Some of the spacing is Type 164G deep but again is Type 140G wide. Some pieces are Type 140G deep and a couple are 6mm deep. There is an inked mark from a raised space in the space left for the initial which is slightly thinner than the em quad. The initial space is slightly narrower at 15.5mm than the 16.4mm that two ems of Type 164G would measure. All three of these proof sheets indicate that the printer was not using spacing that was a square of the type body.

To state again, this is an area which needs more time and research than has been possible for this study. There seems to be a lot of variation, as one might expect at such an early stage of printing development, in whether the printer(s) were working to a measure based on the square of their type body and when. The earliest dated item, based on ems was the *Türkenkalender* of 1454, which was followed by the bulk of the 42-line *Bible,* printed '*c.*1454–55'. In 1457 Fust and Schöffer were working in ems for their *Psalter,* but not totally in 1459 for their *Rationale divinorum officiorum.* The printer of the 36-line Bible, '*c.*1459–60', was not working in ems. Mentelin was not working in ems for his *Biblia Latina* of '*c.*1460–61' but was for his *Summa theologica* of 'not after 1463'. A summary of some of these various workings in ems or not is given in a table at Table 3.6.

---

[62] Pirożyński, p. 32.
[63] Wehmer, *Mainzer Probedruck*, Tafel 7 and Tafel 9.

Table 3.6. Summary of editions discussed in text with unjustified setting, showing which which were set to an em measure and which were not. The Donatus proof and 40-line *Bible* proof sheets are included as they both show the end of the text line, a space for an initial and inked ems at the end of the line. The fragments of many early Donatus editions are not included here as they do not give enough evidence.

Date	Title	Type size	Line length in mm	Line length in ems	Initial spaces in ems	Proof of line length	Printer
1454	*Türkenkalender*	164	125	15	yes	inked space	?Gutenberg
[*c.*1454–55]	*Biblia latina (42-line)*	147	91?	not in ems	no	(longest line?)	?Gutenberg
		140	91?	11?	yes	(longest line?)	
[*c.*1458]	*40-line Bible proof*	164	102/109?	not in ems	no evid.	line + spacing	
[*c.*1458]	*Donatus proof*	164	152	not in ems	no	line + spacing	
[*c.*1460]	*Biblia latina (36-line)*	164	96	not in ems	yes & no	inked space	
1457	*Psalter*	286	216	15	yes	inked space	Fust & Sch.
1458	*Canon Missae*	286	230	16	yes	inked space	Fust & Sch.
1459	*Psalter*	286	215	15	yes	inked space	Fust & Sch.
1459	*Rationale*	91	91?	20?	yes & no	(longest line?)	Fust & Sch.
1460	*Constitutiones*	91	124	27		(longest line?)	Fust & Sch.
		118	65	11		(longest line?)	
[*c.*1461]	*De vita christiana*	91	87	19	yes	inked space	Fust & Sch.
1462	*Biblia latina (48-line)*	118	94?	16?	yes	(longest line?)	Fust & Sch.
[*c.*1461]	*Biblia latina*	118	91?	not in ems	no	(longest line?)	Mentelin
[*c.*1460–69]	*Catholicon*	82	87	21	yes & no	blind impressed space	
[*c.*1460–69]	*De articulis fidei*	82	87	21	yes	blind impressed space	
[*c.*1460–69]	*Dialogus rationis*	82/95	84?	18 (95)	yes (95)	(longest line?)	
[*c.*1460–69]	*De articulis fidei*	82	82	20	yes	inked space	

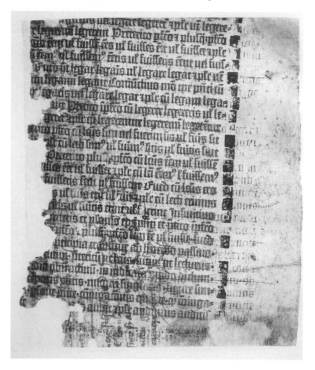

Figure 3.16. Housed in the Jagiellonian Library, Cracow, shelfmark Inc.2267. Page [3a] is a proof sheet of a 27-line Donatus, *Ars minor*, [*c*.1458],[id00314650] and shows raised and inked spacing in the margin. (Reproduced from Wehmer, *Mainzer Probedruck*.)

SIGNIFICANCE OF THE EM QUAD

The em quad is such a fundamental part of the printing method that it ought to be in the forefront of any scholar's mind when trying to unravel some of the problems of understanding fifteenth-century printing methods. It is so fundamental that it is a little surprising that it has hardly been mentioned in the literature of printing history. Some writers have been aware of ems and have mentioned them in their discussions of early printing, but they seem to have concentrated mostly on the work of Aldus Manutius at the end of the fifteenth century. Burnhill was very aware of Aldus' use of ems as his basic 'in-house' measurement but failed to take this any further to look at the printing by other printers and see they were all also using their own ems as a basis. Barker was aware of Aldus and other early printers working to a unit of measurement but did not see that the em of each typeface was the unit for each printer. Frans Janssen, in his paper on the indented paragraph, noted that the em quad

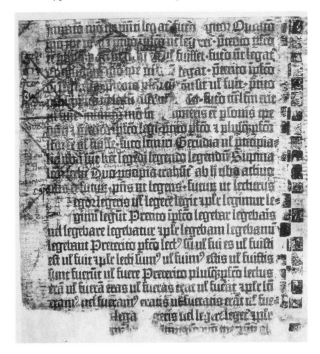

Figure 3.17. Housed in the Jagiellonian Library, Cracow, shelfmark Inc.2267. Page [4a] is a proof sheet of a 27-line Donatus, *Ars minor* [*c*.1458], [id00314650] and shows raised and inked spacing. (Reproduced from Wehmer, *Mainzer Probedruck*.)

is used as the basic unit for indenting in Aldus' *Hypnerotomachia Poliphili* but did not take this use of the em any further.[64] He omitted to state that all the elegantly balanced '*cul-de-lampe*' shaping of texts in the *Hypnerotomachia Poliphili* are managed in steps of an em. Neil Harris, in his exhaustive study of bearer type in the *Hypnerotomachia Poliphili,* also might have commented that the em was essential to Aldus' layout in this edition.[65] Aldus could not have produced this edition to such a high standard if he had not been working closely with his ems.

However, as has been shown in this chapter, the use of the em was not confined to Aldus and was in use by printers from as early as 1454 with the printing of the *Türkenkalender.* Other complicated text settings, such as text and commentary in different type sizes, the inclusion of illustrations, ornamental initials, a time line such as with the *Fasciculus temporum* and

[64] Frans, A. Janssen, 'The indented paragraph', *Technique and design in the history of printing* (Amsterdam: Hes & De Graaf, 2004), pp. 39–56 (p. 45).

[65] Neil Harris, 'The blind impressions in the Aldine *Hypnerotomachia Poliphili* (1499)', *Gutenberg-Jahrbuch*, 79 (2004), pp. 93–146.

printing in two colours, were all made possible because printers worked in a standard unit. To try to do any of the above, without a standard unit of measure, would have been technically difficult, if not impossible. If one measures some of the complicated settings, either of text and commentary or with inset initials or illustrations, the relationship between the type size(s) and the dimensions of the woodcut material, which might not be apparent in millimetres, can be clearly seen in terms of ems.

Knowing the measure and the basis to which a printer was working could also be another tool in helping to identify previously unknown editions. Zainer's use of his em was integral to his page layout, and could be used as an indentifying factor. Janssen, in another paper, picks out and tabulates a number of layout and design points as a means of identifying early previously un-identified editions. He includes the number of lines on a page, use of typeface, use of headlines etc. but does not mention perhaps the most significant one, the set measure of the text.[66] He discusses the type area and the proportions of height to width of text, but not the text width on its own.[67] Perhaps the text width, and the em on which it was based, should also be added to this list of design points.

The consideration of whether a printer was working in ems or not might also be of use when applied to some of the questions raised by some of the undated early editions. The em factor might not provide all the answers but it is another aspect to be taken into consideration. A few of examples are brought together here; for some it seems that an understanding of the em is the solution, for others it can only offer another angle.

As already mentioned in this chapter, the understanding that the spacing between the letters in A M E N in *Dialogus rationis* is in ems of Type 95G (and not of Type 82G) clearly indicates that this edition was printed with type on a body of 95G and not with a body of 82G that has been leaded – this edition is not the earliest example of leaded lines as has been suggested by some writers.[68]

It is very likely that the *Catholicon* will remain a puzzle that cannot be solved that easily. However it was set to a fixed measure based on ems and it does show rising spaces, which I am not sure ties in with a theory that it was printed from 2-line slugs.

Various suggestions have been made about how the type of the 42-line *Bible* was altered from being size Type 147G, to Type 141G to the final Type 140G. Perhaps the type for the 42-line *Bible* was originally cast on a larger 147G body for the first few pages, was not filed down but was re-

---

[66] Frans A. Janssen, 'Layout as means of identification', *Technique and design in the history of printing* ('t Goy-Houten: Hes & De Graaf, 2004), pp. 101–111 (p. 106).

[67] Janssen, 'Layout', p. 108.

[68] Hellinga, 'Analytical bibliography', p. 96, recounts the opinions of Zedler and Ruppel, and adds that in her opinion the type was recast on a larger body.

cast on a smaller 141G body for a short one-page trial, and then finally on a 140Gbody for the printer to work to a sound basis of line lengths and initial spaces based on em quads of Type 140G.[69]

A copy of the *Missale speciale* or *Missale abbreviatum* has not been personally examined, but from facsimiles of their pages it seems that the initial spaces are not in ems of the type face and neither is the line length of the longest line.[70] It would be useful to examine a copy closely for any raised spaces that might give evidence of line length. Even if the two editions had been printed at a date later than the original casting of the type (*c*.1455?) and had been printed as late as *c*.1473 as suggested by Allan Stevenson from his study of the paper used, it would have been expected that the printer would have been clearly working in ems by the 1470s.[71] This could suggest that they were printed earlier.

These are only a few examples of some of the questions raised by some of the early editions. It would be good to see bibliographers grasp the use of the em alongside their use of millimetres when considering incunabula, especially when looking at the earliest printed editions.

---

[69] This is an area where there has been a large amount of discussion, which is still ongoing. It is not proposed to enter into the arguments here of whether Gutenberg was using cast type from a mould or not. Even listing all the references about Gutenberg, the printing of the 42-line *Bible*, the various states of the type (or not type) the paper used, etc. is beyond the scope of this book, although some of the references are in the *Bibliography*. However the evidence found on the printed pages show that the em could be brought into the discussion in this area.

[70] *Missale speciale* [*c*.1473?] (im00732500) and *Missale abbreviatum* [*c*.1473?] (im00735500).

[71] Stevenson, Allan, *The problem of the Missale speciale* (London: Bibliographical Society, 1967).

4 BLIND IMPRESSIONS FROM (BEARER) TYPE

Almost all Zainer's editions have at least one example of a blind impression on one of the pages. These impressions are most usually made by un-inked type letters that have been pressed into the paper, making a very obvious mark. Such blind impressions are not unique to Zainer. They occur in the editions of many other fifteenth- and sixteenth-century printers in Germany, France, Italy, Spain, England and the Low Countries, from as early as 1457 with blind impressions of type-high pieces of wood in the *Psalter Romanum,* 1457 (ip01036000) printed by Fust and Schoeffer in Mainz (from personal observation) to some lines of blind type in *In natalen Iesu Christi* printed by Konrad Dreher in Erfurt in 1572 noted by David Paisey in his article about blind impressions.[1]

Being fairly widespread and also fairly noticeable has meant that these blind impressions have been the subject of discussion by other writers. They have all written from slightly different angles. Adolf Schmidt wrote in 1897 about blind impressions and the instability of the platens of early presses.[2] He suggested that the early printers used type-high spacing or type as a support for the platen.[3] He then described a number of editions in which he had found blind impressions and what had caused them.[4] Schmidt wrote again in 1927, adding to his previous work by concentrating in more depth on editions by further printers in whose work he had found blind impressions.[5]

Victor Scholderer described the blind impressions he found in the editions printed in Augsburg by Anton Sorg, at the press at SS Ulrich and Afra, and by Günther Zainer, and wondered if there was any particular Augsburg connection to the practice.[6] David Paisey also took the more generalist approach as he describes the occurrence of blind impressions over a century and a half of printing and across many countries.[7] He offered a succinct introduction to the subject as he noted the difficulty of spotting the blind impressions, how they were not always noted in

[1] David Paisey, 'Blind printing in continental books', in A.L. Lepschy, J. Took, D. Rhodes, eds., *Book production and letters in the western renaissance* (London: Modern Humanities Research Association, 1986), pp. 220–233 (p. 229).
[2] Adolf Schmidt, 'Untersuchungen', p. 15.
[3] Adolf Schmidt, 'Untersuchungen', p. 16.
[4] Adolf Schmidt, 'Untersuchungen', pp. 17–21, 24–27.
[5] Adolf Schmidt, 'Technische Beiträge zur Inkunabelkunde', *Gutenberg-Jahrbuch,* 2 (1927), pp. 9–23.
[6] Scholderer, 'Notes', pp. 1–6.
[7] Paisey, pp. 220–233.

catalogues and how, even when noted, they could later be found to have disappeared. Bühler's article concentrated on one printer as he described the blind impression marks found in four editions printed by Johann Prüss in Strassburg.[8]

More recently two other writers focus on a specific edition. Randall McLeod writes about the blind impressions found in Castiglione's *Il Libro del Cortegiano*, 1528, printed by Aldus Romano and Andrea d'Asola in Venice.[9] He documents some of the sequence of printing as evidenced by reading the text in the blind impressions. Neil Harris makes an exhaustive study of the Aldine blind impressions in *Hypnerotomachia Poliphili*.[10] The conclusion of these scholars is that the impressions occur where there are fewer lines of set matter on the page than usual. The typesetter has added a line, or lines, of type or other material, at the foot of the page, as a support or bearer, to help balance the platen of the press, and although these extra lines were (usually) not inked they made an impressed mark onto the paper. None of these writers asked the question whether a bearer was always necessary; they have accepted the presence of a bearer line or lines and assumed it was there for support, but have not investigated further to see how necessary the support was for a particular occasion.

Accuracy of recording is difficult. Despite the number of blind impressions that Zainer has in his editions, and the number that have been recorded by the other scholars, these are still rare finds in early printed editions. Not only are they rare but they are often difficult to spot. Many blind impressions can only be seen with a raking light, not always possible in some well-lit modern reading rooms. Harris noted this particular difficulty with the *Hypnerotomachia Poliphili*, and stated that the blind impressions are '. . . at best faint and in the majority of copies wholly invisible.'[11] He describes trying to find dark corners in which to investigate with a torch.[12] On a couple of occasions a very clear impression was noted in one copy in one library, and then it was realised that the same mark had not been noticed in another copy of the edition in a different library. On revisiting the earlier library, and knowing which leaf to scrutinise, a very faint impression which had been overlooked before was discerned.

Blind impressions can be very copy specific.[13] An impression may be

---

[8] Curt Bühler, 'A note on a fifteenth-century printing technique', *University of Pennsylvania Chronicle*, 15 (1949), pp. 52–55.

[9] Randall McLeod, 'A angels fear to read', in Joe Bray, Miriam Handley, Anne C. Henry, eds., *Marking the text: the presentation of meaning on the literary page* (Burlington: Ashgate, 2000), pp. 144–192.

[10] Neil Harris, 'The blind impressions in the Aldine *Hypnerotomachia Poliphili* (1499)', *Gutenberg-Jahrbuch*, 79 (2004), pp. 93–146.

[11] Harris, 'Blind impressions', p. 131.

[12] Harris, 'Blind impressions', p. 132.

[13] Paisey, p. 222.

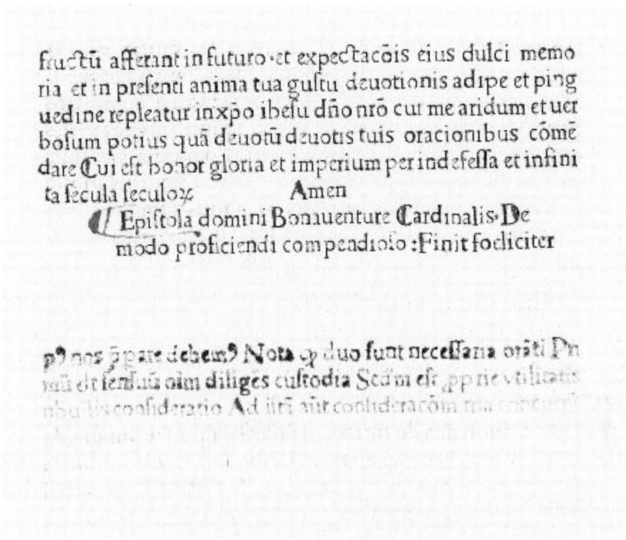

fructu afferant in futuro·et expectacois eius dulci memo
ria et in presenti anima tua gustu deuotionis adipe et ping
uedine repleatur in xpo ibesu dño nro cui me aridum et uer
bosum potius qua deuotu deuotis tuis oracionibus cóme
dare Cui est honor gloria et imperium per ind efessa et infini
ta secula seculo℣ Amen
⁋ Epistola domini Bonauenture Cardinalis·De
modo proficiendi compendioso :Finit fodiciter

p⁹ nos ƺ pare debem⁹ Nota ꝯ duo funt necessaria orsti Pri
... di femsui olm diliges custodia Scd̄m est ppne utilieas
... lis consideratio Ad iiñ aut consideracoim ma ...

Figure 4.1. Partially inked bearer lines in leaf [c7v] of *De adhaerendo Deo*. The top eight lines are part of the text. The bearer lines, from line 12 position, have been caught by the ink dabber at the top, and then later rubricated. (Bodleian Library, Oxford.)

found in one copy and be completely invisible in another. They also vary in clarity and depth of impression. In his Appendix Harris lists all the variations he found through 66 different copies of the *Hypnerotomachia Poliphili,* and he classifies them as 'readable', 'visible' and 'trace'.[14] One blind impression I discovered has only been found in one of the Bodleian copies of *De adhaerendo Deo.*[15] It has not been found in any of the other 13 copies looked at. Page [c7v] has only eight lines of printed text and the remainder of the page is made up with three lines of space and 23 bearer lines. As a blind impression of type this is a particularly fine example. It is most visible in impression at the top where it has also been partially inked (the inking in a nice curved shape from the ink dabber) Further, the rubricator added a red stroke to the initial 'A' of this partial, unintentionally inked, section of text (Figure 4.1).

Blind impressions are also transient; Paisey found examples where impression marks, noted previously, had disappeared.[16] He suggests that later handling such as rebinding or cleaning might be the cause. Harris suggests a number of causes for the variations found in blind impressions such as the packing on the press, and the strength of the pressman's pull.

[14] Harris, 'Blind impressions', pp. 133–146.
[15] Shelfmark Auct. 6 Q 4.3 (2).
[16] Paisey, pp. 221–222.

He also mentions binding practice having an effect, stating that blind impressions tend to be faintest in quires at either end of a copy, as, being nearest to the binder's hammer, they are more likely to be flattened.[17] My evidence from Zainer's editions does not support Harris's point, and some of the strongest of impressions have been noted in the end quires of two editions, *Aurea Biblia* 1476 and *Vocabularius Bibliae*.

Although the subject of blind impressions caused by bearer lines has already been addressed by other writers it was thought worthwhile to consider Zainer's use of them to add to the discussion. Almost every one of Zainer's editions has a blind impression caused by inserted lines of type, or odd letters or a type-high piece of wood. Two editions in particular, the 1476 edition of *Aurea Biblia* and *Vocabularius Bibliae* [*c*.1476] have a high incidence of bearer lines and are considered in more detail to try to find out why. The aim was to discover whether Zainer had a particular method of working that made the use of bearer lines necessary; where and when he used bearer lines, and what material he used for them.

Firstly the number of lines to a page that Zainer used as standard was noted and then by how many lines the type-block was short of the standard to see if that bore any relation to his use of a bearer. The number of bearer lines being inserted each time was also noted as was the position of the bearer line(s). This should help to determine if the lines were actually serving as supports or had just been left in the forme from the previous print run, perhaps to save some time when imposing the new forme. But before considering whether the lines were really needed as support it is important to first consider the mechanics of the early printing press and the stability of its platen.

The stability of a fifteenth-century platen

As stated in the *Introduction* there is little information about the workings of the fifteenth-century, wooden printing press and the first image of a printing press does not give much useful detail, especially about the platen which cannot be seen in the image. Other presses in existence in the 1450s, from which the printing press might have derived, were fruit presses and paper presses. If one starts with a paper press, used for pressing the excess water out of a stack of newly formed sheets, raises the bed a little and provides some method of sliding the type smoothly in and out under the platen one can get some idea of what the first press might have looked like.

The wooden press, as we believe it to be, had a platen made of wood or metal suspended from a wooden frame, the hose, and attached to a spindle.[18] The spindle was fitted with a screw thread so it could be wound down and pressure put on to the platen, and the hose stopped the platen from turning. Under the platen was the bed of the press on which the type was placed, locked up in some way to stop it falling over. There was some method of moving the type in and out from under the platen. From the early illustrations the screw appears to be made of wood. It is not known when this was replaced by a metal one but evidence of one press working with a wooden screw in the 1480's can be found in the diary/day book of the press of San Jacopo di Ripoli in Florence. Jacopo the joiner/carpenter is paid for a screw and housing for the press in 1482, and later in 1483 for arranging the spindle of the press.[19]

The key parts of the press, the screw and spindle that pushes down on the platen and presses it onto the paper and inked type, can be seen in printer Jodocus Badius Ascensius' mark from Paris in 1520.[20] The attachments holding the platen to the screw are also visible (Figure 4.2). In this illustration one can see that the main thrust of the spindle is delivered centrally through its point where it makes contact with the platen. The platen is suspended from the spindle and screw mechanism. The attachments used for this provide some restrictions to its movement but still leave the platen quite unstable, and able to tilt towards any one edge or corner.

The forme holding the page or pages of type is placed on the bed of the press under the platen. The platen is screwed down with great pressure onto the forme of type.[21] However, because of the inherent instability of the platen, the type has to be located as near to the centre as possible under the platen. This is a technical point that any printer with experience of letterpress automatically takes into consideration when

---

[18] In a letter to Johann Amerbach on 24 September 1481, Adolf Rusch asked Amerbach to have his caster make four platens for him, as he had before. Halporn, p. 15, letter AK1:1. In *Printing presses* (London: Faber, 1973), p. 26, James Moran also quotes the Rusch letter to Amerbach, and adds that it is not known when the use of metal in parts of the wooden press began.

[19] Conway, *Diario*, p. 232 and p. 270. Alan May, 'The one-pull press', *Journal of the Printing Historical Society*, new series 11 (2008), pp. 65–89, describes the turning of a wooden screw when constructing his one-pull wooden press. The screw had to be made with the correct 'slope' to enable enough pressure to be transmitted for printing on a pull of the press bar. Hans-Jürgen Wolf, *Geschichte der Druckpressen* (Frankfurt: Interprint, 1975), pp. 55 and 60, suggests that the first metal screw was introduced by Nürnberg carpenter and screwmaker Leonhard Danner (1497–1585) in the sixteenth century.

[20] Ascensius used a similar illustration for his mark from 1507, but this image shows the detail of the spindle more clearly.

[21] The images of wooden hand presses all show the operator working with great physical effort. This is not exaggerated. It was quite a surprise to me to find out how much force had to be used to pull down the platen of a wooden press with a metal screw, previous experience having been with an iron hand press with springs and levers to aid the downward pressure. Gaskell (p. 124) states that a press with a metal screw will have almost twice the power of one with a wooden one.

hose

spindle

platen

Figure 4.2. Illustration of printing press *c*.1520, showing screw, spindle and platen, from the device of Jodocus Badius Ascensius. See also Figure 4.4 for photograph of the hose. (Moran, *Printing presses,* Faber & Faber, p. 24.)

deciding where to position the type in the forme, so it can be placed centrally in the press and keep the platen balanced. All hand presses, be they made of wood or iron, and most jobbing platen presses, have to have the type area placed centrally, or the platen will tilt from the horizontal.[22] If one tries to print the forme with a tilted platen the type at one end receives little or no pressure and so does not print properly, and the type at the other end receives too much pressure and digs into the paper. This is shown, perhaps with some exaggeration, at Figure 4.3. This means that if there were a short number of lines of type in the forme it could cause an imbalance of the platen. To counteract this something needs to be added at the foot of the forme to support the platen, as a bearer. David Paisey also adds that there is risk of damage to the tympan and the screw of the press if the platen tilts.[23]

---

[22] John Southward, *Practical printing*, 3rd edn (London: Powell, 1887) vol. 2, p. 377, describes the necessity of centring the forme under the centre of the platen. 'Southward' was one of the printing industry's technical manuals used by apprentices from the end of the nineteenth and through the twentieth century.

[23] Paisey, p. 221.

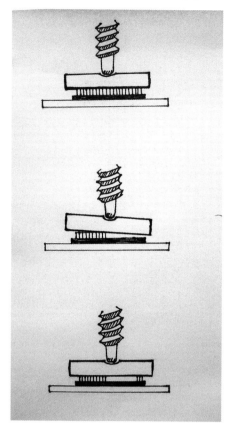

Figure 4.3. Very simplified diagram showing (top) a balanced platen over a forme full of set type. The pressure from the screw only operates through the spindle (middle). A tilted platen when some lines of type are removed from the forme and there is no support at that end, and (foot) the platen rebalanced by the insertion of some supporting bearer lines of type (which would not have been inked).

Practical experiment 4.1 – balance of the platen

To discover to what extent the platen was unstable some experiments were undertaken using the reconstructed wooden common press in Cambridge University Library.[24] The press had been built in 1969 under the supervision of Philip Gaskell and to specifications as described in Stower's printers' manual of 1808.[25] The press has a platen

---

[24] Date of experiments 1 December 2005. With thanks to Nicholas Smith for allowing use of this press and for kindly casting some lines of Linotype for use with these experiments.
[25] Stower, pp. 302–345.

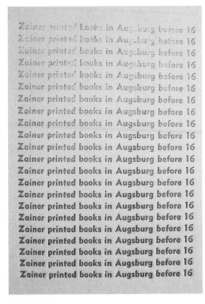

Figure 4.4. The results of printing with a tilted platen. Heavy impression at the foot of the leaf, on the right, gradually changing to very light impression at the head of the leaf on the left. The photo on the left shows the printed side of the leaf and the photo on the right shows the impression marks on the verso.

size of 35 × 52cm and a metal screw. The packing was a printers' woollen blanket and the platen had been attached firmly to make it as stable as possible.

The experiment was to test, in stages, how many lines of text needed to be removed from a type block of 34 lines before the balance of the platen was affected. Barcham Green hand-made, cotton-rag paper, damped overnight was used and 34 lines of type were locked in a chase and placed centrally on the bed of the press, and its position marked.

The type was inked before each impression. The bed was wound under the platen and the central position marked for further printings. Sheets of damped paper were printed at each stage. The first impression was made as a standard to judge the subsequent impressions.

When two lines were removed from the foot of a centrally-positioned text block of 34 lines of type, the platen remained stable. Removing two further lines made no visible difference. When two further lines were removed (a total of six lines) the platen began to tilt, so that the type at the head of the page received visibly lighter pressure whilst that at the foot received visibly more pressure. When a further six lines were removed (a total of twelve lines) the impression at the head was so light that the type

Figure 4.5. Tightly tied platen on wooden press in the University Library, Cambridge.

had barely printed whereas the three lines at the foot had impressed so heavily that the shoulders of the type had printed as well as can be seen in Figure 4.4.

The press at Cambridge, built in the 1969, is obviously not the same press as Zainer used in the 1470s. However this experiment does show that with a solidly constructed wooden press, with an iron screw and the platen tied as tightly as possible (Figure 4.5) the removal of up to four lines of type, about 12 per cent of the total caused little difference to the printing performance, but the removal of six lines, about 17 per cent of the total, could produce some visible imbalance of the platen.

Practical experiment 4.2 – the effect of bearer lines

A second experiment was made to see how the addition of lines of type as support, as bearer lines, might affect the balance of the platen and consequently the printing performance of the press.

Barcham Green hand-made, cotton-rag paper, damped overnight, was used, and the same wooden press in Cambridge University Library. As before the type was inked before each impression and the bed was wound under the platen to a central marked position.

When 25 lines of type were missing, a one-line bearer inserted at the foot of the forme did not provide sufficient surface area to work successfully as a support. The single line showed extremely heavy impression and the remaining nine lines at the top of the forme still showed a bias of lighter impression on the first line and heavier on the ninth line. It needed a block of eight bearer lines as support at the foot to balance the platen sufficiently for even printing. Similarly when the forme had 22 lines, a single line was not enough to support the platen as it took too much pressure itself. It needed a block of three or four lines to provide enough support. The experiment suggests that one line of type was sufficient as a bearer only when the forme was short by a few lines of type.

It seems, from this second experiment, that adding lines of type-high material as support where the forme is short by a number of lines (as a rough guide by more than five lines short) does work as a printing technique. It also shows that the more lines that the forme is short, the more bearer lines have to be used; being twenty-five lines short needed eight lines of support, being twelve lines short needed three lines of support. However experiment 4.1 suggests that if a page is short by four or fewer lines then no bearer should be necessary. These conclusions will be looked at later in the light of Zainer's practice.

ZAINER'S USE OF BEARERS IN HIS EDITIONS

As was stated earlier, blind impressions made from bearer type seem to feature somewhere in almost every edition that Zainer printed. In the period being studied, 1473–1478, he printed 28 chancery-folio editions. Examples of using bearers have been found in 21 of these editions. He also printed one quarto, seven royal-folio editions, one median-folio and one imperial-folio edition, all with at least one example of bearer type, making a total of 30 out of 38 editions with bearer type. In his article on Augsburg printing, Scholderer comments on the high incidence of bearers in the editions of Anton Sorg, and that 13 of Sorg's 25 editions have a bearer.[26] It would seem that Zainer had an even higher incidence of editions with bearers than this.

There are seven chancery-folio editions without evidence of bearers. They range from the German edition of *Historia Griseldis*, [*c*.1473] to three different editions of *De periculis contingentibus*, [*c*.1473, *c*.1474 and *c*.1475] to Aesop's *Vita et fabulae*, [*c*.1476] *Die vierundzwanzig goldenen Harfen* [14]76 and *Vitae sanctorum patrum* [1478–80]. Being spread through the time period there seems to be no chronological basis to their not having bearers. However it must be borne in mind, as mentioned by David Paisey, that although evidence of bearer type is no longer visible now does not mean that it was not there originally.[27] They vary in number of leaves;

---

[26] Scholderer, 'Notes', p. 3.
[27] Paisey, p. 221.

there are four single-quire editions, the first four listed above, and three multiple-quire editions. The single-quire editions all have a blank first leaf, which is sometimes missing in the copies looked at. Interestingly this leaf carries a full page of bearer type in the *c.*1476 *De periculis* edition, so perhaps the earlier editions also had had them and they are just not visible. *Vita et fabulae* has uneven number of line lengths all the way through as the typesetter juggled setting the fables in two languages and inserting over 200 woodcuts. However, having looked through three different copies, no sign of a bearer has been found. The two copies of *Goldene Harfen* and the six copies of *Vitae sanctorum* have also shown no evidence. There seem no marked differences, from a practical printing view, to explain why these editions do not have bearers. *Vita et fabulae* in particular has such irregular numbers of lines that one would expect to see bearer lines. However there are few extant copies and it has been possible to look at three of them; the one in John Rylands Library is in a Victorian binding so would be unlikely to show anything; the one in the Bodleian Library has had a bad attack of damp, to the extent that the latter part of the copy is rotting and very fragile, so this might have affected any marks; but the copy in Munich was in good condition but no evidence of bearer type could be found.

Recording the occurrences of blind impressions

The total number of copies of each edition consulted is given in *Bibliography – Primary Sources, section 1*. Each occurrence of a blind impression on a particular page was noted with its leaf number, its line-position, the number of bearer lines being inserted and the material being used, the number of printed lines on the page, and the number of lines of type that the page is short. The number of lines on the page included the headline in those editions that had one. The figures given in the following tables have all been assembled from this master list and are as accurate as possible. More than one copy of each edition has been used as the basis for these tables.[28]

Differences in printing practice through a print run could easily cause variation in depth of impression noted 500 years later, as could binding practice at any time. When printing on a hand press there are a number of variables that all have to be controlled by the skill and judgement of the operator. Variations in dampness of paper, and in the dampness of the packing which will absorb moisture from having damp sheets pressed onto it, and variations in pressure applied to the platen as the bar of the

[28] It has been assumed that if an impression of bearer type is found on a particular page in one copy then the bearer would have been in position for the entire print run, even though the marks may no longer be visible in some copies. Looking through multiple copies has helped give a better chance of finding all the marks that might have been made in an edition.

screw is tightened will all affect the depth of impression of the type into the paper. A skilled pressman will achieve a more regular impression through a print run than an unskilled one. Paisey suggested the use of a mask, a layer of paper placed over the blind type, which might have affected the depth of the impression.[29] A further experiment was carried out to see what the difference was between printing with and without a mask.

Practical experiment 4.3 — blind impression through a frisket

This experiment was made to see if there is a visible difference between a blind impression of type onto dampened paper pressed directly onto the paper from an impression made when pressed through a paper mask. Barcham Green hand made paper, dampened the night before was used with a forme of type ready for printing and an Albion hand press. A sheet of thin paper was laid over half the type area, and then the sheet of dampened Barcham Green paper was laid across the whole forme and an impression made.

A visible difference could be seen. Where the type metal made direct contact with the sheet of paper being impressed there was a clear mark with crisp edges and a shiny surface on the paper where the metal of the flat letter forms had made contact. Where the type had been masked by an intervening piece of paper the mark was much less crisp, the edges were blurred and the damp sheet of paper had not been pressed as flat by the type letters.

This experiment showed that type metal pressed directly onto a damp sheet of paper makes a sharp mark with crisp edges and leaves a slight sheen on the impressed area. The masked impression is much duller. It would suggest that Zainer's crisp impressions were made from type metal directly onto the printed sheet but it is impossible to say how the less clear impressions were made; perhaps with a mask, or perhaps without and have blurred a little through the centuries from handling. It would seem that later handling has a large part to play as it is much easier to find examples of blind impressions in copies in contemporary bindings than in copies that were rebound in the nineteenth or twentieth century. Harris also found this and suggests it is hardly worth opening some copies in national collections to look for blind impressions.[30]

---

[29] Paisey, p. 221.

[30] Harris, 'Blind impressions', p. 130 and also see end of his footnote 46 where he adds that he found the most legible impressions in copies in their original bindings.

A QUARTO EDITION

Zainer's earliest dated edition, *Büchlein der Ordnung der Pestilenz,* is a small quarto which has one occurrence of a blind impression. The last page [e8v] has only 15 lines rather than the standard 24 lines of text. Two lines of Ms, acting as bearer lines, have been inserted at the 23- and 24-line positions.

TWENTY-ONE CHANCERY-FOLIO EDITIONS

Seven of the chancery-folio editions showed no signs of bearers, leaving only 21 editions that did have them. Nine of these editions only have one occurrence each of bearer type, eight of these comprise blocks of text, and the ninth is a line of sorts.[31] The statistics are brought together at Table 4.1. Eight editions have between two and ten occurrences of bearer lines and three editions have between 11 and 21 occurrences. The two editions with the highest number of occurrence of bearer lines, 21 and 50, are unusual. They are unusual, when compared with the rest of Zainer's editions, for their high number of occurrences and also, as will be discussed later, for the positioning of their bearer lines.[32]

Table 4.1. The number of occurrences of bearers found in 28 chancery-folio editions.

Number of occurrences of bearers being used	Number of editions
0	7
1	9
2	5
4	1
7	1
10	1
11	1
14	1
21	1
50	1
Total 136	**28**

[31] When counting occurrences of bearer lines in Zainer's editions, each occurrence is only counted once per edition; it is not counted each time it is found in a number of copies of that edition

[32] Harris, 'Blind impressions', p. 93, found forty pages with bearing material in the Aldine 1499 edition of *Hypnerotomachia Poliphili.*

Table 4.2. The different material used for bearers in 21 chancery-folio editions where bearers were found. Those listed as 'unable to discern' were of type, but it was impossible to tell whether they were of text or sorts.

Number of bearer lines	Number of occurrences				
	Text	Sorts	Wood	Spaces or upside down letters	Total
1	6	63		7	76
2	2	31	3		36
3	4	2			6
4	1	1			2
5	3				3
14	1				1
15	1				1
18	1				1
20	2				2
23	1				1
27	1				1
34	1				1
Total	24	97	3	7	131
Unable to discern					5
Total					136

Material used for bearer lines

Zainer used a variety of material for his bearers; lines of text, lines of assorted letters (listed as 'sorts' in the Tables), lines made up of a few letters interspersed with spacing, type high spacing material or upside down letters, and pieces of wood. The lines of text can be of interest as they have presumably already been used as part of a printed page.[33] The various materials used are tabulated in Table 4.2. None of the materials used are peculiar to Zainer, and Paisey, with his survey of over 200 different editions, mentions them all.[34] Lines of sorts seem to be the most frequently used, making up 71 per cent of the total. These were more often the least used letters from the type case such as rows of ℞s or ¶s as shown at Figure 4.6.[35] Sometimes Zainer would set the line solid, as a complete row of the same sort and sometimes he would space out perhaps

---

[33] More detail about the evidence provided by lines of text used as bearer type is discussed under 'Bearer lines as evidence of printing practice' later in this chapter.

[34] Paisey, p. 223.

[35] The ℞ was generally used in liturgical texts. Zainer first uses it in *De planctu ecclesiae*, 1474, where it seems to be being used as a contraction for the word '*Registrum*', perhaps referring to a common text of the period Gregory the Great's *Registrum epistolae*. See A. Cappelli, *Dizionario di abbreviature latine ed italiani* (Milan: Hoepli, 1912). With thanks to Alan Coates for suggesting this link.

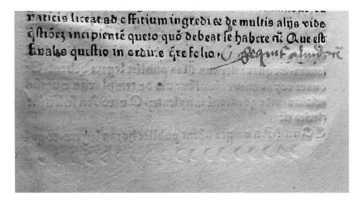

Figure 4.6. Albertus de Ferrarriis, *De horis canonicis,* leaf [a4v] with 29 lines of text and a 1-line bearer of ¶s at the 35-line position. (Ulm Stadtbibliothek.)

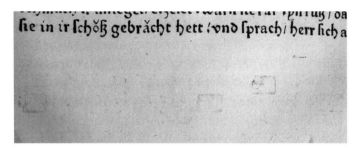

Figure 4.7. Giovanni Boccaccio, *De claris mulieribus,* leaf [m1r] with 28 lines of text and two bearer lines of upside-down letters or quads , interspersed with spacing, at 31- and 32-line position. (Ulm Stadtbibliothek.)

three or four or five of the sorts with under type-height spacing to fill the line. Sometimes the sorts are mixed letters. Sometimes what could be upside-down sorts are spaced out in a line as illustrated at Figure 4.7. Sorts were not used for bearers when he was inserting more than four bearer lines.

Sometimes, on just under 18 per cent of the occasions, lines of text as shown at Figure 4.8 are used. Zainer use lines of text as bearers most often where there is a need for more support, and consequently more lines to be inserted. 33 per cent of the uses of text are for single or pairs of bearer lines and 67 per cent are for when he was adding three or more lines. I have only found three occasions where Zainer uses type-high pieces of wood as a bearer, making up just two per cent of the total. All these materials would have been near to the compositor's hand so he could make up a line as quickly and as easily as possible.

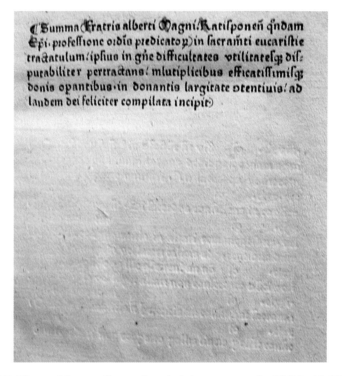

Figure 4.8 Albertus Magnus, *Summa de eucharistiae sacramento*, leaf [b3r] with 18 lines of printed text and 14 blind impressed lines of text from [b2v] from 21- to 34-line position. (Ulm Stadtbibliothek.)

Number of bearer lines

Table 4.3 shows the number of bearer lines inserted, and also the number of lines in relation to the number of lines that a leaf is short of the standard.[36] Single lines as bearers are the most common, being more than half the total use, just over 56 per cent. Pairs of lines are the next most common in use making up 29 per cent of the total; the total of single lines and pairs of lines comprising 86 per cent of the total usage. As can be seen from the table single lines are inserted most often when the leaf is short of only a small number of lines. Zainer did insert a single line once when he was eleven lines short of text on a leaf in the 41-lines-to-a-leaf edition of *Legenda aurea* [not after 1478] (ij00091000). Here the eleven lines missing represent 27 per cent of the total text area, 10 per cent more than the 17 per cent that was found to be the point at

[36] Zainer's standard number of lines of type to a page varies slightly between editions as discussed in Chapter 2, *Initial Observations & Basic Findings* under 'Number of lines'.

Table 4.3. Occurrences of different number of bearer lines inserted in 21 chancery-folio editions, related to the number of lines by which a leaf is short of the standard number of lines — the standard number being 34 lines.

Number of bearer lines inserted	Number of lines short of standard (34)																				Total
	1	2	3	4	5	6	7	8	9	11	12	13	14	15	16	21	22	26	30	34	
1	4	7	23	17	10	5	4	1	5	1											77
2		4	21	3	6	2	2	1				1									40
3					1	1			1	1							2				6
4							1				1										2
5								1	1				1								3
14														1							1
15															1						1
18																	1				1
20																2					2
23																		1			1
27																			1		1
34																				1	1
Total	4	11	44	20	17	8	7	3	7	2	1	1	1	1	1	2	3	1	1	1	136

which bearers were shown to be needed in Experiment 4.1. When the type page was short by more lines than eleven lines he previously had always inserted multiple bearer lines.

A striking point about this table is the high percentage of occurrences of bearer lines (almost 50 per cent) when the page was only three or four lines short of the standard — where Experiment 4.1 suggested a bearer would not be necessary. The occurrences that have caused these high totals in these two columns have come from two editions, and will be discussed later; three quires of *Vocabularius Bibliae* provided 44 of these occurrences, and 16 further occurrences came from five quires of *Aurea Biblia*, 1476.

Other blind impressions from type

Apart from material set in lines right across the full measure of the text, Zainer also on occasions used a single letter or two inserted at the end of short lines, as in *Sermones de sanctis* 1475 (Figure 4.9) or in the bottom right corners where there was 4- or 6-line space in the corner of the forme, as in the 1476 edition of *Aurea Biblia* (Figure 4.10). Neither of these occasions seem to be in places where support for the platen might be necessary. They occur on the inside of the forme, where there is type providing support all round, and not on an outside edge or corner where they would

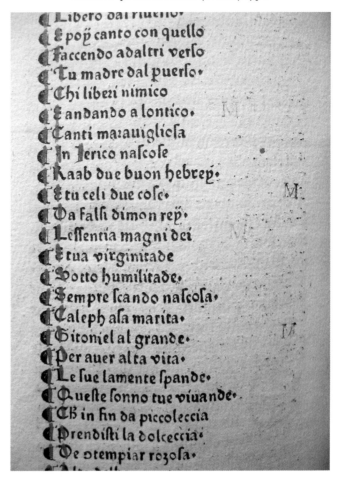

Figure 4.9. Page [r1v] of *Sermones de sanctis*, 1475, showing one column of text with short lines. Bearer letters have been inserted occasionally at the middle or end of some of the lines – perhaps to support the sheet of paper being printed. (Ulm Stadtbibliothek.)

be needed to balance a platen. Admittedly they are positioned in the forme where there is a larger than usual white space. It could be that the blind impressed letters have been inserted to support the paper and keep it from picking up ink from the furniture. Damp paper is heavier than dry and it is floppy, so has a tendency to fall into low places on the forme. Printers have used a number of methods to stop this such as a supporting frisket, or pieces of string as discussed in Chapter 2, and this may be another such attempt. If this is the case it was not very successful as on both occasions the leaf seems to have picked up as much ink as usual.

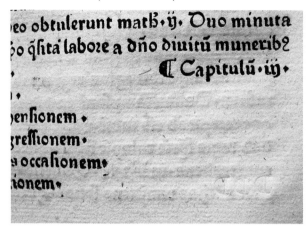

Figure 4.10. *Aurea Biblia,* 1476, page [a3v] with 35 lines of text. Blind impressions from three paragraph signs inserted as support in bottom right corner at 35-line position, next to the central margin. (University of Reading Library.)

Position of bearer lines

As the bearer lines are being added for support it would be expected to find them positioned as near to the foot of the type block area as possible so as to best maintain the balance of the platen. The majority of the single bearer lines (40 per cent) are inserted just beyond the type block, at the 36-line position with 20 per cent at the 35-line position, 17 per cent at the 34-line position, 13 per cent at the 33-line position, 6 per cent at the 32-line position and 4 per cent, i.e. three occasions, of a single bearer at the 37-line position. Where pairs of bearer lines were inserted the 36-line position is again the most used. 72 per cent of the double bearer lines are at the 35/36-line position, with 11 per cent at the 36/37-line position, and only one or two occurrences in the other line positions. There are no bearer lines positioned higher up the type block than the 31-line position.

If the typesetter was keeping the same skeleton of furniture in the forme for every conjugate pair of pages he set, one would expect to find the bearer lines being repeated in the same position through a single edition. Table 4.4 shows that this is broadly the case. The bearer lines do occur in almost the same line position within an edition, although there are one or two slightly wilder positions. There may be a chronological link with the positioning of the bearer lines in the earlier editions, as, up to 1475, they do not have any bearers inserted beyond the forme of 35 lines. The later editions have bearer lines in the 36- and occasionally the 37-line position. The pattern of the position of bearer lines is very different in the chancery folios from that found in the large folios.

Table 4.4. The line position of single- and double-bearer lines in Zainer's 34-line, chancery-folio, editions.

Title	Single bearer lines — Line position							Double bearer lines						
	32	33	34	35	36	37	Total	31/32	32 & 35	33/34	34/35	35/36	36/37	Total
De mysterio missae			2	4			6							
Historia Griseldis			2				2							
De claris mulieribus (Ger.)	5	5	1	2			13	1						1
De claris mulieribus (Lat.)		3	6	1			10							
Aurea Biblia, 1475									2					2
Aurea Biblia, 1476		2	2	2	14	2	22							
De horis canonicis				2			2							
Vocabularius Bibliae				5	7	1	13			1	2	25	5	33
Documenta moralis					8		8							
	5	10	13	16	29	3	76	1	2	1	2	25	5	36

NINE LARGER FOLIO EDITIONS

All Zainer's larger folio editions have at least one blind impression from bearer type. *Pro rata* there are fewer blind impressions in the large-folio editions than the chancery-folio editions – only 32 occurrences through nine editions (Table 4.5). The chancery folios averaged 6.5 blind impressions per edition and the larger folios averaged 3.5 blind impressions per edition.

Table 4.5. Number of occurrences of bearers being used in 9 royal/imperial/median-folio editions.

Number of occurrences	Number of editions
1	1
2	2
3	3
4	1
5	1
9	1
Total 32	9

The larger-folio editions, on royal, median or imperial paper, are all printed with two columns to a leaf. As was discussed in Chapter 2, the evidence from pages that Zainer printed crookedly shows that he printed these editions one leaf at a time.[37] This means he could have worked sequentially through the quires. If Zainer was working sequentially he would have had greater control of his copy-fitting and should not have had the problem of having to adjust the number of lines as he worked through the quires, as he often had to do with the chancery folios. When he came to the end of the text, if he found he was short of text to fill the column he could have left it short and added bearer lines if he felt them necessary.

Bearers are almost always found in Zainer's larger folios when one column has full number of lines and the other is short. Usually the left-hand column is set to the full number of lines, as one would expect being the first one to be set, and the second, right-hand, column runs short. There are only two occasions where this differs and the left-hand column is short. On one occurrence the left-hand column has 31 lines of text and 15 bearer

---

[37] The evidence for how many leaves he printed at a time with Zainer's one median-folio edition, the *Decameron*, is confusing. Unfortunately it has only been possible to examine two copies, and it has not been possible to build up enough evidence from these to come to any firm conclusions. However because the text was set in two columns of type to a page it has been included here with the other large-folio editions.

lines of text are added, and the other occasion the left-hand column has 44 lines and one line of sorts is added at the 50-line position to balance the forme. There is no indication from the content of the text why this might have occurred, such as an obvious beginning of a new section of text, and on these two occurrences it may just have been the result of poor copyfitting.

Material used for bearer lines

As with the chancery folios as seen in Table 4.1, the bearers in the royal/imperial folios are made up from sorts or lines of text matter as shown in Table 4.6. Sorts are only used to make up one-, two-, three- or four-line bearers and are used in 37 per cent of the total occurrences. Bearer lines from text make up the other 63 per cent of the occurrences. This is quite different from the chancery folios where bearer lines from sorts occur 71 per cent of the time and from text matter only 18 per cent of the time. In the large folios text is never used for the one- and two-line bearers, although one- and two-line bearers from text are found in the chancery folios. Both formats have three-line and one four-line bearers from both sorts and text. As with the chancery folios, all the remaining bearers in the large-folio editions over four lines come from text. Possible bibliographic

Table 4.6. Different material – either text matter or odd sorts – being used for bearers in 9 royal/imperial/median-folio editions.

Number of bearer lines	Number of occurrences	
	Text	Sorts
1		6
2		3
3	3	3
4	1	
6	1	
13	2	
15	1	
20	2	
22	1	
23	2	
25	2	
30	'1	
47	'1	
48	1	
50	2	
Total	20	12

clues that can sometimes be found in the content of the text are discussed later in this chapter in the section 'Bearer lines as evidence of printing practice'. There are no bearers from type-high wood in the large folios.

Number of bearer lines

The number of bearer lines inserted shows some correlation to the number of lines missing from the column. If the text is only a few lines short then only one or two lines are inserted. If the whole column is missing then a full, or almost full, column of bearer lines is inserted. An interesting example of a column of text being used as a bearer is found on page [ff8v] of *De planctu ecclesiae,* where the entire 59 lines of the right-hand column from page [ff9r] is used, complete with large 10-line woodcut initial and the headline, and with all the lines in the same position as in the original forme. Table 4.7 shows that single- and three-line bearers are the most used, each making up 21 per cent of the total. In all the examples given in Table 4.7 the bearers are added to one column to bring it up to

Table 4.7. Occurrences of the different number of bearer lines in the royal/imperial/median folios, related to the number of lines a leaf is short of the standard. (The figures in italics show the standard number of lines in the edition).

Number of bearer lines inserted	Number of lines short of standard																			
	51	*51*	*51*	*50*	*50*	*51*	*37*	*37*	*37*	*50*	*38*	*50*	*50*	*50*	*50*	*50*	*50*	*51*	*59*	
	3	**4**	**7**	**9**	**10**	**12**	**14**	**15**	**16**	**18**	**19**	**20**	**23**	**24**	**28**	**31**	**42**	**51**	**59**	**Total**
1	1	1	1		1		1		1											6
2						1		1								1				3
3					1	1						1		2	1					6
4				1																1
6					1															1
13											1									1
14																		1		1
15										1										1
20													1		1					2
22															1					1
23														1						1
25																1				1
30																	1			1
47						1														1
48																		1		1
50																		1		1
58																			1	1
Total	1	1	1	1	3	3	1	1	1	1	1	1	1	3	3	2	1	3	1	30

the full measure of the other on the leaf. There are two anomalies that are not included in this table; one arises on leaf [C7v] of *Quadragesimale*, 1475 and the other on leaf [n4v] of *De planctu ecclesiae*. They both have only one short left-hand column of text, one with 25 lines and the other with 12 lines. Bearer lines have been added to the right-hand column, but not to make up to the full number of lines of the usual text page. *Quadragesimale* has 25 bearer lines inserted in the right-hand column to balance the 25 lines of text, and *De planctu ecclesiae* has 13 bearer lines added to the left-hand column to balance its 12 lines of text. In both cases the text block, with its bearer type, is at the top of the forme. This would seem impossible to print in the usual manner as there is not a full forme of type to place under the press and keep the platen balanced. Perhaps the printer folded the sheet of paper in half so it would fit into the press, and then ran the forme, turned by 90°, with its short type block, under the platen (Figure 4.11). However no other evidence, such as extra impression of the top lines through both leaves, for this method has been found to support this theory, and this remains a puzzle.

Position of bearer lines

The bearer lines are all positioned within the area of the type block, and almost always, however many lines they comprise, are based at the foot of the type block. The only occasions where they do not sit on the bottom line are the two anomalies mentioned in the previous paragraph. This differs from the chancery folios where 48 per cent of the bearers had their base position at one or two lines beyond the type block. In the large folios, where multiple lines of type matter have been used, they are positioned as a block from the base line. There is one further difference from this, in the 1473 edition of *Rationale divinorum officiorum* on leaf [dd10r], where 23 bearer lines are spaced out down the column to fill the space of 50 lines of text. There is a block of 14 lines in the 1- to 14-line position, 2 lines at 24- & 25-line position, 2 lines at the 35- and 36-line position, 3 lines from 46- to 48-line position, and a further 2 lines at the 49- and 50-line position.

BEARER LINES AS EVIDENCE OF PRINTING PRACTICE

It was hoped that a close examination of Zainer's use of bearers might help throw light on aspects of his printing practice. Recording and analysing the number of lines of text by which a page is short, together with the number of bearer lines inserted, both aspects that might affect the balance of the platen, might help explain why Zainer used bearers. This method, of recording the number of lines that a page is short and where a bearer is inserted, can also be used to analyse the editions printed by other printers for comparison. Also by examining the content of the

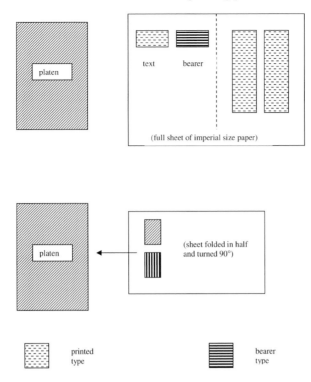

Figure 4.11. *De planctu ecclesiae,* leaf [n4v]. Diagram showing (top) sheet of imperial size paper with 12 lines of text printed at top of page. The platen would not be balanced if a forme, with the type just set at the top, was placed under the platen. The only way to keep the platen balanced would be to turn the forme and print by folding the sheet of paper and feeding it horizontally into the press (bottom). This is feasible and an expedient solution to the problem.

text matter that Zainer used for bearers, it might be possible to follow how he progressed through printing the quires of his editions. There is also a small anomaly of the use of sorts that do not seem to have ever been used in Zainer's printing – they might have been part of Zainer's fount or they might have come from outside sources.

Balancing the platen

From Experiment 4.1 it seems that removing two lines of text from a forme of 34 lines, i.e. just under six per cent, made no difference to the balance of the platen. Six lines of type needed to be removed before a clear tilt to the platen could be seen. Zainer's use of bearers in his large folios, and the later group of six chancery folios basically all fit in with this theory. There are only two occasions, both in royal folio, *Liber Bibliae*, where he inserted a bearer line when the type block was less than six lines short. However it is very different for the remainder, the earlier chancery folios. As shown in Figure 5.11, with these editions he was inserting lines of bearer type most often when his forme was short of between one and six lines. He uses bearers 76 per cent of the time when the text is short between one and six lines, compared with using bearers only 24 per cent of the time when the text is short by seven lines or more. It would seem, taking into account the results from the experiment, that he might not have needed to use bearers for any of these instances, and that his lines of (bearer) type did not have a role of supporting the platen on many occasions. Zainer's practice here seems to be in contradiction to the assumptions made by other scholars, that these lines of type are for support, and needs an explanation.

In an attempt to discover the causes of Zainer's practice the five chancery-folio editions where he has a much higher usage of bearers than any of the others were studied again. When each of these five was examined separately it became obvious that Zainer was inconsistent in his use of bearers through the quires of these editions; there seems to be no pattern linked with a need to balance the platen. In the Latin edition of *De claris mulieribus* bearers are only used in quires [a], [c], [f], [h], [i], [k] and [l]. Of the eleven uses of bearer lines in this edition, eight are when the type block is short of six lines or less, and on only three instances is the type block short by more than six lines. Further there are instances through this edition of pages with a short number of lines of text that do not have bearer lines inserted. For example page [h9r] has 32 lines of printed text and a bearer in the 35-line position while page [i3v] has 32 lines of printed text and no visible bearer. The same occurs in the German edition of *De claris mulieribus*; the bearers are only in quires [a], [b], [e], [k], [l], [o] and [p] despite there being other short pages in the edition where no bearers are visible. In *Documenta moralis* the bearers are only in quires [a], [d], [k] and [l] from the 28 quires that make up the edition, and the bearers are all inserted when the leaf is short by only two or three lines of text.

Even more extreme examples of his irregular use of bearers are found in the two editions that have the most number of occurrences of bearers, the *Aurea Biblia,* 1476, and the undated *Vocabularius Bibliae.* In *Aurea Biblia,* there are 21 instances where Zainer uses bearers. However they occur in only five of the 16 quires that make up this edition. Only in five of these instances might the use of support be thought necessary; where there are 12 printed lines of text on the page, and where there are 26-, 28-, 29- and 30-lines on a page. Then there are eleven instances of bearers on 31-line pages and five on 32-line pages, none of which should need support.

Further, there are a number of pages in the remaining quires with 32 lines that do not have bearers. Pages [c9v], [c10r], [e1v], [f9v], [f9r], [i7v] and [i8r] all have 32 lines of text and no bearer. No other pages with 31 printed lines have been found for comparison.

The case of *Vocabularius Bibliae* is very similar. There are 50 instances of bearers and they are found in only four of the 28 quires; quires [a], [b], [c] and [e]. The majority of them occur on pages where there are 32 lines of printed text – one would think them to be quite unnecessary for balancing the platen on these pages. There are other occasions through this edition with 32 lines of printed text on the page and no bearers. For example pages [x6r] and [A5v] both have 32 lines of text, and page [A6r] has 31 lines of text, and none have a bearer. There is no remarkable pattern to the position or the use of the bearer lines that might suggest why they were there. Throughout quire [c] there are almost always 32 lines to a page and 2 bearer lines are inserted in the 35- and 36-line position.

As these are all chancery folios, and Zainer is printing two conjugate pages at a time, one has to consider how many lines of text are in the conjugate page; perhaps that page had more lines than usual and had exacerbated the tilt of the platen. The pages were reconsidered, this time as conjugate pairs, and this did not seem to be the case.

There are one or two possible explanations why these 'unnecessary' bearers might be there. Having added the bearer lines in one forme, perhaps a forme where they were necessary, they then remained as part of the skeleton, when the text was changed, throughout the printing of all the pages in the quire (or of three quires in the case of *Vocabularius Bibliae*). It would have saved the time involved in removing the bearer lines and inserting a piece of furniture in their place in the forme. This would only have been a small saving, especially as the bearer lines would not have been needed to be replaced later in these quires. As their supporting use as bearers were not necessary these lines of type are essentially being used as furniture, filling out lines of space in the forme.

The fact that these bearers only occur within a limited number of quires suggests that there might be different workmen handling the different quires, one feeling the need for adding bearers and the other not. Evidence for more than one compositor working for Zainer around the same time as *Aurea Biblia*, *Documenta moralis* and *Vocabularius Bibliae* in 1476 has been found from textual analysis of the *Decameron*, printed c.1477. The conclusions of Bertelsmeier-Kierst can help as she found variant spellings, according to two different dialectal pronunciations of a number of words. One of the most marked features was the different use of consonants; the Bavarian 'b' and standard German 'p'. Bertelsmeier-Kierst found that the use of 'b' and 'p' fell clearly into quires; for 29 of the quires 'p' was dominant (used for 99 per cent of the time) and for 14

Table 4.8. The division in the quires of the *Decameron*, as noted by Bertelsmeier-Kierst, and based on dialectal spellings as characterised by the use of either b or p. She suggests that this gives evidence of at least two different compositors working on this edition.

	Words spelt with p rather than b	Words spelt with b rather than p
Quires	a,b,c,d,e,f,g,h,I,k,l,m,n,o,p,q, y,z,A,B, E,F,G, N,O,P V,X	r,s,t,v,x C,D,E, H,I,K,L,M, Q,R,S,T
Total	29 quires	14 quires

quires 'b' was dominant (used for 81 per cent of the time) and she states that Zainer had at least two compositors, of different language/dialect backgrounds, working on the *Decameron* for him (Table 4.8).[38]

Another explanation might be that, rather than two different workmen making up the formes, Zainer had more than one press, with one being in such a poor state that its platen was more than usually unstable. In this case bearer lines might have been needed where only a line or two of text was removed from the text block. Alternatively he may have started with a press with an unstable platen, on which the two *De claris mulieribus* editions were printed in 1473. As his workshop grew he could have added a new press and ran both side by side so that the later editions were printed partly on the older press and partly on the newer one.

There does seem to be a change in practice with his six, later, chancery-folio editions. These were printed around 1477 and 1478, and use a new typeface, Type 96G, with 41 or 42 lines of text to a page, but with almost the same text area. They show a much reduced incidence of use of bearers than any of the earlier editions, only one per edition when compared with an average of six per edition for the earlier chancery folios, and no occurrences of bearers when the page was less than six lines short of text. Perhaps this is another indication of a new, and more stable, press.

[38] Bertelsmeier-Kierst, p. 250. Other information in Akihiko Fujii, *Günther Zainers druckersprachliche Leistung* (Tübingen: Niemeyer, 2007) from an analysis of the typesetting in Günther Zainer's editions from 1471–1477 shows a similar division of labour, and at least two typesetters working, although with neither of these sets of findings do we know how many presses were in use. Fujii states (p. 115) that the evidence he found shows that the compositors were mostly working sequentially, and from looking at two of Günther's editions that were studied by Fujji, it is obvious that, although there might be a change of typesetter from one quire to the next, there is no break in the text. For example in Günther's German *Bible*, [1475/76] (ib00627000) there is a continuing sentence from the end of quire [f] to the beginning of quire[g] – with both quires (according to Fujii) being set by different people. This text would have been difficult to copyfit that accurately in advance. The edition looks to have been printed sequentially. It seems that perhaps Günther moved his compositors around to work on different texts at different times rather than on different sections of the same text at the same time.

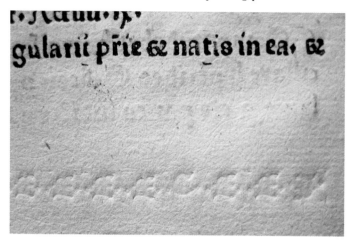

Figure 4.12. *Aurea Biblia,* 1476, with a bearer line comprising a row of .ff. and a single .C. at foot of leaf [c9v]. The character at right hand end is upside down. (University of Reading Library.)

Material used for bearers

Where Zainer has used odd sorts to make up his bearer lines on the face of it they do not give much information. However the different sorts used seems to fall into a chronological pattern of use. Lines of Ry have only been found in five editions, printed in 1473 and 1474; *De mysterio missae,* 29 May 1473, *De claris mulieribus* [*c.*1473] (both German and Latin editions), *Rationale divinorum officiorum,* 3 December 1473, *Liber Bibliae,* 9 April 1474. A printed paragraph mark, ¶, has only been found in three editions. It is found in the dated edition *Aurea Biblia,* 1476, and two undated editions, *Vocabularius Bibliae* [*c.*1476], *De horis canonicis* [*c.*1476]. As the use of ¶ as a bearer is restricted to just these three editions it suggests that the two undated editions may have been printed around the same time as the dated one.

Further evidence that might help in dating editions comes from some other lines of sorts. Two bearer lines comprising a unusual combination of a row of C's with an .ff. character and a second line made up from a row of .ff. and a single C. are used through the edition of *Aurea Biblia,* dated June 1476 (Figure 4.12).[39] They are used twice in the first and third quires, and ten times in the last quire of this edition. A combination of the two sorts has been found in a shorter line as bearer on leaf [d4r], RH

---

[39] The .ff. is not a standard character in the fount but was used by Zainer when printing *De planctu ecclesiae.* Cappelli, *Dizionario,* suggests that the .ff. could be used as an abbreviation for referring to the legal book, Justinian's *Pandectae digestum.*

column, of the royal-folio, 1476 edition, *Quadragesimale*. Apart from these two dated editions they are also used once as bearer lines in the fourth quire in the undated edition *Documenta moralis*. Combined with C in exactly the same formation implies that the lines used in the two chancery-folio editions are identical, and therefore that the two editions could have been printed at the same time. If so, this would help give a firmer date for the latter edition, *Documenta moralis*.

Where several lines of (continuous) text have been used for the bearer lines it is sometimes possible to discover the original use of the lines. The lines of text being used for bearers had to have been set already as part of the edition. For the bibliographer this is helpful evidence as to which leaf has been printed first, assuming that the type would have been used for printing before being used as a bearer. It can also give an indication of how the printer approached setting his type and copy fitting: whether he had enough type to set the text for the entire quire at once for instance.

Chancery folios

Where the text can be read, with Zainer's chancery folios, both the bearer lines and the leaf where they originated have always been found in the same quire. The bearer lines have come from a bifolium located further out in the quire than the leaf where they are used as bearers. This indicates that Zainer was printing his outermost bifolia first and progressing inwards to the centre of his quires (Figure 4.13).

De adhaerendo Deo, [1473] – 5-bifolia quire [c]; bearer lines on [c7v] come from [c9v]
Summa, 1474 – 5-bifolia quire [b]; bearer lines on [b3r] come from [b2v]
Vocabularius Bibliae, [1476] – 5-bifolia quire [a]; bearer lines on [a7r] come from [a3r]
Documenta moralis, [1476] – 5-bilfolia quire [a]; bearer lines on [a2v] come from [a10v]

The implications of this are that either Zainer had enough type to set the entire quire at once, or he 'cast-off' the copy and estimated how the text would fit. This evidence links with the information about Zainer's copyfitting, discussed in Chapter 2, of some of the examples found of his adjusting the number of lines in the centre bifolium of his quires. It is most likely that he did not have enough type to set the text for an entire quire at one time. His increased number of adjustments to the number of lines to a page as he worked towards the centre of the quire, suggests someone who had enough type perhaps to set the text for both sides of one or two sheets at one time, but no more, and then distribute and reset the type for the next sheets.

Other examples show that, as well as the text for bearers coming from a

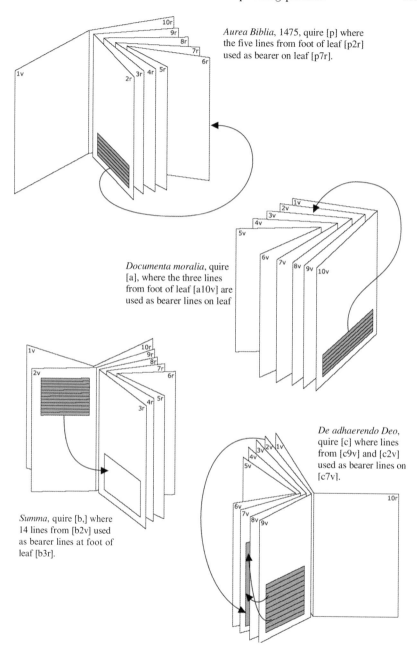

Aurea Biblia, 1475, quire [p] where the five lines from foot of leaf [p2r] used as bearer on leaf [p7r].

Documenta moralia, quire [a], where the three lines from foot of leaf [a10v] are used as bearer lines on leaf

De adhaerendo Deo, quire [c] where lines from [c9v] and [c2v] used as bearer lines on [c7v].

Summa, quire [b,] where 14 lines from [b2v] used as bearer lines at foot of leaf [b3r].

Figure 4.13. Diagrams showing various movements of lines of text to provide bearers in four different chancery-folio editions.

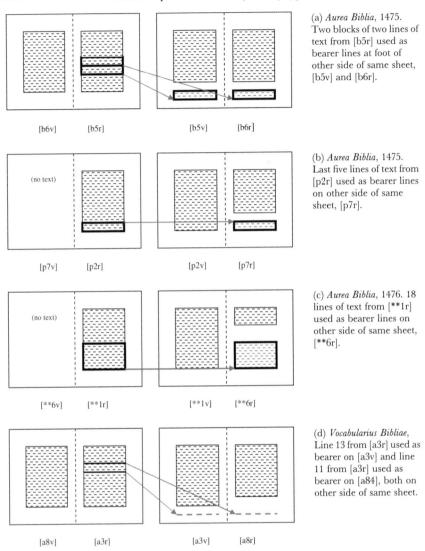

(a) *Aurea Biblia*, 1475.
Two blocks of two lines of
text from [b5r] used as
bearer lines at foot of
other side of same sheet,
[b5v] and [b6r].

(b) *Aurea Biblia*, 1475.
Last five lines of text from
[p2r] used as bearer lines
on other side of same
sheet, [p7r].

(c) *Aurea Biblia*, 1476. 18
lines of text from [**1r]
used as bearer lines on
other side of same sheet,
[**6r].

(d) *Vocabularius Bibliae*,
Line 13 from [a3r] used as
bearer on [a3v] and line
11 from [a3r] used as
bearer on [a84], both on
other side of same sheet.

Figure 4.14. Diagrams of chancery-folio editions showing the lines of type used for bearers that have come from the other side of the same sheet, the outer side, which has just been printed.

bifolium further out in the quire, the text used for bearers had come from the other side of the same bifolium, the side that had just been printed (see Figure 4.14).

Aurea Biblia, 1475 – 5-bifolia quire [b]; bearer lines on [b5v] come from
[b6r],
— 4-bifolia quire [p]; bearer lines on [p7r] come from [p2r]
Aurea Biblia, 1476 – 3-bifolia quire [**]; bearer lines on [**6r] come from
[**1r]
Vocabularius Bibliae, [1476] – 5-bifolia quire [a]; bearer lines on [a3v] come
from [a3r]
— bearer lines on [a8r] come from [a3r]

As discussed in Chapter 2, it seems, from the evidence of set-off on the
pages, that Zainer was working to the same method described by Moxon
in the seventeenth century, where he would have been printing the first
side of the sheet of paper in the morning and printing the reiteration in the
afternoon while the paper was still damp.[40] Working the reiteration while
the sheet was still damp was important as it saved having to re-damp the
stack of sheets. This would mean that the lines of text being used as
bearers would have had to be removed from the forme that had just been
printed and inserted immediately into the forme about to be printed. The
forme for the reiteration was not made up and ready to go straight on the
press; it was still waiting for bearer lines to be added. This suggests that he
was working with just one chase holding the forme for this edition, and is
a further indication, along with his adherence to fixed measures discussed
in Chapter 2 under 'Skeletons' that he might have been keeping the same
skeleton of furniture from one forme to the next.

Evidence about how some other printers progressed in working
through an edition can be found from other scholars. Schmidt found
from the evidence of bearers in Anton Sorg's printing of Ambrosius,
Expositio evangelii, 1476, that Sorg took type for bearers from a bifolium
further out in a quire, from further within in a quire and from other quires
altogether.[41] There seems to be no regular pattern to his method of
working, and perhaps he was setting type for more than one quire at one
time. Harris found with Aldus in 1499 that the bearer lines were coming
from the same quire, the previous quire, a quire right at the end of the
edition to be used in a quire at the beginning of the edition, and from
another edition altogether. He found none coming from the other side of
the same leaf.[42] Harris suggests that different quires of this edition were
being worked on by different workmen simultaneously, which could
explain the leaps that the lines of type made between quires when being

---

[40] Moxon, p. 297, described printing the white paper, turning the heap, and printing the
reiteration, as one continuing operation. On p. 306 he described printing the reiteration while the
ink on the first side is still wet.

[41] Schmidt, 'Technische', pp. 11–12.

[42] Harris, 'Blind impressions', see Appendix, pp. 136–146 for where bearer lines were found and
their origins.

used as text, and then being used as bearers.[43] Both these examples seem to show a difference in approach from Zainer, and might suggest that he was working with a smaller printshop and fewer compositors and press-men than the others. To do a full comparison with the methods of other printers is beyond the scope of this study, however the discoveries so far do suggest a line of enquiry for the future.

Royal, median and imperial folios

With the large folios, where the impression can be read and the source located, the text almost always comes from a preceding page to the one being printed, either immediately before or from the page before that. Apart from *Liber Bibliae*, where the bearer comes from a previous leaf, the lines of type are taken from the recto side to be inserted as bearer lines in the verso of the same leaf, hardly allowing time for the ink to dry (some examples are shown at Figure 4.15). This is similar to some of the bearers in the chancery folios where a quick removal of text from one forme to the next was found. This is another indication, along with the regular findings of the crooked printing of text areas on conjugate pages discussed in Chapter 2, that Zainer was working sequentially through his large-folio quires.

Liber Bibliae, 1474 – bearer on [D12r] comes from the recto of the previous leaf [D11r].

De planctu ecclesiae, 1474 – bearer on [ff8v] comes from previous side of same leaf [ff8r]

Sermones de sanctis, 1475 – bearer on [b8v] comes from previous side of same leaf [b8r]

Rationale divinorum officiorum, 1475 – bearer on [a2v] comes from previous side of same leaf [a2r]

Quadragesimale, 1475 – bearer on [C9v] comes from previous side of same leaf [C9r]

Quadragesimale, 1476 – bearer on [x7v] comes from previous side of same leaf [x7r]

 – bearer on [y8v] comes from previous side of same leaf [y8r]

Decameron [*c*.1477] – bearer on [Q5v] comes from previous side of same leaf [Q5r]

However there is one anomaly in the 1476 edition of *Quadragesimale* where the bearer lines on [G7v] comes from the recto of the following leaf [G8r], implying that page [G8r] had been printed before [G7v]. This example throws up a number of possibilities as to how it came about. This could indicate that Zainer had enough type to set the text for two royal-folio

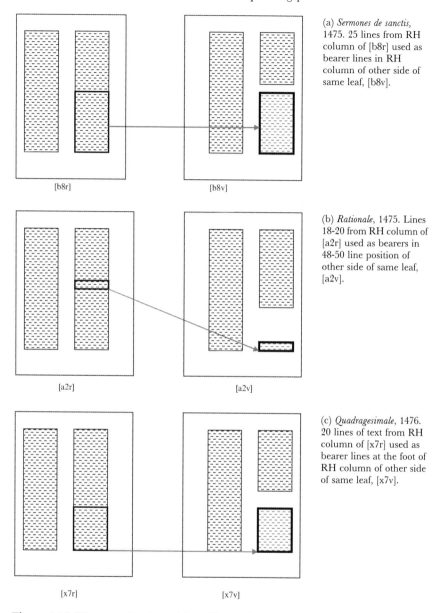

(a) *Sermones de sanctis,* 1475. 25 lines from RH column of [b8r] used as bearer lines in RH column of other side of same leaf, [b8v].

(b) *Rationale,* 1475. Lines 18-20 from RH column of [a2r] used as bearers in 48-50 line position of other side of same leaf, [a2v].

(c) *Quadragesimale,* 1476. 20 lines of text from RH column of [x7r] used as bearer lines at the foot of RH column of other side of same leaf, [x7v].

Figure 4.15. Diagrams showing origins of bearer lines in some royal folios.

pages at a time, and that he might have been operating more than one press, with more than one compositor, and was not forced by lack of type to working in strict progression. However quire [G] is the last quire of the edition and has 10 leaves. Perhaps, because Zainer had almost reached the end of printing all the text, he may have been able to copyfit the text for the last few pages with some confidence, and so set the text for [G8r] before [G7v].[44]

All these examples show how near were the leaves with the bearer lines to the leaves where they were inserted. They were in the forme of the page that had just been printed, in process of being dismantled, and so could be easily lifted and inserted into the forme for the new page as bearer type. Apart from the one occasion where the bearer type came from a page after the one where it was inserted, all these uses of bearers show that Zainer was printing his large-folio editions seriatim, working from beginning to end, printing one side of a one page at a time.

Schmidt found a much bigger distance between where the lines of type had been used as text and where they were used as bearers and gives as example Eggestein's printing of Lombardus, *Sententiarum* [*c*.1471]. He found that the bearer lines inserted on the last leaf of Book 3 came from leaf 126 in Book 2, and that the bearer lines at the end of Book 4 came from the last leaf of Book 3, and he suggests that this indicates that all three parts of the book were being printed at the same time.[45] This is indication of a difference in approach to use of bearers between Zainer and another printer, and evidence of different printing practices in the printshop.

Evidence for type handling

Another point that can sometimes be deduced from reading the blind impressions is how the compositor physically handled his type. The order in which the lines are inserted in the forme to be used as bearers is not always the same as when they stood to be printed as text. An example of transporting the lines to be used for bearers, just a few lines at a time, can be seen in one copy of *De adhaerendo Deo* (illustrated at Figure 4.1). The text is clear enough to detect its source, [c2r/9v], and also to see how the text from [c2r/9v] was picked up and placed on [c7v]. The top five lines of the blind impressed section came from the bottom five lines of [c9v], lines 29–33. The next nine lines of the blind impressed section come from the next nine lines up on [c9v], lines 17–25. The last eight blind impressed lines come from lines 13–20 of [c2r] (Figure 4.16). On this occasion the compositor was not working from one forme directly to the next. There was one bifolium in between the two; between where the lines were used

---

[44] In quire [G] the last page [G10v] is blank, so Zainer only had the remaining text for [G8r], [G8v], [G9r], [G9v] and [G10r] to set/copyfit, and this edition is a reprint of his 1475 edition.

[45] Schmidt, 'Untersuchungen', p. 24. Efforts were made to check Schmidt's findings against the Bodleian copy of *Sententiarum*. Unfortunately only the bearer lines on the last leaf were visible. Also the quiring given in the Bodleian catalogue does not match Schmidt's collational formula and it was impossible to translate Schmidt's leaf 126 into a quire reference.

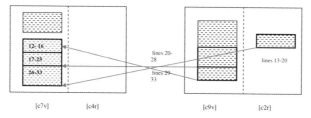

Figure 4.16. *De adhaerendo Deo*, [c.1473]. Diagram showing from where text lines on [c9v] and [c2r] are taken to be used as bearer lines on a different leaf in the same quire, [c7v].

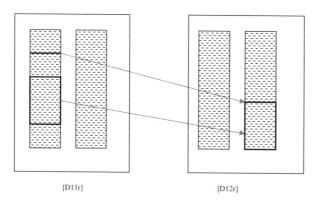

Figure 4.17. Diagram showing where 23 text lines, 18–39 plus line 10, from [D11r] were used as bearer lines on the following leaf of same quire [D12r] in *Liber Bibliae*.

as text, and where they were used as bearers. It also shows that he was comfortable picking up and moving blocks of type matter of between five and nine lines at one time.[46]

Another example of type handling can be seen in *Liber Bibliae*. This edition has two columns of 50 lines of text and on page [D12r] the RH column has only 27 lines of text. The remaining 23 lines (line position 28–50) are bearer type taken from the LH column of the previous leaf in the quire [D11r]. Twenty-one lines of text (lines 18–38) were moved as one block from [D11r] and inserted, and then he found he was still short of a line, so line 10 of text from [D11r] was placed in line position 50 at the foot of [D12r] (see diagram at Figure 4.17).

---

[46] Lines of type are tricky to move. They need support at the head and foot from thin strips of wood, and to be tightly squeezed on all sides when being lifted. One line is easy, but more than five or six lines, need more strength in the fingers, depending on the length of the line and size of hands. Moving blocks of set type around is always easier if the type has just been cleaned as the residual liquid helps the type letters stick to each other. The compositor might also have used page cord to tie the set lines of type more securely for moving. Moxon describes tying up the page of type on a galley with page-cord on pp. 219–220, but we have no knowledge of how early this was used.

Table 4.9. Occurrences of bearer lines in some chancery-folio editions by other printers showing how often they were inserted, and by how many lines a page was short of the standard.

Chancery-folio editions	Standard no. of lines	3	4	5	6	7	8	10	12	13	17	21	24	26	38	40	Occurrences of lines on a page that are less than standard text area
						Number of lines short of standard											
Adolf Rusch																	
De vita solitaris	34				1												1
Georg Reyser																	
Manuale	33											1					1
Didascalicon	33						1			1							2
Expositio	35			1							1						2
Heinrich Knoblochtzer																	
Sermones dominicales	38									1					1		2
Günther Zainer																	
Etymologiae	38	1							1								2
Legenda aurea	44					1											1
Historia Griseldis	35		1														1
Belial	35			1						1							2
Johann Schüssler																	
Summa de potestate	35							1						1			2
Johann Bämler																	
Belial	30					1											1
Von dem Ursprung	28						1										1
Anton Sorg																	
De oculo murali	40							1									1
Praeceptorium divinae legis	39										1						1
Quinquaginta	38												1				1
Expositio	40															1	1
(SS U & A) Speculum	52								1			1	1				3
Konrad Dinckmut																	
Erklärung der zwölf Artikel	37							1									1
Michael Wenssler																	
De consolatione philosophiae	30											1					1
Fratres Vitae Communis																	
Casus breves	30														1		1
Total		1	1	2	1	2	2	3	2	3	2	3	2	1	2	1	28

Table 4.10. Occurrences of bearer lines in median-, royal and imperial-folio editions by some other printers, showing how often they were inserted and by how many lines a page was short of standard.

Median-, royal- and imperial-folio editions

Title/printer	Standard no. of lines	Number of lines short of the standard												
		3	4	6	12	14	19	21	23	33	35	38	40	
Johann Mentelin														
Biblia germanica	61				1									1
Mariale	61												1	1
Heinrich Eggestein														
Sententiarium	42										1			1
Adolf Rusch														
Decretum	56		1											1
Aggregator . . .	55							1						1
Günther Zainer														
Rationale	50											1		1
Johann Schüssler														
Antiquitates judaicae	50	1		1										2
Anton Sorg														
Speculum	52									1				1
Sensenschmidt														
Flores	40												1	1
Friburger, Gering & Crantz														
Sermones	36			1										1
Rationale	46								1					1
Michael Greyff														
Quadragesimale	51					1								1
Praeceptorium	43						1							1
Total		1	1	2	1	1	1	1	1	1	1	1	2	14

OTHER PRINTERS WITH BEARERS

Tables 4.9 and 4.10 list the use of bearers by some other printers. This is not an exhaustive list, as, to document all the various uses of bearers by other printers is beyond the scope of this book. The first place to look was in copies of editions where other scholars had found bearers being used. It is almost never possible to look at the same copy of an edition that was examined by others however these figures of bearer use by other printers are offered here for a gentle comparison. They seem to suggest, with regard to the number of lines a page of text is short, that their purpose is most likely to be one of support.

The examples given by Harris in *Hypnerotomachia Poliphili* all seem to be about support. Many of the examples are where the lines of text narrow to a *cul-de-lampe* shape on the page, ending with a line of only one or two characters or a single flower. These single-character lines are very vulnerable during printing, as they have to take the full weight of the impression by themselves. They are liable to dig heavily into the paper, and also wear very quickly. The addition of bearer lines here is also, I suggest, to spread the impression rather than just to balance the platen.

Tables 4.9. and 4.10 seem to show that other printers used bearers far less frequently than Zainer. The other printers are using bearers only once or twice per edition compared with Zainer's average of four to six times. Where they did use bearers they occur in more necessary positions, i.e. where the page is short of six or more lines of text, and their most obvious use is to provide support to stop the platen tilting. The only printer found so far who inserted a bearer when the page was only three or five lines short was Johann's brother Günther. None of the other printers inserted bearer lines, as Johann did, when the text page was only one or two lines short as shown in Table 4.3.

This suggests that Zainer's practice of keeping lines of type in the forme, where its role seems to be more as furniture than providing support, is particular to him. He did not do this with every edition, but the use of bearer lines, where the page was less than six lines short of the standard, has been found in 10 of his chancery-folio editions, between 1473 and 1476 and in one royal folio in 1474. After 1476 all his uses of bearers are when the text page is short by more than six lines. As mentioned above this could be due to different workmen or different presses, but it seems to be a practice unique to Zainer during his first years.

5 CLOTH IMPRESSIONS

Another series of markings are found on the leaves of Zainer's editions. They look as though they have been made by fabric having been impressed onto the paper. At least one example has been noted in almost every copy of every edition that has been looked at for this research.[1] The fact that they are so common in Zainer's editions suggests that they would be worth investigating to see if their presence carried any indication of Zainer's methods.

THE APPEARANCE OF THE CLOTH IMPRESSION MARKS

The marks are blind impressions on the paper of the book. The weave of cloth is sometimes crisply visible and, for the purposes of this work, it will be assumed that the marks have indeed been made by a cloth. Sometimes, along with the impression mark, there is a cloth-shaped stain on the paper (Figure 5.1) and sometimes there is only a stain but no impression mark.

The impression marks are not always easily visible, and a raking light is much more use for spotting a mark than a direct, bright light above. Sometimes a particular copy has been washed and/or rebound and all evidence of marks that might have been there have vanished. The best copies for finding impression marks are those that are as close as possible to their contemporary state and even better if the binding has come a little loose so one can see whether the impression mark goes over the centrefold of the sheet.

There is variation in the size and the shape of the marks. They are usually somewhat larger than the text area, although they may well be quite unrelated to the text area. The edges of the cloth are usually visible beyond the text area and to varying distances. Some marks are made by cloths that go only a few millimetres beyond the text, sometimes they just miss a line or two or an edge of the text, and others go right off the edge of the leaf. Sometimes they go across the inter-columnar margin and into the outer margins (Figure 5.2).

The depth of the impression can vary; sometimes it is clear and deeply impressed, and other times it is much more difficult to discern. Sometimes there is only a slight cockling of the paper, or more of a stretch of the

---

[1] The only editions where they have not been found are in copies that have probably been 'washed' or in editions with a very small number of leaves, such as a single-quire booklet with only ten leaves (five chancery-folio sheets). An edition with only a few leaves could easily escape having a leaf with an impression mark (see occurrence rates in Table 5.2).

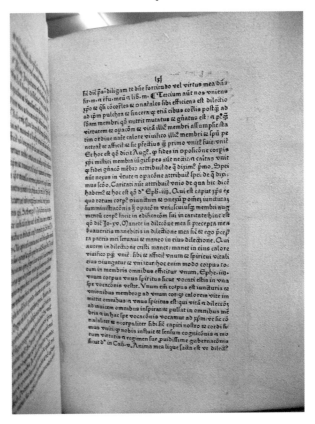

Figure 5.1. Cloth-shaped stain mark on [g5r] of Albertus Magnus, *Summa de eucharistiae sacramento*, 1474. (Ulm Stadtbibliothek.)

paper than a true cloth impression. Sometimes the impression shows ragged edges with fraying threads of varying lengths, or an edge with simple blanket stitching, or occasionally a selvedge[2] (Figures 5.3 and 5.4). For the chancery folios, the cloth impressions are spread over two conjugate leaves but in the royal/imperial folios the impressions are only on one leaf (Figure 5.5). Some of the royal/imperial-folio sheets do have two cloth impressions, one on each conjugate leaf, but this is less common. The marks usually vary somewhat in shape, so apparently are made by different cloths. Sometimes they are impressed on the same side of the sheet and sometimes on opposite sides. For example one of the BSB copies of *Quadragesimale* had cloth marks on conjugate leaves [*5/*6],

---

[2] The edges are not 'hemmed'. Hemming involves folding over the raw edge to enclose the loose threads at the edge, which gives a double or triple layer of cloth, and then sewing. These edges have been blanket stitched over the raw edges of a single layer of fabric.

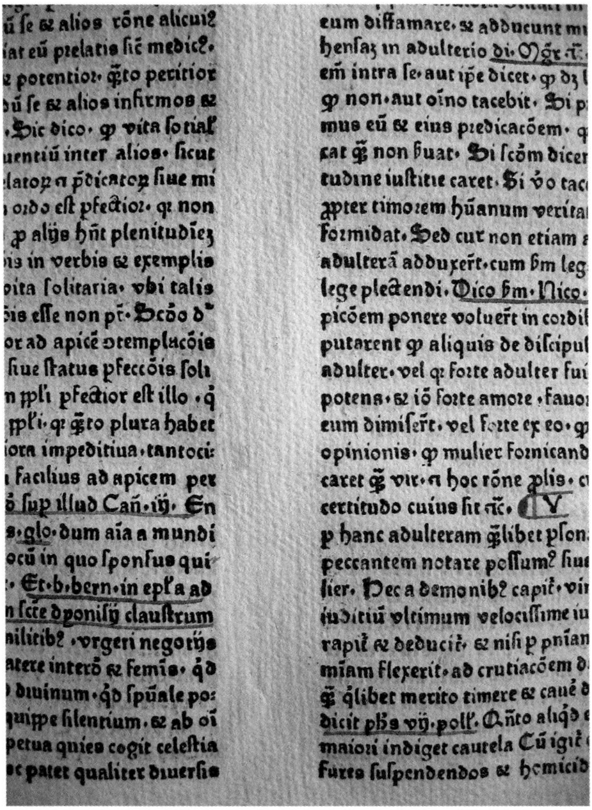

Figure 5.2. Weave pattern from impressed cloth visible in inter-columnar margin of Gritsch, *Quadragesimale*, [14]76. (Ulm Stadtbibliothek.)

both impressed on the outer side of the leaf (and the marks made by different cloths). However conjugate leaves [i1/i10] in the same copy had marks impressed on different sides of the paper.[3]

THE NATURE OF THE CLOTHS

From observations of the cloth marks, it could be seen that the cloths had varied both in their size and quality. More than one cloth was used to make the marks, and more than one for each copy and for the print run of each sheet, but it has not been possible to count the number of different cloths used. The general appearance suggests that many different cloths were being used. The size of the various cloths varies only slightly, they are almost all smaller than the sheet of paper.

[3] *BSB-Ink* G-392, shelfmark 2° Inc.c.a.486a.

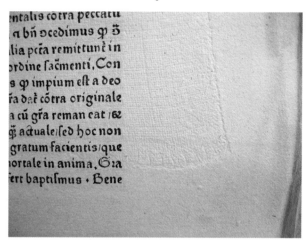

Figure 5.3. Cloth impression on [o4r] in Albertus Magnus, *Summa de eucharistiae sacramento*, 1474, showing neat blanket stitching over an unfolded edge at foot of cloth and selvedge edge to the right. (Ulm Stadtbibliothek.)

Some have a selvedge edge; some very occasionally have two selvedge edges, which means they have come from quite a narrow strip of woven cloth. Many have one or two raw edges. Sometimes the edges have frayed – perhaps from repeated use – occasionally with long, loose threads, up to two or three centimetres long, straggling out from the main piece of cloth. At other times one edge is blanket stitched, perhaps to reduce the fraying. The impressions that show a selvedge or a stitched edge are found least frequently. When recording the cloth impressions, it was not realised at the time whether the kind of edges shown by the cloths might have been of significance. Only those with stitched edges were noted, but those with selvedge edges were not. Further research on this needs to be done to determine the occurrence rate of cloths with selvedge or stitched edges for all the editions recorded. However, an example of the occurrence rates for stitched edges can be seen in five of the copies of *Summa* which were looked at and recorded. 75 cloth impressions were noted in total and only three of these showed a stitched edge.[4] The weave and thread count varies for cloths within a copy. The coarsest, and most prominent because it was much coarser than other cloths, was approximately six threads per centimetre (Figure 5.6). Other cloths had a much finer weave with up to twelve or fifteen threads per centimetre. This variety in the thread count suggests that the cloths came from a variety of sources.

In the opinion of Dr Ruth Barnes, fabric expert at the Ashmolean

---

[4] It is not clear that the presence of stitched or selvedge edges are significant in any way, so these comments are just for the record.

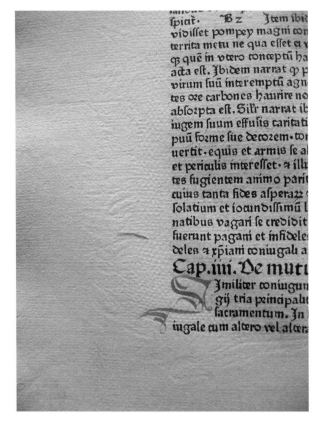

Figure 5.4. Long frayed edges on a cloth impression mark on [k4v] of Gallensis, *Summa collationum*, 1481. (Gutenberg-Bibliothek Mainz.)

Museum in Oxford, the cloths were all made from linen, because the threads in the imprints are straight and show a crisp definition.[5] She looked at cloth impressions in the Bodleian copies of *Summa* and *Rationale* (1473).[6] The impressions in these editions showed a cloth with a simple weave pattern and she suggested the cloths had not come from rags because the threads, as could be seen in the impressions, were generally quite strong rather than worn; rather she suggested they might have come from off-cuts of fabric. She felt that, from the impression marks she had seen, the cloths had probably been deliberately made up, perhaps from off-cuts, for their purpose.

[5] Date of consultation 24 January 2006. My thanks to Ruth Barnes for her help and expertise. To be absolutely sure of this a microscopic analysis of the imprint would need to be done.

[6] *Bod-inc.* A-149, shelfmark Auct. Q sup.2.25 and *Bod-inc.* D-183, shelfmark Auct. 5 Q 2.21. These editions were chosen because they showed good, clear impression marks, and may not be representative of the whole range of different marks.

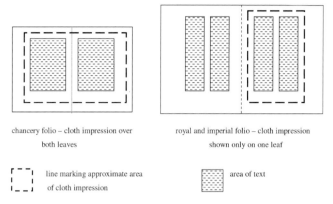

chancery folio – cloth impression over   royal and imperial folio – cloth impression
both leaves   shown only on one leaf

┌ ─ ─ ┐   line marking approximate area   ▦   area of text
│   │
└ ─ ─ ┘   of cloth impression

Figure 5.5. Diagram showing approximate position of cloth impression on chancery- and royal imperial-folio leaves.

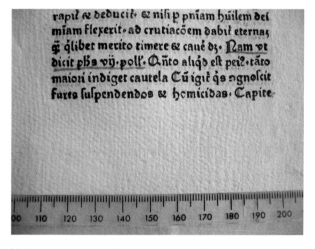

Figure 5.6. Cloth impression mark showing coarse thread count on Gritsch, *Quadragesimale*, [14]76. (Ulm Stadtbibliothek.)

HOW THE CLOTH IMPRESSIONS MIGHT HAVE BEEN MADE

As part of the printing process

Writing at the turn of the twentieth century, Adolf Schmidt had noticed the cloth marks in books printed by Johann Zainer.[7] Schmidt postulated that they had been made as part of the printing process. He suggested this because the impression marks so closely follow the printing area, usually

---

[7] Schmidt, 'Untersuchungen', p. 59.

being only just a bit bigger than the text block. He also suggested that they were made from the frisket covering and that a method of covering the frisket, by stitching it to hold it in place, could have caused the impression marks on the printed pages.[8]

Having offered this as proof that the cloth marks were part of the printing process, Schmidt extended his argument by using it as a basis for another theory. The fact that the cloth marks covered two pages of text in Zainer's chancery folios and one page of text in his royal/imperial folios, and given that he considered the impression marks to be part of the printing process, lead him to deduce that Zainer printed his chancery folios two pages at a time, and the royal/imperial folios one page at a time.[9]

If the stitch marks were to come from a stitched frisket one would expect them to show up all the way round. The stitching that has been observed as part of these cloth impression marks does not go all round the edge of the mark. It has only ever been noted by this author along one side of the cloth impression mark. It seems unlikely that the marks were caused by the stitching on the frisket. During the printing process it should be impossible for any part of the frisket covering to be under pressure and so make an impressed mark. However it was thought worthwhile to explore this angle a little further.

Descriptions of early printing practice were sought to see if they mention a cloth being used as part of the printing process that might substantiate Schmidt's theory. An early description of printing given in *De la vicissitude ou varieté de chose en l'univers*, published in Paris in 1579, and later translated into English in 1594, mentioned a 'moyst linnen cloth' being placed on the tympan 'to keepe the leafe from mackling'.[10] Scrutiny of Moxon, writing almost one hundred years later, reveals his discussion on printing the second side of a sheet, the reiteration.[11] He described using a damp cloth when printing the reiteration of a sheet to help prevent set-off onto the tympan from the newly-printed first side, and then the set-off itself being off-set onto the side being printed. He

---

[8] Schmidt does not quote Moxon although he may have known of his writing. Moxon, p. 278, describes covering the tympan and frisket with vellum. When covering the tympan, the stretched, damped skin is held in place with nails, but as the frisket is made of iron, nails cannot be used to hold it tight, so the skin is stitched in position round the frame.

[9] Other evidence, discussed in Chapter 2, indicates that this probably was Zainer's method of printing – however Schmidt's reasoning behind his argument here might not be correct.

[10] Louis Leroy, *Of the interchangeable course, or variety of things in the whole wide world*, tr. Robert Ashley (London: C. Yetsweirt, 1594) ff. 21v–22r). This is perhaps the first mention of a cloth being used as part of the printing process. For the meaning of the word 'mackling' *The Oxford English Dictionary* states that the word comes from the Latin verb *maculare*, to spot or stain, now generally only existing as its opposite 'immaculate'. German uses the word 'die Makulatur' for waste paper or rubbish.

[11] Moxon, pp. 306–307.

advised pasting a cloth onto the tympan, roughly larger than the text area, instead of a sheet of wastepaper, as a protective tympan sheet. When the cloth became dirty from a build up of ink it could be removed and rinsed out in lye to clean it.

Taking his information from Moxon, Gaskell also mentions the use of a tympan cloth when describing the procedure of printing the reiteration. He states 'the tympan sheet, no longer needed as a guide to the alignment of the sheets, was replaced by a linen cloth, which was less likely than paper to take set-off (ink mark) from the impressions of the first forme; but if set-off did occur and threatened to set back and spoil subsequent impressions of the first forme, the tympan cloth could be rubbed over with lye to clean it.'[12]

Perhaps the cloth impression marks came from tympan cloths rather than from a hem-stitched frisket as suggested by Schmidt. If this were the case then Schmidt's thought of the cloth marks giving evidence for one page or two being printed at a time still applies. As long as the cloth marks are linked with the printing process this will be the case.

As part of the paper damping process

Alfred Schulte, paper historian at the Gutenberg Museum in the 1930s, also wrote about the cloth impressions found in Zainer's editions, suggesting that the marks were made when the sheets of paper were being damped.[13] Throughout the hand-press period paper was damped before printing, although it is not known what precise method was used for this damping process in the fifteenth century. Schulte discounted the idea that the marks were made as part of the papermaking process because the cloths (or, more likely at that time, felts) would then have been larger than the paper, not smaller. He noticed that the stitching on the cloths, where visible, was only through a single layer of fabric. A hem with a double layer of fabric would have left too deep an impression, and he suggests that the cloths were specially 'hemmed' simply so as not to leave too heavy a mark. Schulte states that wet cloths were interleaved with the sheets of paper and the whole pile left under a weight to dampen. As an historical reference for this paper-damping method Schulte suggested that a hint might be found in Gessner's manual of 1740, where the use of cloths by copperplate printers was described. He quoted Gessner about the need to wash the cloths to remove size picked up from the paper and also about the need to keep the damping vat uncontaminated. This does not seem to be a very helpful reference as there is no

---

[12] Gaskell, *Bibliography*, p. 131.

[13] Alfred Schulte, 'Über das Feuchten des Papiers mit nassen Tüchern bei Johann Zainer und einigen anderen Frühdruckern', *Gutenberg-Jahrbuch*, 66 (1941), pp. 19–22.

actual mention of paper being damped with cloths, only a passing mention that copper printers had to rinse out their cloths.[14]

Other sources were sought to find if there was any historical evidence to support Schulte's theory. Moxon, writing in the seventeenth century, was not much help because he described an alternative damping practice, dragging folded quires (25 sheets) of paper through a trough of water and then stacking them flat, interleaved with a dry quire, until all the paper needed for the job had been wetted. A board was placed on top and then a weight, and the whole pile left overnight ready to be printed the next morning.[15] In 1793 Kircher described the process similarly but advised turning the pile every day for 4 to 5 days before use.[16] He added a caveat that care must be taken not to leave it too long in summer when the weather is warmer in case the paper starts to go mouldy.[17] Neither of these sources mentions a cloth anywhere as part of the damping process.

However an article by Johan Gerritsen about the author Viglius's visit to Froben's Basel printshop in 1534, where he described the printing process in a letter to a friend, included the phrase that '[the pressman] must wet . . . the paper in order that it shall more easily receive the impressed letters, by means of some interposed dampened linen cloths . . .'.[18] He did not give a more detailed description, but this is a categorical statement that the paper was damped by using cloths in the early sixteenth century. Perhaps this sixteenth-century method was a process continued from sixty years earlier; if so it would just be one of many long-lived practices.

Other processes that might have caused the marks

Papermaking

When paper is being made the newly couched sheets are stacked in a pile interleaved with papermakers' 'felts' and the pile is then put under immense pressure to remove the surplus water. It could be that the marks seen on Zainer's pages came from this first heavy pressing, depending on what kind of material was being used as a 'felt'. Felt had

---

[14] C. F. Gessner, *Die so nöthig als nützliche Buchdruckerkunst und Schriftgiesserey* (Leipzig, 1740/41). Schulte's footnote cites looking under the key words *Tücher, Papierfeuchten, Feuchtevass*, amongst others. So far, despite searching under all the key words that Schulte suggests, it has not been possible to verify an actual mention of damping with cloths. Schulte was writing when all the books in the Gutenberg Museum had been packed away to keep them safe during the war and acknowledged that further research needed to be done.

[15] Moxon, pp. 278–281.

[16] E. W. G. Kircher, *Anweisung in der Buchdruckerkunst* (Braunschweig, 1793; repr. Darmstadt: Renate Raecke, 1983), pp. 30–36.

[17] Kircher, p. 32.

[18] Johan Gerritsen, 'Printing at Froben's: an eyewitness account', *Studies in Bibliography*, 44 (1991), pp. 144–164 (p. 151). The original Latin letter stated "*adhaec etiam pilas papyrumque, quo facilius litteras, impressas recipiat, interpositis quibusdam humectantibus linteolis madefacere, . . .*" (p. 162).

been made and used by the Greeks and Romans, centuries before, so was known and available in the fifteenth century. Dard Hunter said that it was unlikely that the early papermakers used woven woollen cloths, but were more likely to use felted fibres.

It is not likely that the old craftsmen employed woven wool cloth such as the makers of handmade paper use at present, but a more compact, matted substance of hair or wool. The woven material that is used by modern papermakers is called felt, but the name is a misnomer, as felt is a compressed mass and does not necessarily consist of warp and weft.[19]

It was not until the eighteenth century that 'felts' were purpose-made, woven, woollen blankets; some three hundred years after the marks were made on Zainer's pages.[20] The marks on Zainer's pages are from woven cloths, because all show warp and weft, and it seems unlikely that these marks were made by fifteenth-century papermakers' 'felts'. Hunter further mentions that in some 'old paper, especially Italian and Dutch, it will be noticed that many of the sheets retain the impressions left by the material upon which they were couched'.[21] Close inspection of Zainer's paper does indeed reveal other 'hairy' impression marks that were more likely left by his papermakers' felted couching cloths. These marks are quite different from the cloth impression marks that are being discussed here.

Clear impression marks are not found on every sheet of Zainer's books. Perhaps there is another fact that needs to be taken into account that could affect how a cloth might impress into paper. Conservators at the Bodleian Library were consulted and in their opinion the amount of size, either in or on the sheet, might make a difference as to how much the fibres could be impressed.[22] Hunter also mentions sizing of the sheets by the papermakers but states that there was very little sizing done on paper that would be used for printing books (compared to paper for writing) in the fifteenth and sixteenth centuries.[23] Hunter states that sizing was not necessary for type impression, and the sizing that was done had no special formula: many had heavy sizing, some had a little and a few of the volumes he had looked at showed no evidence of sizing at all. Zainer's paper bears many different watermarks implying a number of different sources and perhaps different amounts of sizing, if any. Perhaps this variation in sizing might account in part for why not all Zainer's pages

---

[19] Dard Hunter, *Papermaking: the history and technique of an ancient craft,* 1943 (New York: Dover repr. 1978), p. 179.

[20] Hunter, p. 181.

[21] Hunter, p. 186.

[22] Date of consultation 17 May 2005. My thanks to them for their time and observations made.

[23] Hunter, p. 194. Sizing, dipping the dried sheets in a solution of animal glue, was a subsequent process carried out by the papermakers, when deemed necessary and dependent on the final use of the sheets.

bear impression marks. When planning the practical experiments it was decided to use a sized paper to see if the sizing made any difference to how the paper received an impression mark. These experiments showed (amongst other things) that it was impossible to make any impression on the eighteenth-century account book paper that had a hard sizing.

Further opinion about whether the marks might have been made as part of the paper making process was sought from modern-day hand-papermaker Christine Gibbs of Griffin Mill. She thought that sizing would not affect how much a sheet of handmade paper would accept impression.[24] Her experience of making conservation paper to match that of earlier centuries might help throw light on this area. She suggested that the amount of beating the pulp receives, and consequently how much the fibres compact, would be more likely to cause a difference to how a sheet receives an impression, than how much sizing was on the paper. She said that paper would be pressed and re-pressed during its curing period to smooth out irregularities, and, agreeing with Hunter, said that marks of the material on which the sheets have been couched can be seen on some early papers.

If impression marks were left on early paper as part of the papermaking process it seems unlikely that they would have left a mark with a stitched or frayed edge halfway across the sheet. As represented in images of early papermaking, and also as with the method of today's hand papermakers, the felts are always larger than the sheet of paper that is being couched onto them. If so, there is no way that stitched or frayed edges could leave marks across the sheet. All in all it seems most unlikely that Zainer's cloth impression marks were made as part of the papermaking process.

As part of the drying and pressing process after printing

A post-printing process should also be considered. The marks occur so often throughout Zainer's books that they seem to be coming from his workshop, and not from some later bookbinding process which might well have been carried out in various different workshops. Perhaps they could have been caused as part of a final pressing after the ink had dried, and the pages were pressed before being sold.[25] This seems unlikely as the look and strength of these marks implies that they had to be made as part of a wet process, not when everything was dry.[26]

[24] Date of correspondence 1–7 November 2005. My thanks to Christine Gibbs for her advice.

[25] The sheets would probably not have been pressed immediately after the reiteration had been printed and both the paper and the ink were still wet. In his book of engravings *Nova Reperta* (Antwerp: *c.* 1600), Johannes Stradanus includes an engraving of a printing office *c.* 1570 which shows the printed sheets hanging up to dry over ropes (following the method used by papermakers when drying their paper). The illustration is shown in Moran, *Printing Presses,* p. 28.

[26] See below where Experiment 5.1a showed that it was not possible to emboss dry paper with a dry cloth.

There remain two different theories as to how the marks were caused, either during the printing process or from the paper damping process just prior to printing. Two different methods of investigation were decided on to try to discover which theory, if either, might be the correct; (1) to record the cloth marks that occurred in as many copies of Zainer's editions as possible to see if there might be patterns to their occurrence that could give clues as to their purpose or why or when they had occurred, and (2) to undertake some practical experiments to try to recreate the cloth marks myself.

Recording the cloth impression marks

Clear cloth impression marks were recorded, for every copy of every edition looked at that contained marks. When recording the fabric impressions, both the leaf on which they occurred was noted and the side of the leaf on which the impression mark was made (inner or outer). This notation of which side of which leaf they occurred was done firstly, so an individual mark could be found at a later stage, and secondly to see if there was any pattern to their occurrence that might be interpreted later. None of the editions looked at had printed foliation, pagination or signatures. Sometimes the first leaf of the quires had a light pencilled signature, which helped when counting through the quire to the next pencil signature. Consequently accurate recording the leaf of each clear cloth mark was a slow process and there were times, usually where there were no pencilled signatures, when I lost my way amongst the quires, so there may be an occasional misrecording.

Only impressions where it could be seen from which side they had been impressed were recorded. The depth of impression and crispness might vary but if the side from which they had been impressed could be seen then that mark was included. Any doubtful, 'looks like an impression mark but I can't see where it's coming from' examples were omitted. This often occurred when the edge of the mark could not be clearly discerned. Altogether this means that there could be more marks than have been recorded.

A table was built up for each edition, and each copy seen of that edition, from the various libraries visited. Leaf references were given as conjugate pairs for the chancery folios where the cloths spread across two leaves, and as individual leaves for the royal/imperial folios. One example is given opposite (Table 5.1). As the numbers of impression marks being recorded built up, it began to emerge that their location in the copies showed no obvious pattern of occurrence. If one leaf in one copy had an impression mark then that same leaf in another copy of the same edition might not

Table 5.1. An example of a table recording the clear cloth impression marks, by leaf, inner and outer side, from six copies of Aquinas, *Quaestiones quodlibet*, 1475. Each edition had such a table, but because it was not possible to discern a pattern that could be related to the use of reiteration cloths, the others have not been included.

QUAESTIONES QUODLIBET

Leaves in quire	Bodley Inner	Bodley Outer	BSB Inc.c.a.416 Inner	BSB Inc.c.a.416 Outer	BSB Inc.c.a.416a Inner	BSB Inc.c.a.416a Outer	BSB Inc.c.a.416b Inner	BSB Inc.c.a.416b Outer	Ulm StB Inner	Ulm StB Outer	Mrman Westr Inner	Mrman Westr Outer	Total
[*8]	*2/7	*4/5					*4/5	*1/8, 2/7		*2/7			
[a10]	a2/9	a1/10, 5/6		a3/8, 4/8		a3/8		a1/10, 2/9, 5/6					
[b10]	b1/10, 2/9			b3/8, 5/6	b4/7	b5/6	b2/9	b1/10	b4/7		b5/6		
[c10]		c4/7		c3/8		c4/7	c5/6		c3/8	c2/9			
[d8]	d4/5	d2/7, 3/6	d2/7		d1/8	d2/7	d2/7		d4/5				
[e10]				e2/9		e3/8, 4/7					e3/8, 5/6	e4/7	
[f10]				f5/6	f3/8			f1/10, 2/9			f2/9	f3/8	
[g10]	g4/7			g2/9	g4/7						g3/8		
[h10]	h3/8			h1/10, 2/9						h3/8			
[i8]				i1/8		i2/7	i2/7	i1/8				i3/6	
[k10]	k3/8				k1/10	k5/6		k1/10, 3/8, 5/6			k5/6	k4/7	
[l10]		l2/9, 5/6		l1/10, 4/7		l1/10	l2/9			l4/7	l1/10		
[m10]	m4/7			m1/10, 4/7			m1/10			m4/7			
[n10]		n3/8		n4/7	n2/9				n5/6	n5/6	n4/7		
[o8]			o4/5		o2/7	o4/5		o2/7, 3/6					
[p10]		p1/10	p3/8, 4/7		p3/8, 4/7					p1/10			
[q10]	q2/9, 4/7	q1/10, 3/8	q1/10, 4/7, 5/6		q1/10	q5/6				q4/7	q1/10	q3/8	
[r10]		r3/8	r2/9		r2/9	r3/8, 5/6		r1/10	r5/6			r5/6	
[s10]		s5/6		s5/6			s1/10				s2/9		
[t10]	t5/6		t4/7, 5/6		t1/10		t1/10	t4/7			t3/8		
[v10]				v1/10						v3/8			
[x10]			x1/10			x4/7, 5/6			x3/8, 4/7				
[y10]										y2/9	y3/8		
[z10]				z3/8	z3/8	z3/8		z3/8	z2/9		z1/10		
Total	12	14	11	19	13	15	9	17	8	10	13	6	147

have one.[27] Some of the other editions also have cloth impressions on the same leaves through different copies, and, unusually, in one edition, *Summa,* a cloth impression occurs on the same leaf in six of the nine copies that had clear enough marks to be counted.

The marks do not appear in equal numbers through the quires of the books; one quire in one copy might have three cloth impressions and another quire have none. Sometimes only one or two marks occur throughout the whole book, as with the copy of the 36-leaf *Deutsche Chronik,* and other times there are as many as 90, as in the BSB copy of the 407-leaf *De planctu ecclesiae.*[28]

The total number of clear marks noted in each copy of an edition was generally fairly similar, but there also could be a wide variation, as with the 1478 edition of *Sermones.*[29] In the Bodleian library copy only 32 marks were noted whereas in comparison the copy from the BSB which showed 88, with the other copies of this edition having totals somewhere in between. The cause of this could be that a copy had by chance been compiled from more or fewer sheets that bore marks, or it could be because the different copies had been treated differently since they were printed. In the case of the 1478 edition *Sermones,* the Bodleian copy had been rebound in the nineteenth century, and very heavily pressed, whereas the Munich copy was in a late gothic (original?) binding.

It was thought it might be more useful to see how often the marks occurred, both through copies of one edition and also across the whole range of editions, than trying to find a pattern of their locations within the copies. Table 5.2 lists twelve different chancery-folio editions and eight royal/imperial-folio editions from the 38 editions included in this research. The number of copies of each edition looked at (column 1), which varies from as few as two to as many as thirteen. The numbers of copies that showed clear marks within each edition (2) varies also and there are only four editions in which all copies looked at had clear impression marks.

The number of sheets in each copy is given (3), calculated from the number of leaves as listed in the *GW*. Where there are an odd number of leaves, because an extra single leaf was inserted when the edition was printed, this is noted as a half sheet in the table. To try to even out the extremes in the number of occurrences in any one copy, it was decided to see how many cloth impression marks were noted per number of sheets

---

[27] Although at first glance Table 5.1 seems to show that *Quaestiones* has marks occurring on the same leaves, this can possibly be explained by the fact that this edition generally has a high occurrence rate of marks when compared with the other editions (21%, see Table 5.2). With a one in five chance of a sheet having a mark it is therefore more likely to have a number of marks occurring on the same leaves than some of the other editions looked at.

[28] *De planctu ecclesiae, BSB-Ink* A-461, shelfmark 2° Inc.c.a.305.

[29] *Bod-inc.* L-075, shelfmark Auct. 6 Q inf.2.10 and *BSB-Ink* L-122, shelfmark 2° Inc.c.a.801.

Table 5.2. The occurrence rates of clear cloth impression marks in copies of 22 different editions. * See Table 5.1 for details of recorded cloth marks found in 6 copies of *Quaestiones*.

Title	Date printed	(1) No. of copies looked at	(2) No. of copies with clear marks	(3) No. of sheets per copy	(4) Total no. of sheets in the copies with clear marks	(5) Total no. of clear impression marks	(6) Rate of occurrence of impression marks ($(5) \div (4)$)
Chancery folios							
Deutsche Chronik	1473	2	1	18	18	2	11%
De mysterio missae	1473	8	6	67.5	405	73	18%
De adhaerendo Deo	[1473]	13	10	20	200	32	16%
Claris mulieribus (lat)	1473	5	5	59	295	41	13.90%
Claris mulieribus (ger)	[1473]	4	2	74	148	12	8.10%
Summa	1474	11	9	91.5	823.5	150	18.20%
Aurea Biblia	1475	5	4	80	320	55	17.20%
Quaestiones *	1475	8	6	116	696	147	21.10%
Aurea Biblia	1476	8	6	160	480	68	14.20%
Vocabularius Bibliae	[1475]	3	2	139.5	279	62	22.20%
De horis canonicis	[1476]	4	3	13	39	7	17.90%
Documenta moralis	1476	6	5	191	955	166	17.40%
Royal and imperial folios							
Rationale	1473	4	4	134.5	538	126	23.40%
Liber Bibliae	1474	9	6	133	798	334	41.90%
De planctu ecclesiae	1474	6	4	203.5	814	252	31.00%
Rationale	1475	3	3	128.5	385.5	85	22.10%
Quadragesimale	1475	5	5	135.5	677.5	203	30.00%
Sermones	1475	10	8	121.5	972	142	14.60%
Quadragesimale	1476	6	4	135.5	542	174	32.10%
Sermones	1478	7	6	190	1140	389	34.10%

looked at in total for each edition. The three right-hand columns give, (4) the total number of sheets for all the copies looked at that had clear marks, (5) the total number of clear impressions, and (6), which is the total of column (5) divided by column (4), gives the percentage occurrence of impressions through the total number of sheets. Table 5.2 gives a minimum occurrence rate − the marks probably all occur at a higher rate than shown in the table. From the table it can be seen that the occurrence rates range from as low as 8.1 per cent through an edition to as high as 41.9 per cent.[30] Because of the variation in the number of impressions noted from copy to copy within the editions, the figures in the table would have been more accurately representative if based on a larger number of copies. Unfortunately it has not been possible to find more than one or two copies with impression marks to record for some editions, for example it has only been possible to record impressions from one copy of *Deutsche Chronik*.

Within the chancery-folio group of editions the occurrence rate varies between the lowest at 8.1 per cent for German edition of *De claris mulieribus* and the highest at 22.2 per cent for *Vocabularius Bibliae*. Both these editions are ones for which the sample was small; the recording being based on only two copies. *Deutsche Chronik* showed an occurrence rate of 11 per cent. These are the least reliable of the figures (being based on fewer copies) and if the figures from these three editions are ignored then the remaining editions have occurrence rates that are quite close, varying from 14.2 per cent to 21.1 per cent, with a mean occurrence rate from these more representative editions of 17.1 per cent. The two editions with the most copies having been recorded, perhaps give the most reliable rates of occurrence. *De adhaerendo Deo,* with ten copies recorded, gives a rate of 16 per cent and *Summa de eucharistiae sacramento,* with nine copies, has a rate of 18.2 per cent. These last two figures also give a mean occurrence rate of 17.1 per cent. It would seem that a pattern in frequency of occurrence is showing in these chancery folios.

The royal/imperial-folio group is based on a more balanced number of copies from each edition and gives occurrence rates that are fairly close, all between 22 per cent and 42 per cent apart from one anomaly, the 1475 edition of *Sermones*, which has a much lower rate of occurrence at 14.6 per cent. This edition is a puzzle because it is one for which the marks have been recorded from eight different copies, so implying that the figures should be some of the most reliable. When checking the original data very low numbers of marks were found in all eight copies. This suggests that whatever was the cause of the cloth impression marks something different was happening with this edition. If the occurrence rate from this edition is

[30] The 8.1 per cent occurrence rate is for an edition in which only 2 copies have been looked at and recorded so may not give very accurate figures.

omitted the remaining seven editions have a mean occurrence rate of 30.7 per cent, almost double the mean of the chancery folios. Although the occurrence rates are fairly close within each group there does seem to be a difference between the rates of the chancery-folio and the royal/imperial-folio groups of editions. Possible reasons for this will be examined later.

There is also evidence of a possible chronological basis to some of the cloth marks because three of the earliest editions, *De mysterio missae*, *De adhaerendo Deo* and *Deutsche Chronik*, all printed before the end of May 1473, have marks which show no visible edges to the cloth; suggesting that the cloth was bigger than the sheet of paper. This could be because the edges of the copies had been trimmed off, but two of the copies of *De adhaerendo Deo* show deckle on the fore-edge and foot.[31] This indicates that there had been minimum trim on these copies, and that trimming is not the reason for there being no visible edge to these cloth marks. All Zainer's editions after May 1473 show impression marks with edges to the cloth. This might suggest a change in practice to use smaller cloths but further research is needed to solidify this point.[32]

Some later editions printed by Zainer, after the cut-off date of 1478 of this research, were also examined to see if cloth impressions could be found. Marks were found in some editions printed through the 1480s and the latest was found in the Bodleian library copy of *Imitatio Christi* printed in 1487.[33]

Practical experiments − printing

Schmidt suggested that the cloth impression marks had been caused as part of the printing process. If the marks had been part of the printing process, or had been caused by a tympan cloth when the reiteration was being printed, one would expect to find the marks consistently on either the inner or the outer side of the sheet; if the printer had printed the outer side of the sheet first, and then the inner side second, using a cloth to help prevent set-off, then one would expect to find the cloth marks always impressed on the first outer side. To test Schmidt's suggestion, when recording the impression marks, their occurrence on the inner or outer side of the sheet was noted, to see if a pattern might be found that would give a reason for the marks. However the impressions occur roughly the

[31] Munich copy *BSB-Ink* I-391, shelfmark Clm 23817 and Augsburg copy Hubay 40, shelfmark 2° Inc 145.

[32] A possible reason for this change is discussed below under 'Evidence for Zainer's printing practice'.

[33] Cloth impression marks were found in the following editions printed by Zainer, held in the Bodleian Library: *Biblia Latina*, 1480 (ib00567000) *Bod-inc.* B-276, shelfmark Auct. M 3.7; and Thomas a Kempis, *Imitatio Christi*, 1487 (ii00015000) *Bod-inc.* T-103, shelfmark Auct. 5 Q 6.7; and in Mainz in the Gutenberg Museum Bibliothek copy of Johannes Gallensis, *Summa collationum*, 1481 (ij00331000) GM Ink 36.

same number of times on the inner side of the sheet and the outer. On counting the total number of clear impression marks recorded from the fifteen editions which show the most marks, of a total of 1857 impression marks 900 were on the inner side of the leaf and 957 on the outer which suggests no real bias to either side. Schmidt's theory is not supported by the location of the marks on inner or outer side of the sheets.

To determine further whether some part of the printing process might have caused the marks, and also to establish whether they could be made with dry paper or whether water had to be part of the process, a series of experiments was undertaken. Two sets of experiments were carried out to try to establish (1) if the cloth impression marks could have been made in some way as part of the printing process as suggested by Adolf Schmidt, and (2) to see if they might have been caused during the paper damping process as suggested by Alfred Schulte.

First it was necessary to establish whether it was possible to make a cloth impression on paper as a dry process or if the paper needed to be damp. Then, to discover if other factors might influence the depth and crispness of the impression, or whether an impression was made or not, further experiments were planned along with the two main experiments. For this it was decided to try some different papers and also vary the hardness of the packing to see if either might make a difference to the result.

Experiment 5.1

An Albion iron hand press was used for the first set of experiments. It has an 18 × 24 inch platen and is capable of considerable pressure − it can print an area of text measuring 13 × 19 inches easily, and this experiment would be working with a text area of approximately half this.

(*a*) (28 August 2005) To see if it is possible to make a blind impression mark of a dry cloth by impressing it onto dry paper. This experiment was kept as basic as possible by trying simply to impress cloth into paper. A hard packing, which might give a better resistance and so help in pressing the cloth into the paper, was placed on the tympan comprising a sheet of cardboard within the tympan and acetate sheet on the tympan sheet.

Two types of paper were used, an eighteenth-century account book paper made from linen rag and with a heavy sizing, and Somerset etching, a mould-made cotton rag paper, 250gsm weight. This paper was chosen because it was designed for taking the heavy impression of an etching press.

No type was used for this experiment, just a type high piece of wood 150 × 270 mm, (6 × 11 inches) covered with a dry linen cloth, and placed on the bed of the press. Each paper was placed in turn on the press, and pressure was applied with the platen brought down as far as possible. No impression mark was made on either sheet, which suggests that it is unlikely that cloth can be impressed into dry paper with the pressure of an iron hand press.

(*b*) (28 August 2005) To see if it is possible to make a blind impression mark of a cloth, this time damped, by impressing it onto damp paper. Damping the paper softens the fibres, (and the sizing if the paper is sized) and should help a sheet of paper receive impression. The packing remained the same as with the first experiment before and the same papers, 18th-century account book and Somerset etching papers were used, this time both damped.

As before no type was used for this experiment and the same a type high piece of wood covered this time with a damp (placed in water and then wrung out until the excess drips were removed) linen cloth, and placed on the bed of the press. The paper was damped by sponging one sheet with a moist sponge, placing a dry sheet on either side and placing in a polythene bag with a wooden board on top, and leaving overnight. (As paper absorbs moisture it expands, which can cause the sheets to cockle. One method to avoid this cockling is to put a large flat board on top of the sheets with a heavy weight on the top). The damped papers were placed in the press, and pressed as above onto the damp cloth.

Only the slightest blind mark of a fabric weave was visible on the Somerset etching paper. No mark was made on the harder-sized account book paper. This experiment showed that this was not an efficient way to impress cloth into paper. Although damping the paper made a slight difference on the Somerset paper the mark had nothing like the depth of impression of those seen in Zainer's editions. It was decided not to continue experiments with the eighteenth-century paper because its sizing had made the surface very hard to make any impression.

(*c*) (14 October 2005) To see if it is possible to make cloth impression marks when type is used on the press, with a softer packing and different papers (with different sizing). The previous hard packing was removed and a softer packing of a traditional woollen blanket inserted in the tympan. Two different papers were tried, a 230 gsm Hähnemühle etching, and a 210 gsm Zerkall etching paper, both damped overnight as method described in (*b*).

This time 20 point type set to a text block size of 150 × 270mm, the same dimensions as had been used previously for pressing the cloth on its own. A damp linen cloth placed on the tympan as described by Moxon as a 'tympan cloth'. The paper was placed on this cloth on the tympan when being printed.[34]

---

[34] Moxon, p. 306.

A deep impression of the type area onto the paper was achieved but not of the cloth. (In Zainer's editions the cloth is impressed into the paper, across the type letters and into the non-type areas. Here only the type letters were impressed and so sign of cloth weave was made at all). With this experiment the soft packing and the damp paper ensured that the type pressed deeply into the paper but no cloth weave impression mark could be seen in either paper. Again it was obvious this was not the method of impressing cloth onto paper. It was also noticeable that as everything was damp (cloth, paper, packing, tympan) a surprising amount of water was squeezed out.

(*d*) (15 October 2005) To see if it is possible to make cloth impression marks with a coarser cloth and by raising the surrounding non-printing areas to type height. The same packing and papers and type were used as with experiment (c). The paper was placed on cloth on tympan and printed as above. Again only a slight weave mark could be discerned behind where the type had pressed on the softer Zerkall paper but none on the non-type areas, the margins.

These last three experiments all seem to be showing the same thing – the cloth marks on the pages of Zainer's editions were not caused as part of the printing process.

The first experiment quickly established that the paper had to be damp before any impression of a linen cloth could be made in it. The remaining experiments showed that there is no way of achieving the kind of cloth impressions that Johann Zainer had on his pages by the printing process. It was just possible to make a cloth weave mark over the areas where the type pressed but quite impossible to make the weave marks over the spaces where there was no type. Zainer's books clearly show weave impressions across the gutters and into the margins of his pages. Logically, and now proved practically, these could not have been executed as part of the printing process. This means that Adolf Schmidt came to the wrong conclusion and that the printing process was not the cause of Zainer's impression marks.

Practical experiments – paper damping

A further set of experiments was carried out to see if the cloth marks could be recreated through a paper damping process. The first experiment aimed to discover if paper could be damped successfully by interleaving with damp cloths. Ideally each sheet should be of equal dampness to enable consistent printing. The second experiment was to see if clear cloth impression marks could be made when using this paper damping method. The third experiment was to determine if moisture would spread laterally across the sheet, from beyond the area of damp cloth, as well as vertically.

Experiment 5.2

(*a*) (26 October 2005) To see if paper can be successfully and evenly damped by interleaving damp cloths between sheets of paper with a light pressing ('Damp' being a cloth that is wetted in water and then wrung out by hand to remove excess water). Also to see if cloth impression marks might be made on the sheets of paper when using this method.

A pile of sheets of Hähnemühle 230gsm etching paper, interleaved every 8 sheets with a damp linen cloth, was made, placed in a plastic bag to prevent drying, a heavy board and a 56lb weight placed on top, and left overnight. The next day the paper was evenly damped but only very slight cloth marks could be discerned and no evidence of weave pattern could be seen. There was some cockling in the paper owing to the unevenness of the moisture penetration. The paper dried out cockled. This experiment showed that this was a successful method of damping paper, but perhaps not quite enough weight on the top to help prevent the paper cockling.

(*b*) (27 October 2005) to see if cloth marks can be made when damping paper with cloths using heavier pressing.

This time Barcham Green Chatham, a flax-fibre, hand-made, paper was used. This paper was chosen because, being made of flax fibres, it was the nearest available paper to that made in the fifteenth century from linen rags. The paper was stacked as above but with cloths interleaved every 10 sheets, the pile placed in between boards and placed in a copying press which was screwed down as tightly as possible and left for two nights.

This method produced even, lightly damped sheets with crisp clear cloth impression marks transmitted both upward, and downward as a reverse image, through the stack. The hemmed edges (here a bulky hem with three layers of cloth rather than a stitching over a single edge) were clearly visible through three sheets and slightly visible through sheets four and five. The weave marks were clearly visible on the first sheet and slightly visible on the second. The edge of the cloth showed clearly through the first two sheets and then only slightly through third and fourth sheets. There was no cockling in the sheets.

This seemed a successful method of both damping paper and creating the cloth impression marks. If one had wanted slightly fewer sheets to be marked then the amount of pressure somewhere between experiments 2 (a) and (b) would probably suffice. If the number of clearly marked sheets, between 2 and 6, had occurred in a quire of 25 this method would also give a rate of occurrence between 8% and 24%, very like that found in Zainer's editions. From these two experiments it seems highly likely that

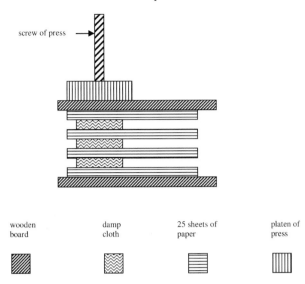

screw of press

wooden   damp   25 sheets of   platen of
board   cloth   paper   press

Figure 5.7. Diagram showing how quires of royal/imperial size paper might have been damped, with damp cloths inserted every 25 sheets, positioned on one half of the stack, and pressed.

the cloth impression marks found in Zainer's editions came from his method of paper damping. The edges of the cloth showed more clearly than the central area.

(*c*) (1 December 2005) One further experiment was conducted to see if moisture transferred sideways through the pile of sheets of paper (under pressure) from inserted damp cloths. The same Barcham Green cotton rag hand-made paper as above was damped by inserting a damp cloth, on the left half of the sheet every 25 sheets of paper, and building a stack of 150 sheets. A heavy board was put on the top and the half of the pile, containing paper and cloths, was put in the press, screwed down, and left overnight (Figure 5.7).

The moisture penetrated evenly upwards and downwards through the stack but only very slightly sideways across the sheets. The edges of the sheet were still quite dry as was the other half of the sheet where the cloths had not been positioned. This experiment clearly shows that if Zainer had been damping this way, and only inserted cloths on one half of the sheet (as seen in the marks in his royal/imperial-folio editions) only that half would have been damp, and could have been printed on both its sides, verso and recto. The moisture would not have transmitted sideways to enable him to print the other half of the sheet. He could only have printed the other half of the sheet after a second damping session.

Figure 5.8. Linen cloth and its imprint impressed into the paper, after inserting damp cloths into a stack of dry paper and leaving in a press overnight.

Experiment 5.2 showed that it is certainly possible to damp paper by damping with cloths; in fact it is a much neater method of paper damping than pulling quires through a trough of water and stacking the wet sheets. It also showed that it is possible to produce flat sheets of evenly damped paper with perfect cloth impression marks on the sheets that would have made Zainer proud (Figure 5.8). It also appeared from the experiment that if Zainer's marks had come from paper damping then he would have had to have added very heavy pressure, perhaps using a press of some kind, to achieve them. The marks made in the above experiment impressed upwards through two or three sheets and, in mirror image, downwards through two or three sheets. The impressions were crispest on the sheets next to the cloth and then became more indistinct on the sheets further away from the cloth. With less pressure on the stack only the two sheets either side of the cloth showed a mark, and then only a very slight one. If Zainer had been damping by this method, and had inserted a wet cloth in every quire of 25 sheets, then one might expect to see clear cloth marks roughly two sheets per quire under lighter pressure, to four to six sheets per quire under heavier pressure. This gives an occurrence rate of 8 per cent under light pressure or of between 16 and 24 per cent under heavy pressure. These rates tally well with that found of impressions in Zainer's books, given in Table 5.2, where only the clearest marks were noted. If the marks had been made when the stack of sheets was damped, as per the method described above, it would account for the differences in crispness and depth of impression seen in Zainer's editions; those marks that were clearest having been on the sheets touching the damp cloth and those that were more indistinct being on the sheets further away from the cloth when the paper stack was prepared. The leaves which had a 'doubtful' mark, and that were not recorded, could perhaps have been those leaves even further away from the cloths. A difference in the amount of pressure put on the stack also made a difference to the number of sheets, above and below the cloth, that were impressed by the cloth. This could explain the puzzle posed by the 1475 *Sermones* edition which had a much lower rate of marks through all the copies recorded; perhaps just not as much pressure was applied when damping the paper for this edition than with other editions.

Damping being the reason for the cloth marks' existence would also account for the irregular occurrence through different copies of an edition and also explain why some of the smaller editions, i.e. only comprising a single quire of five sheets of paper, might exist with no cloth marks as the occurrence rate was too low. With an occurrence rate of as low as 8 per cent to 16 per cent, an edition of only five sheets could easily escape having a sheet with a cloth impression mark on it.

EVIDENCE FOR ZAINER'S PRINTING PRACTICES

It seems that only paper damping could be responsible for making the cloth impression marks, and that even that process would have had to be carried out under pressure. If the theory that the marks were caused when the paper was damped before printing is accepted, then this knowledge may help in understanding how Zainer printed his pages.

For the chancery folios, where the cloth impressions show that the conjugate leaves of the sheet of paper were damped and printed at the same time, nothing new seems to be added to what is described by Moxon. Zainer would have damped the paper a day (or two) before printing, printed both conjugate leaves on one side of the sheet in one pull the next morning and printed the reiteration of the leaves in the afternoon while the paper was still damp.[35]

Order of printing the pages on royal/imperial-folio sheets

However for the royal/imperial folios the cloth marks seem to tell a different story. The cloth impressions only cover half of the sheet of paper, and sometimes there is a second, separate, cloth mark on the other half. These marks, on only one half of the sheet, would suggest that Zainer was only damping half of the sheet (one leaf) at a time, and then printing both sides of this leaf, and then at a later time damping the other half of the sheet, and printing the conjugate leaf on both its sides.

---

[35] Moxon, p. 297.

It might be thought that damping half of the sheet would have been enough to moisten the entire sheet so he could print both royal/imperial-folio leaves. Practical experiment 5.2(c) was carried out to see how far the moisture would spread laterally from damping only one half of the sheets of paper in a stack.[36] This experiment showed that the moisture did not spread sideways across the sheet, when stacked under pressure, and that if Zainer had used this paper-damping method he would only have succeeded in damping one half of each of the sheets, and consequently would have been able to print only that half. The other half of the sheet, where there was no cloth, would not have absorbed enough moisture to be printed. This lack of transmission of moisture sideways was another point emphasised by Schulte. He further suggested that the cloths were deliberately made smaller than the paper so the edges would be dryer, for ease of handling when printing and to reduce the risk of the paper tearing when being fixed to the press.[37]

Another point arises as a result of the earlier experiment 5.2 (b) where it became clear that to achieve heavy enough pressure to produce the cloth impressions Zainer might have used a press and placed the stack of paper being damped in it. If he had wanted to damp the whole sheet rather than just one half he would have needed a press with a very large platen, large enough to cover the entire area of a royal/imperial-folio sheet. With the sheets which had two cloth impressions, the second was probably caused when the sheets were damped later for the second print run on the other half of the sheet. Wet cloths would have been inserted as before, but on the other half of the stack, and some cloths, coincidentally, would have been placed on a sheet that had had an impression mark before. The figures in Table 5.2 show a difference between the occurrence rates of the marks in the chancery folios and the royal/imperial folios. The royal/imperial folios show roughly twice as many impression marks. The figures, combined with evidence from the practical experiment above, suggest that the sheets were damped twice for two separate printing sessions.

It would seem, taking the evidence of the positioning of the marks and their occurrence rates, that Zainer damped the sheets for the royal/imperial folios twice, and then did four separate print runs to print the four pages, two for each damping. However Schulte put forward the theory that Zainer damped four times and then printed and dried with the royal-folio books.[38] He suggested this because he thought the ink would

---

[36] See Experiment 5.2c.

[37] Schulte, p. 19. This reason for small cloths suggested by Schulte could possibly be why Zainer changed from having cloths much larger than his sheets to those that fitted well within the paper dimensions.

[38] Schulte, p. 19.

need to dry before the reiteration was printed. The evidence from Zainer's printed pages, which are covered with ink spots and marks from set-off, suggest that he never waited for the ink to dry, and that he would have printed the reiteration while the paper (and ink) were still wet. Also the occurrence rates of the cloth impressions only show roughly twice as many marks, rather than four times, than for the chancery folios.

Evidence for a one- or two-pull press

If the evidence of the cloth impressions is indicating that Zainer only damped and printed his royal/imperial-folio paper one leaf at a time, perhaps the impressions can also be seen as an indicator of whether Zainer was using a one- or two-pull press.[39]

Lotte Hellinga's research on the change from a one-pull to two-pull press shows that this transition occurred through the period in which Zainer was working, the 1470s and 80s.[40] She stresses that the introduction of the two-pull press was transitional, and printers may well have used both styles of press alongside each other.[41] Hellinga's detailed survey of quarto-format editions printed (a) as half-sheets on a one-pull press and later (b) as full sheets on a two-pull press, gives clear evidence when the two-pull press was introduced.

[quarto] . . .is, however, the format for which the distinction between half-sheets and full sheets, and therefore the use of the one-pull and the two-pull press can be established beyond doubt in the vast majority of instances.[42]

Hellinga established from her survey that the introduction of the two-pull press began in Rome with printer Georg Lauer in 1472.[43] From there it spread to Naples and Venice and then to Paris in 1477, to Strasburg in 1481 and Mainz in 1484.[44]

The evidence from the cloth impression marks in Zainer's royal/

---

[39] It is not known what the first printing presses looked like or how they operated. It is generally accepted that the first presses were one-pull machines with small platens that could only print a limited printing area of text. The bed/stone of the press, carrying the inked type, and with a sheet of paper laid over the top, was positioned under the platen of the press. The platen was pulled down to press the paper onto the type and then the bed was wound/slid out and the process repeated for the next sheet. At some later date the two-pull press was introduced whereby, after the first pull, the type bed was wound further in and a second pull was made on the other half of the sheet. Lotte Hellinga, 'Press and text in the first decades of printing', *Libri, tipografi, biblioteche: ricerche storiche dedicate a Luigi Balsamo* (Florence: Leo S. Olschki, 1997), pp. 1–23. Hellinga (p. 3) gives a succinct summary of the first printing presses and the differences between a one- and two-pull press.

[40] Hellinga, 'Press and text', pp. 1–23. In 'Reconstructions' p. 276, footnote 7, Frans Janssen cites Lotte Hellinga's article in *Gutenberg-Jahrbuch*, 75 (2000), p. 153, for information about the two-pull press. This article does not seem to give any information about the transition to a two-pull press apart from Hellinga's footnote 15 which cites her article 'Press and text' already referred to here.

[41] Hellinga, 'Press and text', p. 3.

[42] Hellinga, 'Press and text', p. 5.

[43] Hellinga, 'Press and text', p. 13.

[44] Hellinga, 'Press and text', p. 23, Appendix III.

imperial folios (one leaf being printed at a time) suggests that he was working with a one-pull press throughout the 1470s including his *Biblia Latina* printed in 1480, which fits in with the chronology established by Hellinga.

It might be thought that Zainer could have used larger cloths for damping the paper for printing his royal/imperial-folios; damping the entire sheet so he could have printed both conjugate leaves on the same side of the sheet with the one print run if he had been operating a two-pull press. The cloth impressions give no evidence of this and suggests that he did not have a two-pull press, and that he continued to print all his royal/imperial folios one side of one leaf at a time – each sheet being put into the press and printed four times.

Without straying too far, some other evidence can be considered that further supports the theory of cloth impression marks indicating that Zainer printed one leaf of royal/imperial folio at a time. If he had printed two conjugate leaves at the same time one would expect to find the areas of printed text on both leaves to be in line with each other, i.e. the position of the text would be the same on each leaf. However instances appear, as discussed earlier in Chapter 2, in his royal/imperial folios where the conjugate leaves have obviously been printed at different times because the text areas are not in line with each other. These examples give clear evidence of each page being printed independently and suggest a one-pull press and substantiate what the cloth marks are saying, that the conjugate leaves were printed separately. It seems most likely that Zainer printed both sides of one leaf for the edition, in two print runs, one after the other, after the first paper damping operation, and then both sides of the other leaf, in two print runs, after the second damping.

These findings do not contradict those of Hellinga as an indicator of a one-pull press. The cloth impressions are only useful in relation to royal/imperial-folio editions that have marks, and Hellinga's research only concerns quarto editions that have watermarks. The two approaches can both bring a different light on the same subject and complement each other.

However there remains the question as whether cloths were used for damping the paper when printing royal/imperial-folio sheets on a two-pull press. For full sheets to be printed on a two-pull press the entire area of the sheets would have to have been damped, presumably using larger cloths, or perhaps folding the sheets of paper in half before damping. If the sheets had been folded before damping one might expect to find some mirror-image cloth mark impressions. These have not been found in any of Zainer's editions, neither have any full royal/imperial folio size cloth marks, Viglius' description above tells of cloths being used for damping as late as 1534, well after the transitional period to a two-pull press, but does not state the dimensions of the sheets of paper being damped. However examples of large cloth marks, covering both conjugate leaves, have been found with Sensenschmidt and Frisner's printing of Justinianus *Codex* in 1475.[45] Cloth marks were noted in the Bodleian Library's copy on both leaves of [k2/9], [n1/10], [n5/6] and [G1/10]. Also in the same edition was supporting evidence from set-off on pages [o5v/6r] and [o5r/6v] of the red printing, showing that the conjugate pages were printed at the same time.

OTHER PRINTERS WITH CLOTH IMPRESSION MARKS

Almost all Zainer's editions have cloth impression marks, which most probably were caused when he damped his paper. If Zainer was using this method of damping paper then perhaps other printers were doing likewise. It was thought worthwhile to discover if cloth impression marks could be found in editions by other printers. If they were found it would be interesting to see if there was any connection between them, and also between them and Zainer, either geographically or through influence from training.

Printers listed by Schmidt and Schulte

Both Schmidt and Schulte mentioned other printers in whose works they had found similar marks. Both writers advised looking at the work of other printers, and Schmidt suggested that the cloth marks might be a helpful tool in distinguishing books from unknown presses.[46] Schmidt had looked at the editions by Mentelin in Strassburg (where Zainer had learnt to print) and not found any marks in his books. However he had found some marks in editions printed by Konrad Winters in Cologne. Schulte, as a paper historian, had made his observations from the Gutenberg Museum's collection of watermarked leaves. He had looked at leaves from editions printed by other Ulm printers, Konrad Dinckmut and Johann Reger and had not found any cloth marks. However he had found some on leaves from the press of Michael Greyff, and Johann Otmar, in Reutlingen. He had been unable to find any evidence of cloth impressions from the editions of six different Strassburg printers he had looked at, including their mentor Mentelin, or in six copies of the work of Johann's brother Günther.[47] He suggested that because he had not found widespread examples of cloth impressions that the method was not used for long or by many printers.[48]

---

[45] Justinianus, *Codex*, 1475 (ij00575000) *Bod-inc.* J-269, shelfmark Auct. 3 Q inf.2.4.

[46] Schmidt, 'Untersuchungen', p. 61. Schmidt was hoping that if the cloth mark had been caused by the tympan or frisket as part of the printing process then one cloth would be particular to one press, which would help in identifying unknown presses.

[47] Schulte, p. 20.

[48] Schulte, p. 20.

Both historians had been looking in what would seem the most obvious places where one might find other examples of cloth impressions, the places where Johann Zainer may have been most influenced such as Strassburg and Augsburg, or perhaps where he might have passed on his influence, such as Ulm, or Reutlingen where he had been born. All these towns were quite close to him apart from Cologne where Konrad Winters printed.

Some royal-folio editions by all the above printers listed by Schulte and Schmidt, mainly from the collection at the Bodleian library but also a few in the BSB, were scrutinised for cloth impression marks. Editions printed through the 1460s and 70s as well as a few in the 1480s were looked at to try to establish the earliest appearance of a cloth impression and to try to discover whether they might still occur in the 1480s. As with a number of Zainer's editions many of these had been rebound and the pages of some may have been washed, leaving no detail of anything. Cloth impression marks were found in some editions printed in the 1470s by both Mentelin and Heinrich Eggestein in Strassburg; *Mariale* and *Summa de casibus* by Mentelin, and *Consilia* and *Decretalium* by Eggestein.[49] No cloth marks have been found in the editions of Günther Zainer, Winters or Otmar which I inspected. Of the three specific editions in which Schmidt and Schulte had seen cloth impressions, only one, *Quadragesimale* printed by Michael Greyff in Reutlingen, was in the Bodleian.[50] This copy showed one or two possible cloth marks. However another edition also printed by Greyff, *Sermones dominicales*, had many clear cloth marks.[51] The impression marks in this royal-folio volume started very close to the centre fold line in the gutter and spread across to right off the edge of sheet. This evidence suggests that the cloths might have been large enough to cover both halves of the royal-folio sheet, but that Greyff quite specifically chose not to, and only covered the half of the sheet he was going to print.

Printers working in places where Zainer printed

Following the approach of Schmidt and Schulte further editions by printers in Strassburg, Augsburg, and Ulm were scrutinised for cloth impressions. In Strassburg cloth marks were also found in three editions by the 'R' printer, *De sermonum proprietate, Speculum historiale* and the *Catholicon* and in editions printed by another printer in Strassburg known

---

[49] Albertus Magnus, *Mariale* [not after 1473] (ia00272000) *Bod-inc.* A-120, shelfmark Auct. 4 Q 2.17; Astenanus, *Summa de casibus* [not after 1473] (ia01161000) *Bod-inc.* A-468, shelfmark Auct. 1 Q inf.2.23; Nicholas de Tudeschis, *Consilia* [not after May 1475] (ip00028000) *BSB-Ink* T-495, shelfmark 2° Inc. s.a.945a; and Innocent, *Decretalium*, 1478 (ii00095000) *Bod-inc.* I-13, shelfmark Auct. 3 Q inf. 2.13.

[50] Johannes Gritsch, *Quadragesimale* [not after 1478] (ig00493500) *Bod-inc.* G-255, shelfmark Auct. 6 Q 3.1.

[51] Hugo de Prato Florido, *Sermones dominicales super evangelia et epistolas* [c.1478] (ih00505000) *Bod-inc.* H-229, shelfmark Auct. 5 Q inf.1.13.

as 'the printer of Henricus Ariminensis (?Georg Reyser)'. [52] There were clear impressions in the Bodleian copies of *Didascalion* and *Expositio* and cloth shaped stains in the *Henricus Ariminensis* and *Quadragesimale*.[53]

In Augsburg no cloth impressions have been found so far in any of Günther Zainer's editions but they do occur in some editions printed by another Augsburg printer, Anton Sorg, who learnt to print in Günther's workshop.[54] His *Quinquaginta* and *Praeceptorium divinae legis* both have clear cloth marks.[55] In Ulm Konrad Dinckmut showed cloth marks in his books. They are much lighter marks than Zainer's; only one mark found so far had anything like the depth of impression of some of Zainer's, but they are clearly visible in his editions, *Erklärung der Zwölf Artikel*, *Postilla super epistolas*, *Sermones de sanctis* and *Legenda aurea sanctorum* .[56]

Printers working in other locations

To try to establish whether cloth impressions occurred further away than Zainer's immediate field of influence, editions by printers in other printing towns were looked at. So far cloth impression marks have been found in the books of five further printers; three working in or close to southern Germany in Esslingen, Nürnberg and Basel, and two further away; in Brussels and Paris. Cloth impressions were found in copies of four editions by Konrad Fyner in Esslingen, *Expositio in Job*, *Conclusiones de diversis materiis moralibus*, *De adhaerendo Deo* and *Manipulus curatorum*.[57]

[52] The 'R' printer's editions are not signed and their printer is named after a very characteristic 'R' in his roman type face. The editions are ascribed to Adolf Rusch, or to Rusch and Mentelin for some of them. Rusch was Mentelin's son-in-law, and after Mentelin's death in 1479 continued to run Mentelin's press. Hrabanus Maurus, *De sermonum proprietate, sive opus de universo* [before 20 July 1467] (ir00001000) *Bod-inc.* H-233A, shelfmark Auct. 1 Q inf.2.11; Vincent of Beauvais, *Speculum historiale* [c.1473] (iv00282000) *Bod-inc.* V-133, shelfmark Douce 307–9; and Johannes Balbus, *Catholicon* [c. 1473] (ib00023000) *Bod-inc.* B-012, shelfmark Auct. M 1.12,13. For information about Georg Reyser see Geldner, *Die deutschen Inkunabeldrucker*, pp. 63–64.

[53] Hugo de Prato, *Didascalion* [not after 1474] (ih00532000) *Bod-inc.* H-242, shelfmark Auct. 6 Q 5.7; Byw. F 2.10; Nikolaus Stör, *Expositio officii missae* [not after 1473] (ie00165000) *Bod-inc.* E-080, shelfmark Auct. 6 Q 3.23; Henricus Ariminensis, *De quattuor virtutibus cardinalibus* [c.1472–75] (ih00019000) *Bod-inc.* H-014, shelfmark Auct. 5 Q 4.34.

[54] Steinberg, *Five hundred years of printing*, new edn., p. 23. It has not been possible to discover from where Steinberg found this information to verify it.

[55] Augustinus Hipponensis, *Quinquaginta*, 1475 (ia01298000) *Bod-inc.* A-554, shelfmark Auct. 7 Q 3.18; Johannes Nider, *Praeceptorium divinae legis* [c. May 1475] (in00199000) *Bod-inc.* N-093, shelfmark Auct. 5 Q 4.12.

[56] *Erklärung der Zwölf Artikel*, 21 Aug 1485 (ie00102000) *Bod-inc.* E-056, shelfmark Auct. 6 Q 4.30; Guillelmus Parisiensis, *Postilla super epistolas*, 1486 (ig00681000) *Bod-inc.* G-323, shelfmark Auct. 4 Q 4.15; Hugo de Prato Florido, *Sermones de sanctis*, 1486 (ih00514000) *Bod-inc.* H-233, shelfmark Auct. 4 Q 4 30; and Jacobus de Voragine, *Legenda aurea sanctorum*, 1488 (ij00121000) *Bod-inc.* J-051, shelfmark Auct. 3 Q inf.1.17.

[57] Thomas Aquinas, *Expositio in Job*, 1474 (it00236000) AUG Hubay 1981, shelfmark 2° Ink 320; Johannes Gerson, *Conclusiones de diversis materiis moralibus* [1474-75] (ig00206000) AUG Hubay 883, shelfmark 2° Ink 42; Johannes Gerson, *De adhaerendo Deo* [not after 1475] (ij00306000) AUG Hubay 1202, shelfmark 2° Ink 320; Guido de Monte Rochen, *Manipulus curatorum* [1476-78] (ig00573000) AUG Hubay 973, shelfmark 2° Ink 116.

In Basel Michael Wenssler used cloths to damp his paper for *Manuale confessorum* and *De morali lepra*.[58] In Konrad Creussner's edition of *De sanguine Christi*, printed in Nürnberg, the cloth impressions were very small, just covering the text area of a single chancery-folio the leaf.[59] The Community of Brothers in Brussels also used cloths to damp their paper and marks were found in their *Polycraticus sive de nugis*.[60] Cloth marks were also found in a royal-folio edition printed in Paris by Michael Friburger, Ulrich Gering and Martin Krantz in *c*.1475. Their *Summa de casibus conscientiae* showed many very clear marks made by cloths that just fitted within the (trimmed) leaf dimensions of 319 × 230mm.[61] So far no cloth marks have been found in the Italian editions that have been looked at but further research might turn some up.

The occurrence rate of cloth marks in the editions cited above that were printed by Reyser, Fyner and Wenssler is close to that of Zainer but the occurrence rate in the one Friburger, Gering and Crantz edition is much higher.[62] Table 5.3 provides a summary of the editions showing cloth impressions, together with their approximate date of printing. There does seem to be a geographical link between many of these printers; the city of Strassburg. Mentelin, Eggestein, Rusch and ?Reyser all printed in Strassburg and Zainer also started printing there. Fyner and Wenssler also have Strassburg connections; Wenssler having been born and living there before going to University in Basel, and Fyner having learnt printing there in Eggestein's printshop.[63] Friburger, Gering and Krantz also came from the Rhineland so it is possible they brought the practice of using cloths for damping paper to Paris with them.[64] Dinckmut, working in Ulm may have learnt his printing from Zainer and likewise Sorg in Augsburg may have learnt from Günther Zainer; again Strassburg connections.

There may also be a chronological aspect. So far no cloth marks have been found in editions printed earlier than 1467, with Rusch in Strassburg, or later than Dinckmut in 1488. A wider body of evidence would be useful. The fact that cloth impressions have been found in editions beyond the small area of southern Germany could suggest that

---

[58] Johannes Nider, *Manuale confessorum*, 1475 (in00180000) AUG Hubay 1500, shelfmark 2° Ink 106; Johannes Nider, *De morali lepra* [not after 1475] (in00190000) AUG Hubay 1503, shelfmark 2° Ink 106.

[59] Sixtus, *De sanguine Christi*, 1473 (is00580000) UBW Hubay 1939, shelfmark I.t.f.87.

[60] John of Salisbury, *Polycraticus sive de nugis curialium* [1479-81] (ij00425000) UBW Hubay 1287, shelfmark I.t.f.206.

[61] Bartolomaeus de Sancto Concordio, *Summa de casibus conscientiae* [*c*.1475] (ib00170500) *Bod-inc.* B-087, shelfmark Auct. 1 Q 1.25.

[62] 74 cloth impression marks were found in the Bodleian copy over 127 leaves giving an occurrence rate of 58 per cent, much higher than with any of Zainer's editions.

[63] Geldner, *Inkunabeldrucker*, pp. 113 and 206.

[64] Colin Clair, *The chronology of printing* (London: Cassell, 1969), p. 14.

Table 5.3. The location of printers and the number of editions printed by them that have been found so far with cloth marks.

Place	Date	Printer	Number of editions
Found by the author			
Strassburg	c.1467	Rusch	1
	c.1473		2
	[na1473]	Mentelin	2
	1472–75	?Reyser	4
	1475	Eggestein	1
	1478		1
	1478	Knoblochtzer	1
Nürnberg	1473	Creussner	1
	1475	Sensenschmidt	1
Esslingen	1474	Fyner	2
	c.1475		1
	1476–78		1
Augsburg	1475	Sorg	2
Basel	1475	Wennsler	2
Paris	c.1475	Friburger, Gering and Crantz	1
Reutlingen	c.1478	Greyff	2
Ulm	1473	J. Zainer	6
	c.1473		3
	1474		3
	1475		5
	1476		3
	c.1476–77	5	
	c.1477		1
	c.1478–81	9	
	1487		1
	1485	Dinckmut	1
	1486		2
	1488		1
Found by other researchers			
Reutlingen		Otmar	1
Cologne		Winters	1

this was a relatively widespread method, used with more or less skill in its application. Viglius' eyewitness account of 1534 of the practice being used by Froben in Basel also supports the theory that this might have been a widespread method, both chronologically as well as geographically. It would be interesting to discover if cloth impressions are found from further afield.

It seems, from observations and practical experiments, that these cloth impressions are most likely to have been made as part of a pre-printing, paper-damping, process. Also this is a technique that was not restricted to Zainer. If one accepts that this was a method of paper damping then it throws some light on Zainer's printing practice, and that of the other printers using this method, for the royal/imperial-folio editions. The cloths were quite specifically positioned on one half of each sheet, on one leaf, with the aim of only damping and then printing both sides of that leaf. This method of printing does not fit in with a two-pull press and could only have been used with one-pull practice. Only one edition has been found so far; Sensenschmidt and Frisner's printing of *Codex* in 1475, which shows a double-size cloth, covering the entire sheet of royal-size paper, and indicates that he was probably printing both conjugate pages at a time on a two-pull press.[65] The evidence from the cloth impressions supports evidence from set-off and poor register found in Zainer's editions that indicate that he was printing his chancery folios two conjugate pages at a time and his royal/imperial folios one page at a time.

[65] For further information about this edition see Margaret M. Smith, 'Printing red underlines in the incunable period; Sensenschmidt and Frisner's 1475 edition of Justinian's *Codex*', *Journal of the Printing Historical Society*, 10 (2007), pp. 45–57. Smith does not comment about the cloth impression marks.

6 POINTS AND POINT HOLES

Some of the incunable editions, usually those in the larger royal- and imperial-folio formats, have small holes pierced through the leaves, named point holes or pin holes.[1] The number and position of the holes can vary, but are usually located in a margin or unprinted area of the leaf. The direction in which the holes were punctured and their size also varies and all these variations can change from printer to printer, from one edition to another by one printer, and over time. The reasons for the existence of these holes and of these differences will be explored in this chapter.

ACHIEVING ACCURATE REGISTER

Accurate positioning of the sheet on the type block to print the first side of the sheet of paper, and then accurate repositioning to print the reiteration is difficult, even when using modern paper with straight edges. If the positioning is inaccurate, on either the first or second print-run, then the areas of printed text on the two sides of the leaf will be out of alignment with each other, or poorly 'backed up'. The printers in the incunable period were working with handmade paper, which has uneven deckle edges, and also could vary in dimensions from sheet to sheet. These irregularities mean that the printers could not have relied on positioning the edges of the sheets as a method for attaining accurate alignment. Therefore the safest way for them to have proceeded was to have used a system of positioning that did not rely on using the edges of the sheet for register. One solution was to hold the sheet in a fixed position in some sort of a frame – a fixed position that could be recreated for printing the reiteration, and having a frame that could be accurately and repeatedly positioned on the type area. How the paper was held in the frame and how that frame was positioned repeatedly with accuracy is the core of this discussion.

---

[1] As will be discussed later in the chapter these holes have been made by small metal points fixed to the tympan or paper holding frame. Some scholars have termed them pin holes. However both Moxon and Gaskell call them 'point holes', and state that they are made by 'points'. In *Johannes Gutenbergs zweiundvierzigzeilige Bibel: Ergänzungsband zur Faksimile-Ausgabe* (Leipzig: Insel, 1923), p. 40, Paul Schwenke uses the German terms *die Punkturen* and *die Punkturlöchern* (points and point holes) and Kircher, *Der Buchdruckerkunst* (opposite p. 16) in 1793 shows *Punctur* on his diagram of a press. It was decided to use the terms points and point holes here.

The use of a tympan and frisket

One method of achieving accurate register is by using the paper-holding apparatus, found on wooden presses from the sixteenth to the eighteenth century, and on iron hand-presses through to the present day; the frame assemblage known as a tympan and frisket. The tympan comprises two pieces, an inner and an outer tympan frame, one fitting inside the other, with packing material sandwiched in between (Figure 6.1). Two small pieces of metal, known as points, are attached to the outer tympan on which the sheets of paper can be accurately positioned (Figures 6.1 and 6.3 for

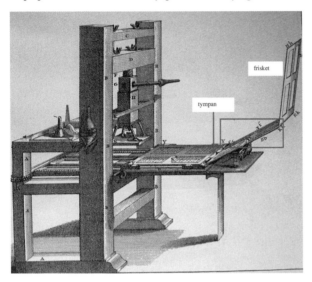

Figure 6.1. Illustration of a two-pull, eighteenth-century, wooden press from Fertel, Dominique, *La science pratique de l'imprimerie* (St. Omer, 1723), p. 230. The tympan frame is hinged to the press, and the frisket hinged to the tympan. There is a cut-out mask on the frisket. The points can just be seen, at centre of the sides of the tympan frame, located at letters 'Ff' and 'Ff'. A close up of the points is shown below; they can be seen projecting up from their supporting plates by which they are attached to the tympan. (St Bride Library.)

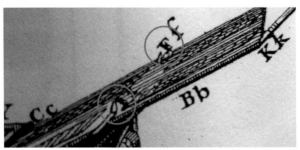

Figure 6.2. From Stumpff's *Schweizer Chronik,* 1548, the earliest illustration to show the open tympan and frisket assembly, with a sheet of paper being lifted off the points on the tympan, located in its central gutter. (Reproduced from Hans-Jürgen Wolf, *Geschichte der Druckpressen* (Frankfurt: Interprint, 1975), p. 56, Fig. 68.)

close up illustration of a point). The points have a two-fold role, in that they both support the paper on the tympan and are also used for accurate register of the sheets. The tympan is hinged to one end of the bed of the press. The frisket is another frame, hinged at the other end of the tympan, away from the press bed and covered with a paper sheet or parchment to mask out the non-printing areas surrounding the type block, and keep the margins of the printed sheets clean (Figure 6.1). The frisket, with its mask, also serves to support the sheet of paper and keep it on the points, when the tympan is folded down, and keeps the paper off the inked type until the platen is lowered for printing. With the tympan hinged to the press, and therefore always in the same position relative to the bed of the press, the paper being printed could always be accurately placed onto the type block for printing. The tympan and frisket apparatus also allows the printer to place the sheet of paper on, and lift it off, the type block cleanly, with no slurring or smudging. Both tympan and frisket have to be large enough to hold a full sheet of paper, even if only one half of the sheet is being printed.

It is not known when exactly this apparatus was first introduced and there is very little information about how paper was accurately positioned on the press in the incunable period. The 1499 illustration from *Danse*

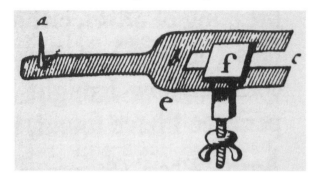

Figure 6.3. Illustration from Moxon, p. [75], showing the seventeenth-century construction of a point (a). Moxon gives the explanation of the diagram on p. 78. The point is made of wire, riveted into a hole in the iron plate (e). The plate is fastened to the tympan by a point-screw (f). The plate has a notch (b–c) so that the position of the point can be adjusted; the points can be placed further in for smaller sheets of paper, or further out for larger sheets. (Dover Publications.)

macabre at Figure 1.1 shows a press with hinges, although what was attached to the hinges is not in view. The earliest illustration to show the tympan and frisket in position on the press and being used does not appear until almost a century after Gutenberg began printing in Mainz, in 1548 in Stumpff's *Schweizer chronik* (Figure 6.2).[2] By the time of this illustration the points are fixed half-way down the tympan, making their holes in the central gutter of the sheet being printed.

Documentary evidence from the San Jacopo di Ripoli press in 1476 mentions having a two small pieces of metal put on the frame for marking the face and holding it, and a month later having a frame with a drum and hinges made – these items could possibly be a tympan with points and a hinged frisket covered with parchment.[3] There is no information about where on the tympan the pieces of metal were attached. At some later date the points changed from being fixed in one position to being adjustable. Moxon gives a description of the construction of a point; it was made from a thin piece of wire, filed down to a sharp end with the other end being riveted onto a plate. The position of the plate could be adjusted for the size of the paper (Figure 6.3).[4]

[2] Moran, p. 26. Falconer Madan also lists early press illustrations in 'Early representations of a printing press 1499–1600', *Bodleian Quarterly Record*, 4 (1924), pp. 165–167.

[3] Conway, *Diario*, ff. [2r] and [2v] of the original dated December and January 1476. Conway suggests on p. 317 in her Glossary that this is an early mention of points being added to the tympan frame and that at the time there was no correct word for 'points', hence the long-winded description given.

[4] Moxon, p. 78 with illustration on plate 9 [p. 75]. As well as being adjustable lengthwise, Moxon (p. 64) also states that holes were drilled in different positions in the tympan frame for locating the point-screws, depending on whether the printer was printing 12° or 16° format.

Evidence from point holes

Evidence of the use or not of a tympan and frisket can be found from holes made by the points in the fore-edge margins of some of the editions printed in the incunable period. Point holes and their evidence have been the subject of some discussion by scholars through the last century. Alfred Pollard mentioned the variable nature of point holes and described the reduction in the number of the holes in a leaf over time, and through the period a printer was working, as being a useful indicator for dating some editions.[5] Paul Schwenke, writing in 1923 about the 42-line *Bible*, discussed the use of points and point holes, and stated that they were not just for fastening, but also for register.[6] He was not sure if Gutenberg used a frisket or not, but because of the inked raised spaces visible beyond the text area, he thought that it was unlikely.

In his research into the printing of the *Mainz Psalters* and *Canon Missae* in 1954, Irvine Masson had a section on point holes.[7] Masson had measured the distances between the point holes in many of the early printed editions, and the dimensions of the areas delineated by the point holes. He noted that the hole positions were almost always related to the text area, either lined up with an edge of the text or centred over the inter-columnar margin. When talking about type page, Masson was describing the width of the visible text area, not the width of the whole area of type plus spacing (see Chapter 3, *Type and Ems*, where it is shown that the total line length was often a good 20mm longer than the line length of visible text in the editions Masson was describing). The holes line up with the position of the visible text. This suggests that the original positioning of the points was based on visual markers in the forme, i.e. the edges of the text, and not the edge of the full set width of the line of type plus spacing. Masson leaves a question as to whether the paper-holding frame was hinged to the press.[8]

Kenneth Povey replied to Masson and extends some of his comments.[9] Povey thought that the paper-holding frame was not attached to the press. He suggested a different method of how the paper-holding frame might have been constructed and how the printer might have achieved accurate register with such a frame, assuming the editions were printed one page at a time.

In his 1998 article Martin Boghardt provides a very detailed study of point-hole patterns in royal-folio editions.[10] Boghardt argues that the paper-holding apparatus had to be detached from the press for both sides

---

[5] Pollard, *BMC*, 1, pp. xiv–xv.

[6] Schwenke, *Johannes Gutenbergs Bibel*, p. 40.

[7] Masson, pp. 16–22.

[8] Masson, p. 21.

[9] Kenneth Povey, 'Pinholes in the 1457 Psalter', *The Library*, 5th series, 11 (1956), pp. 18–22.

[10] Martin Boghardt, 'Pinhole patterns in large-format incunabula', *The Library*, 7th series, 1 (1998), pp. 263–289.

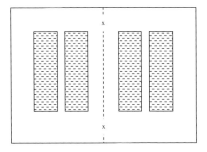

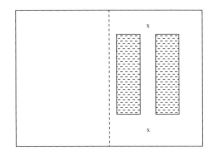

(a) Point hole positions, at head and foot, centred on the central gutter. In these positions the holes would not usually be visible in the bound copy.

(b) Point hole positions, at head and foot, centred on the inter-columnar margin.

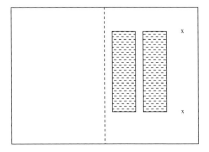

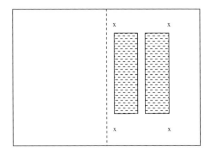

(c) Point hole positions in the fore-edge margin, here shown aligned with the head and foot of the text block.

(d) Four point hole positions at head and foot, aligned with sides of text block.

Figure 6.4. Diagrams showing various positions of point holes in relation to the text block. Here they are shown all as 'x', single punctured (and therefore in one direction). However they could all be double punctured, implying that the sheet has been taken off the points, turned over, and relocated onto the points from the other side. If this is done accurately only one hole may be visible, and it is impossible to say in which direction it is punctured. Sometimes there may be more than two holes, as the printer has fumbled, when printing the reiteration when trying to locate the first hole onto the point.

of the leaf to be printed for the very early incunables.[11] He cites the small size and neatness of the holes, their being in one direction only, no double puncturing, and their pattern on the sheet being asymmetrical, as reasons for the paper-holding apparatus being separate from the press. He states, as Pollard, that there was a tendency for the number of holes to reduce

[11] Boghardt, p. 267.

over time.[12] He also traces the changes in hole patterns from various printers and suggests that once changed a printer stayed with the change.

This may not always be the case. Some printers might stay with a new printing method as noted by Pollard and Boghardt, but others did not.[13] For example Günther Zainer printed his *Catholicon* edition (ib00021000) in 1469 with two point holes centred on the inter-columnar margin (Figure 6.4 (b)). He then printed *Rationale divinorum officiorum* (id00404000) in 1470 with no visible point holes (Figure 6.4 (a)); this, Boghardt suggests, is Günther moving to this method permanently.[14] However a later royal folio, *Biblia Germanica*, [not after 1474] (ib00627000) printed by Günther, had a mixture of visible point holes. On some leaves the holes were centred on the inter-columnar margin, and on others placed in the fore-edge margin (Figure 6.4 (c)); all are punctured in both directions. Boghardt does not mention the point holes in this edition; perhaps the copy he viewed did not have any surviving holes.

Hellinga suggests that the point-hole evidence is better understood as evidence of a specific printing press, and whatever paper-holding apparatus was used with it, rather than a practice used through the whole print workshop.[15] This would explain the evidence from the above mentioned editions printed by Günther; that he perhaps had a new press or a new frame, with points centred on the central gutter, which he used to print his *Rationale,* but that he still kept his earlier presses, one with a frame with points on the outer margin, and one with a frame with points located over the inter-columnar margin, on which he printed the *Biblia Germanica.*

Point holes are difficult. They are elusive and some of the evidence they provide can be inconclusive. Where the holes are clearly visible there is no problem – they are there, and can give clues of printing practice. However when they are not visible, and there is therefore no evidence, that is not to say that they had not been there originally. There are examples of a number of holes clearly visible in one copy of an edition printed by Zainer, and then only found one or two of them in a second copy. Sometimes the holes are removed when the copy is trimmed during binding, and sometimes later cleaning efforts or different storage or pressing can encourage the holes to close up; perhaps the reason Martin Boghardt did not see any holes in the copy of Günther Zainer's *Biblia Germanica* that he looked at. The holes, especially the very fine ones, can easily vanish as the paper fibres are pressed back across the hole (Figure 6.5). Other evidence, about the nature and quality of the holes,

---

[12] Boghardt, p. 266.

[13] *BMC*, 1, p. xxiv. When writing about Mentelin and his point holes, Pollard states that this printer made a change to his typographical practice then stuck to it.

[14] Boghardt, p. 276.

[15] Lotte Hellinga, 'The interpretation of measurements of pinholes and analysis of ink incunabula', *The Library*, 7th series, 2 (2001), pp. 60–64 (p. 64).

Figure 6.5. An example of a small neat point hole made from recto to verso at foot of page [d4v] of *Rationale divinorum officiorum*, 1473. (Ottobeuren Abbey.)

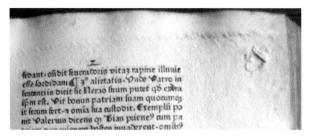

Figure 6.6. An example of a large torn point hole at head of page [d6r] in *Sermones*, 1478. (Ulm Stadtbibliothek.)

can also be confusing. If one is lucky it can be possible to see from which direction the hole was made, either from the verso or the recto side of the leaf. The paper fibres, pushed through by the point, will be visible on the side of the sheet where the point emerged. However if the same hole was later used for a point going through the paper in the opposite direction, or if a later hole is torn, then it is very difficult, if not impossible, to say in which direction the hole was made first (Figure 6.6). Although the evidence provided by point holes may sometimes be incomplete, it is still important and can add another piece to the jigsaw of understanding early printing methods. Some of the evidence from point holes in editions by some other printers through the earliest years of printing will be discussed here before looking at Zainer's point holes.

One aspect of point holes in early editions, as discussed by Masson, is that their location on the page can almost always be related to the position of the text on the page. Point holes along the head and foot margins of the paper are almost always aligned with the side edge(s) of the text block, and likewise point holes on the fore-edge margin of the sheet are almost always aligned with the head and foot edges of the text block (Figure 6.7). If the reason for the point was only to hold the paper then there would be

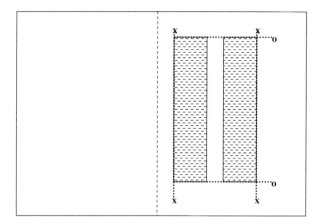

Figure 6.7. Diagram showing point holes (x) in head and foot margins aligned with the sides of the text block. Point holes in the fore-edge margin (o) align at the head and foot with the head and foot of the text block.

no need for any alignment to the type in the forme on the press. However if the points were used for alignment then there is every reason for their position to be related to the text area. Although it is not possible to offer a satisfactory explanation for point holes being so aligned the fact that they were so aligned does suggest that at least part of their role was for registration. When the points were later placed in the central gutter, as seen in illustration at Figure 6.4(a), this alignment of the holes with the text was no longer important.

Evidence of not using a tympan and frisket

There were a number of different reconstructions of the wooden press built in the twentieth century. Frans Janssen gives a good summary in his article on common presses, and discusses on what evidence the reconstructions were based; on early representations in illustrations or printer's devices, or on technical descriptions in manuals, or on surviving presses from previous centuries.[16] Janssen lists twenty-five reconstructions in chronological order, with the sources on which the reconstructions were based. Janssen's main emphasis in his article is focussed on how the spindle was guided when lowering and raising the platen. There is no mention of the paper-holding apparatus, what it might have been originally, and when a tympan and frisket might have been introduced. Janssen does mention the early sketches, showing parts of a press, by Leonardo da Vinci, but the discussion is about the spindle and occasionally about the

---

[16] Janssen, 'Reconstructions', p. 274.

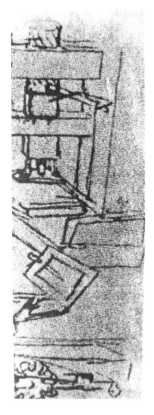

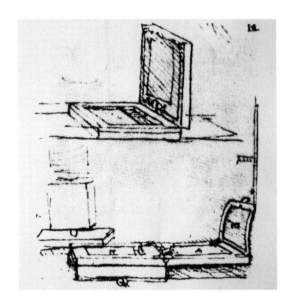

Figure 6.8. Sketches made by Leonardo da Vinci, *c.*1495, showing (left) part of a printing press, with a half-open tympan and frisket in the foreground from *Der Buchdruck*, p. 158. Sketch on the right shows more detail of the tympan and frisket assembly. By this period a hinged tympan and frisket would have been an established part of the press. (Claus Gerhardt, *Der Buchdruck: Geschichte der Druckverfahren,* Stuttgart: Hierseman Verlag, 1975.)

platen and whether it was made of metal or wood, and not about accurate positioning of paper (Figure 6.8).[17] Every one of these reconstructions, including those that purport to be replicas of the press Gutenberg would have been using, shows a press with a hinged tympan and frisket. The reconstructions that are styled as 'Gutenberg's press' are all incorrect, as such a hinged tympan and frisket was probably not introduced until some

---

[17] Janssen, 'Reconstructions' (p. 275), gives a date of *c.*1480–82 for these sketches, but Claus Gerhardt, *Der Buchdruck: Geschichte der Druckverfahren,* vol. 2 (Stuttgart: Hiersemann, 1975), p. 158 suggests 1495. Whichever date is correct, the illustration itself does show some kind of tympan and frisket hinged to the bed of the press. There is perhaps some kind of support for the paper indicated, but no clear evidence of points is shown.

years after Gutenberg was printing. Boghardt made it quite clear in his
article, that where the holes are all single-punctured, and are made only
in one direction, the indications are that the paper was not removed; it
stayed on the points until both sides of the leaf had been printed. A
hinged tympan and frisket, as seen in these reconstructions, would not
have been used.[18]

The evidence for the paper not being removed and repositioned onto
points comes from the pinholes in the 42-line *Bible* and other editions
printed in the first few years. The first 10 leaves of the 42-line *Bible* have
10 point holes, all going from recto to verso. The holes are neat and tiny,
as though made with a fine sewing needle. There is absolutely no
suggestion of any point going back through the hole in the other
direction. Also it is physically nearly impossible to remove a sheet of
damp paper from 10 points, turn the sheet over and then re-position
every hole on the 10 points to print the other side of the page.
Apparently whatever was being used to hold the sheets of paper when
printing the 42-line *Bible*, the paper was held in the same position on the
same points until both sides of the first leaf had been printed. The same
exercise would then have been repeated to print both sides of the
conjugate leaf. The impossibility of re-positioning over multiple points
also applies to other editions with six holes; the remainder of the 42-line
Bible, the 1457 *Psalter, Canon missae,* 1458, the 1459 *Psalter, Rationale
divinorum officiorum,* 1459, the 36-line *Bible* [c.1458/9]. The printers of all
of these editions would not have been using a tympan and frisket, as
shown in Stumpff's illustration, for placing their sheets of paper
repeatedly and accurately on to the press.

There are other early editions, Fust and Schöffer's *Constitutiones,* 1460,
and *Biblia Latina,* 1462, Mentelin's *Summa theologiae* [not after 1463],
Homiliae [not after 1466] and *De arte praedicandi* [not after 1466] that have
four holes but differ from the editions described above because they show
double puncturing in all four corners (Figure 6.4 (d)). Sometimes one can
clearly see two holes in each corner, perhaps only one or two millimetres
apart, occasionally as far as three to four millimetres apart. It is sometimes
obvious that the holes were made in both directions, one from recto to
verso and the other from verso to recto, in each corner of the page. At
other times the evidence is not so clear and one can only see one hole or
none at all. The holes are still very small and neat, as with the single
puncturing seen in the earlier editions with six holes. The implication, of
holes being punctured in two directions, could be that the printer
removed the sheet from the points, turned it over and then re-positioned
the paper over the points to print the other side. This is not easy to achieve

---

[18] Boghardt, p. 267.

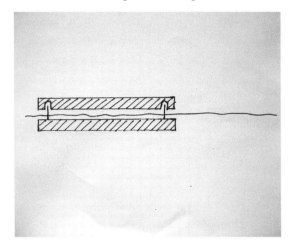

Figure 6.9. Diagram showing side view of a possible two-part frame (similar to the two-part papermakers' mould and deckle but without the screen fixed to the mould) for holding paper. The paper is laid over the points in the bottom half, and the points located into holes in the top section, clasping one half of the sheet of paper in between them.

accurately as the double holes are suggesting and it is difficult to understand how it was done.

Boghardt suggests a separate paper-holding frame, not attached to the press, but does not go into much detail such as how the paper was held, how paper and frame might have been accurately positioned on the text, and how packing material was added.[19] With only the evidence of the point holes any thoughts about how a frame, entirely separate from the press, might have been used can only be speculation. Perhaps the paper was held in a simple two-piece frame (similar to a papermaker's mould and deckle, but without the mesh across the mould), not attached to the press, with fine points in the corners of the bottom section. The top section could be lifted off, the paper positioned, and then the top section replaced, to grip the paper (Figure 6.9). The frame would still need to be positioned accurately, and perhaps it was constructed to locate exactly on/over the forme holding the type. Packing material, necessary to cushion the type from the platen when printing, would still have to be placed on the frame before the platen was lowered, and the top packing sheet, which would have picked up ink, would have needed to be changed fairly regularly or cleaned to avoid set off. This would have been a fairly slow process, perhaps a bit slower than with the later tympan and frisket. However, printing was still a much faster method of reproducing texts

[19] Boghardt, p. 267.

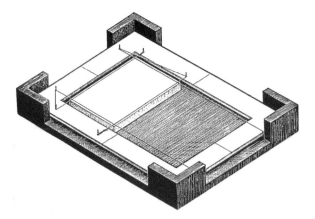

Figure 6.10. Illustration from Kenneth Povey, *Pinholes in the 1457 Psalter*, p. 21, showing raised sides at the corners of the coffin of the press and his suggested paper- holding frame located exactly into the corners. The image also shows the type block in position at left hand end of press bed, and Povey's suggested arrangement of pins and strings for registration of the paper. (The Bibliographical Society.)

than manuscript, so even a method that might seem to later eyes to be quite slow and laborious, would have been markedly faster than writing texts by hand.

Povey suggests that the paper-holding frame was built to locate exactly into four raised sides at the corners on the coffin of the press (see Figure 6.10).[20] This would be theoretically possible, if the printer was working with a skeleton forme, always sited in the same position on the bed of the press. Such raised corners can still be seen on the beds of the iron hand-presses today. Povey's method would provide a foolproof locating system for the frame. It could also be possible to locate a smaller, half-size, frame into two raised corners in the front half of the bed. That still leaves a question mark over how the frame was constructed. It may have been a single frame with points as suggested by Povey or it may have been a two-part frame, also with points and receiving recesses, as at Figure 6.9. Povey suggests folding the sheet of paper in half (which gives a straight edge for any alignment) before placing the sheet on the frame, and lining the folded edge up with the strings he has added as a visual aid to register.[21]

To add to this discussion, in 2007 Alan May built a reconstruction Gutenberg press based to some extent on Dürer's drawing of 1511, on

---

[20] Povey, p. 21.

[21] Povey, p. 20. A printer would be very wary of trying to achieve accurate register by laying a sheet of paper into position by eye and relying on this for accurately printing the reiteration. It might be possible for a few copies, but would be very difficult to keep up any standard on a full day's work.

other kinds of contemporary presses, and engineering principles. May was very aware of the problem of the point holes being punctured in one direction, and the impossibility of re-fixing a sheet of paper back onto 10 points. His solution has been to make the holes with a fine pin on the folded sheet before printing and then to use them purely as an aid to register and not for fixing the paper.[22] His press is provided with an innovative paper holding apparatus comprising two separate frames, hinged at either end of the press bed; the first a frisket folded down over the type and on which the paper is positioned and the second, the tympan with its packing material. This method of printing works, not just for single sheets but for longer print runs and for accurately printing the reiteration. May's press offers a possible explanation for the very fine holes that are only punctured in one direction.

By June 1466 Mentelin had printed his *Biblia Germanica* and the leaves show three hole positions.[23] It is just about possible to relocate a sheet of paper with three holes, back onto three points and the printer's struggle to do this is evident. The holes in Mentelin's *Bible* are larger than the example of neat holes shown in Zainer's *Rationale*, 1473 at Figure 6.5. Many holes in Mentelin's *Bible* are torn and messy and some are double or treble holes as the printer has tried to relocate the first hole onto the point for the reiteration. Heinrich Eggestein, also in Strassburg used a three-hole pattern from 1466, starting with his *Biblia Latina*.[24] Boghardt describes these holes '. . . often they are ragged or consist of two punctures very close to one another, and the direction in which the holes were made is often not discernible'.[25] The evidence of torn and messy holes suggests that the printer was trying to relocate onto points fixed to a frame, and possibly that that frame was hinged to the press. This could perhaps be the first use of a tympan. Positioning onto points on a frame fixed to the press at a sloping angle is much more awkward to do than when the frame is flat on a bench. These messy holes suggest awkwardness. Perhaps because the earlier editions discussed above, with neat double-punctured, point holes in four corners, do not show signs of awkwardness they too might possibly have been made by a frame separate from the press.

As soon as the frame is hinged to the press at an angle, and that frame is folded over to lower the paper onto the forme, there has to be some kind of support for the paper or it will fall off. This is where the frisket, with its covering, could be used. The covering can support the paper being printed and also keep the margins from picking up stray ink from the

[22] May, pp. 76–79.
[23] *Biblia Germanica* [not after June 1466] (ib00624000).
[24] *Biblia Latina* [not after 24 May 1466] (ib00530000).
[25] Boghardt, p. 273.

forme. Some printers used pieces of string to support the paper, and impressions of the string and their knots can be clearly seen in some editions.[26] As mentioned in Chapter 2, under 'Inking', string impressions are evident in the *Catholicon* (ib00022000) printed by Adolf Rusch in Strassburg in *c*.1470, placed in the inner, outer and inter-columnar margins and also in the outer and inter-columnar margins of his *Speculum* (iv00282000) printed in *c*.1473. Impressed string marks were also found with Georg Reyser's edition of *Missale Herbipolense* (im00663900) printed a few years later, printed in 1481. Whether string was used on its own as a means of support for the paper, or along with a cut-out mask on the frisket, cannot be said with any certainty.

The position of the points on the frame or tympan changed, and for some years was generally fixed to the top end of the tympan. At some later date, presumably with the firm establishment of tympan and frisket and fixed points in the centre of the frame, the holes and their evidence vanish into the central gutter. It seems that different printers progressed towards this method at different times. Boghardt states that it was not until 1483 that Peter Schöffer printed a royal folio without point holes in the fore-edge margin, whereas Mentelin was doing so by 1473.[27] Boghardt also demonstrates the variety of hole patterns used by different printers, and their reduction in number from ten holes to six, to four, to three, to two, in different positions and configurations.[28] In light of Boghardt's findings, the information about how Zainer handled his sheets of paper for printing, both on and off the press, is brought together here.

Zainer and point holes

It is not known how Zainer registered his sheets of paper accurately on the press. He must have had some method, although, from the poor register in some of his editions, it obviously was not a foolproof method. His smaller chancery and median folios and the larger, royal and imperial folios need to be considered separately.

Chancery and median folios

For his chancery folios there is the slimmest of evidence to show how he might have held the sheets for printing. There are no visible point holes in any of the outer margins of his chancery and median folios. However one

---

[26] String (or elastic) is still used today by handpress printers, strung across the frisket frame to give extra support for a particularly large sheet of paper. Lewis Allen describes the use of elastic around the frisket frame to support the paper in *Printing with the handpress* (New York: Van Nostrand Reinhold, 1969), p. 39.

[27] Boghardt, pp. 273 and 276.

[28] These are all brought together in his overview with diagrams on p. 284 and in his appendix pp. 285–287.

or two examples of point holes have been found located in the middle of the central gutter of the sheet, between the text blocks. These would not usually be visible, because they would be covered up by the sewing thread. The rare examples can only be seen when the binder has folded the sheet crookedly, so exposing a point hole. All the following examples are in copies that are still in their original bindings which means that it is unlikely that the holes are surviving sewing holes from an earlier binding. One example is found in the Cambridge University Library copy of *Documenta moralia* [*c*.1476].[29] Sheet [i2/9] has been folded crookedly and one hole can be seen in the central gutter on leaf [i9] at the foot, *c*.47mm from the foot of the text. Another example, again of just one hole, was spotted in a slightly loosely bound copy of *Vita et fabulae* [*c*.1476] in the Bodleian.[30] The hole is centred between the text blocks and in line with the foot of the text on sheet [o1/10]. A further example is on sheet [b5/6] in a copy of *Summa de eucharistiae sacramento* in Augsburg.[31] Again the hole is located centrally between the two text blocks and this time 28mm below the text. The last example found has four holes, two at the head and two at the foot of centre-quire sheet [g5v/6r] in a BSB copy of *Vitae sanctorum*, printed *c*.1478.[32] The holes at the head are very close together; one pierced in each direction, and located *c*.25mm above the head of the text (and only two millimetres from the trimmed edge of the paper). The holes at the foot are located at *c*.33mm and *c*.35mm from the foot of the text, also with one hole in each direction. All the holes are centred on the central gutter between the two text blocks. The distance between the holes at head and foot is *c*.250−252mm (Figure 6.11).

It is not known what might have been making these holes. Presumably they were made by points when fixing the paper, and for registration, but it is not known in what manner this was achieved. The first three examples do not tell very much apart from suggesting that Zainer might have been using points to locate his paper. On one occasion the hole is in line with the text, and for the other two it is positioned at some distance below the text. Unfortunately they are all instances of only one hole being visible, so there is no chance of discovering how far apart two holes were. There is also no indication to what the points might have been fixed. The last example, with two holes in each position, and each being pierced in different directions, does suggest that the sheet was lifted off the points after the first printing, and relocated to print the reiteration − perhaps an indication of his use of a tympan and frisket with attached points. Alternatively, because the paper has to be placed on and lifted off

---

[29] CUL, OATES 999.
[30] *Bod-inc.* A-053, shelfmark Douce 252.
[31] Hubay AUG 39, shelfmark 2° ink 320.
[32] *BSB-Ink.* V-251, shelfmark 2° Inc. s.a. 650b.

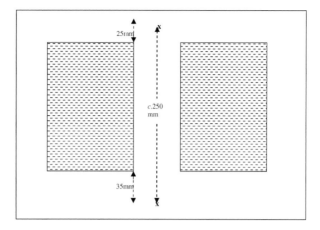

Figure 6.11. Diagram of leaves [g5/6] of BSB copy of *Vitae sanctorum*, shelfmark 2°
Inc.s.a.650b, showing location of double-punctured pinholes, one in each direction in
each position, at head and foot on central line of sheet. The holes lie about 250mm apart.

the type cleanly and accurately, there might equally have been some kind
of unattached paper-holding frame, perhaps with some central points.[33]
   One other example of using points in one of Zainer's chancery folios is
found in an extra half-leaf in *De mysterio missae* in 1473, an apparently
unusual practice. This leaf must have been printed later, after it was noted
that some text was missing; it has just 17 lines of text on each side of the
leaf rather than the standard 34 lines. It is sewn into quire [k] between
leaves [k7] and [k8] and is printed with the chain lines of the paper
running across the leaf rather than down, which would be usual for a folio
sheet. The leaf is not the full height of the rest of the edition, being around
210mm high rather than the full height of 315mm of a chancery sheet. It is
the full width of the rest of the edition, plus the surplus 'tab' for the fold
into the quire. (see diagram and photo at Figure 6.12). There are two
point holes on the fore-edge *c.*160mm apart and in some copies the holes
are double punctured. There are also five blind-impressed letter Rs set in
a line 34mm from the left-hand side of the text. These are impressed from
both sides so were used as bearers for printing both recto and verso of this

---

[33] Placing a damp sheet of paper onto inked type, and removing it, cleanly and accurately is very
difficult to achieve just by hand. There is always some small movement during the operation that
results in slurring of the letters on the paper. Ideally the paper wants to be supported on all four sides,
and often across the centre as well for a large sheet. It should be placed over the type, but held off from
the type until the moment of impression. The lowering of the platen pushes the paper down onto the
type for printing. With the raising of the platen, the paper may remain on the type until it is physically
lifted off. Some paper-holding frame must have been used by printers right from the start – it is
unlikely that they could have managed such clean printing if they had been laying the paper on by
hand.

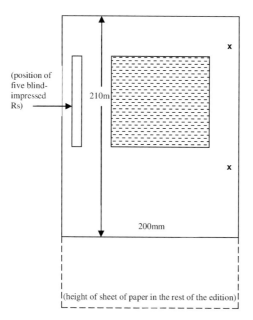

Figure 6.12. Diagram of inserted leaf in quire [k] in *De mysterio missae* showing position of point holes (x) at 160mm apart, of blind-impressed letter Rs and text area of only 17 lines of text. (Usual height of edition *c*.295mm.)

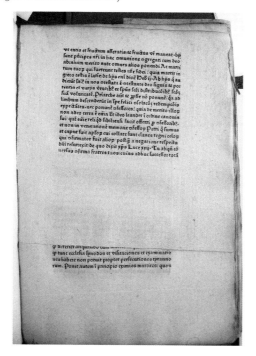

The inserted leaf in quire [k] in *De mysterio missae*. (Ulm Stadtbibliothek.)

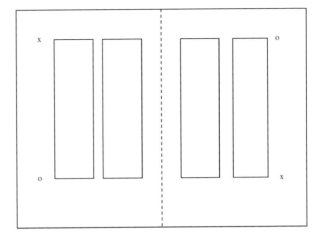

Figure 6.13. Diagram showing pattern of point holes, as found in conjugate leaves in *Rationale divinorum officiorum*, 1473, and *Liber Bibliae*, 1474. The holes punctured from verso to recto are diagonally opposite each other, and the holes punctured from recto to verso are also diagonally opposite each other, on the sheet. x = hole punctured from verso to recto side of leaf; o = hole punctured from recto to verso side of leaf.

leaf. This leaf could have been printed two-up on a full chancery-folio size sheet of paper, but if this had been the case there would have been evidence from four points (two sets for each printing) along the long edge of the sheet. I have not seen evidence of point holes in a row like this on this leaf and suggest that it was more likely that these small single leaves were printed one at a time. The space of 160mm between the point holes does not tally with any other spacing between points found in Zainer's editions; perhaps Zainer added an extra point into a frame already in existence, or had a new frame made especially for printing this extra leaf.

Royal and imperial folios

Zainer only printed ten large folios (nine royal and one imperial), all before 1480, and after that date all his books were printed on smaller paper. Eight were printed within the period of this study. As with the chancery folios the evidence is again incomplete but what is of interest is that there are very obvious changes in Zainer's method sometime between 1473 and 1478. To try to get the best picture of the existence of point holes it has been particularly important to look at more than one copy. As stated above, point holes can close up, or be removed by trimming, depending on their storage, handling and rebinding, through the centuries. One copy of an edition may show a point hole on a leaf that cannot be seen in a different copy. Most of the findings discussed here are of composite findings with notes from more than one copy.

Zainer's first two royal folios, *Rationale*, 1473, and *Liber Bibliae*, 1474, show a very similar pinhole pattern. They have very neat tiny holes for the most part and the positions of the holes are closely related to the text area. They are in line with the top of the text and with the foot of the text and lying approximately 39/40mm, the equivalent of seven ems, out from the text area. Many of them seem to be single-punctured holes, but occasionally some double-punctured ones are evident, sometimes a much as five to seven millimetres apart. It has been possible in a number of the copies to see the direction in which the holes were made.

When looking at a conjugate pair of leaves the holes at the top left and bottom right corners are punctured from the verso to the recto side, and those at top right and bottom left corners are punctured from the recto to verso side. However an element of caution has to used when considering these point hole findings as not all holes are found in every copy. The clearest example of the diagonally opposite holes, and with the majority apparently single-punctured, was noted in the Museum Meermano-Westreenianum copy of *Liber Bibliae*.[34] Other copies did not show this as clearly; occasionally there were leaves with double-punctured holes at the head or the foot and there were leaves with larger holes and leaves with no holes. As the Meermano copy showed the clearest evidence throughout the edition this could suggest that the observable variation in size and existence of the point holes is copy specific. There could be a number of reasons for this. The existence of double-punctured holes in one direction or torn holes is most likely due to the printer fumbling while ensuring the paper is placed in the correct position. The non-existence of holes is more difficult to explain – perhaps they were probably there originally and their disappearance could be due to different handling after printing through the centuries.

It was established from other evidence of set-off marks and cloth impressions (discussed in earlier chapters) that Zainer was printing one page at a time. Because of the neatness of the holes, and one or two occasions of inky drag marks in the inter-columnar margins, it is possible that for these two editions he was working with a paper-holding frame that was detached from the press.[35] The frame may have been large enough to hold a full sheet of paper, with either two or four points on it, or it may just have clasped the one half of the sheet that was being printed with two points. Where there are double-punctured holes there is some suggestion of poor register, but these occasions are rare in both these editions. The overall look of these two editions generally shows a careful approach.

---

[34] MMW catalogue 817, shelfmark 4 A 1.

[35] See Chapter 2, *Initial Observations & Basic Findings*, under 'Inking', and see Figure 2.4 of marks from the sheet dragging on the type when being lifted off the forme.

The registration is good for the most part and the presswork is clean; both factors that are not always evident in Zainer's work.

Zainer's next edition with visible point holes is an imperial folio, *De planctu ecclesiae,* dated October 1474, six months after *Liber Bibliae.* It is his largest edition, in both number and size of leaves, and with the text set in wider and longer columns than his royal folios. Zainer's use of points with this edition is very different from the two earlier royal-folio editions. Out of the 43 quires in total almost half of them, 22, quires [e, f, B–T, dd and ee] show no visible evidence of point holes. Of the remaining 21 quires some have evidence of point holes at the top, some at the foot and some in both positions. Quires [a, b, c, d, k, l, m, n, V, X, Z, aa, bb and cc] all have holes in the fore-edge margin and quires [d, g, h, i, k, A, Y and Z] have holes in mixed positions; some in the fore-edge margin and some in the central gutter. Sometimes there is evidence of double puncturing and sometimes there are only single holes in each position. Some of the sheets in some quires have no evidence of holes in one of the leaves of a sheet but there are holes clearly visible in the conjugate leaf. The holes, on every leaf where they are visible, are roughly the same distance apart, *c.*332mm and roughly the same distance from the text area, *c.*45/46mm. Again their position relates to the text area, lining up almost with the head and foot of the text and being eight ems to the side.

Zainer could have been in the process of changing from using points in the fore-edge margin to points in the central gutter for this edition, which would account for the quires where there are no visible holes. In the leaves where there are point holes on one leaf but not on its conjugate leaf then it could be that the first leaf was printed on a press, using fore-edge-margin holes and the second leaf printed using a press with a central-gutter hole system. The fact that this edition is split in its use of point holes does suggest two different methods of holding the paper and two presses. Because this was a very large edition, it is quite possible that Zainer would have used more than one press for printing it.[36]

The next four royal-folio editions, *Rationale,* 1475, *Quadragesimale,* 1475 and 1476, and *Sermones,* 1475, have very little evidence of point holes. Only one quire, quire [x] in *Sermones,* 1475, shows two point holes in the fore-edge margin. Apart from this one quire it is likely that the rest of these four editions were printed with points in the central gutter. If *De planctu ecclesiae* was printed during a transitional phase in Zainer's paper-holding methods then it could be expected that the editions printed after *De planctu* might be working with holes in the central gutter. Evidence of inky

---

[36] Other evidence from Zainer's use of lines of bearer type discussed in Chapter 4 also suggests that Zainer might have had more than one press. The information about press at SS Ulrich and Afra as discussed by Scholderer ('Notes', pp. 5 and 6) states that there were at least six and perhaps as many as ten presses, in Augsburg in 1474.

drag marks as discussed above, indicating that the paper had not been lifted cleanly off the type after printing, was noted in *Quadragesimale*, 1475, and *Sermones*, 1475 (see Figure 2.4). This suggests that the paper-holding frame was still separate from the press and being manually lifted off. There are also some impressed marks, probably from string, and some inky string marks were noted in copies of all four editions, indicating that Zainer may also have been using string to support his sheets of paper during printing (Figure 2.5). It is not possible to tell how Zainer located this frame accurately on the type block – perhaps it was made to fit exactly over the chase, or whatever was used to make up the forme.

The last royal-folio edition being considered for this study is *Sermones*, 1478. This edition shows evidence of a complete change in method of holding the paper. After having printed four editions without visible point holes in 1475 and 1476, this edition has visible point holes in the fore-edge margin again. However, these are completely different holes from any produced by Zainer before. They are large and messy, almost always double-punctured, sometimes triple- or quadruple-punctured where the printer has struggled to re-locate a hole over a point. They are often torn and show evidence of being made in both directions (Figure 6.6). Because the holes are generally so large they are easier to see and consequently to measure and record. Even so a number of different copies were consulted to assemble the information.

The point holes occur at three different distances apart from each other; *c.*290mm, *c.*330mm and *c.*345mm. The point holes are also positioned differently in relation to the text. Holes that are *c.*290mm apart are found in three different positions (Figure 6.14). They are located level with the text at head and foot (a), at *c.*38mm below the text at head and foot (b), and at *c.*18mm below the text line at head and foot (c). With the holes that are *c.*330mm apart, one hole is level with the head of the text and the other at *c.*38mm below the foot of the text (d). With the point holes that are *c.*345mm apart, the top hole is again level with the head of the text while the lower hole is located at *c.*60mm below the foot of the text (e). There are still a few leaves where only one hole, at either the head or the foot, could be found, and also a few where no hole at all has been found.

There are a number of implications that arise from the point holes being different distances apart. If the points are fixed to a frame, or tympan, then the three different distances would suggest at least three different frames or tympans. Having holes *c.*290mm apart was a common distance for Zainer. 290mm (50 lines of text set in Type 116G) is his standard text-column height for his royal folios. Where he had previously used fore-edge margin points in two of his earlier editions, they were this same 290mm distance apart. 330mm is also a familiar dimension for Zainer as it is the text-column height of his imperial folio *De planctu*

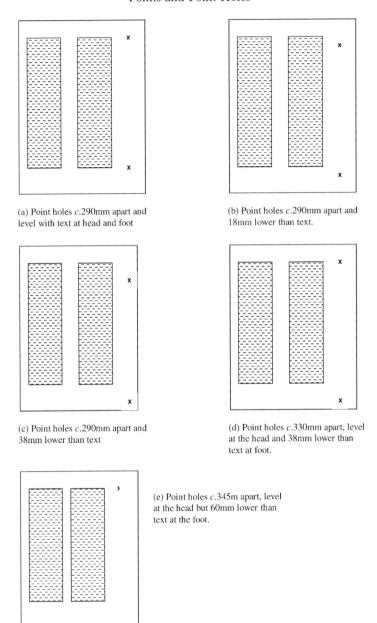

(a) Point holes c.290mm apart and
level with text at head and foot

(b) Point holes c.290mm apart and
18mm lower than text.

(c) Point holes c.290mm apart and
38mm lower than text

(d) Point holes c.330mm apart, level
at the head and 38mm lower than
text at foot.

(e) Point holes c.345m apart, level
at the head but 60mm lower than
text at the foot.

Figure 6.14. Diagrams showing distances apart of point holes in the observed copies of
Sermones, 1478, and their locations relative to the position of the text on the page.

ecclesiae. Where he had used fore-edge margin points in this edition they were also *c.*330mm apart. So for both these sizes he may already have had paper-holding frames in his printshop. The 345mm distance is a new one for Zainer. Nothing has been found in any of the examined editions that might explain a frame with points 345mm apart. It might have been used for his single-leaf *Almanacs*, which had larger text areas than any of his other editions, but on checking the dimensions, the height of their text areas proved to be larger than 345mm. If one accepts that three different distances between points means three different paper-holding frames, then this suggests that Zainer used at least three different presses for printing *Sermones*, 1478, and perhaps he had a totally new press, large enough to take a frame with points 345mm apart.

It is also interesting to see which quires were printed with point holes in the same position. Most of the quires were printed with every leaf in the quire having point holes in the same position. 17 quires [f, g, l, m, n, o, D, K, L, M, N, P, Q, R, S, T and V] were printed with holes 290mm apart and level with the text, six quires [h, i, k, B, F and G,] were printed with holes 330mm apart and six quires[r, s, t, v, x, y and z] were printed with holes 345mm apart (Table 6.1).

Only three quires, [a], [b] and [c,] are printed with holes 290mm apart and with the holes located *c.*38mm below the text area. These three quires contain the tabulated 'contents table' of the edition and would most likely have been printed at the end of the job, and perhaps quite separately from the printing of the rest of the edition. The fact that they were the only quires printed with this hole position could support the theory that they were printed separately.

Most of quire [d] and [I] and all of [e] and a few other odd leaves have visible holes only at either the head or the foot. They may never have had holes in the second position or the holes may have been there once and have since been obscured. Two leaves, [c10] and [V6] have no printed text on either page and no point holes. Their conjugate leaves [c1] and [V1] have both printed text and two double-punctured point holes, punctured in each direction; the link of point hole with text is further evidence that Zainer was printing one page at a time, supporting the similar conclusion from the cloth impression evidence of the previous chapter.

There remain seven quires with mixed point-hole patterns. Apart from one anomaly every leaf within these mixed quires had its reiteration printed on a frame with the holes the same distance apart. The mixing of hole patterns is seen when comparing the holes in one leaf with the holes in its conjugate leaf. For example page [q1r] was printed with a frame with holes 290mm apart, as was its reiteration [q1v]. At some later date its conjugate page [q8r] was printed using a frame with holes 345mm apart, as was its reiteration [q8v]. This could suggest that the recto and verso of

Table 6.1. The different point hole patterns in leaves in the quires in *Sermones*, 1478.

Distance between holes	290mm	290mm	290mm	330mm	345mm			
Head position	Level with text	18mm below head	38 Mm below head	Level with head	Level with head			
Foot position	Level with text	18mm below foot	38 mm below foot	38mm below foot	60 mm below foot	Hole at head or foot only	Three holes	No hole visible
Leaves in quires	f 3–10 g l m n o p1–4 q1,2 C3–5 D E 1–8 H 9,10 I 7,8 K L M N O 5–7,10 P Q R S T V1–5	p 7,8	a b c 1–9	h i k p 5,6 A 4–8 B C1,2,6,7,8 E 9,10 F G H 1–8	q 3–8 r s t v x y z A 1–3	d 9,10 g 2,3,5 O1–4,8,9	q2	d1,4,7,8 e f1,2 I 1–6 V 6

each were printed on the same press, or, if not the same press, then on a second press with a paper-holding frame with points the same distance apart.

The one anomaly is leaf [q2] which has three point holes; one level with the head of the text, one 290mm away and level with the foot of the text and the third at 38mm below the text. Its conjugate leaf [q9] has two holes *c.* 330mm apart. On this occasion it seems that the recto and verso of leaf

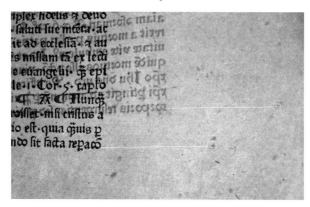

Figure 6.15. Leaf [Q3] of *Sermones*, 1478, showing position of point holes in relation to text on both recto (bottom arrow) and verso (top arrow) sides of the leaf. This image shows what happens when registration, by locating the holes onto the points for the printing the reiteration, is not accurate. The distance, from end of line of text to point hole, is exactly the same in both cases. (Ulm Stadtbibliothek.)

[q2] were not printed on same press; the recto was printed with holes 290mm apart, then paper removed from tympan and the verso was printed on a press, or with frame with holes, 330mm apart. This is the only leaf where holes in three different positions have been found.

Another indication that this edition shows a change in practice is suggested by the large number of instances of poor register. Good registration was never one of Zainer's best attributes but in this edition it is exceptionally poor. Examples of poor register show clearly that the points were crucial for accurate registration. The photo at Figure 6.15 is one of many examples found through this edition which show the relationship between position of the paper on the point and location of text area.

The changes in Zainer's method for holding his paper over the five-year period of this study are summarised below.

(i) He began in 1473, perhaps with his paper held in a frame large enough to hold a full sheet of paper on points in all four corners, the frame perhaps being separate from the press.

(ii) From late 1474 until 1476 he tried working with a frame, still separate from the press, with two points fixed in some manner that meant they made holes in the central gutter of the sheet. These frames may have been made to fit exactly over the forme.

(iii) By late 1477 to 1478 he was working with a tympan and frisket assembly hinged to his press, with a large enough frame for a whole sheet of paper, and he hung the sheet of paper by two points at one end. He printed one page, removed the paper, and turned it over and refixed the sheet to the points, re-using the holes that were punctured in the paper for the first printing, to print the reiteration of that leaf. At some later stage he printed first one, then the other side of the conjugate leaf.

A NOTE ON FRISKETS

It is not certain whether Zainer used a frisket, or some kind of mask to keep the non-printing areas of the paper clean. Because there are frequent inky marks and smudges found in the margins of his editions it seems he might not have always used a frisket. However Zainer's use of a frisket, or some kind of frame with a cut-out mask, could be the cause of some of the blind-impressed linear marks found in some editions.[37] The impressed lines noted in some copies of some of the chancery folio editions usually occur along the foot of the text and run for perhaps only 20–80mm along the foot. Occasionally they are found on the same leaf in different copies of an edition but more usually they are inconsistent. They may or may not have been caused by the edge of a frisket. Only one example has been noted where a possible frisket covered over some of the printed area by mistake. In the BSB copy (shelfmark 2° Inc.c.a.221) of the Latin edition of *Historia Griseldis* the frisket has bitten into the border on page [a1r], cutting out a small section of top right and bottom left corners. This may have been caused by inaccurate positioning of the forme on the bed of the press, and could have been cured by moving the forme slightly, or by trimming more from the frisket to clear the border completely.

Blind impressed lines were also noted very occasionally in some of the royal-folio editions, but again there occurrence was not consistent, and not seen on any leaf in more than one copy.

How Zainer achieved register

Despite the evidence assembled above of point holes, supporting strings and tympans and friskets, it is still not possible to say with any certainty how Zainer achieved register for his earliest royal folios and his chancery folios. If, as at (i) above, he held the paper in a frame and printed both sides of one leaf, and then on a separate occasion printed both sides of its conjugate leaf, he would definitely have needed some method of accurately positioning the paper-holding frame on the type.

How Zainer achieved register with centre point holes as (ii) above is more problematical. He had to align the paper over centrally located

---

[37] See Chapter 2, *Initial Observations & Basic Findings,* under 'Impression and Impressed marks (i)'.

points – perhaps he folded the sheet and lined up as Povey suggested above. This frame still located into the four corners on the bed of the press (iii) above, is perhaps the easiest to understand because Zainer was, for reasons given above, using a frame hinged to the press, a tympan and frisket. With points fixed to the frame and the frame fixed to the press he should have had no problems with register.

All this can at best be speculative because there is so little hard evidence, and much of that evidence is apparently conflicting or can be interpreted in different ways. What is less speculative are the changes noted in Zainer's hole quality and position, from marginal and small, to not visible, to marginal and messy – this latter suggesting his use of a press with tympan and frisket.

7 CONCLUSIONS

The aim of this research has been to make a close study of one printer, Johann Zainer, to collate the facts and information found within copies of his books, and interpret these findings to throw light on his printing practices. To keep the project to a workable scale it was decided to concentrate on just 38 of the editions printed by Zainer in his first six years, 1473–1478. The results of this study show that working with this inductive approach has been successful. New information has been discovered about Zainer and his printing practices, and also aspects of fifteenth-century printing practices that have not previously been discussed.

This has always been a study based on measuring and measurements. Perhaps this is not too surprising as the book printer through the centuries has always had to work strictly to fixed measurements to achieve what is generally taken for granted by the reader, the layout and the readability of the text on the page. Copies of 38 of Zainer's editions were measured; the dimensions of each copy, the width of its margins and the dimensions of its text areas were all measured and recorded. Further, each copy was looked through for other items, such as occurrences of blind impressions from cloths or type letters, of ink-smudges, ink-slur, set-off and off-set ink, and the positions of point holes, which were all noted and recorded. This information was collated with bibliographic information from the incunable bibliographies and library catalogues. One or two copies of some editions printed beyond the cut-off date of 1478 were also examined to try and establish if later books showed the same evidence as those of the earlier period.

PRACTICAL EXPERIMENTS

The data collected from measuring was interpreted, partly on the basis of my printing experience, and also with the help of some practical experiments. The experiments were carried out in three areas; to discover by how much paper might stretch when damped, and then by how much it might shrink on drying (Chapter 2); to look at the stability of a wooden press when part of the type block is removed from the forme (Chapter 4); and to test the various theories of the causes of the cloth impression marks (Chapter 5). All the experiments helped in the fundamental understanding of different aspects of the printing process; paper behaviour, press handling and paper damping.

Understanding by how much a sheet of paper might stretch when damp and then shrink on drying is important to understanding the variations in measurements that might be found when recording the data for this study. The experiment showed that tolerances of between one and two per cent were acceptable, which agreed with Gaskell[1].

Zainer often used lines of bearer type with no obvious reason and to try to understand why he might have used bearers so irregularly an experiment was set up to test the stability of a wooden press. The pressure of the wooden press is transmitted through the end of a spindle. The experiment showed that the platen of a wooden press was unstable and that support would be necessary to balance the platen if more than 15 per cent of the text lines removed from the type block. Support was not necessary if removing only one or two lines from a text block comprising 30 or more lines. Also the more lines removed, the more lines need to be inserted at the foot of the text block to balance the platen. Possible explanations for Zainer's eccentric use of bearer support, where he used bearers right through some quires and not at all in others, could be that he had more than one press, and one had a more unstable platen than the other or that he had more than one pressman, and they worked with different methods.

The last experiment, to try to establish the method that might have caused the blind impressions marks of cloths, involved testing different hypotheses suggested by other scholars. Again the experiments proved essential not only for explaining that the cloth marks had been made as part of Zainer's paper-damping process, but they also showed that the spread of moisture through the stack only travelled up and down and not horizontally.

New information

Some of the evidence discovered from this study is new and has not previously been discussed. Other aspects had been discussed in the literature but the findings from Zainer bring new evidence to the discussion. Perhaps the most important was establishing that Zainer was working to a unit of measurement based on the em of his text face. Zainer was not alone in working like this and evidence was found to show that the em of the text type had been used by other printers as the basis for their page layout from as early as 1454, although not firmly established until *circa* the mid-1460s. One or two editions printed in the 1450s do not seem to have their text width based on their em, but by the mid-1460s the em of the text type being used could be clearly seen to be the unit of measurement to which every printer was working. As in Zainer's editions,

---

[1] Gaskell, *Bibliography*, p. 13.

the spaces left for initials, indents for paragraphs or chapter headings can all be measured in each printer's em. All the editions listed in *Bibliography, primary sources – section 3* were measured and almost all of them (with the omission of the one or two mentioned above) were working to a unit of measurement based on the ems of their text type. This provides a foundation against which to test the editions of yet other printers.

That the em, the square of the type body, has been used as the basis of almost all printing right from the beginning is a significant factor in our understanding of early printing. Printing is complex, involving the handling of many small pieces of metal and a number of processes, all needing skill and experience, to produce good clean work. There is a very high risk of error, especially in inexperienced hands. Having a fixed unit of measure to which to work shows that, despite the many errors seen, the basis of printing in the incunable period was not haphazard, but did have a sound mathematical foundation.

Other new evidence for printing practice came from the interpretation of the cloth impression marks, which showed how Zainer was damping his paper. The experiment showed, unexpectedly, that the moisture would not transmit horizontally through the stack of paper, but only vertically. This meant that if Zainer only damped one half of the sheet he could only print that half. This information could be used for the question of the introduction of the two-pull press – if the cloth impression only covers one leaf, only one half of the sheet will be damp and only one half of the sheet can be printed and therefore it will most likely have been printed on a one-pull press. Zainer was not the only printer damping his paper with wet cloths and cloth impression marks were also found in the editions of other printers, from Rusch in 1467 to Dinckmut in 1488, and from as far apart destinations as Brussels, Basel and Paris. Among the examples found from other printers was a very small cloth mark, covering a single chancery-folio leaf in an edition by Creussner in 1473, and a very large cloth mark, covering two royal-folio leaves and indicating the use of a two-pull press, by Sensenschmidt and Frisner in 1475. Cloth marks were found in editions by Mentelin in Strassburg, from whom Johann probably had originally learnt to print, and by Dinckmut in Ulm, who probably learnt from Zainer. The information from paper damping and its significance for indicating the use of a one-or two-pull press tied in with Hellinga's findings for the introduction of the two-pull press for quartos.

Other aspects previously discussed by scholars included the occurrence of point holes. With Zainer the nature and location of point holes in his editions indicated that he was perhaps using a press with an unattached paper-holding frame in his first three years, and then later, and definitely by 1478, was using a press with a hinged tympan and frisket fixed to the press for holding the paper.

Also mentioned by earlier scholars was the use of bearers. Zainer seemed to use them more often than his contemporaries, and more often than would seem, from the practical experiment, to be technically necessary. Their occurrence in some quires of an edition and not others could mean that there was a difference in balance of the platens in Zainer's presses.

All these factors offer small clues about the nature of Zainer's printing press. They suggest that Zainer had a press with a fairly small platen; just large enough to cope with printing two chancery-folio leaves together, perhaps measuring *c*.300mm × 400mm (about 50mm shorter than a sheet of A3 paper today). At least one of his presses was fairly unstable, as it seems that support for the platen, in the form of bearer lines, was necessary even when the type area was short of only two or three lines of text. Because of evidence of loose lock-up indicated by the number of raised, inked spaces, he may not have been locking up his type in a chase but instead placing the lines of type in a tray or galley, which was in turn placed into position on the bed of the press. The one-way point holes suggest that his paper was clasped in a separate frame until *c*.1478 when his two-way point holes, with strong evidence of their link with the register of the sheets of paper, indicate his use of a tympan and frisket. The cloth impressions marks show that he was not using a two-pull press.

There are also clues about Zainer's printing methods. Evidence from the material used for bearers occurring in two different editions, and his uneven use of bearers through an edition, suggests more than one press in his printshop, and more than one edition being printed at one time. He worked from the outside of his quires towards the centre for his chancery folios, but sequentially through his royal-folio editions.

Quality control did not seem to be one of Zainer's prime concerns. Extraneous ink marks are found regularly through all his editions, as are poorly imposed pages. These were obviously not things that bothered him. The overall picture of his printing is that it was done in a hurry, which rather spoils his exciting use of woodcut illustrations and initials.

The question of chronology

Apart from applying the information discovered about Zainer to the consideration of the operation of the printing press and the practices of the printer in the 1470s, it is also possible to use the information about Zainer's printing practices to help with the chronology of some of his undated editions. There is no bibliography that gives a chronological list of all Zainer's editions. Amelung did list the editions he was describing in a chronological order, but he does not list all Zainer's editions.[2] Many of

[2] Amelung, *Der Frühdruck*.

Zainer's editions were undated, and some just have a printed year but no month or day. When there is a lack of printed evidence from the colophon for the date then other methods must be sought.

Changes in practice can indicate a chronological progression. However this statement must be viewed with caution as the direction of a printer's progress can reverse, and having established that a certain printer did have a change in practice at a certain date, there is nothing to say that he stayed with that practice and did not revert back to an earlier practice at a later date. However if the evidence for a change in practice comes from more than one source, then it becomes more robust; an accumulation of small bits of evidence can support each other.

If a chronology for changes in practice can be established then these can be used to help to establish when some previously undated editions might have been printed. For example two aspects of Zainer's printing practice in his early editions can be used to suggest a firmer date of printing for two of them. There are five editions that all have a narrow central gutter, which I suggest means that they were printed at a very similar time, and before Zainer changed to a wider central gutter. Also they all have cloth impression marks where the marks go right off the edges of the paper (dates based on Amelung and ISTC).

Deutsche Chronik	February 1473
De mysterio missae	May 1473
De periculis contingentibus	[*c.*1473]
De adhaerendo Deo	[*c.*1473]
Historia Griseldis (Latin)	1473

These are the only five of Zainer's editions that show these two distinctive features. Also the first three editions are all printed in the early versions of Type 116G, the last two use Type 110R. All Zainer's other editions, printed in the first three years use new, later, variant letters in Type 116G, which suggest they were printed after this group. *Deutsche Chronik, De mysterio missae* and *De adhaerendo Deo* all use the same set of initial letters. *Historia Griseldis* (Latin) uses a new set of initials, used by five subsequent editions, which suggests it may have been printed after *De adhaerendo Deo* (Table 7.1).[3]

There are other editions printed in or allocated to 1473 that show different practice. *De claris mulieribus* (German) [not before 14 Aug 1473] has a wide central gutter and cloth marks with edges within the confines of the sheet of paper.[4] It seems likely that any edition printed with the

---

[3] See further information about Zainer's initials and his use of them in the *Appendix* and Table App.1.

[4] This dating is from Amelung p. 78 who states that Steinhöwel dated the dedication of this edition on 14 August 1473. A copy in Budapest has a purchase date of 1473.

wide central gutter and visible edges to the cloth marks will have been printed after the group of five listed above and about the same period as *De claris mulieribus* (German). *De Claris mulieribus* (Latin) is dated 1473, also has the new variant letters of Type 116G and the second set of ornamental initials as well as the wide central gutter and cloth marks within the edges of the sheet of paper. It may have been printed before the German edition but because it shares so many features with the German edition the two will most likely have been printed at about the same time and after the block of five listed above. Both the *De claris mulieribus* editions share these same production features with the Swabian and German editions of *Historia Griseldis*, and none of this group of four have any of the features of the earlier group of five as shown in Table 7.1. Table 7.1a lists nine of Zainer's chancery-folio editions in the chronology suggested by ISTC together with the order given by Amelung in *Frühdruck*. Table 7.1b lists the same editions but in the order suggested by the different printing practices.

The use of a particular combination of sorts and letters as bearer type in some undated editions *c.*1476 also help with firming up the chronology. The same sorts in bearer lines are used in the dated *Aurea Biblia*, 1476 and the undated *De horis canonicis*, and *Vocabularius Bibliae*, suggesting that all were in the printshop either at the same time or at least with some close overlap in their production.[5]

Bringing together Zainer's change in typeface along with his change of gutter width can help to clarify the chronology with two later undated editions. Aesop's *Vita et fabulae* and the *Decameron*, are both printed with the very short-lived Type 117G.[6] *Vita et fabulae* has a wide central gutter that had been used for the previous three years and the *Decameron* has a narrow central gutter, being re-introduced and subsequently used for the next seven or eight years. These two factors suggest that *Vita et fabulae* was printed before the *Decameron*. Another aspect can be introduced to firm up this chronology. Around the same time Zainer introduced a change in quiring pattern; *Vita et fabulae* was quired in 10s, as had been most of Zainer's editions up to that time but the *Decameron* was quired in the alternating 8- and 10-leaf quire pattern peculiar to Zainer, and only used for 8 editions (see Table 7.2). All come together to suggest that *Vita et fabulae* printed first, and *Decameron* later, it being the last edition printed with Type 117G before Zainer changed to his new text type Type 96G. This Type 96G was used on its own for two editions only and thereafter with display type Type 136G.

The chronological use of typeface together with quiring pattern could also be used for strengthening the dating of Zainer's three different

---

[5] See Chapter 4.
[6] See Chapter 1, *Introduction*, under 'Zainer's typefaces'.

Table 7.1a. Some of Zainer's early chancery-folio editions with printed or ascribed dates of 1473, in chronological order suggested by ISTC and Amelung.

Rank	Date	Title	Text type	Centre gutter	Cloth over edge	Printed initials
1	11 Feb 1473	*Deutsche Chronik*	116*/110	narrow	yes	1a
2	29 May 1473	*De mysterio missae*	116*a	narrow	yes	1a
3	1473	*De claris mulieribus* [Latin]	116ab	wide	no	2a
4	[not before 14 Aug 1473]	*De claris mulieribus* [German]	116*ab	wide	no	2a
5	1473	*Historia Griseldis* [Latin]	110	narrow	yes	2a
6	[c.1473]	*Historia Griseldis* [Swabian]	116ab	wide	no	2a
7	[1473]	*De periculis contingentibus*	116a	narrow	yes	spaces
8	[1473]	*De adhaerendo Deo*	110	narrow	yes	1a
9	[c.1473–74]	*Historia Griseldis* [German]	116ab	wide	no	2a

Table 7.1b. The same editions but in an order suggested by Zainer's printing practices, of a wide or narrow centre gutter, and cloth marks over the edge of the paper, along with the use of different printed initials. Four of the editions have the same ranking, two move up (earlier) and three move down (later).

Rank from above table	New rank	Date	Title	Text type	Centre gutter	Cloth over edge	Printed initials
1	1	11 Feb 1473	*Deutsche Chronik*	116*/110	narrow	yes	1a
2	2	29 May 1473	*De mysterio missae*	116*a	narrow	yes	1a
7	3	[1473]	*De periculis contingentibus*	116a	narrow	yes	spaces
8	4	[1473]	*De adhaerendo Deo*	110	narrow	yes	1a
3	5	1473	*Historia Griseldis* [Latin]	110	narrow	yes	2a
4	6	[not before 14 Aug 1473]	*De claris mulieribus* [German]	116*ab	wide	no	2a
5	7	1473	*De claris mulieribus* [Latin]	116ab	wide	no	2a
6	8	[c.1473]	*Historia Griseldis* [Swabian]	116ab	wide	no	2a
9	9	[c.1473–74]	*Historia Griseldis* [German]	116ab	wide	no	2a

editions of Voragine's *Legenda aurea*. There has been variation in their dating in different bibliographies, but ISTC lists them as follows:

(ij00087000) [*c*.1476] no reason given for dating in ISTC
(ij00088400) [not after 1477] purchase note BSB 1477, Amelung – paper source 1477
(ij00091000) [not after 1478] purchase note 1478 Chicago copy

ISTC dates (ij00087000) to [*c*.1476] but gives no reason for this. Amelung states that the dating of (ij00087000) is 'firm' but gives no reason. (ij00091000) is dated to [not after 1478] from a purchase note in the Chicago copy, and (ij00088400) to [not after 1477] from a purchase note of 1477 in the BSB copy. Amelung adds to the information about the (ij00088400) edition that its paper was made in the Urach papermill in 1477. Two of these editions therefore have attributed dates that are well founded. The (ij00087000) edition remains with a doubtful date of [*c*.1476] which in light of new information could be improved. There are some other factors to be added that might help. (ij00088400) is printed in Type 96G only. (ij00087000) and (ij00091000) both use Type 96G together with Type 136G, which suggests they were printed later. (ij00088400) and (ij00091000) are both quired in alternating 8s and 10s, whereas (ij00087000) is quired only in 8s. (ij00088400) and (ij00091000) both use the same printed ornamental initials right through whereas (ij00087000) only uses one initial for the incipit. All these factors indicate that (ij00087000) was probably printed after the other two editions and not earlier as suggested by ISTC. In 1476 Zainer was still using Type 117G, a wide central gutter and quiring in 10s – (ij00087000) does not fit in with his printing practice of the time. It is more likely that edition (ij00087000) should be dated [after 1478]. To summarise:

(ij00088400) [not after 1477] purchase note 1477, paper source 1477, quired 8&10, Type 96G, printed ornamental initials 5, 5a, 6, printed folios in Arabic numerals.[7]
(ij00091000) [not after 1478] purchase note 1478, quired 8&10, Type 96G & Type 136G, printed ornamental initials 5, 5a, 6, no printed folios.
(ij00087000) [after 1478] quired 8, Type 96G & Type 136G, one printed ornamental initial 5, spaces for initials, no printed folios.

There is one last edition, *Praeceptorium,* which could perhaps also be dated earlier. At present it has a suggested date of [not after 1479] from a note of date of purchase in a BSB copy. However by 1479 Zainer was quiring in 8s

---

[7] See Appendix for details of ornamental initials.

Table 7.2a. Some chancery-folio editions in as near as possible chronological order following Amelung and ISTC.

Rank	Date	Title	Text type	Centre gutter	Number of leaves in quire	Reason cited by ISTC or Amelung
1	[14]76	*Die 24 goldenen Harfen*	117	wide	10	MS inscription 1476
2	[not after 1476]	*Documenta moralia*	116b/117	wide	10	none given
3	[c.1476–77]	*Vita et fabulae*	117	wide	10	use of Type 117
4	[c.1476]	*Decameron*	117	narrow	8&10	
5	[c.1476]	*Legenda aurea* [ij00087000]	96/136	narrow	8	
6	[not after 1477]	*Legenda aurea* [ij00088400]	96	narrow	8&10	purchase note 1477 – BSB copy
7	9 Mar 1478	*Sermones*	96	n/a	8&10	
8	[not after 1478]	*Legenda aurea* [ij00091000]	96/136	narrow	8&10	purchase note 1478 – Chicago copy
9	[not after 1478]	*Sermones* [ia00331000]	96/136	narrow	8&10	purchase note 1478
10	[not after 1478]	*Postilla*	96/136	narrow	8&10	none given
11	[c.1478–80]	*Vitae sanctorum*	96/136	narrow	8&10	none given
12	[c.1478–80]	*Sermones* [ia00332000]	96/136	narrow	8	after *Sermones* [A-331]
13	[not after 1479]	*Praeceptorium*	96/136	narrow	8&10	purchase note 1479 – BSB copy

Table 7.2b. The same editions in revised chronological order based on width of centre gutter, quiring pattern and use of different typefaces. Only two editions keep the same ranking, two move up and the remaining nine move down.

Rank from above table	New rank	Date	Title	Text type	Centre gutter	Number of leaves in quire	Reason for my moving
2	1	[not after 1476]	Documenta moralia	116b/117	wide	10	last use of Type 116/first use Type 117
1	2	[14]76	Die 24 goldenen Harfen	117	wide	10	
3	3	[c.1476–77]	Vita et fabulae	117	wide	10	
4	4	[c.1476]	Decameron	117	narrow	8&10	
6	5	[not after 1477]	Legenda aurea [jj00088400]	96	narrow	8&10	Type 96 only
7	6	9 mar 1478	Sermones	96	n/a	8&10	
8	7	[not after 1478]	Legenda aurea [jj00091000]	96/ 136	narrow	8&10	
9	8	[not after 1478]	Sermones [ia00331000]	96/ 136	narrow	8&10	
10	9	[not after 1478]	Postilla	96/ 136	narrow	8&10	
11	10	[c.1478–80]	Vitae sanctorum	96/ 136	narrow	8&10	
13	11	[not after 1479]	Praeceptorium	96/ 136	narrow	8&10	number of leaves in quires
5	12	[c.1476]	Legenda aurea [jj00087000]	96/ 136	narrow	8	number of leaves in quires, Type 96 with Type 136 for heading
12	13	[c.1478–80]	Sermones [ia00332000]	96/ 136	narrow	8	

and *Praeceptorium* is in alternate 8s and 10s. The group of editions printed in alternate quires of 8 and 10 leaves stand so clearly apart from the later editions, when Zainer worked almost exclusively in quires of 8, that *Praeceptorium* should probably be part of the 8- and 10-leaf quire group, and dated to [*c*.1478].

FURTHER RESEARCH

This study has shown that, from focusing on the printing practices of one printer, the information discovered can bring results, in both a deeper understanding of that particular printer and in a wider understanding of printing practices in general in the incunable period. Similar comparative studies of other printers could provide more information and all go towards building up a larger picture of fifteenth-century printing practices.

Apart from similar studies there is further research that could be done in certain areas. There is still more evidence to be collected for cloth impressions. There must be many more examples of cloth impression marks, in copies of editions by other printers. It will take time to discover them but it would be worthwhile to keep adding them to the list and interesting to see how widespread was the method of damping paper with cloths.

It would be interesting to explore the early printers' use of the em of their typeface further. The use of the em is another tool that could be used to help unravel some of the so far unsolved puzzles in the first two decades of printing. It should be possible to add whether the em was used as a basis for printing to the information about many of the early Donatus editions, for instance, and see if any findings about ems correlate with what has been discovered about the different states of the typefaces.

The information from the textual analysis carried out by other scholars, has indicated at least two compositors setting the text for an edition. It could prove useful to consider the information from these studies together with any findings about printing practice. Unfortunately it proved difficult to do this with the *Decameron* and Bertelsmeier-Kierst's findings as it was not possible to obtain conclusive enough evidence from the *Decameron*. However it could be worth further comparing Fujii's findings from Günther's editions to see if they link with any other technical evidence of printing practice.

Another area worthy of exploration is the link between printer and binder. There were strong indications that there was a connection between Zainer and the Ulm binder and printer Konrad Dinckmut over a number of years. It would be interesting to discover the extent of this connection, and if it could be determined whether it was the printer or the binder (or the customer) who had the final say in the dimensions of the finished copy.

Zainer's printing practices were similar to those of his contemporaries. The marks and mistakes shown in his editions can also be found in those of his contemporaries. However he showed them more regularly and more clearly than his fellow printers which made him an ideal subject for this study.

APPENDIX

ZAINER'S DECORATIVE INITIALS

Zainer used at least nine different sets of decorative initials, although not all seem to have been as full alphabets. They are discussed in *BMC* and also by Amelung but some of the information is confusing. To try to clarify the situation the different sets of initials used by Zainer from 1473–1478 have been brought together here. Sketches of the different sets of initials are included to show the differences described in *BMC* as 1a, 1b, 1c and 2a and 2b. They are reproduced as near to actual size as the photocopier will allow.

The initials are listed with their height in millimetres and also as the number of lines of type with which they were designed to fit. None of sets form complete alphabets; they seem to comprise only the letters that were needed. The most complete is set 4, which was being printed with both Latin and German text and includes U, V and W, but no J or X. Where more than one of the same initial has been used on a page it is evident that some letters had at least one, and on one occasion as many as five sorts, of the same design. For many of the letters there was also a variant of the basic design.

Table App.1 shows the editions in which the various letters have been found. There seems to be a chronological basis to the introduction of a new design of letters but not necessarily to their final use; letters from 2 are used in *Aurea Biblia*, 1475 along with 1b, and letters from 1a are used in *Vocabularius Bibliae* [*c*.1476], perhaps because all the letters from 1c had been used and he was still short of a letter E so went back to an earlier fount. Some editions, such as *De mysterio missae*, used initials and also left spaces for them to be inserted later by hand, for which I could discern no reason. This is also commonly found in the work of other printers

Johann's 3-line initials are very similar to those used by his brother Günther as illustrated, with multiple variations, by Albert Schramm.[1] This area of Zainer's initials, and their closeness in design to those of his brother could benefit from further research.

---

[1] Albert Schramm, 'Günther Zainer, Augsburgs erster Drucker', in M. Breslauer and K. Koehler, eds., *Werden und Wirken* (Leipzig: Koehler, 1924), p. 374.

1a. 3-line initials (Type 116G), 17mm high, *BMC* 1a. Lombardic in design. Only 19 letters have been noted, 18 of which plus the alternate design of A are shown here. There is also a Q. Those illustrated here have been traced from *Büchlein der Ordnung* reprinted in Klebs and Sudhof, *Die ersten gedruckten Pestschriften* (1926). The Z is back to front. Used in *Büchlein der Ordnung*, *Deutsche Chronik*, *De mysterio missae*, and one letter in *De adhaerendo Deo*.

1b. 3-line initials (Type 116G), 17mm high, *BMC* 1b. Similar in design to 1a, but with wider letter shapes and ornamented with black beads. Gently traced through heavy acetate sheet to protect the pages, from original copy of *Rationale* in Ulm Stadtbibliothek. A total of 21 letters have been found with alternate designs of G and S. Used in *Summa, Liber Bibliae, De planctu ecclesiae, De periculis, Rationale* 1475, and *Sermones de sanctis*. Also used later in *Quaestiones* and *Vocabularius Bibliae*.

1c. 3-line initials Type 116G), 17mm high, *BMC* 1c. Similar letter design as above, some letters with white beads, others without. Traced as above from original copy of *Documenta moralia*. 18 different letters have been found with many with variant designs. There are four different designs of E and S, three A, two D, F, I, L, M, N, and U. The E with small black bead may belong to 1b. Used in 10 different editions from June 1475 until 1476.

2. 4-line initials (Type 116G), 22mm high *BMC* 2a. 20 letter shapes with leaves noted, plus S which is a serpent. Those shown traced from Amelung, *Frühdruck*, plus two traced from original copy of *Historia Griseldis* in Ulm. An alternate M of two birds, alternate D (also used as a Q) and G of a serpent. Only part of the alphabet is illustrated here. Used in 1473 in both editions of *De claris mulieribus* and all three editions of *Historia Griseldis* plus later in *Aurea Biblia* 1475, *De horis canonicis* and in the quarto *De legendis antiquorum* [*c*.1478].

3. 10-line initials (Type 116G), 56mm high, *BMC* 3a & 3b. Illustrated in full by Amelung, *Frühdruck*, pp. 62–63, and titled by him as the romanisches Alphabet. Fits with 10 lines of Type 116G. First used in *Liber Bibliae* April 1474. Amelung shows 24 letters but in reality there are only 22 as the D is the E upside down, and the J is the L upside down.

4. 5-line initials (Type 117G), 29mm high. A different Lombardic design, cut especially for Aesop's *Vita et fabulae*. Those shown traced Amelung, *Frühdruck*, pp. 96–98. There are 24 letters in total and most have two variant designs. Towards the end of the edition a third version of A and N were introduced. Only part of the set is illustrated here, and none of the variant designs shown.

5. 10-line initials (Type 96G), 48mm high, *BMC* 2b. Illustrated in full

Table App. 1 listing the use of different sets of Zainer's printed woodcut initials in his editions. The 'special initials' listed in the far right column are individual initials that were not part of any matching set.

Design number allocated	Date	Spaces	3-Line Type 116 – 17mm high			4-Line Type 116 – 22mm high	10-Line Type 116 – 56mm high	5-Line Type 117 – 29mm high	10-Line Type 96 – 48mm high	7-Line Type 96 – 33mm high	4-Line Type 96 – 19mm high	Spec initial	Border
			1a	1b	1c	2	3	4	5	5a	6		
Büchlein	1473		✓									✓U	✓
Deutsche Chronik	1473		✓									✓A	✓
De mysterio missae	29 May 1473	✓	✓									✓I	✓
De periculis contingentibus	[1473]	✓											
De adherendo Deo	[c.1473]	✓	1✓									✓D	✓
Historia Griseldis (Latin)	1473					1✓						✓L	✓
Historia Griseldis (Swabian)	[c.1473]					✓							
De claris mulieribus (Latin)	1473					✓						✓S	✓
De claris mulieribus (German)	[nb415ag1473]				✓								
Historia Griseldis (German)	[c.1473–74]					1✓					✓D		
Rationale	3 Dec 1473	✓										✓Q	✓
De periculis contingentibus	[1474]			✓									✓
Summa	1474			✓									
Liber Bibliae	9 Apr 1474			✓			✓					✓Q	✓
De planctu ecclesiae	26 Oct 1474			✓			✓					✓O	✓
De periculis contingentibus	[b417 Jun 1475]			✓									

Rationale	18 Mar 1475	✓								✓	
Sermones de sanctis	1475	✓								✓	
Aurea Biblia	17 Jun 1475			[1]✓	✓	✓	✓				
Quadragesimale	20 Oct [14]75				✓	✓	✓				✓
Quaestiones	1475			✓	✓	✓	✓				
Quadragesimale	[14]76			✓	✓	✓	✓				
Aurea Biblia	1476			✓	✓	✓	✓				✓
De horis canonicis	[c.1476]			✓	✓	✓	✓				
De periculis contingentibus	[c.1476]			✓	✓	✓	✓				
Vocabularius Bibliae	[c.1476]			✓	✓		✓				
Documenta moralia	[na1476]			✓	✓	✓	✓				
24 goldene Harfen	[14]76			[1]✓	✓	✓	✓				
Aesop	[c.1476]	✓						✓A			
Decameron	[c.1476]	✓									
Legenda aurea (ij00088400)	[na1477]	✓	✓						✓		
Sermones quadragesimales	9 Mar 1478	✓	✓						✓		
Legenda aurea (ij00091000)	[c.1478]	✓	[1]✓						✓		
Legenda aurea (ij00087000)	[c.1476]	✓	[1]✓						✓		
Vitae sanctorum	[c.1478–80]	✓									
Sermones (ia00331000)	[na1478]	✓									
Praeceptorium	[na1479]	✓									
Postilla	[1478]	✓									
Total		13	4	9	10	9	10	1	4	2	2

Figure App. 1. Initials 1a, 1b, 1c.

Figure App. 2. Initials 2, 3, 4.

by Amelung, pp. 67–68, and titled by him as the rococo Alphabet. Amelung shows 18 letters, which includes a variant D. The letters were cut to fit with 10 lines of the new text type, Type 96G, and used from some time in 1477 in the three editions of *Legenda aurea* and Albertus Magnus' *Sermones*.

5a. 7-line initial (Type 96G), 33mm high, *BMC* 2b. The letter U only, of same romanisch design as 3 above. Used in two editions of *Legenda aurea*, and some later editions after the period of this study. Amelung p. 102.

6. 4-line initials (Type 96G) 19mm high, *BMC* 2b. Three variations of 22 letter designs based on birds, leaves and flowers, and designed to fit with the new Type 96G. Used in two editions of *Legenda aurea* and some later editions after the period of this study. Only three versions of one letter, F, illustrated here, and not the full alphabet (from photographs of *Legenda aurea* in Ulm Stadtbibliothek).

There are also a few one-off letters not illustrated here, listed as 'special initials' in Table App.1:
10-line (Type 116G) Q in *Rationale divinorum officiorum*, 1473 (Amelung p. 85) and *Summa de eucharistiae sacramento*.
6-line (Type 116G) U used in *Büchlein der Ordnung* (Amelung p. 70).
6-line (Type 116G) A in *Deutsche Chronik*.
6-line (Type 116G) D in *De adhaerendo Deo*.
6-line (Type 116G) I in *De mysterio missae*, 1473 (Amelung p. 73).
6-line (Type 116G) L used in *Historia Griseldis* (Latin) (Amelung p. 83).

As well as letters with extensions of letter to form a partial border not illustrated here:
A in *Mönch von Salzburg*, 1473 (Amelung p. 72).
S in the Latin edition of *De claris mulieribus* (Amelung p. 75).
D in the German edition of *De claris mulieribus* (Amelung p. 77).
S used in *Biblia Latina* (Amelung p. 64).

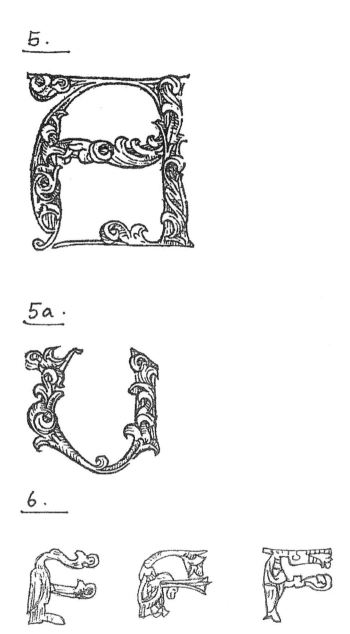

Figure App. 3. Initials 5, 5a, 6.

GLOSSARY

ascender – strokes of *lower-case* letters that stand up above the body of the letter.

beard – as used by Moxon refers to the *shoulder* of a piece of type below the bottom line of the *face* (see diagram at Figure 3.1).

bed (press) – flat surface on which the type *forme* is placed for printing.

bifolium (plural **bifolia**) – a *sheet* of paper folded once to produce two *leaves,* which are *conjugate.*

bleed (ink) – ink soaking into and through the paper so visible on the reverse.

blind impression – an un-inked impressed mark on a sheet of paper.

body (type) – the size, from front to back, of a piece of type, today measured in points based on 72 points to an inch. For the fifteenth-century type is customarily measured in millimetres over 20 lines of text. (see Figure 3.1).

chase – a rectangular frame in which the type and associated *furniture* are locked up.

composing stick – a small wooden (later metal) tray for holding the type letters and *spacing* as the lines of type are set.

conjugate leaf – a leaf, joined to another, as part of a *sheet* folded once. A sheet of paper, folded in half, provides two *conjugate leaves.*

conjugate pages – two pages of text on the same side of a sheet of paper in a folio.

deckle edge – the edge of a sheet of hand-made paper, often uneven, formed where a little of the pulp seeps between the papermaker's mould and deckle, when the sheet is made.

depth of drive – the depth to which a *punch* is driven into the *matrix,* which in turn is the basis for the distance from the printing *face* of a piece of type to the *shoulder.*

descender – strokes of *lower-case* letters that hang below the body of the letter, or below the baseline.

edition – a bibliographical entity; a particular printed work, be it broadside or book or pamphlet, printed in a number of copies.

em – here used as a measure that is the square of the type *body* size.

en – a measure that is half an *em.*

feed-edge – the edge of a sheet of paper that has a fixed position on the press, it is always the edge of the sheet that is positioned on the press first.

foliation – the numbering of leaves of a book.

folio – used to describe the format of a book. Also a sheet of paper folded in two, giving two *leaves* (a bifolium) or four pages. Also a *leaf* with a *page* on each side.

foot – the bottom edge of a book or the bottom of the *type block* or *text page.*

footsticks – wooden lengths of *furniture,* placed in the chase at the foot of the forme.

fore-edge – the front edge of a book.

forme – the combination of *furniture* and type letters locked up in the *chase*.

forme (inner) – the pages of type that are printed on the inside of a folded sheet before the folding.

(outer) – the pages of type that are printed on the outside of a folded sheet before the folding.

fount – a complete set of type letters, including punctuation, numerals, signs, etc., cast to the same body size and typeface design. There should be sufficient quantities of the various letters for them to be used without running out of any particular letter much before another. The records from SS Ulrich and Afra in Augsburg described founts of 40,000 characters being ordered.

furniture – spacing material, usually as lengths of wood, lower in height than the type face, placed around and between the *type blocks* to support and fill out the *forme* in the *chase*.

frisket – iron frame, attached to the *tympan*, usually covered with parchment or a sheet of paper, that supports and masks part of the sheet of paper being printed.

galley – a two- or three-sided wooden or metal tray used for storing or transporting set type matter.

gathering – see *quire*.

gutter – used here for the central margin between *text areas* on two *conjugate leaves*, or the space between two *type blocks* (see also *inter-columnar margin*).

hanging indent – a line or paragraph that begins with the text protruding out into the margin at the left, beyond the *text area*, rather than being indented into the *text area*.

head – the top of a book or the top of the *type block* or *text page*.

headline – the top line, above the text giving a running title or chapter number or folio/page number.

imposition – positioning of *type block(s)* on the sheet to be printed, so that the pages are in correct reading order when printed.

impression – the pressure applied when printing a sheet of paper. Also the impressed mark from printed type (or anything else), either blind or inked, on a sheet.

indent – the space at the beginning of a line, often for a new paragraph.

ink balls – a pair of wooden-handled instruments, shaped like large darning mushrooms, with a leather-covered, round head, filled with wool, used for inking the type.

inter-columnar margin – the space between two columns of text (see also *gutter*).

leaf – two *pages* back to back.

ligature – two or more letters linked to each other, and often cast as one sort.

line length – the length of line as seen on the page, also called *text-page width*.

lock-up – term used for the procedure of keeping all the lines of type tightly together to avoid any movement during the printing process.

lower-case – the minuscule or small letters of the alphabet.

margin – the white space surrounding the type area (see also *inter-columnar margin* and *gutter*).

matrix – a mould, usually of copper, into which a *punch* has been struck and from which the face of the letter is cast.

measure – the width to which the type and spacing is set, not always the same as the visible *line length* on the page.

off-set – inked marks that occur when freshly printed text is transferred onto another surface and then re-transferred from this to another surface. This can occur, by mistake, when ink from a freshly printed page transfers to the tympan, and then from the tympan back to the sheet being printed on the press (see also *set-off*).

packing – paper or fabric of various density inserted between outer and inner *tympan* layers to cushion the surface of the type letters in the *forme*, when being printed, from the pressure of the *platen*.

page – one side of a *leaf*.

platen – a rectangular solid of wood (or later iron), part of the press used to impress the paper onto the inked type. The size of the platen limits the size of the *type block* that can be printed.

point holes – holes made by the points in the sheet of paper, when the paper is placed on the points for printing, sometimes called pinholes by others..

points – small pieces of metal fixed to the *tympan* on which the sheet of paper is placed before printing. Also used for accurate *register* when printing the *reiteration*.

punch – a piece of steel with a letter engraved at the end, driven into a piece of copper to make a *matrix*.

quad – short for quadrat, a term used for large spacing. It is cast to the depth of the type *body* (but lower than the type letters in height) in various thicknesses; most usually an *en* or *em*, or 2-, 3- or 4-ems thick.

quire – a gathering made up of the *leaves* of a folded *sheet* or of a number of folded *sheets*, one inside the other.

quire (papermakers') – 24 or 25 sheets of paper / a twentieth of a ream.

recto – the upper face of a leaf (the right-hand *page* of an open book).

register – the adjustment of pages printing back to back so the text areas exactly align.

reiteration – the second side of a *leaf* or *sheet* to be printed.

set width – the thickness of a physical type letter from one side to the other.

set-off – marks made in error from the wet ink of a freshly printed page onto another page, or other surface, placed on top of it.

shank – the entire body of a piece of type which supports the letter at the top (see Figure 3.1).

sheet – a piece of paper, usually printed flat, either one, two, four, eight or more pages at a time, and then folded after printing, before being gathered into a *quire* and being bound up into the finished book. Fifteenth-century editions were usually printed on either of four basic sheet sizes.

shoulder – the top of the *shank* of a piece of type. In early printing it often caught ink and printed. Later it was filed down so as not to mark the page (see Figure 3.1).

skeleton – the basic *forme* of *furniture* and *chase* but without the *type block*.

sort – general term for any piece of type.

spine – the back of a book.

spacing – pieces of type, cast to various thicknesses and of the same *body* size as the type face but standing lower. Used to fill the space between words, paragraphs, or fill out the end of lines.

stone – level surface on which to impose the *forme* and ensure all the type letters stand evenly.

text area – the area on the page covered with printed text – see *text page*.

text page – the text part of the page as printed on the page. See also *type block*.

text-page width – see *line length*.

tympan – a frame covered with fabric or parchment, hinged to the press bed, on which the paper is fixed for printing. It comprises two frames, one fitting inside the other, between which *packing* can be inserted.

type block – all the printed matter set and ready to go in the *forme* for printing.

type face – the top, level, printing surface of a piece of type (see Figure 3.1).

typeface – the design of the letterforms in a fount.

type page – see *type block*.

upper case – all the majuscules or large letters in a fount.

verso – the lower face of a *leaf*, the other side to the *recto* (the left-hand *page* in an open book).

BIBLIOGRAPHY

Primary sources

Primary sources used for this research are divided into three separate sections. Section 1 lists the copies of the editions printed by Zainer between 1473 and 1478 that were used as the basis for this research. Section 2 lists copies of other editions printed by Zainer that were looked at but not used as a basis for core information. Section 3 lists copies of editions by other printers that were also studied.

Other Primary Sources – the Bibliographies and Catalogues consulted throughout this research – are listed above under 'Abbreviations'.

The lists give:

Date of printing from ISTC, printed in the edition or, if in square brackets, assigned later.

Author's name.

Title – usually following orthography of the Bodleian Library.

ISTC number.

Location:

ANT – Plantin-Moretus Museum, Antwerp
AUG – Augsburg Stadt- und Staatbibliothek
BL – British Library, London
BOD – Bodleian Library, Oxford
BSB – Bayerische Staatsbibliothek, Munich
CUL – Cambridge University Library
JRL – John Rylands Library, Manchester
MEM – Stadtbibliothek, Memmingen
MMW – Museum Meermano-Westreenianum, The Hague
MZ – Gutenberg Museum Bibliothek, Mainz and Stadtbibliothek, Mainz
OTTO – Ottobeuren Abbey
RUL – Reading University Library
SBU – Stadtbibliothek, Ulm
UBW – Universitätsbibliothek Würzburg
WIN – Royal Library, Windsor

Library catalogue number, where applicable; see 'Abbreviations' above.

Library shelfmark.

A concordance is given at the end from ISTC numbers to Hain, *GW* and Goff numbers.

Section 1: editions and copies printed by Zainer used as the basis for this research

ISTC date	ISTC	Author	Title	Library	Cat. no.	Shelfmark
11 Jan 1473	is00762800	Heinrich Steinhöwel	*Büchlein der Ordnung*	BL	II 520	IA. 9103
				BSB	S-570	Rar.707
				AUG	1937	1 an 4° Ink 232
11 Feb 1473	is00765000	Heinrich Steinhöwel	*Deutsche Chronik*	BL	II 520	IB. 9105
				BSB	F-157	2° Inc.c.a.288m
				SBU	501	15003,1
29 May 1473	ia00287000	Albertus Magnus	*De mysterio missae*	BOD	A-124	Auct. 6 Q 4.3 (1)
				BL	II 520	IA.9108
				JRL		R12105.1
				BSB	G-391	2° Inc.c.a.163
				BSB	G-391	2° Inc.c.a.163a
				BSB	G-391	2° Inc.c.a.163b
				SBU	16	14973
				MMW		3 C 17
				AUG	35	2° Ink 305
				UBW	35	I.t.f.58
				UBW	35	I.t.f.59a
				UBW	35	I.t.f.60
[1473]	it00316000	Thomas Aquinas	*De periculis contingentibus* (printed in first form of Type 116)	BOD	T-232	Auct. 6 Q 3.14
				BL	II 520	IB.9107
				BSB	T-418	2° Inc.s.a.1133
				AUG	1933	2° Ink 305
				UBW	2048	I.t.f.60
[c.1473]	ia00218000	Johannes de Castello	*De adhaerendo Deo*	BOD	A-097	Auct. 6 Q 4.3(2)
				BOD	A-097	Auct. 1 Q 5.57
				JRL		5689
				BSB	I-381	2° Inc.s.a.24
				BSB	I-381	2° Inc.s.a.24a
				BSB	I-381	Clm 4365/4
				BSB	I-381	Clm 7566/2
				BSB	I-381	Clm 23817/3
				SBU	316	14988–14991
				CUL		997
				AUG	40	2° Ink 145
				AUG	40	2° Ink 106
				AUG	40	2° Ink 359
				WIN		1057991
				UBW	18	I.t.f.66
				UBW	18	I.t.f.87
				UBW	18	I.t.f.147
1473	ip00402000	Francesco Petrarca	*Historia Griseldis* (Latin)	BOD	P-165	Douce 204*
				BL	II 522	IB.9117
				JRL		20912
				BSB	P-268	2° Inc.c.a.221
				BSB	P-269	2° Inc.c.a.221a
				CUL		996
[c.1473]	ip00403000	Francesco Petrarca	*Historia Griseldis* (Swabian)	BOD	P-167	Douce 204(1)
				BSB	P-271	Rar. 705/1
				SBU	414	14993
				SBU	415	14993,1
[not before 15 Aug 1473]	ib00720000	Giovanni Boccaccio	*De claris mulieribus* (German) (Steinhöwel dedicated his translation, on 14 August 1473)	BL	II 521	IB.9113
				BSB	B-561	Rar.704
				BSB	B-561	Rar.705
				BSB	B-561	Rar.706
				SBU	125	14992

ISTC date	ISTC	Author	Title	Library	Cat. no.	Shelfmark
1473	ib00716000	Giovanni Boccaccio	*De claris mulieribus* (**Latin**)	BOD	B-376	Douce 216
				BL	II 521	IB.9110
				BL	II 521	IB.9111
				JRL		15996
				AUG	403	1 an 2° Ink 139
				BSB	B-559	2° Inc.c.a.191
				CUL		995
				WIN		1057852
				UBW	448	I.t.f.67
3 Dec 1473	id00407000	Giullelmus Duranti	*Rationale divinorum officiorum*	BOD	D-183	Auct. 5 Q 2.21
				BL	II 521	IC.9115
				BSB	D-326	2° Inc.c.a.204
				BSB	D-326	2° Inc.c.a.204a
				BSB	D-326	2° Inc.c.a.205
				AUG	735	2° Ink 311
				AUG		2° Ink 310
				OTTO	149	Inc 200
[*c.*1473–4]	ip00404000	Francesco Petrarca	*Historia Griseldis* (**German**)	BSB	P-272	2° Inc.s.a.62/2
[1474]	it00317000	Thomas Aquinas	*De periculis contingentibus*	BL	II 520	IB.9109
				BSB	T-419	2° Inc.s.a.1133a
				BSB	T-419	2° Inc.s.a.1135c
				BSB	T-419	2° Inc.s.a.1151m
				AUG	1994	2° Ink 116
1474	ia00335000	Albertus Magnus	*Summa de eucharistiae sacramento*	BOD	A-149	Auct. Q sup.2.25
				BL	II 522	IB.9129
				BSB	A-156	2° Inc.c.a.260
				BSB	A-156	2° Inc.c.a.260a
				BSB	A-156	2° Inc.c.a.260b
				BSB	A-156	2° Inc.c.a.260c
				SBU	24	14974
				MMW		3 C 18
				AUG	39	2° Ink 319
				AUG	39	2° Ink 320
				AUG	39	2° Ink 91
				OTTO	13	Inc 25
9 Apr 1474	ib00336000	Petrus Berchorius	*Liber Bibliae moralis*	BOD	B-155	Auct. 6 Q1.22
				JRL		2193
				BSB	B-291	2° Inc.c.a.269
				BSB	B-291	2° Inc.c.a.269b
				BSB	B-291	Clm 28359
				SBU	103	14948,1
				MMW		4 A 1
				AUG	322	2° Ink 324
				AUG	322	2° Ink 323
26 Oct 1474	ip00249000	Alvarus Pelagius	*De planctu ecclesiae*	BOD	P-076	Auct. 5 Q 1.11
				BOD	P-076	Auct. Q sub.fen.1.8
				JRL		17288
				BSB	A-461	2° Inc.c.a.304
				BSB	A-461	2° Inc.c.a.305
				SBU	409	14975
18 Mar 1475	id00408000	Giullelmus Duranti	*Rationale divinorum officiorum*	BOD	D-184	Auct. 1. Q 1.24
				BSB	D-328	2° Inc.c.a.368
				BSB	D-328	2° Inc.c.a.368a
				MEM		3/159
				AUG	736	2° Ink 356
				UBW	794	I.t.f.130
				UBW	794	I.t.f.131

ISTC date	ISTC	Author	Title	Library	Cat. no.	Shelfmark
[before 17 Jun 1475]	it00318000	Thomas Aquinas	*De periculis contingentibus* (date from use of initials 1b as *Aurea Biblia* uses 1c.)	BOD	T-233	Auct. 6 Q 3.26
				JRL		R4561
				BSB	T-420	2° Inc.s.a.1135
				UBW	2050	I.t.f.49
1475	il00158000	Leonardus de Utino	*Sermones de sanctis*	BOD	L-083	Auct. 5 Q 2.2
				BOD	L-083	Broxb. 67.2
				BSB	L-111	2° Inc.c.a.421
				BSB	L-111	2° Inc.c.a.421a
				BSB	L-111	2° Inc.c.a.421b
				BSB	L-111	2° Inc.c.a.421c
				SBU	340	14983
				SBU	341	14983,1
				MMW		4 A 2
				AUG	1303	2° Ink 362
				OTTO	269	Inc 130
17 Jun 1475	ir00012000	Antonius Rampigollis/ Bindus de Senis	*Aurea Biblia*	BOD	B-345B	Auct. 5 Q 4.35
				BSB	B-520	2° Inc.c.a.407
				BSB	B-520	2° Inc.c.a.407a
				SBU	452	14980
				OTTO	375	Inc. 24
				UBW	1802	I.t.f. 117
20 Oct [14]75	ig00490000	Johannes Gritsch	*Quadragesimale*	BOD	G-251	Auct. Q sub.fen.1.16
				BSB	G-391	2° Inc.c.a.378
				BSB	G-391	2° Inc.c.a.378a
				BSB	G-391	2° Inc.c.a.378b
				SBU	245	14981
1475	it00185000	Thomas Aquinas	*Quaestiones de duodecim quodlibet*	BOD	T-146	Auct. 5 Q 4.4
				BSB	T-251	2° Inc.c.a.416
				BSB	T-251	2° Inc.c.a.416a
				BSB	T-251	2° Inc.c.a.416b
				BSB	T-251	2° Inc.c.a.416c
				SBU	535	14982
				MMW		1 D 28:1
				WIN		1071428
				UBW	2001	I.t.f.147
[14]76	ig00491000	Johannes Gritsch	*Quadragesimale*	BOD	G-252	Auct. 5 Q 2.14
				BSB	G-392	2° Inc.c.a.486
				BSB	G-392	2° Inc.c.a.486a
				BSB	G-392	2° Inc.c.a.486b
				BSB	G-392	2° Inc.c.a.486c
				SBU	246	14984
1476	ir00014000	Antonius Rampigollis / Bindus de Senis	*Aurea Biblia*	BOD	B-345C	Auct. 5 Q 5.33
				RUL		240-RAM
				BSB	B-552	2° Inc.c.a.523
				BSB	B-552	2° Inc.c.a.523a
				BSB	B-552	2° Inc.c.a.523b
				BSB	B-552	2° Inc.c.a.509a
				SBU	453	44966
				CUL		1000
[c.1476]	it00465000	Albertus de Ferrariis/ Albertus Trottus	*De horis canonicis*	BOD	F-018C	Auct. 5 Q 5.18
				BL	II 525	IB.9167
				BSB	F-65	2° Inc.s.a.446
				BSB	F-65	2° Inc.s.a.446a
				MZ		Stb Ink 1288
				UBW	841	I.t.f.206

ISTC date	ISTC	Author	Title	Library	Cat. no.	Shelfmark
[c.1476]	ih00037000	Henricus de Hassia/de Langenstein/ Guillelmus Brito	*Vocabularius Bibliae*	BOD	H-029	Auct. 5 Q 4.14
				BL	II 525	IB.9158
				BSB	G-481	2° Inc.s.a.590
				BSB	G-481	2° Inc.s.a.590a
				UBW	1063	I.t.f. CXXX
[c.1476]	it00319000	Thomas Aquinas	*De periculis contingentibus*	JRL		15699.2
				SBU	544	34834
				BSB	T-421	2° Inc.s.a.1134
				MMW		1 D 28:2
[not after 1476]	ic00320000	Dionysius Cato	*Documenta moralia Catonis* (MS note in Stuttgart copy dated 1476)	BOD	C-135	Auct. 6 Q 2.26
				JRL		R59193
				BSB	D-228	2° Inc.s.a.290a
				BSB	D-228	2° Inc.s.a.290b
				SBU	158	45693
				AUG	545	2° Ink 72
				CUL	1154	998
				CUL	1155	999
[14]76	in00224000	Johannes Nider	*Die vierundzwanzig goldenen Harfen*	BSB	N-179	2° Inc.c.a.509
				BSB	N-179	2° Inc.c.a.509d
				UBW	1559	I.t.f.330
[c.1476–7]	ia00116000	Aesopus	*Vita et fabulae*	BOD	A-053	Douce 252
				JRL		7776
				BSB	A-69	Rar.762
[c.1477]	ib00730000	Giovanni Boccaccio	*Decameron*	BL	II 520	IB.9108A
				BSB	B-556	2° Inc.s.a.218
[not after 1477]	ij00088400	Jacobus de Voragine	*Legenda aurea sanctorum* (BSB – purchase note 1477)	BOD	J-041	Auct. 3 Q inf.1.1
				BSB	I-68	2° Inc.s.a.1246
			(Amelung – printed on 1477 Urach paper)	BSB	I-68	2° Inc.s.a.1247
				BSB	I-68	2° Inc.s.a.1248
				MMW		3 C 19
				AUG	1163	2° Ink 270
				OTTO	242	Inc 222
9 Mar 1478	il00146000	Leonardus de Utino	*Sermones quadragesimales*	BOD	L-075	Auct. 6 Q inf.2.10
				BSB	L-122	2° Inc.c.a.801
				BSB	L-122	2° Inc.c.a.801a
				BSB	L-122	2° Inc.c.a.801b
				BSB	L-122	2° Inc.c.a.801c
				BSB	L-122	2° Inc.c.a.801d
				SBU	342	14977
				SBU	343	34474
				MZ		Stb Ink 1970
				MMW		4 A 3
				AUG	1300	2° Ink 437
				AUG		2° ink 436
				OTTO	267	Inc 118
[not after 1478]	ij00091000	Jacobus de Voragine	*Legenda aurea sanctorum* (Goff – MS date 1478 in Chicago copy)	BOD	J-042	Auct. 5 Q 4.13
				BSB	I-71	2° Inc.s.a.1247a
				BSB	I-71	2° Inc.s.a.1249
				BSB	I-71	2° Inc.s.a.1249a
				SBU	305	33972
[not after 1478]	ia00331000	Albertus Magnus	*Sermones de tempore* (Goff – purchase notes 1478)	BOD	A-147	Auct. 6 Q inf.1.10
				JRL		R14425
				BSB	A-216	2° Inc.s.a.44
				BSB	A-216	2° Inc.s.a.44a
				BSB	A-216	2° Inc.s.a.44b
				SBU	22	40840
				MMW		3 C 21

ISTC date	ISTC	Author	Title	Library	Cat. no.	Shelfmark
[1478]	ig00650000	Johannes Herolt Guillermus	*Postilla super epistolas*	BSB	H-139	2° Inc.s.a.567
				BSB	H-139	2° Inc.s.a.567a
				BSB	H-139	2° Inc.s.a.567b
				BSB	H-139	2° inc.s.a.567c
[c.1478–80]	ih00200000	Hieronymous	*Vitae sanctorum patrum*	BOD	H-109	Auct. 1 Q 3.34
				BSB	V-251	2° Inc.s.a.649a
				BSB	V-251	2° Inc.s.a.649c
				BSB	V-251	2° Inc.s.a.650
				BSB	V-251	2° Inc.s.a.650a
				BSB	V-251	2° Inc.s.a.650b
				SBU	277	52722
				SBU	278	43169
[not after 1479]	in00205000	Johannes Nider	*Praeceptorium divinae legis* (BSB – purchase note 1479)	BSB	N-167	2° Inc.s.a.917
				BSB	N-167	2° Inc.s.a.917a
				BSB	N-167	2° Inc.s.a.917b
				SBU	389	56277
[c.1476]	ij00087000	Jacobus de Voragine	*Legenda aurea sanctorum*	BSB	I-73	2° Inc.s.a.1250
				BSB	I-73	2° Inc.s.a.1250a
				AUG	1160	2° Ink 271
				OTTO	241	Inc 233

Section 2: other editions printed by Zainer and consulted for this study

ISTC date	ISTC	Author	Title	Library	Cat. no.	Shelfmark
[1473]	im00791500	Mönch von Salzburg	*Sequenz von unserer lieben Frauen*	AUG	1463	Ebl.vor1500 no.36
[c.1473]	ip00419700	Petrarca, Francesco	*Vitae huius compendiosa*	BL	II.522	IB.9120
[c.1476]	ib01239950	Brunus Aretinus	*Historia Sigismunde*	BSB	B-408	(with Aesop)
[c.1476]	ig00112800		*Gebetbuch*	BSB	G-52	8° Inc.s.a.62
[c.1478]	ip00542000	Pflaum, Jacob	*Kalendarium 1477–1552*	BSB	P-406	2° Inc.c.a.713
				BSB	P-406	2° Inc.c.a.713a
[c.1477]				CUL		1001
				SBU	425	14868a
				AUG	1651	2° Ink 419
				AUG	1651	2° Ink 624
[c.1477]	ip00543000		*Kalender 1477–1554*	BSB	P-407	2° Inc.s.a.762
	ip00544000		*Kalender 1477–1552*	BSB	P-408	2° Inc.s.a.762a
				AUG	1652	2° Ink 429
				SBU		33972
[1478]	ib00274000	Basilius Magnus	*De legendis antiquorum libris* (early 1478 Amelung)	BOD	B-130	Auct. 5 Q 6.67
				BOD	B-130	Auct. 6 Q 6.38
				BL	II.525	IA.9176
				BSB	B-228	4° Inc.s.a.297
				BSB	B-228	4° Inc.s.a.298
				SBU	98	14793,1
[not before 1478]	ia00226000	Albertus Magnus	*Ars intelligendi, docendi . . .*	BOD	A-101	Auct. 6 Q 4.8
				MMW		3 C 20
				MEM		3, 130
[1478–80]	ia00332000	Albertus Magnus	*Sermones de tempore*	BSB	A-218	2° Inc.s.a.40a
				MZ		Stb Ink 1293
[c.1478–80]	in00216000	Nider, Johannes	*Sermones de tempore*	BOD	N-099	Auct. 3 Q inf.1.17
				BSB	N-175	2° Inc. s a.926
				BSB	N-175	2° Inc.s.a.925a

ISTC date	ISTC	Author	Title	Library	Cat. no.	Shelfmark
[1478–80]	ia00333000	Albertus Magnus	*Sermones et tempore*	SBU MEM	22	45861 3,131
[*c.*1478–80]	id00341935	Donatus, Aelius	*Ars minor*	BOD	D-132	Auct. 2 Q 3.43
[1478–80]	iu00057000	Ulricus Ulmer	*Fraternitas cleri*	MZ SBU	588	GM Ink 70 14994
[1478–82]	ia01399000		*Auslegung*	BSB	G-63	2° Inc.s.a.139
[not after 10 Nov 1479]	ia00499350		*Almanac 1480 (incomplete)*	SBU	232	43155
[not before 18 Jan 1479]	if00243700		*Formulare und deutsch Rhetorica*	BOD	F-084	Auct. 2 Q 4.49
29 Jan 1480	ib00567000	M. Monachus	*Biblia latina*	BOD BOD SBU	B-276 B-276	Auct. M 3.8 Auct. M 3.7 14985
[*c.*15 Jun 1480]	ia00340000	Albertus de Padua	*Expositio evangelorum*	BOD BSB BSB BSB SBU	A-094 A-133 A-133 A-133 26	Auct. 6 Q inf.1.22 2° Inc.s.a.914u 2° Inc.s.a.402 2° Inc.c.a.914sb 15081,1
1480	ig00311000	Gobius, Johannes	*Scala coeli*	BOD BSB MZ	G-163 G-223	Douce 191 2° Inc.c.a.596n Stb Ink 1727a
1480	iv00363350		*Vocabularius ex quo*	BSB BSB	V-308 V-308	2° Inc.c.a.998 2° Inc.c.a.998a
1[4]81	ij00331000	Johannes Gallensis	*Summa collationum*	BOD BOD MEM MZ MZ	J-160 J-160	Byw. F 2.13 Auct. 5 Q 5.48 3, 132 Stb Ink 1192 GM Ink 36
[*c.*1482]	il00047500		*Schwabenspiegel Landrechtsbuch*	CUL		949
[not after 1479]	ip00267000	Peregrinus	*Sermones*	MEM		115/3
[*c.*1482]	is00763000	Steinhowel, Heinrich	*Büchlein der Ordnung (Pest Regiment)*	AUG	1938	4° Ink 200
[14]87	ii00015000	Thomas à Kempis	*Imitatio Christi, et al.*	BOD	T-103	Auct. 5 Q 6.7
	ii00013000			MZ		Stb Ink 251
	ii00390000			BSB BSB	T-184 T-184	8° Inc.s.a.149 8° Inc.s.a.150
[*c.*1487]	ib00895000	Bonaventura	*Meditationes vitae Christi*	BOD	B-442	Auct.1 Q 7.78(4)
[*c.*1490[	ie00059300		*Epistola di miseria*	BOD	E-019	Auct. 7 Q 7.13
[*c.*1490]	ic00989950	Confessionale	*Interrogationes et doctrinale*	BOD MMW	C-416	Auct. 1 Q 7.78(3) 4 F 18:2
[*c.*1490?]	il00204000	Lichtenberger, Johan.	*Prognosticatio*	BOD	P-474	Auct. 4 Q 4.30(2)
? Amelung think not JZ		Lichtenberger, Johan.	*Vocabularius: Curia palatium*	BOD	V-170	Auct. 7 Q 7.26

Section 3: editions and copies by other printers used for this study

ISTC date	ISTC	Author	Title	Library	Cat. no.	Shelfmark
GERMANY						
GUTENBERG (Mainz)						
[Dec 1454]	it00503500	6 leaves	*Eyn manung der cristenheit*	BSB	M-149	Rar.1
[1454–5]	ib00526000		*Biblia Latina*	BOD	B-237	Arch. B b.10
			Biblia Latina	CUL	14	Inc. 1 B 1
			Biblia Latina	BSB	B-408	2° Inc.s.a.197C1
[1454–6]	id00314900	Aelius Donatus	*Ars minor*	BSB	D-243	Rar.103(1o
[1454–6]	id00315100	Aelius Donatus	*Ars minor*	BSB	D-244	Rar.103(1
[1454–6]	id00315600	Aelius Donatus	*Ars minor*	BSB	D-245	Rar.103(1m
[1454–6]	id00315500	Aelius Donatus	*Ars minor*	BOD	D-124	Auct. 2 Q inf.1.50(6)
[1454–6]	id00316100	Aelius Donatus	*Ars minor*	BOD	D-125	Auct. 2 Q inf.1.50(5)
[*c.*1471]	id00317400	Aelius Donatus	*Ars minor*	BOD	D-126	Auct. 2 Q inf.1.50(1)
PFISTER ?(Bamberg)						
[*c.*1460–1]	ib00527000		*Biblia Latina*	ANT		O.B.6.11
			Biblia Latina	UBW	383	I.t.f. I
			Biblia Latina	BSB	B-409	Rar.111a
[*c.*1462–3]	ib00652750		*Biblia Pauperum*	BSB	B-502	Rar.4
FUST & SCHÖFFER (Mainz)						
1457	ip01036000	fragment	*Psalterium*	BSB	P-820	2° L impr.membr.1b
			Psalterium	WIN		1071478
1458	im00736000		*Canon Missae*	BOD	M-284	Arch. G b.4
29 Aug 1459	ip01062000		*Psalterium*	BOD	P-519	Arch. B.a.1
6 Oct 1459	id00403000	Guillelmus Duranti	*Rationale divinorum officiorum*	BOD	D-178	Auct. 4 Q 1.3
25 Jun 1460	ic00710000	Clement V	*Constitutiones*	BOD	C-359	Auct. 4 Q 1.4
14 Aug 1462	ib00529000		*Biblia Latina*	BOD	B-239	Auct. M 1.4–7
[1460–65]	ia01354000	Augustinus	*De vita christiana*	BOD	A-606	Douce 122(1)
Printer of the Catholicon						
[*c.*1460–9]	ib00020000	Johannes Balbus	*Catholicon*	BOD	B-010	Auct. 2 Q inf.1.31(a)
[*c.*1460–9]	it00272950	Thomas Aquinas	*De articulis fidei*	SBU	538	15296
[*c.*1460–9]	it00273000		*De articulis fidei*	BOD	T-117	Auct. 1 Q 5.40
[*c.*1460–9]	im00367000	Mattheus de Cracovia	*Dialogus rationis*	SBU	357	15297
PETER SCHÖFFER (Mainz)						
1466	ic00576000	Marcus Cicero	*De officiis paradoxa*	ANT		R 30.4
13 Aug 1472	ig00362000	Gratianus	*Decretum*	BOD	G-180	Auct. 4 Q 1.5–6
1474	it00520000	Johannes de Turrecremata	*Expositio summa*	ANT		R 32.4
[1470–5]	ia01249000	Augustinus	*De cognitionae verae vitae*	BOD	A-567	Douce 122(2)
JOHANN MENTELIN (Strassburg)						
[*c.*1461]	ib00528000		*Biblia Latina*	BOD	B-238	Auct. M 3.6
[not after 1463]	it00208000	Thomas Aquinas	*Summa theologiae*	BOD	T-171	Auct. 7 Q inf.1.14
				BSB	T-286	2° Inc.s.a.1146a
					T-286	2° Inc.s.a.1146b

ISTC date	ISTC	Author	Title	Library	Cat. no.	Shelfmark
[not after Jun 1466]	ib00624000		*Biblia Germanica*	BOD	B-325	Auct. Y 4.2
[not after 1466]	ia01226000	Augustinus	*De arte praedicandi*	BOD	A-514	Auct. 7 Q 6.6
					A-514	Auct. 7 Q 3.13
[not after 1466]	ij00288000	Johannes	*Homiliae super*	BOD	J-130	Auct. 7 Q 3.24
		Chrysostomus	*Matthaeum*	BOD	J-130	Auct. 7 Q 2.21
[not after 1468]	ia01239000	Augustinus Hipponensis	*De civitate Dei*	BOD	A-525	Auct. 7 Q 1.15
[not after 1472]	in00133000	Nicholas de Lyra	*Postilla*	BOD	N-057	Auct. 4 Q 2.19
[not after 1473]	ia01161000	Astenanus	*Summa de casibus*	BSB	A-794	2° Inc.s.a.103b
				BOD	A-468	Auct. 1 Q inf.2.23
[not after 1473]	ia00272000	Albertus Magnus	*Mariale*	BSB	A-186	2° Inc. s.a.29a

HEINRICH EGGESTEIN (Strassburg)

[not after 24 May 1466]	ib00530000		*Biblia Latina*	BOD	B-240	Auct. M 2.13(2)
[not after 1468]	ib00531000		*Biblia Latina*	BOD	B-241	Auct. M 1.8,9
				BOD	B-241	Auct. M.2.13(1)
[not after 2 Mar 1470]	ib00533000		*Biblia Latina*	BOD	B-243	Auct. Y 3.5,6
1472	ig00361000	Gratianus	*Decretum*	BOD	G-178	Auct. 3 Q 1.1
[before 1471]	ip00479000	Lombardus, Petrus	*Sententiarum libri IV*	BOD	P-222	Auct. 5 Q 2.8
[not after 9 May 1475]	ip00028000	Nicholas de Tudeschi	*Consilia*	BSB	T-495	2° Inc.s.a.945a
1478	ii00095000	Pope Innocent IV	*Decretalium*	BSB	I-176	2° Inc. s.a.152
				BOD	I-13	Auct. 3 Q inf.2.13
[not after1475]	ic01016000	Cyrillus	*Speculum sapientiae*	BSB	B-742	Clm. 7566/1

ADOLF RUSCH (Strassburg)

[before 20 Jul 1467]	ir00001000	Hrabanus, Maurus	*De sermonum proprietate*	BOD	H-223A	Auct. 1 Q inf.2.11
[*c*.1470]	ib00022000	Johannes Balbus	*Catholicon*	BSB	B-10	2° Inc. 144b
[*c*.1470]	id00358000	Jacobus de Dondis	*Aggregator*	BOD	D-157	Auct. 2 Q 1.26
[*c*.1470]	id00405000	Guillelmus Duranti	*Rationale*	BOD	D-179	Auct. 5 Q inf.2.11
[1470–2]	ip00831000	Plutarch	*Vitae parallelae*	BSB	P-625	2° A.gr.b.901
[not after 1471]	is00480000	Servius Maurus	*Commentatum Virgili*	BOD	S-187	Auct. P. 1.1
[*c*.1473]	ib00536500		*Biblia Latina*	BOD	B-244	Auct. M 1.12,13
[*c*.1473]	iv00282000	Vincentius Bellovacencis	*Speculum – 3 vols.*	BOD	V-133	Douce 307–9
[not after 1473]	ip00412000	Francesco Petrarca	*Secretum*	BOD	P-171	Auct. 2 Q 3.30(2)
[not after 1473]	ip00417000	Francesco Petrarca	*De vita solitaris*	BOD	P-391	Auct. 2 Q 3.30(3)
[*c*.1473]	id00354000	Donatus	*Commentum*	BOD	D-154	Auct. O 1.11
[not after 15 Jun 1476]	iv00292000	Vincentius Bellovacencis	*Speculum naturale*	BOD	V-139	Auct. Q sub.fen.1.4,5
[1475–7]	ib00023000	Johannes Balbus	*Catholicon*	BOD	B-012	Auct. Q sub.fen.1.10
				BSB	B-11	2° Inc.s.a.143a
[not after1480]	ib00607000	[printed for Koberger]	*Biblia with gloss*	BSB	B-442	2° Inc.s.a.212

GEORG REYSER (?printer of Henricus Ariminensis) (Strassburg)

1473–4	ia01282250	Augustinus	*Manuale*	BOD	A-583	Auct. 7 Q 3.14
[*c*.1476]	ij00492900	Judaei	*De Judaeorum*	BOD	J-227	Auct. Q sub.fen.2.22
[1473–5]	ie00165000	[Stor]	*Expositio*	BOD	E-080	Auct 6 Q 3.23

ISTC date	ISTC	Author	Title	Library	Cat. no.	Shelfmark
[not after 24 Aug 1473]	ic00870000	Contracti	*Tractus*	BOD	C-439	Auct. 6 Q 5.35
[1473–4]	ih00019000	Henricus Ariminensis	*De quattuor virtutibus*	BOD	H-014	Auct. 5 Q 4.34
[not after1474]	ig00493000	Johannes Gritsch	*Quadragesimale*	BOD	G-253	Auct. 5 Q 2.16
[not after1474]	ih00532000	Hugo de Sancto	*Didascalicon*	BOD	H-242	Auct. 6 Q 5.7

GEORG REYSER (Würzburg)

| 1481 | im00663900 | | *Missale herbipolense* | BOD | M-256 | Auct. 1 Q 1.7 |

C.W. (Strassburg)

| 1473 | iz00013000 | Zacharias | *Concordiantia evangelista* | BOD | Z-002 | Auct. 1 Q inf.2.12 |

HEINRICH KNOBLOCHTZER (Strassburg)

13 Dec 1478	ie00002000	Ebendorfer	*Sermones dominicales*	BOD	E-001	Auct.Q sup.1–22, 23
				BSB	E-2	2° Inc.s.a.738a
				BSB	E-2	2° Inc.s.a.20u/1

ULRICH ZELL (Cologne)

[c.1467]	im00371800	Mat. de Cracovia	*De modo confitendi*	BOD	M-153	Auct. 1 Q 5.31(1)
[c.1467]	ig00238000	Johannes Gerson	*Opus tripartitum*	BOD	G-116	Auct. 1 Q 5.31(2)
[c.1467]	ig00255000	Johannes Gerson	*De pollutione nocturna*	BOD	G-122	Auct. 1 Q 5.31(3a)
[c.1467]	ig00194000	Johannes Gerson	*De cognitione castitatis*	BOD	G-095	Auct. 1 Q 5.31(3b)
[c.1467]	ig00265000	Johannes Gerson	*De remediis*	BOD	G-126	Auct. 1 Q 5.31(4)
[c.1467]	ia01223000	Augustinus Hipponensis	*De agone christiano*	BOD	A-512	Auct. 1 Q 5.31(5)
[c.1467]	ia00524000		*Alphabetum*	BOD	A-213	Auct. 1 Q 5.31(7)
[c.1467]	ia01281000	Augustinus Hipponensis	*Homiliae*	BOD	A-551	Auct. 1 Q 5.31(8)
[c.1467]	ia01355000	Augustinus Hipponensis	*De vita christiana*	BOD	A-607(2)	Auct. 7 Q 4.33(1)
[c.1467]	ia01302000	Augustinus Hipponensis	*Sermo super orationem*	BOD	A-590	Auct. 7 Q 4.33(2)
[c.1467]	ia01265000	Augustinus Hipponensis	*Enchiridion de fide*	BOD	A-543	Auct. 7 Q 4.33(3)
[c.1467]	ij00298000	Johannes Chrysostomus	*Sermo super psalmum*	BOD	J-139	Auct. 7 Q 4.33(4)
[c.1467]	ic00559000	Cicero	*De amicitia, et al*	BOD	C-336	Auct. Q 5.52(1)
[c.1470]	ia01260000	Augustinus Hipponensis	*De disciplina christiana*	BOD	A-541	Auct. 1 Q 5.34(10)

KONRAD WINTERS (Cologne)

1475	ib00539000		*Biblia Latina*	BOD	B-249	Auct. V.3.2,3
[not after1475]	il00144000	Leonardus de Utino	*Sermones quadragesimales*	BOD	L-074	Auct. 5 Q inf.1.9
8 Nov 1476	ir00255000	Werner Rolewinck	*Fasciculus temporum*	BOD	R-107	Auct. 2 Q inf.1.29
8 Nov 1476	ij00086000	Jacobus de Voragine	*Legenda aurea*	BOD	J-029	Douce 250 Auct. 5 Q 5.9

GÜNTHER ZAINER (Augsburg)

12mar[14]68	ib00893000	Bonaventura	*Meditationes vitae Christi*	BOD	B-441	Auct. 6 Q 4.25
				BSB	B-681	2° Inc.c.a.13d Rar.60
30 Apr 1469	ib00021000	Johannes Balbus	*Catholicon*	BOD	B-011	Auct. 3 Q 3.35

ISTC date	ISTC	Author	Title	Library	Cat. no.	Shelfmark
1469	ia01381000	Johannes Aurbach	*Summa de sacramentis*	BOD	A-613	Auct. 1 Q 4.20
				BSB	I-534	Clm/16477/1
[*c*.1470]	ie00140000		*Expositio canonis missae*	BOD	E-067	Auct. 1 Q 3.19(1)
22 Jan 1470	id00404000	Guillelmus Duranti	*Rationale divinorum officiorum*	BOD	D-183	Auct. 6 Q 1.3
				BSB	D-325	2° Inc.c.a.27
1 Jan 1471	ir00215000	Rodericus Zamorensis	*Speculum vitae humanae*	BOD	R-084	Auct. 4 Q 3.21
				BOD	R-084	Auct. 1 Q 4.24
				BOD	R-084	Auct. 5 Q 3.23(1)
				BSB	S-66	2° Inc.s.a.1264
[1471–3]	in00045000	Nicodemus	*Evangelium*	BSB	E-131	2° Inc.s.a.904
[1471–3]	ip01038000		*Psalterium*	BOD	P-496	Auct. 6 Q inf.1.11
18 Jan 1471	io00140400	Ovid	*De arte amandi*	BOD	O-049	Auct. O 3.37
1471	ip00402850	Francesco Petrarca	*Historia Griseldis*	BOD	P-166	Auct. 4 Q 3.14
	ig00112700		*Gebetbuch*	BSB	G-51	8° Inc.c.a.1
26 Jun 1472	ij00074000	Jacobus de Theramo	*Belial*	BOD	J-024	Auct. 6 Q 4.42
12 Jul 1472	ii00191000	Isidorus Hispalensis	*De responsione mundi*	UBW	1181	I.t.f.49
19 Nov 1472	ii00181000	Isidorus Hispalensis	*Etymologiae*	BOD	I-035	Auct. 1 Q 3.22
				BSB	I-627	2° Inc.c.a.129
				BSB	I-627	2° Inc.c.a.130a
[before 1473]	ih00192000	Hieronymous	*De viris illustribus*	BOD	H-103	Auct. 1 Q 3.19(3)
				AUG	1046	2° Ink 268
5 Jun 1473				UBW	1105	I.t.f.49
1473	ig00417000	Gregorius	*Homiliae super evangelia*	UBW	964	I.t.f.49
1473	im00762000		*Modus legendi*	UBW	1499	I.t.f.49
[not after 1474]	ib00627000		*Biblia Germanica*	BOD	B-337	Auct. Y.4.6
JOHANN BÄMLER (Augsburg)						
[b422 Apr 1472]	in00222000	Johannes Nider	*24 goldene Harfen*	BOD	N-102	Auct. 6 Q 5.22
18 Dec 1472	in00223000	Johannes Nider	*24 goldene Harfen*	BOD	N-103	Auct.1 Q inf.1.43
14 Feb 1473	ij00075000	Jacobus de Theramo	*Belial*	BOD	J-025	Auct. 2 Q inf.2.34
[14]74	ia00596000	Johannes Andreae	*Super arboribus*	BOD	A261	Douce 204(2)
[*c*.1473]	ia00573950	Andechs	*Von dem Ursprung und Anfang des heiligen Bergs*	BOD	A-242	Auct. 3 Q 5.11
				BSB	I-56	2° Inc.c.a.229
1476	ij00076000	Jacobus de Therano	*Belial*	BSB	I-57	2° Inc.s.a.1117k
JOHANN SCHÜSSLER (Augsburg)						
28 Jun 1470	ij00481000	Flavius Josephus	*Antiquitates judaicae*	BOD	J-210	Auct. K.1.15
16 Feb 1471	ic00965000	Petrus de Crescentis	*Ruralia commoda*	BOD	C-477	Auct. L 3.31
7 Jun 1471	io00096000	Paulus Orosius	*Historiae*	BOD	O-026	Auct. L 2.10
[na1471]	it00518000	Johannes de Turrecremata	*Expositio in psalmos*	BOD	T-271	Auct. 1 Q inf.1.58
5 May 1472	ia00555000	Ambrosius	*Hexameron*	BOD	A-232	Auct. 1 Q 3.19(4)
2 Jul 1472	ij00064000	Jacobus de Theramo	*Belial*	BOD	J-018	Auct. 1 Q 2.1
5 Mar 1473	ia01363000	Augustinus de Ancona	*Summa de poteste*	BOD	A-499	Auct. 6 Q inf.1.4

ISTC date	ISTC	Author	Title	Library	Cat. no.	Shelfmark
ANTON SORG (Augsburg)						
1474	iv00284000	Vincentius Bellovacencis	*Speculum – 3 vols*	BSB BOD	V-203 V-134	2° Inc.c.a.326 Auct. 6 Q inf.2.1–3
[*c*.24 May 1475]	in00199000	Johannes Nider	*Praeceptorium divinae legis*	BOD	N-093	Auct. 5 Q 4.12
Aug 1475	ia01298000	Augustinus Hipponensis	*Quinquaginta*	BOD	A-554	Auct. 7 Q 3.18
1476	ia00554000	Ambrosius	*Expositio evangelia*	BSB	A-474	2° Inc. c.a.443
[not after 1476]	ij00390000	Petrus de Limoges	*De oculo murali*	BSB	P-356	2° Inc. s.a.982
[*c*.1477]	ij00391000	Petrus de Limoges	*De oculo murali*	BSB	P-357	2° Inc.c.a.593b
[not after 13 Oct 1478]	in00950000	Nicolaus Vischel	*Imago beatae virginis*	BSB	V-236	2° Inc.c.a.593b/1
1475–8	ib00368000	Bernardus	*De consideratione*	BSB	B-308	2° Inc.c.a.593b/4
JOHANN SENSENSCHMIDT (Nürnberg)						
[14]70	ir00150000	Franciscus de Retza	*Comestorium vitiorum*	BOD	F-099	Auct. 4 Q 1.10
[14]70	ig00272000	Johannes Gerson	*De spiritualibus nuptiis*	BOD	G-094	Douce 254
[not after 1470]	ib00388000	Bernardus Clarevallensis	*Flores*	BOD	B-177	Auct. 2 Q inf.2.68
[*c*.1470]	ig00204000	Johannes Gerson	*De regulis mandatorum*	BOD	G-101	Auct. 6 Q 3.11
[1470–2]	ih00154000	Hieronymus	*Regula monachorum*	BOD	H-100(1)	Auct. 1 Q 3.19(2)
11 Sep 1471	ig00427000	Gregory I	*Moralia*	BOD	G-217	Auct. 7 Q inf.1.8
[1474–6]	ig00229000	Johannes Gerson	*De examinatime doctrinarum*	BSB	G-153	Clm 4365/3
1475	ij00575000	Justinianus	*Codex*	BOD	J-269	Auct. 3 Q inf.2.4
FRIEDRICH CREUSSNER (Nürnberg)						
1473	is00580000	Sixtus	*De sanguine Christi*	UBW	1939	I.t.f.87
[not after 1476]	ia00602000	Johannes Andreae	*Lectura super arboribus*	BSB	I-287	2° inc.s.a.62(1)
1477	it00477000	Albertus Trottus	*De ieiunio*	UBW	2091	I.t.f.206
1478	ig00192000	Johannes Gerson	*De arte audiendi*	BSB UBW	G-145 905	Clm 4365/1 I.t.f.87
1479	ic00750900		*Collecta magistralia*	UBW	664	I.t.f.66
KONRAD FYNER (Esslingen)						
[not after 1473]	ip00475000	Petrus Lombardus	*Glossa in epistolas Pauli*	BOD	P-218	Auct. 1 Q inf.2.18
1474	it00236000	Thomas Aquinas	*Expositio in Job*	AUG BOD	1981 T-129	1 an 2° Ink 320 Auct. 1 Q 4.31
[1474–5]	ig00206000	Johannes Gerson	*Conclusiones de diversis*	AUG	883	2 an 2° Ink 42
[not after 1475]	ij00306000	Johannes Chrysostomus	*De adhaerendo Deo*	AUG	1202	2 an 2° Ink 320
1475?	it00228000	Thomas Aquinas	*Catena aurea*	BOD	T-133	Auct. 6 Q inf.2.21
Printer of the Augustinus (Lauingen)						
1473	ia01257000	Augustinus Aurelius	*De consensu evangelistarum*	BSB	A-866	Clm 23817/4
PETER DRACH (Speyer)						
[not after 1475]	ia00328000	Albertus Magnus	*Sermones de tempore*	BSB	A-213	2° Inc.s.a.43
1476	iv00316000		*Vocabularius incipiens*	ANT		R 15.25
18 May 1477	iv00336000		*Vocabularius juris utriusque*	BOD	V-157	Auct. 5 Q 5.34

ISTC date	ISTC	Author	Title	Library	Cat. no.	Shelfmark
KONRAD DINCKMUT (Ulm)						
1478	ij00315000	Johannes de Frankfordia	*Sermones dominicales*	SBU	317	34235
21 Aug 1482	ie00102000		*Erklarung der zwölf Artikel*	BOD	E-056	Auct. 6 Q 4.30
1482	is00764000	Heinrich Steinhöwel	*Büchlein der Ordnung*	SBU	500	15003
1482	ir00051000		*Regimen sanitatis*	SBU	456	15004
1482	is00329000	Michael Puff von Schruck	*Von den angebrannten Weinen*	SBU	449	15005
1484	ij00321000	Johannes Friburgensis	*Summa confessorum*	SBU	319	15006
1484	ij00190000	Jacobus de Voragine	*Sermones de sanctis*	BOD	J-077	Auct. 4 Q 4.29 (1)
1486	ig00681000	Guillelmus Parisiensis	*Postilla super epistolas*	BOD	G-323	Auct. 4 Q 4.15
1486	ih00514000	Hugo de Prato Florido	*Sermones de sanctis*	BOD	H-233	Auct. 4 Q 4.30
1488	ij00121000	Jacobus de Voragine	*Legenda aurea*	BOD	J-051	Auct. 3 Q inf.1.7
LEINHARDT HOLLE (Ulm)						
16 Jul 1482	ip01084000	Ptolemaeus	*Geographica*	BOD	P-528	Auct. P.1.4
KONRAD MANCZ (Blaubeuren)						
[*c.*1475]	ih00239000	Eusebius	*Epistola*	CUL	1198	3895
				BSB	E-121	2° Inc.s.a.20u/1
				UBW	826	I.t.f.87
[*c.*1477]	ij00022000	Jacobus de Paridso	*De animabus exutis*	BSB	I-31	Clm 23817/5
[*c.*1477]	ih00025000	Henri de Gorichem	*De superstitiosis*	UBW	1057	I.t.f.87
MICHAEL GREYFF (or not Greyff now printer of Henricus Arminensis (Georg Reyser?)						
[not after 1477]	iv00337200		*Vocabularius juris utriusque*	BOD	V-159	Auct. 3 Q 4.7
MICHAEL GREYFF (Reutlingen)						
[*c.*1478]	ih00505000	Hugo de Prato Florido	*Sermones dominicales*	BOD	H-229	Auct. 5 Q inf.1.13
[not after 1478]	in00203000	Johannes Nider	*Praeceptorium divinae legis*	BOD	N-096	Auct. 6 Q 4.48
[not after 1478]	ig00493500	Johannes Gritsch	*Quadragesimale*	BOD	G-255	Auct. 6 Q 3.1
JOHANN OTMAR (Reutlingen)						
1 Sep 1483	ie00168000	Stör, Nikolaus	*Expositio officii missae*	BOD	E-081	Auct. 6 Q 4.33
24 May 1484	is00524000	Simon de Cremona	*Postilla super evangelia*	BOD	S-210	Auct. 5 Q 4.9
Aug 1484	ib00950000	Bonaventura	*Sermones de tempore*	BOD	B-452	Auct. 3 Q 5.20
ITALY						
SWEYNHEYM & PANNARTZ (Subiaco)						
29 Oct 1465	il00001000	Lactantius, Lucius Coelius Firmianus	*Opera*	BOD	L-002	Auct. L 3.33
12 Jun 1467	ia01230000	Augustinus Hipponensis	*De civitate Dei*	BOD	A-517	Auct. 7 Q 2.19
SWEYNHEYM & PANNARTZ (Rome)						
1467	ic00503500	Cicero	*Epistolare ad familiares*	BOD	C-255	Arch. Gd.55

ISTC date	ISTC	Author	Title	Library	Cat. no.	Shelfmark
1468	il00002000	Lactantius	*Opera*	BOD	C-003	Auct. N 4.24
ULRICH HAN (Rome)						
5 Dec 1468	ic00655000	Cicero	*De oratore*	BOD	C-227	Auct. L 5.4
1 Apr 1469	ic00630000	Cicero	*Tusculanae disputationes*	BOD	C-291	Auct. L 5.5
17 Oct 1473	it00536000	Johannes de Turrecremata	*Meditationes seu Contemplationes*	BOD	T-280	Auct. 6 Q inf.1.13
PFLUGEL & LAUER (Rome)						
15 Mar 1 474	id00446000	Guillelmus Duranti	*Speculum judicale*	BOD	D-201	Auct. 1 Q inf. 2.2–4
LAUER (Rome)						
[*c.*1470]	it00182000	Thomas Aquinas	*Quaestiones de duodecim quodlibet*	BOD	T-143	Auct. 1 Q 1.2,3
[*c.*1472]	id00219000	Diogenes	*Vitae et sententiae*	BOD	D-076	Bwy. D 2.11
1474	ig00448000	Gregorius	*Decretales*	BOD	G-233	Auct. 3 Q 1.7
VINDELINUS DE SPIRA (Venice)						
[before Sept] 1469	ic00504000	Cicero	*Epistolae ad familiares*	BOD	C-256	Auct. N inf.2.2
[1469]	ic00505000	Cicero	*Epistolae ad familiares*	BOD	C-257	Auct. N inf.2.3
[before Sept] 1469	ip00786000	Plinius	*Historia naturalis*	BOD	P-358	Auct L.1.1
1470	il00238000	Titus Livius	*Historiae Romanae*	BOD	L-116	Auct. L.1.8,9
NICOLAS JENSON (Venice)						
1470	ic00500000	Cicero	*Epistolae ad Brutum, et al.*	BOD	C-284	Auct. L 5.14
1470	ic00672000	Cicero	*Rhetorica ad C Herrenium*	BOD	C-209	Auct. L 3.2(1)
1470	ie00118000	Eusebius	*De evangelica*	BOD	E-047	Auct. 7 Q 2.1
FRANCISCUS RENNER DE HEILBRONN (Venice)						
1471	il00140000	Leonardus de Utino	*Sermones quadragesimale*	BOD	L-071	Auct. 5 Q 3.23(2)
ERHARD RATDOLT (Venice)						
1482	ie00113000	Euclid	*Elementa geometriae*	BOD	E-036	Auct. K 3.19
ANDREAS TORRESANUS (Venice)						
23 Sep 1490	ib00221800	Bartolus de Saxoferrata	*Super secunda parte*	BSB	B-156	2° Inc.c.a.2212
NEUMEISTER (Foligno)						
1470	ib01234000	Brunus	*De bello Italico adversus Gothos*	BSB	B-937	2° Inc.c.a.235
ALBRECHT KUNNE (Trient)						
6 Sep 1475	is00528800	[Simone de Trento]	*Historie von Simon zu Trient*	BSB	H-308	2° Inc.s.a.62(2)
ANDREAS BELFORTIS (Ferrara)						
18 May 1486	ib00448000	Bernardus	*Practica seu Lillium*	BSB	B-334	2° Inc.c.a.1759

FRANCE

MICHAEL FRIBURGER, ULRICH GERING & MARTIN CRANTZ (Paris)						
[not before Jun 1472]	ij00631500	Juvenalis	*Satyrae & Persius Flaccus Satyrae*	BOD	J-327	Holk. D.36
[*c.*1473]	ig00193000	Johannes Gerson	*De auferibilitate Papae*	BOD	G-093	Auct. 4 Q 5.41(2)
[*c.*1475]	ib00170500	Bartolomaeus de Sancto Concordio	*Summa de casibus*	BOD	B-087	Auct. 1 Q 1.25

ISTC date	ISTC	Author	Title	Library	Cat. no.	Shelfmark
13 Apr 1475	id00409000	Guillelmus Duranti	*Rationale divinorum officiorum*	BOD	D-186	Auct. Q sup.2.2
7 Sep1 475	ig00059000	Gambilioni-bus	*Tractatus de maleficiis*	BOD	G-028	Auct. 2 Q inf.1.16
22 Jul 76&77	ib00550000		*Biblia Latina*	BOD	B-259	Auct. M 2.14,15
31 Mar 1475	il00156000	Leonardus de Utino	*Sermones de sanctis*	BSB	L-113	2° Inc.c.a.240
4 Jan 1476/77	ip00757000	Franciscus de Platea	*Opus restitutionum*	BSB	P-556	4° Inc.c.a.85

SWITZERLAND

MICHAEL WENSSLER (Basel)

[not after 1471]	it00219000	Thomas Aquinas	*Summa theologiae*	BOD	T-178A	Auct. 5 Q 2.7
[not after 1473]	ib00769000	Boethius	*De consolatione philosophiae*	BOD	B-388	Auct. N inf.1.30
				BOD	B-388	Auct. O 4.25
[not after 1472]	ib00261000	Barzizius Gasparinus	*Epistolare ad exercitationem*	BOD	B-126	Auct. 2 Q 2.33
[not after 1474]	ij00082000	Jacobus de Voragine	*Legenda aurea*	BOD	J-027	Auct. 4 Q inf.1.11
[not after 1474]	ih00029000	Henricus de Hassia	*Expositiones super orationem*	BOD	H-023(3)	Auct. 6 Q 4.3(3)
1475	in00180000	Johannes Nider	*Manuale confessorum*	AUG	1500	4 an 2° Ink 106
				UBW	1546	I.t.f.60
[not after 1475]	ip00900000	Peraldus	*Summa de vitiis*	UBW	1030	I.t.f.60
[not after 1475]	in00190000	Johannes Nider	*De morali lepra*	AUG	1503	5 an 2° Ink 106
25 Mar 1479	ia01241000	Augustinus	*De civitate Dei*	BSB	A-859	2° Inc.c.a.819b

LOW COUNTRIES

WILLIAM CAXTON (Bruges)

1473	il00117000	Raoul Le Fevre	*Le receuil des histoires de Troyes*	BOD	L-060	Arch. D.1

COLARD MANSION (Bruges)

1477	id00274500		*Dits moraux*	ANT		R 36.2

FRATES VITAE COMMUNIS (Brussels)

1478	it00505800	Johannes de Turnhout	*Casus breves*	BSB	I-527	2° Inc.s.a.1172
[1479–91]	ij00425000	John of Salisbury	*Polycraticus sive de nugis*	UWB	1287	I.t.f.206

BELLAERT (Haarlem)

1484	ij00072000	Jacobus de Theramo	*Belial*	BOD	J-022	Auct. 2 Q 1.19
25oct1484	io00125000	Otto van Passau	*Die 24 Alten*	BOD	O-036	Auct, 6 Q 5.43(2)

VAN DER MEER (Delft)

1488	il00354000	Ludolphus	*Vita Christi*	BOD	L-189	Douce 179

CONCORDANCE – EDITIONS PRINTED BY ZAINER

ISTC	H	GW	GOFF
ia			
ia00116000	HR330	351	A116
ia00218000	429	582	A218
ia00226000	491	590	A226
ia00287000	449	700	A287
ia00303000	551	723	A303
ia00331000	472	775	A331
ia00332000	470	776	A332
ia00333000	471	777	A333
ia00335000	HC456	780	A335
ia00340000	574	785	A340
ia00499350	C2207	1345	
ia01399000	2146	3084	A1399
ib			
ib00274000	HC2689	3706	B274
ib00336000	2794	3862	B336
ib00567000	HC3079	4242	B567
ib00716000	3329	4483	B716
ib00720000	3333	4486	
ib00722500	3334	4489	
ib00730000	3279	4451	B730
ib00895000	HC3551	4745	B895
ib01239950			
ib01240000		5643	B1240
ic			
ic00320000	HC4710	6318	C320
ic00809000	4675	7309	
ic00810000	4674	7310	
id			
id00327630	6338	8822	
id00341935		8996	
id00407000	HC6474	9105	
id00408000	HC6475	9107	D408
ie			
ie00059300	6607	9358	
if			
if00243700	HC7258	10178	
ig			
ig00112800	7509		
ig00311000	9406	10945	G311
ig00490000	8063	11539	G490
ig00491000	8064	11540	G491
ig00650000	8252	11940	G650
ih			
ih00037000	8396	11871	H37
ih00200000	8594		H200
ii			
ii00013000	HC9091		I13
ii00015000	9093		I15
ii00039000	HC9115		I39
ij			
ij00087000			J87
ij00088400	C6389		J100
ij00091000	C6390		J91
ij00331000	7443		J331
il			
il00047500	HC9870		
il00146000	16119		L146
il00158000	16133		L158
il00204000	HC10080		
im			
im00791500	C5387	E806	
in			
in00205000	11785		N205
in00216000	HC11802		N216
in00224000	11849		N224
ip			
ip00249000	891		P249
ip00267000	HC12581		P267
ip00402000	HC12814		P402
ip00403000	C4715		P403
ip00404000			P404
ip00419700		E1182	
ip00542000	4264		P542
ip00543000	9730		P543
ip00544000	12689		P544
ir			
ir00012000	HC13681		R12
ir00014000	13682		R14
is			
is00762800	15058		
is00763000	15056		S763
is00765000	15054	10075	S765
it			
it00185000	HC1403		T185
it00319000	HC1376		T319
it00316000	1375		T316
it00317000	HC1378		T317
it00318000	1377		T318
it00465000	593		T465
iu			
iu00057000	HC16083		U57
iv			
iv00325650	C6377		
iv00363350	C6319		
iz			
iz00016500		E1561	
iz00020000		E1569	Z20

CONCORDANCE – EDITIONS BY OTHER PRINTERS

ISTC	H	GW	GOFF	ISTC	H	GW	GOFF
ia				**ic**			
ia00272000	HC461	680	A272	ic00500000	5214	6859	C500
ia00328000	HC469	772	A328	ic00503500	HR5162	6799	C503a
ia00524000	HC7631	1554	A524	ic00504000	HCR5164	6800	C504
ia00554000	900	1602	A554	ic00505000	HC5165	6801	C505
ia00555000	903	1603	A555	ic00559000	5302	6994	C559
ia00573950	971	1639		ic00576000	5239	6922	C576
ia00596000	1053	1718	A596	ic00630000	HR5312	6888	C630
ia00602000	1025	1682	A602	ic00655000	HC5099	6743	C655
ia01161000	HC1889	2750	A1161	ic00672000	5057	6709	C672
ia01223000	HC2084	2870	A1223	ic00710000	HC5410	7077	C710
ia01226000	1956	2871	A1226	ic00750900	HC4458	7159	C136
ia01230000	2046	2874	A1230	ic00870000	HC5678	7457	C870
ia01239000	2056	2883	A1239	ic00965000	HC5828	7820	C965
ia01241000	HC2058	2885	A1241	ic01016000	HC5904	7889	C1016
ia01249000	2092	2938	A1249				
ia01257000	HC1981	2897	A1257	**id**			
ia01260000	HC1963a	2900	A1260	id00020500	HC10414	7954	
ia01265000	HC2028	2903	A1265	id00219000	HC6196	8378	D219
ia01281000	HC1984	2913	A1281	id00274500	HC6283	8319	D274a
ia01282250	2102	2969	A1284	id00314900		8680	
ia01298000	1987	2916	A1298	id00315100		8683	
ia01302000	1991	2995	A1302	id00315500		8687	
ia01354000	C768	3037	A1354	id00315600		8688	
ia01355000	HC2094	3038	A1355	id00316100		8691	
ia01363000	960	3050	A1363	id00317400		8708	
ia01381000	2124	2852	A1381	id00354000	6382	9037	D354
ib				id00358000	HC6395	9042	D358
ib00020000	HC2254	3182	B20	id00403000	HR6471	9101	D403
ib00021000	2255	3183	B21	id00404000	6472	9103	D404
ib00022000	HC2253	3184	B22	id00405000	6461	9102	D405
ib00023000	HC2251	3185	B23	id00409000	6476	9108	D409
ib00170500	HC2525	3452		id00446000	6508	9150	D446
ib00221800	2610	3572					
ib00261000	2675	3676	B261	**ie**			
ib00368000	2887	3914	B368	ie00002000	8370	9173	E2
ib00388000	2925	3928	B388	ie00102000	6668	9379	E102
ib00448000	HC7796	4081	B448	ie00113000	HC6693	9428	E113
ib00526000	3031	4201	B526	ie00118000	6699	9440	E118
ib00527000	HC3032	4202	B527	ie00140000	6795	5983	E140
ib00528000	3033	4203	B528	ie00165000	CR2387	m44069	E165
ib00529000	HC3050	4204	B529	ie00168000	HCR6810	m44065	E168
ib00530000	3037	4205	B530				
ib00531000	HC3036	4206	B531	**ig**			
ib00533000	3035	4208	B533	ig00112700	7508	12981	
ib00536500	HC3034	4209	B534	ig00192000	7661	10724	G192
ib00539000	HC3039	4214	B539	ig00193000	HC7670	10726	G193
ib00550000	HC3058	4225	B550	ig00194000	7690	10728	G194
ib00607000	HC3073	4282	B607	ig00204000	7646	10735	G204
ib00624000	HC3130	4295	B624	ig00206000	7641	10736	G206
ib00627000	3133	4298	B627	ig00229000	7627	10763	G229
ib00652750	3177	4326		ig00238000	HC7653	10774	G238
ib00769000	3355	4514	B769	ig00255000	7697	10809	G255
ib00893000	3557	4739	B893	ig00265000	7705	10825	G265
ib00950000	3515	4813	B950	ig00272000	7715	10727	G272
ib01176000	3838	5433	B1176	ig00361000	7884	11352	G361
ib01234000	HC1558	5600	B1234	ig00362000	7885	11353	G362
				ig00417000	7948	11418	G417

ISTC	H	GW	GOFF
ig00427000	7928	11429	G427
ig00447000	HC7999	11451	G447
ig00448000	8001	11453	G448
ig00493000	8059	11541	G493
ig00493500	8060	11543	G495
ig00573000	HC8158	11727	G573
ig00059000	HC1624	10519	G59
ig00681000	8265	11956	G681
ih			
ih00019000	1649	12193	H19
ih00025000	7809	12222	H25
ih00029000	8394	12242	H29
ih00154000	8585	m07940	H154
ih00179000	8589	12451(II)	H179
ih00192000	8589	12451(I)	H192
ih00239000	6718	9447	H239
ih00505000	8999	n0214	H505
ih00514000	HC9010	0948925	H514
ih00532000	HC9022	n0283	H532
ii			
ii00095000	HC9191	m12156	I95
ii00181000	9273	m15250	I181
ii00191000	9302	m15281	I191
ij			
ij00022000	HC9346	m10818	J22
ij00064000	C5791	m11041	J64
ij00072000	C5821	m11118	J-72
ij00074000	C5805	m11082	J74
ij00075000	C5807	m11063	J75
ij00076000	C5803	m11062	J76
ij00082000	C6399	m11185	J82
ij00086000	C6410	m11193	J86
ij00121000	C6449	m11311	J121
ij00190000	R219	m11605	J190
ij00288000	HC5034	m13306	J288
ij00298000	HC5031	m13329	J298
ij00306000	5025	m13353	J306
ij00315000	HC7352	m13582	J315
ij00321000	7371	m13606	J321
ij00390000	HC9426	m27451	J390
ij00391000	HC9427	m27450	J391
ij00425000	HC9430	m14717	J425
ij00481000	HC9451	m15160	J481
ij00492900	HC9465	7259	J494
ij00575000	9599	7723	J575
ij00631500	9674	m15740	
il			
il00001000	9806	m16541	L1
il00002000	HC9807	m16542	L2
il00117000	HC7048	m17449	L117
il00140000	16124	m17870	L140
il00144000	16116	m17915	L144
il00156000	16131	m17893	L156
il00238000	HC10130	m18494	L238
il00354000	C3762	m19270	L354
im			
im00367000	5803	m21753	M367
im00371800	1342	m21715	T300
im00663900	11309	m24419	
im00736000		m23863	M736
im00762000	11490	m24994	M762
in			
in00045000	11749	m26178	N45
in00095000	11759	m26340	N95
in00133000	10366	m26538	N133
in00180000	11838	m26875	N180
in00190000	11816	m26867	N190
in00199000	11789	m26907	N199
in00203000	HC11781	m26936	N203
in00222000	11846	m26853	N222
in00223000	11847	m26854	N223
io			
io00096000	12101	m28416	O96
io00125000	HC12132	m28517	O125
io00140400	12216	m28610	
ip			
ip00028000	HC12343	m47759	P28
ip00090000	12384	12052	P90
ip00402850	12817	m31580	
ip00402900	C4716	m31578	
ip00412000	12800	m31627	P412
ip00417000	HC12796	m31765	P417
ip00475000	10204	m32577	P475
ip00479000	10183	m32468	P479
ip00757000	13039	m00817	P757
ip00786000	HR13087	m34312	P786
ip00831000	HC13124	m34477	P831
ip01036000	13479	m36179	P1036
ip01038000	13470	m36010	P1038
ip01062000	13480	m36286	P1062
ip01084000	HC13539	m36379	P1084
ir			
ir00001000	HC13669	n0187	R1
ir00051000	13742	m37288	R51
ir00150000	HC13384	10270	R150
ir00215000	HC13940	m38455	R215
ir00255000	6919	m38695	R255
is			
is00329000	C5319	m36507	S329
is00480000	HC14703	m41885	S480
is00524000	HC5823	m42215	S524
is00528800	7733	m42239	
is00580000	HC14797	m42634	S580
is00764000	15057	m43858	S764
it			
it00182000	HC1400	m46335	T182
it00219000	1468	m46499	T219
it00208000	HC1454	m46490	T208
it00236000	1397	m46296	T236
it00272950	C562	m46417	
it00273000	HC1425	m46416	T273
it00477000	589	m47672	T477
it00503500	10741	m19909	

ISTC	H	GW	GOFF	ISTC	H	GW	GOFF
it00505800	HC15685	m14865		iv00292000	C6523	m50635	V292
it00518000	15693	m48192	T518	iv00316000	C6332	m51309	V316
it00520000	15698	m48203	T520	iv00336000	C6359	m12653	V336
it00536000	15724	m48259	T536	iv00337200	C6356	m12663	V339
iv				iz			
iv00282000	C6245	m50882	V282	iz00013000	HC5023	m52010	Z13
iv00284000	C6247	m50570	V284				

SECONDARY SOURCES

Agüera y Arcas, Blaise, 'Temporary matrices and elemental punches in Gutenberg's DK type', *Incunabula and their readers*, Kristian Jensen, ed. (London: British Library, 2003), pp. 1–12.

Aldrich, S. J., 'The Augsburg printers of the fifteenth century', *Transactions of the Bibliographical Society*, 2 (1894), pp. 25–48.

Allen, Don Cameron, 'Some contemporary accounts of renaissance printing methods', *The Library*, 4th series, 17 (1936–37), pp. 167–71.

Allen, Lewis, *Printing with the handpress* (New York: Van Nostrand Reinhold, 1969).

Allen, P. S., *The correspondence of an early printing house: the Amerbachs of Basle*. Second lecture of the David Murray Foundation in the University of Glasgow, 7 June 1932. Glasgow University Publications, 17 (Glasgow: Jackson-Wylie, 1932).

Altman, Ursula, 'Bibliography, books and readers', *Bibliography and the study of 15th century civilisation* (London: British Library, 1987), pp. 68–81.

Amelung, Peter, 'Bologneser Typen in Süddeutschland, ein Beitrag zur Geschichte des Ulmer Buchdrucks im 15. Jahrhundert', in Hans Lülfing, ed., *Beiträge zur Inkunabelkunde*, dritte Folge, vol. 4 (Berlin, 1969), pp. 145–151.

Amelung, Peter, *Der Frühdruck im deutschen Südwesten 1473–1500* (Stuttgart: Württembergische Landesbibliothek, 1979).

Amelung, Peter, 'Humanisten als Mitarbeiter der Drucker am Beispiel des Ulmer Frühdrucks', in Fritz Kraft and Dieter Wuttke, ed., *Das Verhältnis der Humanisten zum Buch* (Boppard: Boldt, 1977), pp. 129–144.

Amelung, Peter, 'Methoden zur Bestimmung und Datierung unfirmierter Inkunabeln', *Buch und Text in 15. Jahrhundert, Arbeitsgespräch in der Herzog August Bibliothek vom 1. bis 3. März 1978* (Hamburg: Hauswedell, 1981), pp. 89–128.

Amelung, Peter, 'Der Ulmer Buchdruck im 15. Jahrhundert. Quellenlage und Forschungsstand', *Villes d'imprimerie et moulins à papier du XIVe au XVIe siècle. Aspects économiques et sociaux* (Bruxelles: Crédit Communal de Belgique, 1976), pp. 25–38.

Ashcroft, Jeffrey, 'Bruder Hans "Teutsch Psalter" – uses of literacy in a late medieval monastery', *Gutenberg-Jahrbuch*, 60 (1985), pp. 125–139.

264   Bibliography

Audin, Maurice, *Les types Lyonnais primitifs conservés au Département des Imprimés* (Paris: Bibliothèque Nationale, 1955).

Audin, Maurice, 'Types du XVe siècle', *Gutenberg-Jahrbuch*, 29 (1954), pp. 84–100.

Barge, Hermann, *Geschichte der Buchdruckerkunst* (Leipzig: Reclam, 1940).

Barker, Nicolas, *Aldus Manutius and the development of Greek script and type in the fifteenth century* (Sandy Hook: Chiswick Book Shop, 1985).

Barker, Nicolas, 'Grammatica Rythmica: copy, text and layout 1466–1681', in A. R. A. Croiset van Uchelen, ed., *Hellinga Festschrift: Forty-three studies in bibliography presented to Dr Wytze Hellinga* (Amsterdam: Israel, 1980), pp. 43–57.

Bauer, Friedrich, *Handbuch für Schriftsetzer* (Frankfurt: Klimsch & Co, 1917).

Bauer, Friedrich, 'Technisches in der Geschichte der Schriftgiesserei', *Gutenberg-Jahrbuch* 2 (1927), pp. 24–29.

Bechtel, Guy, *Gutenberg et l'invention de l'imprimerie* ([Paris]: Fayard, 1992).

Bertelsmeier-Kierst, C., '*Griseldis' in Deutschland. Studien zu Steinhöwel und Arigo* (Heidelberg: Winter, 1988).

Blake, N. F., 'Caxton prepares his edition of the Morte d'Arthur', *Journal of Librarianship*, 8 (1976), pp. 272–85.

Bloy, C. H., *A history of printing ink, balls and rollers, 1440–1850* (London: Wynkyn de Worde Society, 1967).

Boag, Andrew, 'Typographic measurement: a chronology', *Typography papers*, 1 (1996), pp. 105–121.

Bogeng, G. A. E., *Geschichte der Buchdruckerkunst*, vol. 1: *Der Frühdruck* (Dresden: Demeter-Verlag, 1930).

Boghardt, Martin, *Analytische Druckforschung: ein methodischer Beitrag zu Buchkunde und Textkritik* (Hamberg: Hauswedell, 1977).

Boghardt, Martin, 'Blattersetzung und Neusatz in frühen Inkunabeln', *Bibliothek und Wissenschaft*, 29 (1996), pp. 24–58.

Boghardt, Martin, 'Partial duplicate setting: means of rationalisation or complicating factor in textual transmission', *The Library*, 6th series, 15 (1993), pp. 306–331.

Boghardt, Martin, 'Pinhole patterns in large-format incunabula', *The Library*, 7th series, 1 (1998), pp. 263–289.

Bond, W. H., 'Casting off copy by Elizabethan printers: a theory', *Papers of the Bibliographical Society of America*, 42 (1948), pp. 281–291.

Bornschlegel, Franz-Albrecht, 'Etappen der Schriftentwicklung im Augsburger Buchdruck von Günther Zainer bis Johann Schönsperger d. Ä.', in Helmut Gier and Johannes Janota, eds., *Augsburger Buchdruck und Verlagswesen von den Anfängen bis zur Gegenwart* (Wiesbaden: Harrassowitz, 1997), pp. 153–172.

Bowers, Fredson, *Principles of bibliographic description* (Princeton, New Jersey: Princeton University Press, 1949, repr. 1976 and 1994).

Bowers, Fredson, 'Bibliographical evidence from the printers' measure', *Studies in Bibliography*, 2 (1949–50), pp. 154–169.

Bozzolo, Carlo and Ornato, Ezio, *Pour une histoire du livre manuscrit au Moyen-Âge* (Paris: Centre National de la Recherche Scientifique, 1983).

Bühler, Curt, 'A note on the fifteenth century printing technique', *University of Pennsylvania Library Chronicle*, 15 (1949), pp. 52–55

Bühler, Curt, *The fifteenth-century book* (Philadelphia: University of Pennsylvania Press, 1960).

Bühler, Curt, 'The fifteenth century editions of Petrarch's *Historia Griseldis* in Steinhöwel's German translation', *The Library Quarterly*, 15 (1945), pp. 231–236.

Bühler, Curt, 'The margins in medieval books', *Early books and manuscripts: forty years of research* (New York: 1973), pp. 100–108, also *Papers of the Bibliographical Society of America*, 40 (1946), pp. 32–42.

Bühler, Curt, *The university and the press in fifteenth-century Bologna* (Notre Dame, Indiana: Mediaeval Institute, University of Notre Dame, 1958)

Burger, H. O., *Renaissance–Humanismus–Reformation. Deustche Literatur im europäischen Kontext* (Bad Homburg: Gehlen, 1969).

Burnhill, Peter, *Type spaces: in-house norms in the typography of Aldus Manutius* (London: Hyphen, 2003).

Cappelli, A., *Dizionario di abbreviature latine ed italiani* (Milan: Hoepli, 1912).

Careri, Maria, *et al*, eds., *Album de manuscrits français du XIIIe siècle* (Rome: Viella, 2001).

Carter, H., *A view of early typography up to about 1600* (Oxford: Clarendon Press, 1969).

Clair, Colin, *The chronology of printing* (London: Cassell, 1969).

Collins, F. Howard, *Authors' and Printers' Dictionary*, 10th edn. (Oxford: Oxford University Press, 1956).

Conway, Melissa, *The 'Diario' of the printing press of San Jacopo di Ripoli 1476–1484* (Florence: Leo S. Olschki, 1999).

Cook, D. F., 'Inverted imposition', *The Library*, 5th series, 12 (1957), pp. 193–196.

Corsten, Severin, 'Die Drucklegung der zweiundvierzigzeiligen Bibel, technische und chronologische Probleme', *Johannes Gutenberg zweiundvierzigzeilige Bibel, Kommentarband* (Munich: Idion, 1979), pp. 33–67.

Corsten, Severin, 'Die Erfindung des Buchdrucks im 15. Jahrhunderts', in Barbara Tiemann, ed., *Die Buchkultur im 15. und 16. Jahrhundert*, vol. 1 (Hamburg: Maximilian-Gesellschaft, 1995), pp. 125–202.

Corsten, Severin, 'The illustrated Cologne Bibles of c.1478', in Martin Davies, ed., *Incunabula: Studies in fifteenth century printed books presented to Lotte Hellinga* (London: British Library, 1999), pp. 79–88.

Corsten, Severin, 'Das Setzen beim Druck in Formen', *Gutenberg-Jahrbuch*, 59 (1984), pp. 128–132.

Corsten, Severin, and Fuchs, Reimar Walter, eds. with Staub, Kurt Hans, *Der Buchdruck im fünfzehnten Jahrhundert, eine Bibliographie*, 2 vols. (Stuttgart: Hiersemann, 1988–1993).

Dane, Joseph and Lange, Thomas, 'An unrecorded south German incunable with a note on the type', *Huntington Library Quarterly*, 60 (1999), pp. 470–474.

Dane, Joseph, 'Notes on the Huntington Donatus *Ars minor*', *Papers of the Bibliographical Society of America*, 94 (2000), pp. 275–282.

Dane, Joseph, *The myth of print culture* (Toronto: University of Toronto Press, 2003).

Davies, Martin, ed., *Incunabula: Studies in fifteenth century printed books presented to Lotte Hellinga* (London: British Library, 1999).

Davies, Martin, 'A tale of two Aesops', *The Library*, 7th series, 3 (2006), pp. 257–288.

De Vinne, Theodore L., *The practice of typography: modern methods of book composition* (New York: Oswald, 1914).

Dicke, Gerd, 'Heinrich Steinhöwel', *Die deutsche Literatur des Mittelalters, Verfasserlexicon*, 2nd edn, vol. 9 (Berlin: de Gruyter, 1995), cols. 258–278.

Dicke, Gerd, *Heinrich Steinhöwels 'Esopus' und seine Fortsetzer. Untersuchungen zu einem Bucherfolg der Frühdruckzeit* (Tübingen: Niemeyer, 1994).

Dictionary of printing terms (London: Linotype & Machinery Ltd., 1962).

Dobras, Wolfgang, ed., *Gutenberg, aventur und kunst. Vom Geheimunternehmen zur ersten Medienrevolution* (Mainz: Hermann Schmidt, 2000).

Dziatzko, Karl, *Gutenbergs früheste Druckerpraxis* (Berlin, 1890).

Edmunds, Sheila, 'From Schoeffer to Vérard: concerning the scribes who became printers', in Sandra Hindman, ed., *Printing the written word* (Ithaca: Cornell, 1991), pp. 21–40.

Edmunds, Sheila, 'New light on Johannes Bämler', *Journal of the Printing Historical Society*, 22 (1993), pp. 29–53.

Eisermann, Falk, 'Mixing pop and politics; origins, transmission and readers of illustrated broadsides in fifteenth-century Germany', in Kristian Jensen, ed., *Incunabula and their readers* (London: British Library, 2003), pp. 159–177.

Eisermann, Falk and Honemann, Volker, 'Die ersten typographischen Einblattdrucke', *Gutenberg-Jahrbuch*, 2000, pp. 88–131.

Esdaile, Arundell, *A students' manual of bibliography* (London: Allen & Unwin, 1931).

Feather, Norman, *Mass, length and time* (London: Penguin, 1959).

Febvre, L. & Martin, H.-J., *The coming of the book; the impact of printing* (London: New Left Books, 1976).

Ferguson, W. Craig, 'A note on printers' measures', *Studies in Bibliography*, 15 (1962), pp. 212–213.

Fertel, Dominique, *La science pratique de l'imprimerie* (St-Omer, 1723, repr. Farnborough: Gregg, 1971).

Fioravanti, Lionardo, *Dello specchio di scientia universale* (Venice, 1567).

Fischel, Lilli, *Bilderfolgen im frühen Buchdruck: Studien zur Inkunabel-Illustration in Ulm und Strassburg* (Konstanz: Thorbecke, 1963), pp. 15–91.

Flannery, Melissa C., 'San Jacopo di Ripoli imprints at Yale', *Yale University Gazette*, 63, nos. 3–4 (1989), pp. 115–131.

Flood, John L., 'Early editions of Arigo's translations of Boccaccio's *Decameron*', in Anna Laura Lepschy, John Took, Dennis E. Rhodes, eds., *Book production and letters in the western European renaissance. Essays in honour of Conor Fahy* (London: Modern Humanities Research Association, 1986).

Flood, John L., 'Nationalistic currents in early German typography', *The Library*, 6th series, 15 (1993), pp. 125–141.

Flood, John L. and Kelly, William A., eds., *The German book, studies presented to David Paisey* (London: British Library, 1995).

Fournier, Pierre Simon, *The manuel typographique of Pierre-Simon Fournier le jeune*, vols. 1–3, ed. James Mosley (Darmstadt: Lehrdruckerei der Technischen Hochschule, 1995).

Foxon, David F., 'Printing at one pull and distinguishing impressions by point holes', *The Library*, 5th series, 11 (1956), pp. 284–285.

Foxon, David, 'The printing of *Lyrical Ballads*, 1798', *The Library*, 5th series, 9 (1954), pp. 221–241.

Freys, E., 'Makulatur aus der Presse Günther Zainers', *Gutenberg-Jahrbuch*, 19 (1944), pp. 94–96.

Fujii, Akihiko, 'Zum Graphemgebrauch in den Drucken Günther Zainers zwischen 1471 und 1477', in Eijiro Iwasaki, ed., *Begegnung mit dem "Fremdem". Grenze–Traditionen–Vergleiche. Akten des VIII Internationalen Germanisten-Kongresses Tokyo 1990*, vol. 3 (Munich: 1991), pp. 49–59.

Fujii, Akihiko, *Günther Zainers druckersprachliche Leistung: Untersuchungen zur Augsburger Druckersprache im 15. Jahrhundert*, Studia Augustana, 15 (Tübingen: Niemeyer, 2007).

Fuhrmann, Otto, W., *Gutenberg and the Strasbourg documents of 1439: an interpretation* (New York: Press of the Woolly Whale, 1940).

Fuhrmann, Otto, W., 'The Gutenberg 'Donatus' fragment at Columbia University, New York, one of the oldest Mainz imprints', *Gutenberg-Jahrbuch*, 29 (1954), pp. 36–46.

Füssel, Stephan, *Gutenberg and the impact of printing*, trans. Douglas Martin (Aldershot: Scolar, 2003).

Füssel, Stephan, 'Gutenberg-Forschung Neunzehnhundert-Zweitausend', *Gutenberg-Jahrbuch*, 75 (2000), pp. 9–26.

Gaskell, P., Barber, G., and Warrilow, G., 'An annotated list of printers' manuals to 1850', *Journal of the Printing Historical Society*, 4 (1968), pp. 11–31.

Gaskell, Philip, 'A census of wooden presses', *Journal of the Printing Historical Society*, 6 (1970), pp. 1–31.

Gaskell, Philip, *A new introduction to bibliography* (Oxford: Oxford University Press, 1972).

Geldner, Ferdinand, *Die deutschen Inkunabeldrucker. Ein Handbuch der deutschen Buchdrucker des XV. Jahrhunderts nach Druckorten*, 2 vols. (Stuttgart: Hiersemann, 1968–70).

Geldner, Ferdinand, 'Die ersten typographischen Drucke', in H. Widman, ed., *Der gegenwärtige Stand der Gutenberg-Forschung* (Stuttgart: Hiersemann, 1972), pp. 148–184.

Geldner, Ferdinand, 'Inkunabelkunde. Eine Einführung in die Welt des frühesten Buchdrucks', *Elemente des Buch- und Bibliothekswesens*, vol. 5 (Wiesbaden: Reichert, 1978).

Geldner, Ferdinand, *Der Türkenkalender 1454: Faksimile mit Kommentar* (Wiesbaden: Reichert, 1975).

Gerhardt, Claus W., *Der Buchdruck: Geschichte der Druckverfahren*, vol. 2 (Stuttgart: Hiersemann, 1975).

Gerritsen, Johan, 'Printing at Froben's: an eyewitness account', *Studies in Bibliography*, 44 (1991), pp. 144–164.

Gerulaitis, Leonardas Vytautas, *Printing and publishing in fifteenth-century Venice* (London and Chicago: American Library Association and Mansell Information, 1976).

Gessner, Christian Friederich, *Der in der Buchdruckerei wohlunterrichtete Lehrjunge* (Leipzig, 1743), repr. with notes by Martin Boghardt, Frans Janssen and Walter Wilkes (Darmstadt & Pinneberg: Verlag Renate Raecke, 1984).

Gessner, Christian Friederich, *Die so nöthig als nützliche Buchdruckerkunst und Schriftgiesserey* (Leipzig, 1740/41).

Gier, Helmut and Janota, Johannes, eds., *Augsburger Buchdruck und Verlagswesen von den Anfängen bis zur Gegenwart* (Wiesbaden: Harrassowitz, 1997).

Gier, Helmut and Janota, Johannes, eds., *Von der Augsburger Bibelhandschrift zu Bertolt Brecht* (Weissenhorn: Anton Konrad, 1991).

Gilissen, Leon, 'Un élément codicologique trop peu exploité: la réglure', *Scriptorium*, 23 (1969), pp. 150–162.

Gnirrep, W. M., Gumbert, J. P. and Szirmai, J. A., eds., *Kneep en binding: en terminologie voor de beschrijving van de constructies van oude boekbanden* (The Hague: Koninklijke Bibliotheek, 1992).

Gumbert, J. P., 'The layout of the Bible gloss in manuscript and early print', in Paul Saenger and Kimberley van Kampen, eds., *The Bible as book: the first printed edition*, (London: British Library, 1999), pp. 7–14.

Gumbert, J. P., 'Ruling by rake and board. Notes on some late medieval ruling techniques', in P. Ganz, ed., *The role of the book in medieval culture* (Turnhout: Brepols, 1986), pp. 41–54.

Gumbert, J. P., '"Typography" in the manuscript book', *Journal of the Printing Historical Society*, 22 (1993), pp. 5–28.

Haebler, Konrad, 'Bericht über die Kommission für den Gesamtkatalog der Wiegendrucke', *Centralblatt für Bibliothekswesen*, 25 (1908), pp. 96–107.

Haebler, Konrad, *Handbuch der Inkunabelkunde* (Leipzig: Hiersemann, 1925).

Haebler, Konrad, 'Schriftguss und Schrifthandel in der Frühdruckzeit', *Zentralblatt für Bibliothekswesen*, 41 (1924), pp. 81–137.

Haebler, Konrad, *The study of incunabula*, tr. L. Osborne (New York: Grolier Club, 1933).

Haebler, Konrad, *Typenrepertorium der Wiegendrucke*, repr. (Nendeln/Liechtenstein and Wiesbaden: Kraus, 1968).

Halporn, Barbara C., *The correspondence of Johann Amerbach. Early printing in its social context* (Ann Arbor: University of Michigan, 2000).

Hanebutt-Benz, Eva-Maria, 'Die technischen Aspekte des Druckens mit vielfachen Lettern auf der Buchdruckerpresse', in Wolfgang Dobras, ed., *Gutenberg, aventur und kunst. Vom Geheimunternehmen zur ersten Medienrevolution* (Mainz: H. Schmidt, 2000), pp. 158–189.

Hargreaves, Geoffrey D., 'Some characteristics and antecedents of the majuscules in fifteenth-century German gotico-antiqua typography', *Gutenberg-Jahrbuch*, 61 (1986), pp. 162–176.

Härle, Franz, *Das Chorgestühl im Ulmer Münster* (Ulm: Armin Vaas, 2000).

Harris, Neil,'The blind impressions in the Aldine *Hypnerotomachia Poliphili* (1499)', *Gutenberg-Jahrbuch*, 79 (2004), pp. 93–146.

Harris, Neil, 'A mysterious UFO in the Venetian "*Dama Rovenza*" [c.1482]', *Gutenberg-Jahrbuch*, 78 (2003), pp. 22–30.

Harris, Neil, 'Nine reset sheets in the Aldine *Hypnerotomachia Poliphili* (1499)', *Gutenberg-Jahrbuch*, 81 (2006), pp. 245–275.

Harris, Neil, 'Rising quadrats in the woodcuts of the Aldine *Hypnerotomachia Poliphili*', *Gutenberg-Jahrbuch*, 77 (2002), pp. 158–167.

Hartman, Alfred and Jenny, Beat R. ed., *Die Amerbachkorrespondenz*, vol. 1 (Basel: Universitäts Bibliothek, 1942).

Hassler, Konrad Dietrich, *Die Buchdrucker-Geschichte Ulm's* (Ulm: 1840, new ed. Nieuwkoop, 1965).

von Hase, Martin, 'Zwei Probedrucke des lateinischen Belials von Jacopo de Theramo des Augsburger Druckers Günther Zainer im Spielkartenmuseum, Leinfelden', *Gutenberg-Jahrbuch*, 43 (1968), pp. 106–109.

Hellinga, Lotte, 'Analytical bibliography and the study of early printed books with a case study of the Mainz Catholicon', *Gutenberg-Jahrbuch*, 64 (1989), pp. 47–96.

Hellinga, Lotte, 'Compositors and editors: preparing texts for printing in the fifteenth century', *Gutenberg-Jahrbuch*, 75 (2000), pp. 152–159.

Hellinga, Lotte, 'The interpretation of measurement of pinholes and analysis of ink in incunabula', *The Library*, 7th series, 2 (2001), pp. 60–64.

Hellinga, Lotte, 'Manuscripts in the hands of printers', in Joseph B. Trapp, ed., *Manuscripts in the fifty years after the invention of printing: some papers read at a colloquium at the Warburg Institute on 12–15 March 1982* (London: Warburg Institute, 1983), pp. 3–11.

Hellinga, Lotte, 'Notes on the order of setting a fifteenth century book', *Quaerendo*, 4 (1974), pp. 64–69.

Hellinga, Lotte, 'Press and text in the first decades of printing', *Libri, tipografi, biblioteche: ricerche storiche dedicate a Luigi Balsamo* (Florence: Leo S. Olschki, 1997), pp. 1–23.

Hellinga, Lotte, 'Printing types and the printed word. Considerations around new insights into the beginning of printing', *Archiv für Geschichte des Buchwesens*, 57 (2003), pp. 249–264.

Hellinga, Lotte, 'Problems about technique and methods in a fifteenth-century printing house', *Villes d'imprimerie et moulins à papier du XIVe siècle. Colloque International.* Collection Pro Civitate series, no.43 (Brussels: Crédit Communal de Belgique, 1976), pp. 301–313.

Hellinga, Lotte, and Goldfinch, John, eds., *Bibliography and the study of 15th-century civilisation*, papers presented at a colloquium at The British Library 26–28 September 1984 (London: The British Library, 1987).

Hellinga, Lotte and Trapp, J. B., eds. *The Cambridge history of the book in Britain*, vol. 3: 1400–1557 (Cambridge: Cambridge University Press, 1999).

Hellinga, Wytze, *Copy and print in the Netherlands* (Amsterdam: Federatie der Werkgeversorganisatiën in het Boekdrukkersbedrijf, 1962).

Herz, Randall, 'The Innsbruck leaf fragment: a new incunable edition of

"Wunderbare Meerfahrt des Heiligen Brandan" ', *Gutenberg-Jahrbuch*, 80 (2005), pp. 43–65.

Hind, Arthur, *An introduction to a history of the woodcut* (London: Constable, 1935).

Hindman, Sandra, and Farquhar, J. D., *Pen to press. Illustrated manuscripts and printed books in the first century of printing* (Baltimore: University of Maryland, Department of History of Art, 1977).

Hinman, Charlton, *The printing and proof-reading of the first folio of Shakespeare* (Oxford: Clarendon Press, 1963).

Hirsch, Rudolf, *Printing, selling and reading* 1450–1550 (Wiesbaden: Harrassowitz, 1967).

Hirsch, Rudolf, 'Petrarca's 'Griseldis' in early printed editions, ca.1469–1522', *Gutenberg-Jahrbuch*, 49 (1974), pp. 57–65.

Hornschuch, Hieronymus, *Orthotypographia*, ed. Martin Boghardt, Frans A. Janssen, Walter Wilkes (Leipzig, 1608, repr. Darmstadt: Renate Raecke, 1984) .

Hunter, Dard, *Papermaking: the history and technique of an ancient craft* (1943, repr. New York: Dover, 1978).

Ikeda, Sanae, 'Caxton's printing of Christine de Pisan's Fayttes of armes and of chyualrye', *Journal of the early book society*, 10 (2007), pp. 186–200.

Ing, Janet, *Johann Gutenberg and his Bible* (New York: Typophiles, 1988).

International Congress, *Gedenkboek der Plantin-dagen,* 1555–1955 (Antwerp: Antwerp Bibliophiles, 1956).

Janota, Johannes, 'Deutsche Bibeln', *Von der Augsburger Bibelhandschrift zu Bertolt Brecht* (Weissenhorn: Anton Konrad, 1991), pp. 21–26.

Janota, Johannes, 'Von der Handschrift zum Druck', in Helmut Gier und Johannes Janota, eds., *Augsburger Buchdruck und Verlagswesen von den Anfängen bis zur Gegenwart* (Wiesbaden: Harrassowitz, 1997), pp. 123–39.

Janssen, F. A., 'A technical description of letterpress printing in 1780', *Quaerendo,* 7 (1977), pp. 173–183.

Janssen, F. A., 'The indented paragraph', *Technique and design in the history of printing* (Amsterdam: Hes & De Graaf, 2004), pp. 39–56.

Janssen, F. A., 'Inventaire des presses typographiques en bois conservées aux Pays-Bas et en Belgique', in A. R. A. Croiset van Uchelen, ed., *Hellinga Festschrift: Forty-three studies in Bibliography presented to Dr Wytze Hellinga* (Amsterdam: Israel, 1980), pp. 302–316.

Janssen, F. A., 'Layout as means of identification', *Technique and design in the history of printing* ('t Goy-Houten: Hes & De Graaf, 2004), pp. 101–111.

Janssen, F. A., 'Reconstructions of the common press, aims and results', *Technique and design in the history of printing* ('t Goy-Houten: Hes & De Graaf, 2004), pp. 273–285, also in *Quaerendo,* 32 (2002), pp. 175–98.

Janssen, F. A., 'Some notes on setting by formes', *Technique and design in the history of printing* ('t Goy-Houten: Hes & De Graaf, 2004), pp. 133–139.

Janssen, F. A., *Technique and design in the history of printing* ('t Goy-Houten: Hes & De Graaf, 2004).

Jenkinson, Francis, 'Ulrich Zell's early quartos', *The Library,* 4th series, 7 (1926–27), pp. 46–66.

Jensen, Kristian, 'Incunabula at the Bayerische Staatsbibliothek', *Notes and Queries* (March 2000), pp. 1–4.

Johnson, A. F., *Type designs*, new rev. edn (London: Deutsche, 1966).

Kapr, Albert, 'Concerning the beginning of printing in fifteenth-century Strassburg', *Visible language*, 24 (1990), pp. 238–253.

Kapr, Albert, *Johann Gutenberg, the man and his invention*, tr. Douglas Martin (Aldershot: Scolar, 1996).

Kircher, E. W. G., *Anweisung in der Buchdruckerkunst so viel davon das Drucken betrifft* (Braunschweig: 1793) repr. with notes by Martin Boghardt, Frans Janssen and Walter Wilkes (Darmstadt & Pinneberg: Verlag Renate Raeke, 1983)

Kirsop, Wallace,'Les habitudes de compositeurs: une technique d'analyse au service de l'édition', in Giovanni Crapulli, ed., *Transmissione dei testi a stampa nel periodo moderno*, vol.1 (Rome: Ateneo, 1985), pp. 17–47.

Klebs, Arnold and Sudhoff, Karl, eds. *Die ersten gedruckten Pestschriften* (Munich: Münchner Drucke, 1926).

Koch, Ursula, *Holzschnitte der Ulmer Äsop-Ausgabe des Johann Zainer* (Dresden: Verlag der Kunst, 1961).

Kohushölter, Sylvia, 'Lateinisch-deutsche Bücheranzeigen der Inkunabelzeit', in Volker Honemann, Sabine Griese, Falk Eisermann and Marcus Ostermann, eds., *Einblattdrucke des 15. und frühen 16. Jahrhunderts. Probleme–Perspectiven–Fallstudien* (Tübingen: Niemeyer, 2000), pp. 445–465.

Künast, Hans-Jörg, *Getruckt zu Augspurg: Buchdruck und Buchhandel zwischen 1468 und 1555* (Tubingen: Niemeyer, 1997).

Künast, Hans-Jörg, 'Entwicklungslinien des Augsburger Buchdrucks von den Anfängen bis zum Ende des Dreissigjähringen Krieges', in Helmut Gier und Johannes Janota, eds., *Augsburger Buchdruck und Verlagswesen von den Anfängen bis zur Gegenwart* (Wiesbaden: Harrassowitz, 1997), pp. 4–23.

Kyriss, Ernest, *Verzierte gotische Einbände im alten deutschen Sprachgebiet*, 4 vols (Stuttgart, 1951–1958).

Lanckoronska, Maria, 'Der Zeichner der Illustrationen des Ulmer Aesop', *Gutenberg-Jahrbuch* 41 (1966), pp. 275–283.

Legros, L. A., and Grant, J. C., *Typographical printing surfaces; the technology and mechanism of their production* (London: Longmans, 1916).

Lehman, P., 'Blätter, Seiten, Spalten, Zeilen', *Zentralblatt für Bibliothekswesen*, 53 (1936), pp. 411–442.

Leroy, Louis, *De la vicissitude ou verité de choses en l'univers* (Paris, 1579) ff. 19v–20r in English translation by Robert Ashley, *Of the interchangeable course or variety of things in the whole world* (London: C. Yetsweirt, 1594), ff. 21v–22r.

Lieres und Wilkau, Viktoria, in Olga and Paul Hirsch, eds., *Die Initialen des Johann Zainer aus dem Vocabularius Bibliae des Henricus de Hassia* (Frankfurt: Frankfurter Bibliophilen-Gesellschaft, 1923).

Linotype, *Linotype specimens of faces, matrix information* (London: Linotype, 1953).

London College of Printing, *Practical printing and binding*, 3rd edn (London: Odhams, 1965).

McLeod, Randall, 'Where angels fear to read', in Joe Bray, Miriam Handley,

Anne C. Henry, eds., *Marking the text: the presentation of meaning on the literary page* (Burlington: Ashgate, 2000), pp. 144–192.

McKenzie, D. F., 'Printers of the mind: some notes on bibliographical theories and printing house practices', *Studies in Bibliography*, 22 (1969), pp. 1–75.

McKitterick, David, *Print, manuscript and the search for order, 1450–1830* (Cambridge: Cambridge University Press, 2003).

Madan, Falconer, 'Early representations of a printing press 1499–1600', *Bodleian Quarterly Record*, 4 (1924), pp. 165–167.

Madden, J. P. A., *Lettres d'un bibliographe*, 4e série (1875), pp. 230–232.

Mardersteig, Giovani, *The remarkable story of a book made in Padua in 1477* (London: Nattali & Maurice, 1967).

Martin, Henri-Jean and Chatelain, Jean-Marc, 'Mise-en-page et mise-en-texte du livre français', *La naissance du livre moderne (XIVe–XVIe siècles)* (Paris: Editions de cercle de la Librairie-Promodis, 2000).

Maslen, K., 'Point holes as bibliographical evidence', *The Library*, 5th series, 23 (1968), pp. 240–41.

Masson, Irvine, *The Mainz Psalters and Canon Missae 1457–59* (London: Bibliographical Society, 1954).

May, Alan, 'The one-pull press', *Journal of the Printing Historical Society*, new series 11 (2008), pp. 65–81.

Meale, Carol M., 'Wynkyn de Worde's setting copy for *IPOMYDON*', *Studies in Bibliography*, 35 (1982), pp. 156–171.

Monotype, *Monotype super caster manual* (London: Monotype, 1972).

Moran, James, *Printing Presses* (London: Faber, 1973).

[Morgan, Margery M.], 'A specimen of early printers' copy: Rylands English MS.2', *Bulletin of the John Rylands Library*, 33 (1950–51), pp. 194–196.

Mosley, James, 'The enigma of the early Lyonnaise printing types', *La Lumitype-Photon: René Higgonet, Louis Moyroud et l'invention de la composition moderne* (Lyon: Musée de l'imprimerie et de la Banque, 1995), pp. 13–28.

Moxon, Joseph, *Mechanick exercises on the whole art of printing*, ed. H. Davis and H. Carter (London, 1683–84; Oxford: Oxford University Press, 1958; repr. New York: Dover, 1978).

Nash, Ray, *An account of calligraphy and printing in the sixteenth century from dialogues attributed to Christopher Plantin, printed and published by him at Antwerp in 1567* (Cambridge, Massachusetts: Harvard, 1940).

Neddermeyer, Uwe, *Von der Handschrift zum gedruckten Buch: Schriftlichkeit und Leseinteresse im Mittelalter und in der frühen Neuzeit: Quantitative und qualitative Aspekte* (Wiesbaden: Harrassowitz, 1998).

Needham, Paul, *The Bradshaw method. Henry Bradshaw's contribution to bibliography*. The seventh Hanes Foundation Lecture (Chapel Hill: University of North Carolina, 1988).

Needham, Paul, 'The changing shape of the Vulgate Bible in fifteenth-century printing shops', in Paul Saenger and Kimberley van Kampen, eds., *The Bible as book; the first printed editions* (London and New Castle: British Library and Oak Knoll, 1999), pp. 53–70.

Needham, Paul, 'The compositor's hand in the Gutenberg Bible', *Papers of the Bibliographical Society of America,* 77 (1983), pp. 341–371.

Needham, Paul, 'Counting the incunables: the IISTC on CD-Rom' *Huntington Library Quarterly,* 61 (1998), pp. 459–529.

Needham, Paul, 'ISTC as a tool for analytical bibliography', in Lotte Hellinga and John Goldfinch, eds., *Bibliography and the study of 15th-century civilisation* (London: British Library, 1987), pp. 39–54.

Needham, Paul, 'Johan Gutenberg and the Catholicon Press', *Papers of the Bibliographical Society of America,* 76 (1982), pp. 395–456.

Needham, Paul, 'The paper supply of the Gutenberg bible', *Papers of the Bibliographical Society of America,* 79 (1985), pp. 303–374.

Needham, Paul, 'Paul Schwenke, Gutenberg scholarship, the German contribution 1885–1921', *Papers of the Bibliographical Society of America,* 84 (1990), pp. 241–264.

Needham, Paul, 'Pinholes in the Alost editions and evidences of page-by-page printing', p. 18 in 'Fragments of an unrecorded edition of the first Alost press', *Quaerendo,* 12 (1982), pp. 6–21.

Needham, Paul, 'Res papirea: sizes and formats of the late medieval book', in Peter Rück, ed., *Die Rationalisierung der Buchherstellung in Mittelalter und in der frühen Neuzeit* (Marburg an der Lahn: Institut für Historische Hilfswissenschaften, 1994), pp. 123–145.

Needham, Paul, 'The 1462 Bible of Johann Fust and Peter Schöffer (GW4204)', *Gutenberg-Jahrbuch,* 81 (2006), pp. 19–49.

Nelson, Stan, 'Cutting Anglo-Saxon sorts', *Fine Print on Type* (San Francisco: Bedford Arts, 1989), pp. 117–118.

Nesi, Emilia, *Il diaro della stamperia di Ripoli* (Firenze: Bernardo Seeber, 1903).

Nuovo, Angela, 'Il commercio librario a Ferrara tra XV e XVI secolo. La bottega di Domenico Sivieri', *Storia della tipografia e del commercio librario,* 3 (1998), p. 27.

Ovink, G. Willem, 'From Fournier to metric, and from lead to film' (parts 1 & 2) *Quaerendo,* 9 (1979), no.2, pp. 95–127 and no.4, pp. 283–307.

Painter, George W.,'Gutenberg and the 36-line group: a reconsideration', *Essays in honour of Victor Scholderer* (Mainz: Pressler, 1970), pp. 292–327.

Paisey, David, 'Blind printing in continental books', in A. L. Lepschy, J. Took, D. Rhodes, eds., *Book production and letters in the western renaissance* (London: Modern Humanities Research Association, 1986), pp. 220–233.

Parker, Michael, 'Early typefounders moulds at the Plantin-Moretus museum', *The Library,* 5th series, 29 (1974), pp. 93–102.

Partridge, Walter, 'The type-setting and printing of the Mainz *Catholicon*', *The Book Collector,* 35 (1986), pp. 21–52.

Pelgen, Stephan, 'Zur Archäologie der Buchdruckletter: neue Funde zur Schriftgussgeschichte von (Kur-) Mainz', *Gutenberg-Jahrbuch,* 71 (1996), pp. 182–208.

Pettas, W., 'The cost of printing a Florentine incunable', *La Bibliofiila,* 75 (1973), pp. 67–85.

Piccard, Gerhard, 'Die Wasserzeichenforschung als historische Hilfswissenschaft', *Archivalische Zeitschrift,* 52 (1956), pp. 62–115.

Pirożyński, Jan, 'Early imprints from the Gutenberg press in the Jagiellonian Library', *Polish libraries today*, 6 (2005), pp. 30–34.

Plantin, C., *La première, et la seconde partie des dialogues françois* (Anvers, 1567) repr. in R. Nash, *Calligraphy & printing in the sixteenth century dialogue attributed to Christopher Plantin* (Antwerp, 1964), pp. 13–14.

Pollak, Michael, 'The daily performance of a printing press in 1476: evidence from a Hebrew incunable', *Gutenberg-Jahrbuch*, 49 (1974), pp. 66–75.

Pollak, Michael, 'The durability of fifteenth-century type', *The Library Quarterly*, 40 (1970), pp. 371–390.

Pollak, Michael, 'Incunable printing with the form inverted: an untenable theory', *Gutenberg-Jahrbuch*, 48 (1973), pp. 168–183.

Pollak, Michael, 'The performance of a wooden printing press', *The Library Quarterly*, 42 (1972), pp. 218–264.

Pollak, Michael, 'Production costs in fifteenth century printing', *The Library Quarterly*, 39 (1969), pp. 318–330.

Pollard, Graham, *An essay on colophons with specimens and translations* (Chicago: Caxton Club, 1905).

Pollard, Graham, 'Notes on the size of the sheet', *The Library*, 4th series, 22 (1941), pp. 105–137.

Povey, Kenneth, 'On the diagnosis of half sheet imposition', *The Library*, 5th series, 11 (1956), pp. 268–272.

Povey, Kenneth, 'The optical identification of first formes', *Studies in Bibliography*, 13 (1960), pp. 189–190.

Povey, Kenneth, 'Pinholes in the 1457 Psalter', *The Library*, 5th series, 11 (1956), pp. 18–22.

Powitz, Gerhardt, 'Text und Kommentar im Buch des 15. Jahrhunderts', *Buch und Text im 15. Jahrhundert, Arbeitsgespräch in der Herzog August Bibliothek vom 1. bis 3. März 1978* (Hamburg: Hauswedell, 1981) vol. 2, pp. 35–43.

Presser, Helmut, 'Formgesetze im illustrierten Buch des 15. Jahrhunderts,' *Gutenberg-Jahrbuch*, 26 (1951), pp. 75–80.

Presser, Helmut, 'Abdruck einer Type von 1482', *Gutenberg-Jahrbuch*, 35 (1960), pp. 118–121.

Reed, Talbot Baines, *A history of the old English letter foundries* (Oxford: Oxford University Press, 1887).

Reeve, M. D., 'Manuscripts copied from books', in Joseph. B. Trapp , ed., *Manuscripts in the fifty years after the invention of printing: some papers read at a colloquium at the Warburg Institute on 12–15 March 1982* (London: Warburg Institute, 1983), pp. 12–30.

Rehak, Theo, *Practical typecasting* (New Castle: Oak Knoll, 1993).

Reske, Christoph, *The production of Schedel's Nuremberg Chronicle* (Wiesbaden: Harrasowitz, 2000).

Reske, Christoph, 'The printer Anton Koberger and his printing shop', *Gutenberg-Jahrbuch*, 76 (2001), pp. 98–103.

Reuter, Wolfgang, 'Zur Wirtschafts- und Sozialgeschichte des Buchdruckgewerbes im Rheinland bis 1800', *Archiv für Geschichte des Buchwesens*, 1 (1958), pp. 642–736.

Rogers, David, 'A glimpse into Günther Zainer's workshop *c.*1476', *Buch und Text im 15. Jahrhundert. Arbeitsgespräch in der Herzog August Bibliothek von 1. bis 3. März 1978* (Hamburg: Hauswedell, 1981), pp. 145–163.

Rouse, M. A., and R. H., *Cartolai, illuminators and printers in fifteenth-century Italy. The evidence of the Ripoli press* (Los Angeles: UCLA University Research Library, Department of Special Collections, 1988).

Ruh, Karl, *et al,* eds., *Die deutsche Literatur des Mittelalters, Verfasserlexicon,* 14 vols. (Berlin and New York: De Gruyter, 1983).

Rummonds, Richard Gabriel, *Printing on the iron handpress* (New Castle and London: Oak Knoll and The British Library, 1998).

Ruppel, Aloys, *Johannes Gutenberg: Sein Leben und sein Werk,* 3rd edn. (Nieuwkoop: De Graaf, 1967).

Sartori, Antonio, 'Libri e stampatori in Padova', in Antonio Barzon, ed., *Documenti padovani sull'arte della stampa nel sec XV,* Doc XIV (Padua: Tipographia Antoniana, 1959), pp. 111–231.

Sayce, R. A., 'Compositional practices and the localisation of printed books, 1530–1800', *The Library,* 5th series, 21 (1966), pp. 1–45.

Sayers, A. G., and Stuart, Joseph, *The art and practice of printing,* 6 vols. (London: New Era, *c.*1930).

Schmidt, Adolf, 'Technische Beiträge zur Inkunabelkunde', *Gutenberg-Jahrbuch,* 2 (1927), pp. 9–23.

Schmidt, Adolf, 'Untersuchungen über die Buchdruckertechnik des 15. Jahrhunderts', *Centralblatt für Bibliothekswesen,* 14 (1897), pp. 14–27; 57–65; 153–175.

Schmidt, Adolf, 'Zeilenzählung in Druckwerken. Inhaltsverzeichnisse und alphabetische Register in Inkunabeln', *Centralblatt für Bibliothekswesen,* 13 (1896), pp. 13–30.

Schmidt, Friede, 'Papierherstellung in Augsburg bis zur Frühindustrialisierung', in Helmut Gier und Johannes Janota, eds., *Augsburger Buchdruck und Verlagswesen von den Anfängen bis zur Gegenwart* (Wiesbaden: Harrassowitz, 1997), pp. 73–96.

Schmidt, Rolf, 'Die Klosterdruckerei von St. Ulrich und Afra in Augsburg (1472 bis kurz nach 1474)', in Helmut Gier und Johannes Janota, eds., *Augsburger Buchdruck und Verlagswesen von den Anfängen bis zur Gegenwart* (Wiesbaden: Harrassowitz, 1997), pp. 141–153.

Schmidt-Künsemüller, F. A., 'Gutenbergs Schritt in die Technik', in H. Widman, ed., *Der gegenwärtige Stand der Gutenberg-Forschung* (Stuttgart: Hiersemann, 1972), pp. 122–147.

Schneider, Cornelia, 'The first printer: Johannes Gutenberg', *Gutenberg, man of the millennium, from a secret enterprise to the first media revolution* (Mainz: 2000), pp. 124–145.

Scholderer, Victor 'The beginnings of printing at Basel', in Dennis E. Rhodes, ed., *Fifty essays in fifteenth- and sixteenth-century bibliography* (Amsterdam: Menno Hertzberger, 1966), pp. 192–195.

Scholderer, Victor, 'Bolognese type-faces in Germany', in Dennis E. Rhodes, ed.,

Fifty essays in fifteenth- and sixteenth-century bibliography (Amsterdam: Menno Hertzberger, 1966), pp. 106–112.

Scholderer, Victor, 'Early Bolognese type-faces in Germany', *Gutenberg-Jahrbuch*, 1929, pp. 127–133.

Scholderer, Victor, *Johann Gutenberg: The inventor of printing*, 2nd edn (London: British Museum, 1970).

Scholderer, Victor, 'Notes on early Augsburg printing', in Dennis E. Rhodes, ed., *Fifty essays in fifteenth- and sixteenth-century bibliography* (Amsterdam: Menno Herzberger, 1966), pp. 232–236, also in *The Library*, 5th series, 6 (1951), pp. 1–6.

Scholderer, Victor, 'A piety of printers', *The Library*, 4th series, 19 (1939), pp. 156–166.

Scholderer, Victor, 'Printers and readers in Italy in the fifteenth century', in Dennis E. Rhodes, ed., *Fifty essays in fifteenth- and sixteenth-century bibliography* (Amsterdam: Menno Hertzberger, 1966), pp. 202–215.

Scholderer, Victor, 'The shape of early type', *Gutenberg-Jahrbuch*, 21 (1927), pp. 24–5.

Schorbach, Karl, 'Die Buchdrucker Günther und Johann Zainer', *Sammlung bibliothekswissenschaftlicher Arbeiten*, Heft 6. (Halle: 1919–1940).

Schramm, Albert, *Der Bilderschmuck der Frühdrucke, vol. 5: Die Drucke von Johann Zainer in Ulm* (Leipzig: Hierseman 1923).

Schramm, Albert, 'Günther Zainer, Augsburgs erster Drucker', in Martin Breslauer and Kurt Koehler, eds., *Werden und Wirken. Ein Festgruss Karl W. Hiersemann zugesandt* (Leipzig: K. F. Koehler, 1924), pp. 363–391

Schulte, Alfred, 'Über das Feuchten des Papiers mit nassen Tüchern bei Johann Zainer und einigen anderen Frühdruckern', *Gutenberg-Jahrbuch*, 16 (1941), pp. 19–22.

Schwab-Rosenthal, Ruth, *Peter Amelung's Johann Zainer, the elder and younger* (Los Angeles: K. Karmiole, 1985).

Schwenke, Paul, *Untersuchungen zur Geschichte des ersten Buchdrucks* (Berlin, 1900).

Schwenke, Paul, *Johannes Gutenbergs zweiundvierzigzeilige Bibel: Ergänzungsband zur Faksimile-Ausgabe* (Leipzig: Insel, 1923).

Simon, Eckehard, *The Türkenkalender (1454) attributed to Gutenberg and the Strasbourg lunation documents* (Cambridge, Mass: Medieval Academy of America, 1988).

Smeijers, Fred, *Counterpunch. Making type in the sixteenth century, designing typefaces now* (London: Hyphen, 1996).

Smith, John, *The printer's grammar* (London, 1755, repr. Thoemmes Press: Bristol, 1998).

Smith, Margaret M., 'The design relationship between the manuscript and the incunable', in Robin Myers and Michael Harris, eds., *A millennium of the book: production, design and illustration in manuscript and print 900–1900* (Winchester: St Paul's Bibliographies and New Castle: Oak Knoll, 1994), pp. 23–43.

Smith, Margaret M. with Alan May, 'Early two-colour printing', *Bulletin of the Printing Historical Society*, 44 (Winter 1997), pp. 1–4.

Smith, Margaret M., *Form and its relationship to content in the design of incunables* (Cambridge, 1983, unpublished PhD thesis).

Smith, Margaret M., 'Fragments used for "servile" purposes: the St Bride Library frisket for early red printing', in L. L. Brownrigg and M. M. Smith, eds., *Interpreting and collecting fragments of medieval books* (Los Altos Hills: Anderson-Lovelace and London: Red Gull, 2000), pp. 177–88.

Smith, Margaret M., 'From manuscript to print: early design changes, *Archiv für Geschichte des Buchwesens*, 59 (2005), pp. 1–10.

Smith, Margaret M., 'Medieval roots of the Renaissance printed book: an essay in design history', *Forms of the 'medieval' in the 'Renaissance'*, ed. G. H. Tucker (Charlottesville: Rookwood Press, 2000), pp. 145–153.

Smith, Margaret M., 'Printed foliation: forerunner to printed page-numbers?', *Gutenberg-Jahrbuch*, 63 (1988), pp. 54–70.

Smith, Margaret, M., 'Printing red underlines in the incunable period: Sensenschmidt and Frisner's 1475 edition of Justinian's Codex', *Journal of the Printing Historical Society*, new series 10 (2007), pp. 45–57.

Smith, Margaret M., 'Space-saving practices in early printed books', *Journal of the Printing Historical Society*, 6 (2003), pp. 19–39.

Smith, Margaret M., 'The typography of complex texts: how an early printer eliminated the scribes' red', *Typography Papers*, 1 (1996), pp. 75–92.

Smith, Margaret M., *The title page: its early development 1460–1510* (London: British Library, 2000).

Southward, John, *Practical printing*, 3rd edn (London: Powell, 1887).

Southward, John, *Modern printing*, 2nd edn (London: Raithby Lawrence, 1904).

Southward, John, *Modern Printing*, 8th edn (Leicester: De Montfort, 1954).

Sprandel-Krafft, Lore, *Die spätgotischen Einbände an den Inkunabeln der Universitätsbibliothek Würzburg* (Würzburg: Kommissionverlag Ferdinand Schöningh, 2000).

Steele, R., 'What fifteenth century books are about', *The Library*, 2nd series, 4 (1903), pp. 337–54; 5 (1904–5), pp. 337–58; 6 (1905), pp. 137–55; 8 (1907), pp. 225–38.

Steinberg, S. H., *Five hundred years of printing* (London: Penguin, 1955).

Steinberg, S. H., *Five hundred years of printing*, new edn, rev. John Trevitt (London: British Library and New Castle: Oak Knoll, 1996).

Stevenson, Allan, *The problem of the Missale Speciale* (London: Bibliographical Society, 1967).

Stower, Caleb, *The printer's grammar* (London, 1808, repr. London: Gregg, 1965).

Stradanus, Joseph, *Nova Reperta* (Antwerp, *c.*1600).

Sudhoff, Karl, 'Der Ulmer Stadtarzt und Schriftsteller Heinrich Steinhöwel', in Arnold C. Klebs and Karl Sudhoff, eds., *Die ersten gedruckten Pestschriften* (incl. facsimile) (Munich, 1926), pp. 169–211.

Tanselle, G. Thomas, 'The concept of format', *Studies in Bibliography*, 53 (2000), pp. 67–115.

Tanselle, G. Thomas, *Introduction to bibliography: Seminar syllabus* (Charlottesville: Book Arts Press, 2002).

Tanselle, G. Thomas, *Literature and artefacts* (Charlottesville: University of Virginia, 1998).

Tanselle, G. Thomas, 'Printing history and other history', *Studies in Bibliography*, 48 (1995), pp. 269–289.

Tanselle, G. Thomas, 'The treatment of typesetting and presswork in bibliographical description', *Studies in Bibliography*, 52 (1999), pp. 1–57.

Täubel, Christian Gottlob, *Praktisches Handbuch der Buchdruckerkunst für Anfänger*, ed. Frans Janssen and Walter Wilkes (repr. Darmstadt, 1982).

Updike, D. B., *Printing types, their history, forms and use*, 2nd edn (London: Oxford University Press, 1937).

Vietor, J. L. & Redinger, J., *Format-Büchlein* (Frankfurt am Main, 1679) [together with] *Depositio Cornuti Typographici* (Frankfurt am Main, 1677) repr. with notes by Martin Boghardt, Frans Janssen and Walter Wilkes (Darmstadt, 1983).

Voet, Leon, *The Golden Compasses*, 2 vols. (Amsterdam: Van Gendt, 1969).

Voet, Leon, 'The making of books in the renaissance', *Printing and Graphic Arts*, 10 (1966), pp. 34–62.

Voulliéme, Ernst, *Die deutschen Drucker des fünfzehnten Jahrhunderts* (Berlin: Reichdruckerei, 1922).

Wallau, Heinrich, 'Über Puncturen in alten Drucken', *Centralblatt für Bibliothekswesen*, 5 (1888), pp. 91–93.

Wegener, Johannes, *Die Zainer in Ulm. Ein Beitrag zur Geschichte des Buchdrucks in XV. Jahrhundert*, vol.1 (Strassburg: Heitz, 1904).

Wehmer, Carl, 'Augsburger Schreiber aus der Frühzeit des Buchdrucks', *Beiträge zur Inkunabelkunde*, Neue Folge 2 (1938), pp. 108–127.

Wehmer, Carl, 'Gutenbergs Typographie', in Dennis Rhodes, ed., *Essays in honour of Victor Scholderer* (Mainz: Pressler, 1970), pp. 426–483.

Wehmer, Carl, 'Inkunabelkunde', *Centralblatt für Bibliothekswesen*, 57 (1940), pp. 214–232.

Wehmer, Carl, *Mainzer Probedrucke in der Type des sogenannten astronomischen Kalenders für 1448* (Munich: Leibniz, 1948).

Wehmer, Carl, *Zur Beurteilung des Methodenstreits in der Inkunabelkunde*, special offprint, *Gutenberg-Jahrbuch* (Mainz, 1933).

Weil, Ernst, *Der Ulmer Holzschnitt im 15. Jahrhundert* (Berlin: Mauritius, 1923).

Widman, Hans, ed., *Der gegenwärtige Stand der Gutenberg-Forschung* (Stuttgart: Hiersemann, 1972).

Wijnkus, F. J. M., *Elsevier's dictionary of the printing and allied industries* (Amsterdam, London and New York: Elsevier, 1967).

Wilkes, Walter, *Die Entwicklung der eisernen Buchdruckerpresse*, vol. 2 (Darmstadt, 1988).

Wilkes, Walter, *Schriftkegel, Dickte, Schrifthöhe. Masse der Buchdruckletter* (Darmstadt: Technische Hochschule, 1980).

Wilson, Adrian, *The design of books* (San Francisco: Chronicle, 1993).

Wilson, Adrian, *The making of the Nuremberg chronicle* (Amsterdam: Nico Israel, 1976).

Wolf, Hans-Jürgen, *Geschichte der Druckpressen* (Frankfurt: Interprint, 1975).

Wolffger, Georg, *Format-Büchlein,* ed. Martin Boghardt, Frans A. Janssen, Walter Wilkes (Graz, 1672/73, repr. Darmstadt, 1987).

Worstbrock, Franz Josef, 'Frühhumanismus in Deutschland', *Von der Augsburger Bibelhandschrift zu Bertolt Brecht* (Weissenhorn: Anton H. Konrad, 1991), pp. 168–174.

Zedler, Gottfried, 'Über die Preise und Auflagenhöhe unserer ältesten Drucke', *Beiträge zum Bibliotheks und Buchwesen* (1913), pp. 267–288.

Zahn, Peter, 'Untersuchungen von Beschreibstoffen und Druckfarben früher Inkunabeln mit Röntgen-Floureszenz-Analyse im Teilchen- oder synchrotron-Beschleuniger', *Johannes Gutenberg, regionale Aspekte des frühen Buchdrucks. Vorträge der internationalen Konferenz zum 550 Jubiläum der Buchdruckerkunst am 26. und 27. Juni 1990 in Berlin* (Berlin, 1993), pp. 28–46 .

Zapf, Georg Wilhelm, *Augsburgs Buchdruckergeschichte, pt. 1: vom Jahre 1468 auf das Jahr 1500* (Augsburg, 1788).

Zapf, Georg Wilhelm, *Älteste Buchdruckergeschichte Schwabens* (Ulm, 1791).

INDEX

(Page numbers in italic indicate references to illustrations)